The Crusade for Equality
in the Workplace

The Crusade for Equality in the Workplace

THE *GRIGGS V. DUKE POWER* STORY

ROBERT BELTON

edited by
Stephen L. Wasby

 University Press of Kansas

Clinton College Library

Published by the University Press of Kansas (Lawrence, Kansas 66045), which was organized
by the Kansas Board of Regents and is operated and funded by Emporia State University,
Fort Hays State University, Kansas State University, Pittsburg State University, the University
of Kansas, and Wichita State University

Library of Congress Cataloging-in-Publication Data

Belton, Robert K., 1935–2012, author.
　The crusade for equality in the workplace : the Griggs v. Duke Power Story /
Robert K. Belton ; edited by Stephen L. Wasby.
　　　pages　cm
　Includes bibliographical references and index.
　ISBN 978-0-7006-1953-5
　　1. Affirmative action programs—Law and legislation—United States. I. Wasby, Stephen L.,
1937– editor. II. Title.
　KF3464.B43 2014
　344.7301'1330264—dc23
　　　　　　　　　　2013044783

British Library Cataloguing-in-Publication Data is available.

Printed in the United States of America

10　9　8　7　6　5　4　3　2　1

The paper used in this publication is recycled and contains 30 percent postconsumer waste.
It is acid free and meets the minimum requirements of the American National Standard for
Permanence of Paper for Printed Library Materials z39.48–1992.

For husband and dad,
In remembrance of his love of scholarly work,
from Joy, Alaina, and Keith

Contents

Editor's Preface

Robert Belton's *The Crusade for Equality in the Workplace: The* Griggs v. Duke Power *Story* is the definitive legal history of the seminal U.S. Supreme Court employment discrimination case, *Griggs v. Duke Power Co.* (1971), and its related family of litigation. It can also be seen as a detailed primer on the development of legal principles under Title VII of the Civil Rights Act of 1964, using *Griggs* as its fulcrum. The history recounted in this book is the trajectory of Title VII from its origins in the early 1960s through the enactment of the Civil Rights Act of 1991.

In the telling, Belton fully situates the *Griggs* case in the changing legal environment brought about by Title VII's enactment; recounts *Griggs*'s postdecision history through the Supreme Court's late 1980s unraveling of the gains achieved in *Griggs* and other employment cases; and ends with Congress's action to undo the Supreme Court's retrogressive decisions. This is an account of action in the courts; however, the story takes place within bookends of Congress's action, revealing a dialectic between the Court, Congress, and the executive branch that has continued beyond what is told here.

Belton explores the strategy undertaken by the NAACP Legal Defense Fund (LDF) in its litigation campaign; describes the varied backgrounds of the attorneys who litigated the cases in the campaign; reports litigation from a major pre-*Griggs* case; extensively recounts the *Griggs* litigation itself from the district court through the court of appeals to the Supreme Court's decision; and carefully traces further development of *Griggs*'s disparate impact theory, including remedies for deprivation resulting from discrimination and *Griggs*'s relationship to affirmative action.

Unfortunately, Professor Belton did not live to see his book published. His death in February 2012 came after he had completed all but the final details of the book manuscript and before he could write the preface. Thus, it is important that the reader of Robert Belton's book—for it is *his* book—know something about its origins and completion and about my involvement.

A consummate litigator, Belton also became a scholar of employment discrimination law and has been called the leading scholar on Title VII case law. He contributed to the development and advancement of that law in the courtroom, classroom, and legal clinics and through his writing, and here he continues to instruct as he informs us how a major employment discrimination case resulted from the litigation campaign by the LDF, better known for its earlier campaign that brought about *Brown v. Board of Education* and later school desegregation cases. In doing so, he drew on a wide range of sources: interviews with participants; the papers of judges, lawyers, and others, particularly in the Library of Congress; and most especially his deep personal knowledge from having litigated the case.

From time to time, Belton would talk about wanting to write a book to tell the story of the *Griggs* case because he had been so centrally involved in it and had closely watched its aftermath, which he analyzed in his many law review articles. Once he undertook to write the book, the demands of his Vanderbilt Law School professorship and his continued involvement in cutting-edge litigation meant the book grew more slowly than he would have liked, yet the manuscript continued to develop into what it became: the large, rich story of the *Griggs* case and its progeny as those cases proceeded through the courts.

This book is, however, not only such a story. Instead, it is influenced by Belton's direct involvement in the case, although it is much more than a memoir. This is participant history that demonstrates the value of litigation and speaks to the use of litigation to produce social change. While Belton writes objectively about the activity in which he took part and influenced, there is no question as to what his feelings are. The description of facts and court decisions is objective and accurate, but this book was written with a point of view, and Belton's commitment to the notion of disparate impact infuses his writing.

My initial contact with Bob Belton came through my own research on civil rights litigation by interest groups, when I interviewed some of the hardy band of exciting lawyers for the LDF who had participated in its litigation campaigns, particularly involving school desegregation and employment discrimination. Those interviews and Belton's article on private enforcement of antidiscrimination statutes were of considerable use in my book *Race Relations Litigation in an Age of Complexity* (1995).

What began as a research interview turned into continued if not frequent contact over the years between two academics with parallel interests who respected each other's work. Bob, although accepting advice on constructing a book proposal, had been private about his manuscript, which is quite different from his law review articles and his acclaimed casebook, *Employment*

Discrimination: Cases and Materials on Equality in the Workplace. Thus I had not seen the book manuscript before I learned belatedly of his passing. Because it would have been a travesty were the book not to see the light of day, my first thought beyond the sadness of the news of his death was to inquire as to the manuscript's status. The good offices of Vanderbilt Law School Dean Chris Guthrie brought me in touch with Bob's son, Keith, who very much wanted to see his father's book in print and who accepted my offer to prepare the manuscript for submission.

My first reading of the entire manuscript immediately told me that this was a fully formed book needing only a close reading to make minor adjustments and final fine-tuning, including elimination of some overlap or duplication and the tying together of a few loose ends, while maintaining Bob's voice as much as was absolutely possible. The largest task was cutting away footnotes appropriate for law review articles to better fit the much broader audience this book so well deserves. Some further limited revisions were made on the basis of reviewers' suggestions. Ginger Kimler very ably performed the necessary careful editing.

This book is the story Bob wanted to tell—about the *Griggs* case; about the Legal Defense Fund's litigation campaign; about his colleagues at the LDF, about whom not enough has been written; and about the law of equality in the workplace as it came into place in *Griggs* and other LDF cases and was maintained against the Supreme Court's diminution of the LDF's victories.

Although the doing has been bittersweet, I am honored to have been part of completing the task Bob undertook. I want especially to thank Keith Belton for his quick grasp of the world of publishing, for letting me take the lead, and for being supportive of my suggestions. The assistance provided by Dean Chris Guthrie—and the offer to provide more—is much appreciated. I want to acknowledge Alison Gash's assistance in helping me resolve an important matter. Brian Landberg's and Robert Smith's reading of the full manuscript provided useful ideas. It has been a pleasure to work with the University Press of Kansas; Chuck Myers, for whom this was the first project after joining the Press, was helpful and supportive throughout. Keith Belton and I have special thanks for Ginger Kimler for her fine work as executive editor of the project.

This book is dedicated by Bob's wife and children to his love of scholarly work. I wholeheartedly join that dedication.

Stephen L. Wasby
June 2013
Eastham, Mass.

List of Acronyms

ACIPCO	American Cast Iron Pipe Company
ACLU	American Civil Liberties Union
ADA	Americans with Disabilities Act
ADEA	Age Discrimination in Employment Act
CORE	Congress of Racial Equality
EEOC	Equal Employment Opportunity Commission
FEPC	Fair Employment Practices Committee
LCCR	Leadership Conference on Civil Rights
LCCRUL	Lawyers Committee for Civil Rights Under Law
LCDC	Lawyers Constitutional Defense Committee
LDF	NAACP Legal Defense and Educational Fund
LSCRRC	Law Students Civil Rights Research Council
MALDEF	Mexican American Legal Defense and Educational Fund
NAACP	National Association for the Advancement of Colored People
NELA	National Employment Lawyers Association
NLRA	National Labor Relations Act
NLRB	National Labor Relations Board
NORI	National Office of the Rights of Indigents
NWLC	National Women's Law Center
OFCC	Office of Federal Contract Compliance
OFCCP	Office of Federal Contract Compliance Programs
RLA	Railway Labor Act
VEPCO	Virginia Electric and Power Company
WLDF	Women's Legal Defense Fund

The Crusade for Equality
in the Workplace

1. Introduction

On March 8, 1971, the Supreme Court of the United States decided a landmark civil rights case that was the major catalyst for a social movement that has challenged in profound ways the historical dominance of white males in the workplace. The case is *Griggs v. Duke Power Company* (1971),* and this book is the history of the pioneering litigation campaign out of which *Griggs* and its progeny arose. The case was brought by thirteen African American employees who worked as common laborers and janitors at a Duke Power electrical generating facility located in rural Rockingham County, North Carolina. Most of them had not graduated from high school, and they refused to take an intelligence test and a mechanical ability test as a requirement to be considered for jobs historically limited to white persons. They sued Duke Power for violations of their rights under Title VII of the Civil Rights Act of 1964.

The 1964 Civil Rights Act remains the most comprehensive civil rights law ever enacted to implement this nation's commitment to equality. It has been called "the greatest legislative achievement of the civil rights movement . . . [and] arguably the most important domestic legislation of the postwar era."[1] Of the eleven titles in the 1964 Act, Title VII has had the most significant impact on shaping the enforcement of our commitment to equality.[2] Title VII makes it unlawful for employers, unions, and employment agencies to discriminate against any individual with respect to his or her compensation, terms, conditions, or privileges of employment because of such individual's race, color, religion, sex, or national origin.

With some exceptions, such as the Equal Pay Act of 1963 and a portion of the Voting Rights Act of 1965, the view long held before *Griggs* was that our commitment to equality requires only the abolition of policies and practices that are motivated by discriminatory intent. This traditional, intent-based rule of law is known as the disparate treatment theory of discrimination. Persons relying on the disparate treatment theory to challenge race- or sex-neutral

---

* For citations to cases, see the Table of Cases at the end of the book.

discriminatory conduct face difficult evidentiary barriers because, as one court so aptly described the problem, "[d]efendants of even minimal sophistication will neither admit discriminatory animus nor leave a paper trail demonstrating it; and because employment decisions involve an element of discretion, alternative hypotheses (including that of simple mistake) will always be possible and often plausible."[3] The notion of "simple mistake" had been engrafted onto the disparate treatment theory as the "honest mistake" defense. Thus, even if the reason for its adverse employment decision is proven to be mistaken, foolish, trivial, or baseless, the defense allows an employer to escape liability for unlawful discrimination as long as the employer honestly believed that its action was lawful.[4]

In *Griggs,* the Court specifically rejected the argument that only intentional discrimination offends our national commitment to equality when it endorsed a revolutionary and controversial theory of equality—the disparate impact theory. The disparate impact theory is revolutionary because it broadens the meaning of discrimination to impose an obligation on employers and unions to avoid using race- or sex-neutral employment practices that disproportionately disadvantage persons on the basis of race or sex (or other protected characteristics) where they cannot prove that the challenged practices are mandated by business necessity or where alternative practices with less adverse effects exist. The fact that an employer or union was not motivated by discriminatory intent is totally irrelevant under the disparate impact theory. In *Griggs,* the race-neutral practices at issue were the Wonderlic Personnel Test, which allegedly measures general intelligence; the Bennett Mechanical Comprehension Test; and a high school diploma requirement. Neither the tests nor the high school diploma requirement had been adopted or intended by Duke Power to measure the ability of applicants or employees to perform a particular job or category of jobs historically limited to white persons. There was no evidence that Duke Power had intentionally adopted the tests and the high school diploma requirements to limit or restrict blacks to the common laborer and janitor jobs because of their race. Nevertheless, both had the effect of freezing blacks into the racially segregated common laborer and janitor jobs because blacks graduate from high school at a substantially lower rate than whites and because it is undisputed that often blacks perform less well than white persons on pen-and-paper tests. The Supreme Court ruled in favor of the black employees under the disparate impact theory because Duke Power presented no evidence that either the test battery or the educational requirement was mandated by business necessity, namely, that neither provided any information about the potential ability of the black employees to safely and efficiently perform the jobs historically limited to white employees. Prior to *Griggs,* there had not been a single reported judicial decision that specifically endorsed the disparate impact theory. Several lower courts had suggested the theory without categorically endorsing it. The Supreme Court has consistently acknowledged the distinction between disparate treatment discrimination and disparate impact discrimination.

The *Griggs* disparate impact theory is revolutionary in other ways. It ushered in one of the greatest social movements in the history of this nation because it opened up jobs and other employment opportunities, previously limited to white males, in both the public and private sectors for millions of African Americans, women, Latinos/as, Asian Americans, and Native Americans—an outcome that would not have been possible under the traditional intent-based disparate treatment theory of discrimination. *Griggs* changed forever both the course of civil rights enforcement and the public, political, judicial, and scholarly discussion on the meaning of our national commitment to equality. It opened up a completely new remedial approach to eradicating unlawful discrimination in our society. It provided a new perspective for framing the debate about the meaning of *equality,* on which there is unanimity as to the principle in the abstract but also a substantial and ongoing disagreement about how to transform this abstract principle into reality.

Griggs also provided support for a transition from a human relations/administrative civil rights enforcement model to a public law enforcement model. The human relations/administrative civil rights enforcement model tends to view discrimination more as a moral than as a legal wrong. Under the human relations/administrative civil rights enforcement model, dominant prior to the Civil Rights Act of 1964, legal coercion is deemed to be inappropriate even when judicial enforcement authority is provided.[5] Also, the traditional private law model of litigation tends to view judges as arbiters of disputes between private individuals asserting particular rights. On the other hand, the public interest model of litigation, which emerged in the 1960s and 1970s, views judges not merely as arbiters to settle private disputes but also as creators and managers of complex forms of ongoing relief that provides remedies to large classes of persons not before the court and that requires judges to be continually involved in the administration and implementation of judicial decrees.[6] The class action is the principal procedural device in the public law litigation model, and employment discrimination class actions fall within this litigation model.[7]

The disparate impact theory is one of the most controversial developments in civil rights history because, by focusing on protecting groups from the discriminatory effects of race- and sex-neutral practices rather than discrete acts of intentional discrimination against individuals, it supports affirmative action as a remedy for societal discrimination. It has sparked a vigorous and often contentious public, political, and scholarly debate about the legality of affirmative action because it supports affirmative action remedies that otherwise might be unlawful under a constitutional equal protection approach. It also encourages discrimination lawsuits brought largely by white males claiming "reverse discrimination." For better or worse, the theory provokes heated arguments about the limits of our commitment to equality; it seizes our intellect and roils our emotions. It both unites and divides one group from another.

Although *Griggs* was an employment discrimination case, the disparate impact theory has been implemented in voting rights cases brought under Section 5 of the Voting Rights Act and extended to housing discrimination cases. In addition, many states and municipalities that have their own laws prohibiting discrimination in employment and other activities have explicitly endorsed the *Griggs* impact theory or found the theory to be persuasive authority in analyzing discrimination claims based on state civil rights laws. The international influence of the *Griggs* disparate impact theory is manifest in the civil and human rights laws of other countries that have looked to the civil rights legislation and jurisprudence of the United States for guidance in enacting and interpreting their own civil and human rights laws.

The effect of *Griggs* on civil rights enforcement often has been compared to that of *Brown v. Board of Education,* the famous school desegregation case, and a federal judge has stated that "in [his] opinion, [*Griggs*] even more than *Brown* . . . proved to be the most significant in combating racial discrimination."[8] The potential and far-reaching effects that *Brown* would have on discrimination in the public sector were widely acknowledged immediately after the Supreme Court announced that decision on May 17, 1954. Unlike *Brown,* however, the revolutionary effects of *Griggs* on civil rights enforcement evolved, by and large, only over time. Like *Brown, Griggs* is likely to remain a source of critical public and scholarly debate for many generations to come. And like *Brown, Griggs* has been praised and damned.[9] In July 1971, in an unprecedented and unedited television interview of a sitting Chief Justice of the Supreme Court of the United States, Warren Burger, who authored the unanimous decision in *Griggs,* was asked what he regarded as the most important decisions handed down during his first two full Terms. Chief Justice Burger specifically identified only one case: *Griggs.*[10] One scholar of employment and civil rights law stated that "[f]ew decisions in our time—perhaps only *Brown v. Board of Education*—have had such momentous social consequences as *Griggs*";[11] that *Griggs* brought about "one of the great social movements in this, or any, era" because employers could increase dramatically their employment of minorities and women when they discovered, as a result of *Griggs,* that many standards they thought necessary to find qualified employees were not in fact required and were thus liberated from their attachment to non-job-related criteria;[12] and that *Griggs* is in the "tradition of the great cases of constitutional and tort law which announce and apply fundamental legal principles."[13] Others acknowledged that *Griggs* "burst like a bombshell [in civil rights enforcement] in 1971" and "stunned" the legal world, or that it was "the single most important Title VII decision, both for the development of the law and its impact on the daily lives of Americans."[14]

Griggs's legitimacy, like *Brown*'s, has been questioned. One of the harshest critics of laws prohibiting discrimination in employment, Professor Richard Epstein, baldly asserted that "[i]f in 1964 any sponsor of the Civil Rights Act had admitted Title VII on the ground that it adopted the disparate impact test read into it by the Supreme Court in *Griggs,* Title VII would have gone down to thundering defeat and perhaps brought the rest of the [A]ct down with it."[15] Yet, he, too, had to recognize that *Griggs* was the "*first* and single most important Supreme Court decision under Title VII" at the time it was decided.[16] Another critic conceded that *Griggs* "gave civil rights activists a stunning (publicly unheralded) victory" and was a "revolutionary" theory of equality.[17] Others have argued that the Court's interpretation of Title VII in *Griggs* went beyond the original statutory bargain reached between the proponents and opponents of the statute, that *Griggs* rested on "weak doctrinal foundations," or that it had "shaky underpinnings."[18] Still others have attacked the disparate impact theory as a mandate for preferential treatment or "reverse discrimination" or an unwarranted attack on freedom of contract.[19]

Then, eighteen years after *Griggs,* the Supreme Court, composed of a different lineup of Justices, attempted to purge the theory from our civil rights laws in its "civil rights massacre" of 1989. The phrase describes a series of employment discrimination cases the Court decided over a short period of time in 1989 that effectively ended eighteen years of progress under the disparate impact theory. However, in the Civil Rights Act of 1991, Congress codified the disparate impact theory to return it to the status it had before the Court's 1989 rulings.[20] Nevertheless, the Court has continued its judicial assault. For example, in *Ricci v. DeStefano,* decided on June 29, 2009, a divided Court held that the city of New Haven, Connecticut, engaged in "reverse discrimination" when it discarded the results of a firefighter's promotional test that favored white and Hispanic test-takers because the city feared a potential disparate impact racial discrimination lawsuit by blacks who had either failed or received lower scores on the test. *Ricci* makes clear that the disparate impact theory, although codified by Congress in 1991, is still subject to debate and controversy and is far from being a dusty piece of civil rights history.

But how and why did *Griggs* happen? The history of the litigation campaign that led to *Brown* is widely known.[21] However, even though we have a substantial body of literature on *Griggs*—written by legal scholars, political scientists, social scientists, political analysts, and pundits—not only has the full story of the pioneering litigation campaign that led to *Griggs* never been told,[22] but there is currently a great deal of confusion and misinformation about how and why *Griggs* happened. The current literature on the development of the *Griggs* disparate impact theory has focused almost exclusively on the roles of the Department of Justice and the Equal Employment Opportunity Commission (EEOC).[23] In addition, much of the history of the development of the disparate impact theory is simply wrong.[24] For these reasons, a major objective in writing this book is to fill that gap in the civil rights history of the United States by providing an insider's, first-person, behind-the-scenes history of the litigation campaign that led to *Griggs* and much of its progeny. I was one of the architects of the litigation campaign out of which *Griggs* arose and one of the lead attorneys who represented the plaintiffs in *Griggs.* In other published works, I have briefly covered, in broad outlines, bits and pieces of the *Griggs* story,[25] but this book provides a more complete historical record.

What is not so well known about *Griggs* is that it was the result of a deliberate civil rights litigation campaign, launched in 1965 by the NAACP Legal Defense and Educational Fund (LDF), that was almost on par with the *Brown* litigation campaign. Like *Brown, Griggs* did not just happen. The disparate impact theory was not "engineered" by the EEOC or the Department of Justice.[26] It was not a "judicially created doctrine" that had its genesis "*solely* in constitutional law," nor was it "invented" by the Supreme Court.[27] Both the *Griggs* and *Brown* litigation campaigns were major civil rights "crusades"[28] undertaken to use the courts to bring about social change by eliminating entrenched patterns of racial discrimination. I recognize, as have others, that the term *campaign* conjures up an image of military precision or a tightly controlled program to achieve a strategic outcome in a battle.[29] However, the term *campaign,* as used in this book, describes a programmatic, sustained, and focused litigation agenda to bring about social change. The overarching purpose of the employment discrimination campaign undertaken by the LDF, as was true in the *Brown* case and many of its other litigation activities, was judicial decision making, especially in the appellate courts, which would affect persons similarly situated who are not themselves parties. Some such undertakings seek the making of new rules and others the enforcement of existing rules, although this classification often breaks down in practice. These efforts do more than bring about judicial decisions. They may stimulate litigation or bring about other kinds of civil rights developments, such as legislative and administrative reforms.[30]

The LDF, headquartered in New York City, is widely recognized as one of the premier and most successful public interest/civil rights legal organizations in the history of this nation. Its charter declares that its purposes include rendering pro bono legal services to African Americans suffering injustice by reason of racial discrimination. Initially established in 1940 as the legal arm of the NAACP, the LDF has been separate and independent from the NAACP since 1957. Its attorneys are deemed to be the "crusaders in the courts" who fought for the civil rights revolution. The first Director-Counsel of the LDF, Thurgood Marshall, who later became the first African American Justice of the Supreme Court, established the LDF as a separate organization from the NAACP in order to pursue a legal campaign against racial segregation and other forms of racism through litigation. The LDF has probably litigated more cases before the Supreme Court than any other organization except the Office of the Solicitor General of the United States. Marshall led the legal team that prevailed in *Brown* in 1954. Jack Greenberg succeeded Marshall in 1961. Because Greenberg is Jewish, his appointment as Director-Counsel was deemed analogous to Jackie Robinson's selection as the first African American professional major league baseball player.[31] Greenberg played a critical role in launching the LDF litigation campaign out of which *Griggs* and other early landmark disparate impact decisions arose.

A major objective of the book is to tell the story of the LDF's "crusade for justice in the workplace." The story covers a period of roughly thirty-five years, from 1965, when the LDF launched its campaign, through the passage of the Civil Rights Act of 1991. In short, this book is a historical narrative of the birth, maturation, death, and rebirth of the *Griggs* disparate impact theory. It explains the reasons why the LDF undertook the campaign; the goals it sought to achieve; the strategies it adopted; and the legal, political, and practical obstacles that the LDF faced in attempting to achieve its goals. The fundamental objective of the LDF was to play a major, if not *the* major, role in developing a body of law that would, as characterized by the Court in *Griggs,* "remove barriers that have operated in the past to favor an identifiable group of white employees over other employees."[32] Human stories, sometimes heroic, of some of the major participants in the campaign—for example, African American plaintiffs, civil rights attorneys, and federal judges—are told throughout the book. The book also covers the reasons the disparate impact theory laid the foundations for novel civil rights remedies unparalleled in civil rights enforcement, including affirmative action; how the Supreme Court dismantled the theory during its "civil rights massacre" of 1989; and the legal and political events that led to the codification by Congress of the *Griggs* theory in the Civil Rights Act of 1991.

A second objective of this book is to offer some of my own views and reflections about the history of the development of *Griggs* and its progeny. In the interest of full disclosure, it is important for the reader to know that much of the history of the litigation campaign out of which *Griggs* arose is being told from my perspective as one of the legal strategists in the LDF's litigation campaign, as head of that campaign during its critical and formative years, and later as one of its cooperating attorneys. I left the Legal Defense Fund in late 1969 to join one of the first racially integrated law firms in the South, in Charlotte, North Carolina, where I continued to litigate employment discrimination cases before joining the Vanderbilt Law School faculty. The reader also should be forewarned that I served as counsel in a number of the LDF cases and events covered in this book. Although I have attempted to identify and state fairly points of view at odds with my own, "a degree of subjectivity" is inevitable. Further, the reader should be reminded that a lawyer is not at liberty to reveal certain aspects of cases in which he served as counsel because of the professional obligation emanating from the lawyer-client privilege of confidentiality. I have attempted to comply with this standard of professional responsibility in telling the *Griggs* story.

A third objective of this book is to commemorate some of the unsung heroes who were plaintiffs in some of the landmark employment discrimination cases in the campaign. Most of these heroes were African American males and females who, as plaintiffs, were willing to take on powerful employers and unions in the face of the uncertainty of a new and untested civil rights law and who faced the risk of bodily injury, loss of their livelihoods, and other forms of harassment. Many of these unsung plaintiffs-heroes did not receive the publicity and recognition of those who were involved in more public civil rights activities such as sit-ins, demonstrations, and marches. None of these individuals set out to be civil rights heroes or to make history. These plaintiffs-heroes took on the mantle of "private attorneys general" on behalf of hundreds of other similarly situated applicants and employees in order to enforce public policy against discrimination in employment. Unfortunately, many of them will remain nameless forever except in some instances in which their names appear in court documents now warehoused in federal archival depositories. They have, however, earned their rightful place in the annals of civil rights law and history.

The unsung heroes in the litigation campaign also include the numerous African American attorneys who practiced law in the southern states. Many of them were cooperating attorneys in the LDF's broad range of civil rights litigation, including the employment discrimination litigation campaign. And many of them "lived through the nightmare" of practicing law in the southern states in representing African Americans—enduring ordeals such as having a home or car blown up or sabotaged by acid, being caned by a sheriff when attempting to see a client in jail, or facing a show cause order why they should not be held in contempt for asking a judge to disqualify himself because of racial bias.[33] In a number of instances, the African American attorneys were joined by dedicated and courageous white attorneys in "the crusade for equality in the workplace."

In telling the *Griggs* story, it must be acknowledged that the overwhelming majority of the LDF cases were litigated before southern federal judges. Although a number of these judges were hostile to civil rights cases and civil rights attorneys, others played critical roles by endorsing an expansive and liberal construction of Title VII and an old post-Reconstruction statute, 42

U.S.C. 1981, which prohibits only racial discrimination. The decisions authored by some of the liberal judges on the U.S. Courts of Appeals for the Fourth and Fifth Circuits, which include most of the southern states, were particularly influential in the explosive development of employment discrimination law during the first decade of enforcement under Title VII. The Fourth Circuit includes Maryland, North Carolina, South Carolina, Virginia, and West Virginia. Judges on the Fourth Circuit who authored influential and landmark Title VII decisions were Simon Sobeloff, Harrison L. Winter, J. Braxton Craven, and John D. Butzner.[34] The Fifth Circuit, prior to its split in 1981, covered six of the eleven states in the Confederacy: Alabama, Florida, Georgia, Louisiana, Mississippi, and Texas. Some of the judges on the Fifth Circuit who authored influential and landmark Title VII decisions were John Minor Wisdom, Richard Rives, Elbert P. Tuttle, and John Brown; all were liberal Republicans except Rives, who was a Democrat. One of their colleagues on the Fifth Circuit, Judge Benjamin Cameron, derisively characterized Judges Wisdom, Rives, Tuttle, and Brown as "the Four" because of the crucial role they played in deciding civil rights cases that advanced the opportunities of African Americans.[35] These influential and forward-looking judges established a "Southern jurisprudence" because they "wrote a remarkable chapter in the statutory interpretation" that "created a jurisprudence of Title VII which was calculated to simplify the attack on segregated employment systems" and because "other courts of appeals seemed to defer informally to their counterparts in the South who had intimately experienced the relationship between racial prejudice and employment practices."[36] The philosophy of these liberal federal judges was eloquently expressed in one of the earliest Title VII cases in which I was involved when Judge Tuttle proclaimed:

> Racial discrimination in employment is one of the most deplorable forms of discrimination known to our society, for it deals not with just an individual's sharing in the outer benefits of being an American citizen, but rather the ability to provide decently for one's family in a job or profession for which he qualifies and chooses. Title VII . . . provides us with a clear mandate from Congress that no longer will the United States tolerate this form of discrimination. It is, therefore, the duty of the courts to make sure that the Act works, and the intent of Congress is not hampered by a combination of a strict construction of the statute and a battle with semantics.[37]

In recounting the history of the *Griggs* litigation campaign, I have verified my recollections of the narrative in several ways. First, I have examined many of the original LDF case files and documents. Many of these files and documents are housed at the Library of Congress but are not yet open to the general public; special permission from the LDF is required to gain access to these documents. I am one of the few individuals who has been granted access to these materials. Second, I have relied on interviews (conducted by me and others) of a number of the plaintiffs, civil rights attorneys, and strategists involved in the campaign. The narrative draws upon the papers of some of the judges, including Supreme Court Justices, who participated in some of the major cases, and a limited number of EEOC documents. The research also relies on the more traditional research sources, e.g., cases, newspapers, scholarly articles, and civil rights literature.

A NOTE ON MY ROLE IN *GRIGGS*

I served as cocounsel for the plaintiffs in *Griggs,* and my name is on all of the pleadings, legal memoranda, and briefs filed in the case, including the briefs filed in the Supreme Court. I am also listed as cocounsel in other reported proceedings in *Griggs* in the lower courts.[38] However, my name is not listed in the official publication of Supreme Court decisions because I had taken leave during the summer of 1970 from the law firm I joined after leaving the LDF to study for the North Carolina bar. As I was not involved in any cases during this period, including *Griggs,* I did not submit a notice of appearance on behalf of the plaintiffs in *Griggs.* I submitted my application for admission to the Supreme Court on December 15, 1970, which was one day after the oral argument in *Griggs.* I was admitted to the Supreme Court on January 11, 1971, almost two months before the Court decided *Griggs* on March 8, 1971. I did not correct the omission of my name before the decision was officially published in the bound volume of the *United States Reports.* My role in the campaign and in *Griggs* is acknowledged in Jack Greenberg's book.[39]

A COMMENT ON NOMENCLATURE

During my lifetime, I have witnessed the change in nomenclature of persons of African descent from "colored" to "Negro" to "black," and "African American." Throughout this book, I use "black," and "African American" interchangeably.

2. The Emergence of Title VII as a "Poor Enfeebled Thing"

Congress enacted Title VII to "endeavor to eliminate, so far as possible, the last vestiges of an unfortunate and ignominious page in this country's history."[1] That "ignominious page" is this nation's long history of racial discrimination in employment. The history of racial discrimination in employment is a well-documented historical, economic, and social fact.[2] Title VII was the latest effort in the long struggle by civil rights activists and their supporters to pressure Congress to pass legislation to remedy the problem. However, Title VII emerged from the contentious congressional debates as a "poor enfeebled thing"[3] because, as originally enacted, Congress gave the Equal Employment Opportunity Commission (EEOC), the federal administrative agency created to enforce the statute, the authority to seek enforcement only by "informal methods of conference, conciliation, and persuasion."[4] Because the pre–Title VII efforts adopted to redress the problem have been chronicled as well,[5] those efforts to remedy are covered only briefly in this chapter to provide a historical context in which to locate the LDF's litigation campaign that spawned *Griggs* and its progeny.

RECONSTRUCTION CIVIL RIGHTS LEGISLATION

Slavery was enshrined in the Constitution. The masters owned the labor of slaves because slaves were, by law, the property of the masters. After the Civil War, the Reconstruction Congress, through the enactment of constitutional amendments and civil rights legislation based on these amendments, attempted to deal broadly with the problem of racial discrimination.[6] The Civil Rights Act of 1866 was among the first pieces of civil rights legislation Congress enacted during the Reconstruction era and was "one of the most far reaching [civil rights laws] in congressional history" because it extended to all citizens the same rights and privileges "enjoyed by white citizens."[7] But like other civil rights statutes enacted by Congress during the Reconstruction era, Section 1981 lay dormant for many years because of the restrictive interpretations adopted by the Supreme Court.[8] The LDF litigation team played a major role in reviving Section 1981 as a remedy for racial discrimination in employment by private employers. The efforts of the Reconstruction Congress to prohibit racial discrimination against African Americans in the aftermath of slavery and the Civil War were short-lived because of, among other reasons, the rise of a Jim Crow regime and the Supreme Court's legalization of the "separate but equal doctrine" in constitutional equal protection law in *Plessy v. Ferguson.*

FEDERAL EFFORTS

Until the 1940s, action by the federal government to remedy racial discrimination in employment focused largely on federal employees.[9] Although the origins of the social movement for racial equality in the United States cannot be placed within clear temporal boundaries, the mobilization for the two world wars energized the efforts of civil rights activists and their supporters to pressure the federal government to take action to eliminate racial discrimination in employment. However, the federal government did not join the efforts of African American civil rights advocates and their supporters to end racial discrimination in employment even symbolically until the mobilization for World War II began.[10] This symbolic response took place only because of a serious shortage of labor in the private defense industries during World War II and a planned 1941 "March on Washington." Despite a shortage of labor in the private defense industries, "employers, unions, and management strove mightily to keep blacks out of the desirable jobs and high-paying jobs."[11] The response was that A. Philip Randolph, a prominent black civil rights activist, and other black leaders planned a march to protest the substantial exclusion of African Americans from employment in the government and private defense industries.[12] President Franklin D. Roosevelt exerted great effort to have the march called off, but, without a firm commitment to use his powers to obtain equal employment opportunity for blacks, Randolph and his supporters moved forward with plans for the march.

Scheduled for July 1, 1941, the march seemed likely to attract 100,000 blacks to the capital, to protest the denial of equality of employment opportunities for blacks in the federal government and defense industries, but on June 25 the President capitulated and promulgated Executive Order 8802. This order declared that there shall be no discrimination in the employment of workers in defense industries or the federal government because of race, creed, color, or national origin; required all private defense contracts with the federal government to contain a nondiscrimination clause; and created a Fair Employment Practices Committee (FEPC) to monitor the order's nondiscrimination provision. President Roosevelt issued the order strategically to ensure that there would be no strikes by white employees or demonstrations by civil rights activists that would disrupt the manufacture of military supplies as the country prepared for and engaged in war. As one commentator observed, "It was not the hopes of minorities that brought relief, nor even the horrors of racism elsewhere in the world, although the President was surely moved by them," rather "[t]he disquieting reality [was] that President Roosevelt was embarrassed into acting by the threat of a demonstration march on Washington."[13]

The FEPCs set up under Roosevelt's Executive Order were never given direct enforcement authority and were authorized to enforce their decisions finding violations of the orders only through negotiation, moral suasion, or the pressure of public opinion.[14] Even though it was recognized, even at this early date, that remedying racial discrimination in employment presented complex structural and remedial problems, no sanctions were specified. During the first year of the implementation of Executive Order 8802, African Americans filed 75 percent of the employment discrimination charges, Jews 10 percent, and other minorities 15 percent.[15] In 1944, Congress adopted the Russell Amendment,[16] which provided that any agency created by Executive Order and in existence for more than one year could receive federal funds only if Congress specifically appropriated funds for that agency. As a result of the Russell Amendment and fear that Congress would not appropriate funds for the committee's continued existence, the first FEPC was allowed to die a quiet death.

In its final report, the first federal FEPC made a number of recommendations, including one that would not be fulfilled until Congress passed Title VII almost twenty years later. One recommendation was that Congress should enact legislation that "would guarantee equal job opportunity to all workers without discrimination because of race, color, religion, belief, or national origin" because "[t]he mere existence of a Federal policy of nondiscrimination will not in itself result in fair employment practices within the Federal service or by Government contractors."[17] The commission pulled no punches in predicting that dire consequences would occur if its recommendations were not enacted, so "the wartime gains of Negro . . . workers [will be] lost through an unchecked revival of discriminatory practice." Declaring that "[n]othing short of congressional action to end employment discrimination can prevent the freezing of American workers into fixed groups, with ability and hard work of no account to those of the 'wrong' race or religion," the commission said that "[t]his denial of equal opportunity, if allowed to become permanent, cannot fail to create civic discord and to be a cause of embarrassment to the United States in its international relations."[18] Massive civil disobedience often accompanied by violence against African American civil rights activists and their supporters, in fact, preceded the enactment of the Civil Rights Act of 1964.[19]

Starting with Franklin D. Roosevelt, every President until the election of John F. Kennedy in 1961 had issued his own Executive Order on equal employment opportunity or continued the order in effect when he became President.[20] The enforcement of these Executive Orders was mainly through the FEPC administrative enforcement model. None of the early FEPCs had direct enforcement power, and studies of these programs concluded that their impact on the elimination of discrimination in employment was minimal. Other efforts under the FEPC model during the period prior to the enactment of Title VII received mixed reviews, but the consensus is that the FEPC approach, with enforcement authority limited to negotiation and conciliation, proved inadequate to address the complex problems of racial discrimination in employment.[21]

President Kennedy created the President's Committee on Equal Employment Opportunity in his Executive Order 10925 in 1961.[22] The Kennedy order has been deemed the first presidential Executive Order to provide meaningful enforcement authority on nondiscrimination by government contractors.[23] In October 1965, the Kennedy order was superseded by President Johnson's Executive Order 11246.[24] The Johnson Executive Order effected an administrative reorganization, abolishing the President's Committee established by Kennedy and assigning its responsibility and jurisdiction over government contractors to the Department of Labor. These orders led to the creation of the Office of Federal Contract Compliance (OFCC), later the Office of Federal Contract Compliance Programs (OFCCP), within the Department of Labor. The OFCCP was given primary responsibility for the administration and enforcement of Executive Order 11246. The Johnson order prohibited employment discrimination on the basis of race, color, religion, or national origin by firms that contract with the government. It required federal contractors to take affirmative action to ensure that employees are treated in accordance with its broad mandate. Sanctions for a violation included debarment from future government contracts,[25] but whether the sanctions were effectively enforced has been questioned.[26]

STATE AND LOCAL FEPCS

One of the outcomes of the early federal efforts to eliminate racial discrimination in employment through fair employment practices committees was that civil rights activists began to pressure states to follow the federal model. As a result, in the mid-1940s, states began to enact laws to prohibit discrimination in employment, and they also created state fair employment committees to enforce them.[27] New York passed the first of these measures in 1945. By 1964, an additional 200 communities and several additional states had enacted similar measures.[28] These state and local statutes and ordinances created FEP agencies with enforcement authority ranging from the power only to conciliate to full cease-and-desist power. A 1961 study summarized the state statutes and ordinances as having the following in common:

> [T]hey declare discrimination in public and private employment on racial,
> religious, or ethnic grounds to be illegal; they authorize a state administrative
> agency to receive and investigate complaints; they empower the agency to
> eliminate, by persuasion and mediation, any discrimination found to exist;
> if unsuccessful in such efforts, the agency is authorized to proceed by public
> hearings, findings of fact and law, and cease and desist orders, which are
> enforceable by court decree; judicial review is available to a person claiming to
> be aggrieved by an agency ruling; and finally, the state agency is responsible for
> an educational program intended to reduce and eliminate discrimination and
> prejudice.[29]

Some states authorized their FEP commissions to undertake more forceful roles in eliminating employment discrimination, but like their federal counterpart, they did not use that authority effectively.[30]

Two interrelated factors that limited the effectiveness of the FEPCs to eliminate racial discrimination in employment were the theory of discrimination they adopted and the philosophy of the FEPC human relations/administrative enforcement model itself. First, the traditional theory of discrimination in the pre-*Griggs* era was the disparate treatment theory, or intentional discrimination. This meant that conduct that ultimately "forms the basis of a finding of discrimination under fair employment laws is prohibited only when it is coupled with a certain state of mind . . . [and] is essentially an equivocal act accompanied and inspired by the mental element of prejudice. It is the motive that distinguishes the [prohibited] act, not the act itself."[31]

Second, the human relations/administrative enforcement model views discrimination as a moral, rather than legal, wrong. State agencies adopted the human relations/administrative enforcement model even though philosophical differences existed among the persons and organizations that rallied for, established, and staffed FEPCs. As an observer stated it, the dominant groups consisting of interracial groups of citizens

> were doctrinally committed to human relations rather than civil rights. The distinction is that the human rights organizations define the problem only in class terms and look to moral suasion, drawing their support and inspiration from natural law and theology but tending to overlook the instruments of the states, except insofar as they might be made to affirm such principals [sic] rhetorically. The civil rights organizations on the contrary look primarily to law, courts, and statecraft as the primary instruments of progress—and this not only to pronounce but to deliver and protect the rights of the individual as well as the rights of a class.[32]

The informal methods of conference, conciliation, and persuasion were to be conducted in private, without the threat of legal sanctions and without objective standards for compliance. Settlement by moral suasion in many cases did not result in a compulsory order for an employer who violated the law to hire, promote, or award back pay to individuals found to have been victims of unlawful employment discrimination. Many FEPC commissioners did not feel compelled to demand such relief because they considered their main responsibility to be to promote the educational message, rather than to settle complaints by enforcement of the laws.[33] For example, in a 1963 congressional hearing, an official of the California FEPC testified that he was more concerned with the attainment of a proper educational environment than with the full use of the commission's powers to secure new jobs for complainants. Similar testimony was offered by an official from the Missouri commission.[34] A study by the Senate Committee on Labor reported that of the more than 19,000 complaints that had been filed in thirteen states before December 31, 1961, there had been only eighteen court actions.[35] Herbert Hill, the Labor Secretary for the NAACP who studied state FEP commissions, concluded that "[i]t is evident that state commissions [were] much too concerned with avoiding hostility from businessmen, too careful to refrain from interfering with the stability of manufacturing enterprises or union power, and insufficiently concerned with the welfare of the Negro job seeker."[36] Because state and federal FEPC agencies were committed to defining discrimination solely in terms of intent and too often relied upon the human relations/administrative enforcement model, their records of accomplishments to adopt meaningful and effective remedies for employment discrimination were dismal.[37]

FEDERAL LABOR LAWS

Historically, unions discriminated against African American workers by explicitly or tacitly refusing to admit them to union membership or by relegating them to segregated local unions with separate collective bargaining agreements covering segregated jobs with segregated seniority systems.[38] Prior to the enactment of Title VII, the Supreme Court interpreted the National Labor Relations Act (NLRA) and the Railway Labor Act (RLA) in a way that offered some hope that these laws would be construed broadly to provide an effective remedy against racial discrimination in the unionized sector of the workplace. One of the most significant of these early developments was the duty of fair representation in *Steele v. Louisville & Nashville Railroad*. *Steele* arose under the Railway Labor Act, which governs unionization and collective bargaining in the railroad and airline industries, and involved a black railway employee who sought relief from racial discrimination because of a collective bargaining agreement that conditioned seniority on race. The Supreme Court held that a majority union, acting as the collective bargaining agent under federal law, may not enter into contracts that discriminate against African American workers because the law imposes upon the statutory representative—the union—a duty to protect equally the interests of all members of a craft. That duty, the Supreme Court held, is at least as exacting as the duty that the Constitution imposes upon legislatures to provide equal protection to those for whom it legislates.[39] Later, the Supreme Court held that the duty of fair representation extends as well to the NLRA,[40] which governs labor unionization and collective bargaining rights of employees elsewhere in the private sector and is enforced by the National Labor Relations Board (NRLB). However, the duty of fair representation proved to be of limited usefulness where the forms of union discrimination became more subtle and complex.[41]

Although the duty of fair representation is not explicit in the National Labor Relations Act, the NLRB, with its extensive administrative resources, could have applied the *Steele* doctrine against discriminatory practices of employers and labor unions.[42] However, for many years the NLRB remained unresponsive to complaints of race and sex discrimination. The NLRB's attitude toward remedying racial discrimination in the unionized sector apparently was consistent with the attitude of the federal executive and legislative branches during the 1941 through 1961 period because, as one critic of the NLRB concluded, the history of the Board's policy toward racial discrimination in employment was a "slow transformation of a vague public policy into a judicially developed body of law reluctantly enforced by an administrative agency."[43]

TITLE VII BECOMES LAW

The modern story of federal protection against unlawful discrimination in public and private employment began when Congress enacted Title VII as part of the Civil Rights Act of 1964.[44] The Civil Rights Act of 1964 was a historic piece of legislation because, for the first time since Reconstruction, Congress broadly outlawed discrimination in, among other things, places of public accommodations, employment, and federally funded programs.[45] During the more than twenty years preceding Title VII, over 200 fair employment practices bills had been proposed or introduced in Congress to remedy racial discrimination in employment. The first such bill was introduced as early as 1941 during the existence of the first FEPC appointed to implement President Roosevelt's Executive Order. All of them died in legislative committees, or if they were voted out of committee, they died as a result of a Senate filibuster.[46] One of the proposals, introduced in 1946 by Senator Robert Taft, an Ohio Republican, would have outlawed employment discrimination based on race and empowered the federal courts to oversee sweeping injunctive remedies. It has been argued that Senator Taft's bill, if enacted, would have fundamentally altered the course of the development of employment discrimination law and the civil rights movement that emerged in the early 1960s because, among other things, it would have, in effect, sanctioned quota hiring.[47]

The Civil Rights Act of 1964 was enacted against the background of the civil rights movement and civil rights demonstrations in the early 1960s and the presidential election of 1960. President John F. Kennedy narrowly defeated

Richard M. Nixon in the 1960 presidential election but did so only with solid support from black voters. During the first two years of his presidency, President Kennedy failed to follow through on his election promise to civil rights advocates that one of his first acts in office would be to ask Congress to enact strong civil rights legislation. He feared that doing so while the ugliness of racial discrimination was being profoundly telecast on a daily basis would interfere with moving forward with other issues he deemed more important to his domestic and foreign affairs agendas and would adversely affect his chances for reelection.[48] However, the ongoing civil rights demonstrations and growing demand for strong civil rights legislation continued to put pressure on President Kennedy to submit a bill to Congress.

Then there were the Birmingham, Alabama, civil rights demonstrations in May 1963. During the Birmingham protests, "Bull" Connor, the city's police chief, used fire hoses, police dogs, and other weapons against well-behaved demonstrators, many of whom were schoolchildren. The savage responses by Connor and his police force to the civil rights demonstrators made news headlines, nationally and internationally. The events in Birmingham were nightly flashed across television screens, and Americans saw civil rights activists, including children, beaten, attacked by police dogs, and dragged through the streets. The bloody confrontation between the peaceful demonstrators and Bull Connor was one of the major events that led President Kennedy finally to take steps to introduce a civil rights bill in Congress.[49] As Nicholas deB. Katzenbach, who was Deputy Attorney General during Kennedy's administration and was very much involved in the legislative process that led to the 1964 act, stated, "[W]ithout television there wouldn't be a Civil Rights Act."[50] Another official in the Kennedy administration's Justice Department, Norbert A. Schlei, Assistant Attorney General for the Office of Legal Counsel, reported that the "people of the United States went through a sea-change as a result of the events in Birmingham" or "[a]t least the President . . . thought so."[51] President Kennedy is reported to have stated that African American civil rights leaders should not be so harsh on Bull Connor because "after all, he [Connor] has done a good deal for civil rights legislation this year."[52]

On June 19, 1963, in light of the continuing pressure flowing from the civil rights demonstrations, sit-ins, and arrests, President Kennedy finally yielded and transmitted his proposed Civil Rights Act of 1963 to Congress.[53] Title VII, as it finally emerged in the Civil Rights Act of 1964, was not included in the Kennedy bill, which focused primarily on discrimination in voting, places of public accommodations, and public education. The bill had a rather weak proposal on employment discrimination, limited to providing statutory support for executive action under Kennedy's 1961 Executive Order.[54] President Kennedy did not include a strong provision on discrimination in private employment because the subjects covered in his bill—public accommodations, voting, and education—were primarily aimed at the South. Support of northern congressional representatives was deemed absolutely necessary to pass any civil rights legislation in view of the strong opposition by southern senators to all civil rights legislation, and the Kennedy administration feared that corporate America would lobby northern senators to vote against a civil rights act if it included a strong provision prohibiting discrimination in employment in the private sector. President Kennedy's decision not to include a strong provision prohibiting employment discrimination has been called a "raw political calculation."[55] Also, as Katzenbach explained, the Kennedy administration deemed that Republican support was absolutely necessary to pass any kind of civil rights bill, so "we took what the Republicans put in, knowing it was a lousy equal employment provision, but feeling that it was the only one that had any chance at all."[56]

A critical event that provided impetus for the enactment of the Civil Rights Act was the March on Washington that took place on August 23, 1963, several months after President Kennedy transmitted his proposed civil rights bill to Congress. At the March on Washington, 250,000 people gathered beneath the Washington Monument and listened as Dr. Martin Luther King, Jr., delivered his historic "I Have a Dream" speech. This event focused national attention on the pervasiveness of racial discrimination in the United States. Meeting with civil rights leaders after the march, President Kennedy told them that Congressman William McCulloch had warned him that the entire civil rights bill would be fatally compromised in the House if it contained an enforceable equal employment opportunity provision.[57]

The assassination of President Kennedy on November 22, 1963, was a tragic event that played a role in the eventual enactment of the 1964 Act. Vice President Lyndon B. Johnson was sworn in as President immediately after the assassination of President Kennedy and ended up playing a pivotal role in the bill that ultimately became the Civil Rights Act of 1964. The Leadership Conference on Civil Rights (LCCR) also played a major role in the passage of the Act. The LCCR consists of a mix of African American individuals and organizations, whites, men and women, liberal Democrats, moderate Republicans, labor organizations, Protestants and Jews. It was first formed in 1950 by three giants of the civil rights movement, A. Philip Randolph, founder of the Brotherhood of Sleeping Car Porters, Roy Wilkins, Executive Secretary of the NAACP, and Arnold Aronson, a leader of the National Jewish Community Relations Advisory Council, in response to the federal government's elimination of the FEPC that had been created to end racially discriminatory employment practices in the federal government. It is the nation's premier civil rights coalition and has coordinated the national legislative campaign on behalf of every major civil rights law since 1957.

Title VII was the most contentious, controversial, and longest title in the 1964 Act because racial discrimination in employment was deemed to yield less readily than other forms of discrimination to remedial action by conventional regulatory schemes.[58] Title VII has been described as the outcome of a "torrid conception," followed by a "turbulent gestation," that ended in a "frenzied birth."[59] One of the reasons it was so contentious is the perception held by some that discrimination in employment is more difficult to root out than other forms of racial discrimination:

> [A]s a regulatory problem prevention of discrimination in employment present[ed] difficulties not common to the prevention of more overt forms of discrimination, as in voting, in education, or in public accommodations. Personnel decisions involve a multiplicity of factors, some of them subjective. . . . From the point of view of the employer, the principle object of regulation, prevention of discrimination in employment involves government inquisition into an area of decision-making further removed from public control and curtailment of a freedom of choice generally of a far more intimate concern than are involved in the prevention of other forms of discrimination. From the point of view of the beneficiaries of regulation, members of racial and religious minority groups, discrimination in employment seems to yield less readily than other forms of discrimination to correction by conventional regulatory techniques.

The result was that "the delicate task of adjusting the conflicting interest of those affected left the title by far the longest and most complicated in the act."[60]

The 1964 Civil Rights Act was debated by the House Judiciary Committee twenty-two days, by the Rules Committee seven days, by the House six days, and by the Senate eighty-three days. It was amended 105 times. The Senate eventually passed it, but only after cloture had been successfully invoked against a civil rights filibuster for the first time in Senate history. The filibuster lasted 534 hours, 1 minute, and 37 seconds, making the congressional debates surrounding the Civil Rights Act of 1964 the longest debates in the history of Congress. The bill passed the Senate on June 17, 1964, by a vote of 76 to 18. On July 2, 1964, after one hour of debate, the House of Representatives passed the Senate version of the bill by a vote of 289 to 126. Congress had enacted the Civil Rights Act of 1964 by the largest margin of any civil rights statute in the history of the United States.[61] At seven o'clock on the evening of July 2, President Johnson signed the Civil Rights Act of 1964 into law in the East Room of the White House.

TITLE VII AND ITS ENFORCEMENT

The Leadership Conference on Civil Rights had launched a major lobbying effort to try to get Congress to give the EEOC cease-and-desist power or at the very least the right to file suit in its own name in federal court against recalcitrant employers. Proponents of Title VII, like the LCCR, were in favor of a strong administrative agency modeled on the NLRB, which has administrative hearing powers; the authority to make substantive interpretations of the NLRA, to which courts give great deference; and the power to issue cease-and-desist orders. In the end, the LCCR and civil rights supporters lost that fight, after much wrangling, because opponents of a strong EEOC with judicially enforceable cease-and-desist authority were fearful that it would develop into another expensive octopus like the NLRB, would give the federal government too powerful a role in enforcing Title VII against employers, and would usurp the jurisdiction of state FEPCs.[62] Southern Democrats and conservative Republicans preferred no agency at all and were in favor of leaving enforcement totally in the hands of the courts because they feared that a strong administrative agency would potentially harass employers.[63] In the end, a political compromise was worked out in the Senate that deprived the EEOC of any meaningful enforcement authority by first depriving it of quasi-judicial cease-and-desist authority and then depriving it of its authority to prosecute civil actions in its own name and substituting instead authority for individuals to bring a private right of action after first pursuing relief before the EEOC in the administrative process. An observer concluded:

> This presented a rather basic change in philosophy of the title and implied an appraisal of discrimination in employment as a private rather than a public

wrong, to be sure, one which entitles the damaged party to judicial relief, but not one so injurious to the community as to justify the intervention of the public law authorities. It is unlikely that the full implications of the shift in emphasis to private suits were realized by the drafters of the compromise.

However, the observer noted, the EEOC's loss of enforcement authority was recouped when the Attorney General was later authorized to sue over a "pattern or practice of resistance to the full enjoyment" of the rights secured by the title.[64]

Instead of giving the EEOC cease-and-desist authority, Congress assigned plenary enforcement authority to the federal courts to develop the substantive and remedial rules to secure compliance with Title VII. However, the courts could carry out this responsibility only if lawsuits were filed, because courts generally do not have the authority to initiate lawsuits. Although Congress assigned final interpretive authority over Title VII to the courts to flesh out many questions left unanswered by Congress, it established three means of enforcement for the courts to carry out this role: the EEOC, the Department of Justice, and private parties bringing civil actions.

The enforcement plan embraced both a human relations/administrative enforcement model and a judicial enforcement model. The former provides that, if after an investigation the EEOC finds reasonable cause to believe the Act has been violated, it is to endeavor by informal methods of conference, conciliation, and persuasion to eliminate any alleged unlawful employment practice. The judicial enforcement model is found in two different sections of Title VII: (1) the Department of Justice is authorized to bring civil actions aimed at the "pattern or practice" of discrimination, which consists of "something more than an isolated, sporadic incident" of unlawful employment discrimination,[65] and (2) individuals are authorized to go to court after first exhausting administrative remedies at the EEOC.[66]

The EEOC

Title VII was enacted into law on July 2, 1964, but its effective date was delayed one year to provide employers, labor unions, and employment agencies the opportunity to bring their employment policies and practices into line with the title's requirements and to avoid a multitude of claims while such adjustments were being made.[67] This grace period was also intended to give the EEOC an opportunity to organize, to employ a staff, and to establish procedures for its operation.

With its lack of strong enforcement authority, the EEOC was deemed to be a "poor enfeebled thing"[68] and a "toothless tiger"[69] in its role as "gatekeeper"[70] or "screening agent."[71] President Johnson did not appoint the five EEOC commissioners until May 1965, and they did not take office until June 1, 1965, just one month before Title VII became effective.[72] The EEOC was underfunded and understaffed when it began operations. A 1971 study of the federal civil rights enforcement effort reported that the EEOC completely failed to take advantage of the opportunity the grace period provided and concluded that

> [s]ince its inception, the Equal Employment Opportunity Commission has been
> plagued by organizational and personnel problems which have impaired its ability
> to operate at maximum effectiveness. The agency opened its doors on July 2, 1965,
> under inauspicious circumstances. Since the implementing provisions of Title
> VII, passed on July 2, 1964, were not to become effective until 1 year later, it was
> anticipated that the interim year would be used to organize and staff the new
> agency and to establish procedures for its operation. President Johnson, however,
> did not appoint a Chairman and Commissioners until May 10, 1965. Sworn in
> on June 1, 1965, they had only a month to make the Commission operational.
> Consequently, on the date Title VII became effective, EEOC had only a skeletal
> organization and staff and no operational procedures.[73]

The report also noted that the structural deficiencies were compounded by acute staffing problems, high turnover rates, and insufficient personnel; these structural and staffing deficiencies caused the EEOC to suffer from a critical lack of continuity and direction, thereby impairing its ability to operate efficiently and to fulfill its Title VII mandate.[74] However, some have argued that the lack of enforcement accounts in large part for the success the EEOC achieved before Congress gave it enforcement authority in 1972 because, through its conciliation authority, it could assist employers and unions in avoiding litigation by private parties not controlled by the government.[75]

The language and legislative history of Title VII suggest that the EEOC was to complete the administrative process on charges within thirty days, with certain deferral periods for state and local agency actions. During the early years of its operation, the EEOC attempted to process charges within the statutory time periods.[76] The period for the administrative processing of charges, however, increased steadily after the EEOC began operation. A study issued by the

Comptroller General reported that some complainants had to wait about two years for their complaints to be resolved by the EEOC and that other charges remained in its backlog for as long as seven years.[77] According to one source, in fiscal 1972, the last year before Congress gave the EEOC the power to seek judicial enforcement in its own name, the EEOC found reasonable cause against only 1,390 employers; of the 792 of these cases it attempted to resolve, it was successful in whole or in part in only 268 cases.[78] According to another source, the EEOC had a backlog of nearly 80,000 cases as of the close of fiscal 1974.[79]

Because of the overlapping jurisdiction of the NLRB and the EEOC with respect to claims of racial discrimination in the unionized sector of the workplace, an issue arose shortly after the effective date of Title VII about whether individuals could simultaneously pursue claims of racial discrimination before the NLRB and the EEOC. The U.S. Court of Appeals for the Fifth Circuit spoke to this issue in 1966 in *Local 12 United Rubber Workers v. NLRB,* holding that Congress did not intend to establish Title VII as the exclusive remedy for claims of racial discrimination against unions. However, after the *Local 12* decision, the general counsel of the NLRB took the position that it would continue its earlier post–Title VII position of deferring to the EEOC claims of unlawful racial discrimination where similar charges had been filed with the EEOC and the NLRB and the EEOC was actively investigating such claims.[80]

Although the performance of the EEOC has been criticized fairly regularly since it first began its enforcement responsibilities, others have offered more positive assessments of the agency's performance during its early years of operation.[81] The experience of the LDF's litigation team makes it appropriate to acknowledge that the EEOC, during its early years, made significant contributions to the enforcement of Title VII even before Congress gave it judicial enforcement authority in 1972. One of its major contributions has been, and continues to be, the publication of guidelines and interpretations of the substantive provisions of Title VII.[82] The EEOC deemed that it had the authority to issue interpretive guidelines and substantive interpretation of Title VII as an integral part of its specific authority to conduct investigation of charges and its responsibility to find reasonable cause.[83] In many instances, courts have deferred to the EEOC's substantive interpretations, although they are not obligated to do so.[84] The EEOC's early guidelines on testing proved to be pivotal in *Griggs* and other cases.

Forging a working relationship with the EEOC was a component of the LDF enforcement strategy, undertaken to ensure that the EEOC would have some input from a representative of victims of employment discrimination on issues of importance to the administrative enforcement process. Overall, the employees at the EEOC were a group of pioneering individuals dedicated to the philosophy of making Title VII a major engine for the eradication of employment discrimination in the workplace and creative in devising ways to accomplish it.[85] The litigation team eventually established a solid and productive working relationship with all of the units of the EEOC, consulting on a regular basis with personnel in all of them. I also worked out an arrangement with the EEOC to permit Judith Winston, a Howard University student whom the LDF hired while she was in law school, to obtain documents from files in cases in which the litigation team had been retained as counsel.

In the early years of its campaign to enforce Title VII, the LDF's litigation team worked particularly closely with the EEOC's Office of General Counsel and its legal staff because that office regularly filed amicus briefs on novel and difficult substantive and procedural legal issues that arose in private litigation. Although the EEOC could refer cases to the Department of Justice with a recommendation for adjudication, the EEOC instituted, and regularly engaged in, the practice of appearing in such cases as amicus curiae to state the Commission's views as to the proper interpretation and application of Title VII as it soon became apparent that many of the most important interpretations of Title VII would result from private litigation. Although one of the first EEOC commissioners, Samuel Jackson, described the agency's role in appearing as amicus as that of a "guest at someone else's litigation feast,"[86] it became the EEOC's practice to appear as amicus in virtually all cases that it identified as having the potential for influencing development of Title VII law, and EEOC and LDF attorneys worked together. David Cashdan, an attorney who started with the Office of General Counsel of the EEOC in November 1965, stated that he and I worked so closely together on a number of important Title VII cases that "we were joined at the hip."[87] The result was significant contributions by the EEOC's employees to the LDF's Title VII litigation enforcement campaign and, in conjunction with private-party litigation and a more active litigation program by the Department of Justice, the result was a new body of law that transcended anything known under previous fair employment practices statutes and administrative orders.[88]

The Department of Justice

Congress clearly intended that enforcement of Title VII was to come principally through the combination of EEOC conciliation and judicial enforcement under the pattern or practice authority of the Department of Justice, with private litigation to play a subordinate, yet supportive, role to these government efforts.[89] The Department of Justice initially took the position that, except in a few circumstances specifically described in Title VII, it had the exclusive right to represent the EEOC on all Title VII legal issues in court. The statute specifically authorizes EEOC to appear in court on behalf of the Commission in its own name—to compel enforcement of its demands for information to complete its investigations—but it is questionable whether it allowed the EEOC to appear as amicus on substantive and procedural issues in private litigation. After some dispute between the EEOC and the Department of Justice, the EEOC prevailed on its view that it could appear, in its own name, as amicus in private litigation,[90] and it did so regularly in cases brought by the LDF and others.

During the early years after the effective date of the Act, the Justice Department did not assign a high priority to employment discrimination. It focused primarily on issues and cases involving public accommodations, voting, and school desegregation cases in the South immediately after the 1964 Act became effective.[91] It has been reported that the Justice Department's decision not to use its authority to enforce Title VII more vigorously immediately after it went into effect has several explanations. First, it initially failed to appreciate the critical role Congress had assigned to it to combat discrimination in employment.[92] When compared to the vigorous enforcement campaign it undertook to enforce the public accommodations provisions, the Justice Department's neglect of Title VII is apparent. The Department filed thirteen original cases and intervened in three cases under the public accommodation section of the Civil Rights Act of 1964 during the first year after that section became effective,[93] while it filed only one Title VII pattern or practice suit during the same period and only five pattern or practice cases by the end of fiscal 1967.[94] Second, the Department of Justice failed to fill the void created by the ineffective performance of the EEOC and the Office of Federal Contracts Compliance.[95] Third, the growth in manpower and fiscal resources of the Civil Rights Division did not keep pace with the vast responsibilities assigned to it under the civil rights legislation enacted by Congress in the 1960s. In 1971, the Civil

Rights Division was less than half the size of the Antitrust Division, less than two-thirds the size of the Tax Division, and considerably smaller than either the Criminal Division or the Civil Division.[96] In 1971, the Employment Section of the Civil Rights Division consisted of a chief, thirty-two attorneys, and ten research assistants.[97] The inadequate allocation of resources to the Civil Rights Division demonstrates the low priority that the federal government assigned to the elimination of employment discrimination contrary to the intent of Congress. However, the Department of Justice's decision to give priority to the enforcement of school desegregation, voting, and public accommodations rather than to Title VII also contributed to the unparalleled opportunity for the LDF to launch its pioneering employment discrimination litigation campaign.[98]

A comparison of Justice Department and LDF activity illustrates the difference. By 1971, the Civil Rights Division had filed seventy-five Title VII cases—one in 1966, twenty-six in 1968, twenty in 1969, ten in 1970, and eighteen in 1971[99]—all involving discrimination against African Americans, with none prior to 1970 brought against defendants for discrimination against Latinos/as, women, or American Indians.[100] By contrast, between 1965 and 1971, the LDF and its cooperating attorneys were involved in over 150 cases[101]—more than twice as many as the Department of Justice even though all of them were racial discrimination cases.

Private Enforcement

Civil rights advocates were disappointed that Congress did not give the EEOC prosecutorial or cease-and-desist authority.[102] Cease-and-desist authority would have made the EEOC a strong enforcement agency with the authority to hold hearings, to subpoena witnesses, and to seek, if necessary, judicial enforcement of its remedial orders after an administrative finding of unlawful employment discrimination. As one longtime civil rights advocate and commentator observed:

> Paradoxically it was the very weakness of the statute that precluded the EEOC from following the usual pattern of the state agencies in administratively patching-over problems of job discrimination. Respondents before the commission had so little to fear in the form of administrative enforcement and so little awareness of the potential threat inherent in private litigation that they were unwilling to conciliate meritorious claims. All the forces used in the past to cripple and nullify state and

municipal fair employment practice commissions were also mobilized against the EEOC, and a meaningful threat of judicial action was imperative to make Title VII administratively workable.[103]

In retrospect, however, Congress's failure to grant cease-and-desist authority to the EEOC, coupled with the fact that Congress authorized private litigation as one of the enforcement methods for Title VII, turned out to be a gain for dedicated and committed civil rights advocacy groups such as the LDF. Beholden to no one except its client, the LDF could, and did, advance novel legal theories of discrimination and innovative remedies that otherwise might not have been advanced by the EEOC or the attorney general.[104]

When Title VII was passed, the role of private enforcement was expected to be minimal and limited primarily to individual claims of discrimination. Some had doubts about whether much could be accomplished by private parties.[105] However, with its employment discrimination litigation campaign, the LDF undertook a major, if not the major, role in the development of employment discrimination law. The fact that the EEOC was deemed a "toothless tiger" and the absence of meaningful enforcement activities by the Civil Rights Division during the early years of Title VII provided an unparalleled opportunity for private enforcement to play a major role in the development of employment discrimination jurisprudence. The congressional decision to deprive the EEOC of enforcement authority provided private civil rights advocates the opportunity to test out whether Congress's decision to deprive the EEOC of the right to bring suits to enforce Title VII "represented a rather basic change in the philosophy of [Title VII] and implied an appraisal of discrimination in employment as a private rather than a public wrong."[106]

3. LDF's Enforcement Strategy

There were very few opportunities for public interest legal organizations like the LDF to undertake a major law development program on employment discrimination prior to Title VII to show, for example, that employment practices like neutral-seeming tests and seniority systems were highly discriminatory. No right of private enforcement existed under the federal fair employment practice orders and regulations beyond the opportunity to file a complaint. If the complaint was dismissed, or if the complaint was valid but efforts to conciliate failed, no further private recourse was available against private employers, unions, or employment agencies.[1] Some state laws provided aggrieved individuals the opportunity to seek judicial review of adverse commission actions, but the chances of obtaining a favorable judicial ruling were slim.[2] Federal and state courts normally give considerable weight to administrative determinations, presuming them to be correct unless clearly persuaded that the determinations were not supported by substantial evidence.[3] Some private litigation to remedy employment discrimination in federal, state, and local governments was conducted under the Fifth and Fourteenth Amendments,[4] but the constitutional equal protection ban on discrimination is not applicable to private parties absent a showing of state action.

Although claims of discrimination under Title VII can be, and often are, brought by individuals without the assistance of a private civil rights organization like the LDF, litigation, including civil rights litigation, is costly. Even though some courts have deemed employment discrimination litigation to be tort-type cases, and this became particularly true after Congress made compensatory and punitive damages available in the Civil Rights Act of 1991, immediately after Title VII's enactment only a few attorneys in private practice were willing to accept these kinds of cases on a contingency-fee basis as they regularly did in the more traditional tort cases. Costs, litigation expenses, and attorney's fees were, and continue to be, major factors imposing a general limitation on private enforcement to remedy employment discrimination through individual cases precisely because victims of such discrimination rarely have the resources to finance the costs of litigation. William H. Brown III, EEOC chairman from 1969 to 1973, testified before a congressional committee that "the disadvantaged individual is told that in the pinch he must become a litigant, which is an expensive proposition and traditionally the prerogative of the rich. Thus minorities are locked out of the proffered remedy by the very condition that led to its creation, and the credibility of the Government's guarantees is accordingly diminished."[5] The plaintiffs' costs, expenses, and attorney's fees in *Griggs* were over $65,000,[6] and the plaintiffs, who were employees paid low hourly wages, simply were not financially able to shoulder these costs of the litigation.

Another factor limiting private enforcement of laws prohibiting discrimination in employment is that civil rights cases, particularly ones involving claims of race discrimination, generally top the list of unpopular cases among attorneys. In 1963, a year before the enactment of Title VII, the Supreme Court correctly observed that "[l]awsuits attacking racial discrimination . . . are neither very profitable nor very popular. They are not an object of general competition among . . . lawyers; the problem is rather one of an apparent dearth of lawyers who are willing to undertake such litigation."[7] Thus, even assuming that costs were not a barrier, the probability of hiring a private attorney who is willing to represent African American victims of employment discrimination was severely limited in the early stages of the enforcement of Title VII. Private attorneys were generally unwilling to become involved in employment discrimination cases, particularly so when defendants were likely to be large, well-financed corporations that could hire high-priced attorneys and big labor unions, and when the issues involved an untested law and many novel issues. Cognizant of these economic disparities between the plaintiffs and defendants, the United States Court of Appeals for the Fifth Circuit characterized employment discrimination cases as David and Goliath confrontations.[8]

THE LDF CAMPAIGN

The LDF's program was the most expansive and programmatic of those aimed at employment discrimination. By 1967, the LDF was devoting almost 40 percent of its resources to the employment litigation campaign.[9] For years after Title VII became law, no other organization, including the Department of Justice, had a docket of employment discrimination cases approaching the number of active cases the LDF had.[10] The LDF's objective was to establish a body of Title VII law that would provide the most effective relief possible to African Americans. The LDF could not easily have undertaken its program earlier, when it had a much smaller staff. However, the LDF became a "very different organization from that which had planned and successfully brought the *Brown* case."[11] Some important changes took place at the LDF between its *Brown* campaign and the beginning of its employment discrimination litigation campaign in 1965. From 1940 through about 1960, the first two decades of its existence, the LDF's staff consisted of about four or five attorneys. However, in the mid-1960s, when it initiated its Title VII litigation campaign, the LDF's staff grew to seventeen attorneys and its annual income was more than $4 million, raised entirely from private sources. By the early 1970s, the staff had grown to more than 20 civil rights lawyers stationed in New York City and field offices in California and four southern states, and there was a network of about 200 cooperating lawyers, most of them African Americans and mostly in southern states.[12] In addition, the LDF regularly received assistance from social scientists, educators, commercial lawyers, law professors, foundation executives, liberal politicians, corporations, and government administrators.[13] The LDF also had more than 700 cases on its docket.[14] One of the major reasons for the increased docket and the need to hire more attorneys was the set of prohibitions against discrimination in the Civil Rights Act of 1964, as the LDF became involved in the enforcement of all those additional provisions as well as Title VII.

It had been suggested that when the LDF began its Title VII program, "the character of LDF litigation had been so thoroughly transformed that continued management by staff of a decade earlier would have been virtually impossible." Even before the employment discrimination campaign, "there was defense of the Movement: the freedom riders, the sit-in demonstrators, and the multitude of other demonstrators who required counsel during the heyday of Southern civil rights activities." That litigation, along with the employment discrimination litigation, required "extensive lawyering manpower." Thus, while "[t]he controlled, limited constitutional litigation of the *Brown* case could be managed by a handful of lawyers, a close-knit group of talented civil rights advocates, . . . [t]he staggering caseload of Movement activities and the subsequent massive workload of employment discrimination grievances required a substantial number of attorneys, and, concomitantly, the additional resources to handle trials involving questions of fact."[15]

Other individuals and civil rights organizations, including, for example, the NAACP; Lawyers Committee for Civil Rights Under Law (LCCRUL); the Women's Legal Defense Fund (WLDF); the ACLU-sponsored Lawyers Constitutional Defense Committee (LCDC); the National Employment Law Project; and the Employment Rights Project of Columbia Law School,[16] also played important roles in the development of the law during Title VII's first decade. The Women's Legal Defense Fund was founded to advance women's rights, initially litigating through a network of volunteer lawyers. With a grant from the Junior League of Washington to fund a paid staff, Judith Lichtman became the first executive director in 1974. Founded in the summer of 1964 to assist the civil rights movement, the LCDC solicited lawyers to provide volunteer representation for worthy or significant cases. Typically, a volunteer lawyer would travel to a small town in the South and spend a month handling local cases. In December 1968, the LCDC merged with the Roger Baldwin Foundation, a tax-exempt arm of the ACLU.

The Campaign

The LDF launched the employment discrimination enforcement campaign out of which *Griggs* arose in June 1965, the same month and year that I graduated from Boston University School of Law. Based on his many years of civil rights litigation experience with the LDF, Greenberg concluded that the "entire history of developments in civil rights law is that private suits have pioneered the way, and large scale government enforcement has followed."[17] The enforcement of Title VII followed this pattern, with the LDF deciding to initiate its employment discrimination litigation campaign shortly after the enactment of the Civil Rights Act of 1964. In an interview reported in the *Wall Street Journal* on May 28, 1965, less than six weeks before Title VII's effective date, Greenberg characterized the statute as a "weak, cumbersome [and] probably unworkable set of propositions" but "the best available weapon" in civil rights law.[18] Although Congress emphasized cooperation and voluntary compliance as the preferred means of eliminating unlawful employment discrimination, it was highly unlikely that this "preferred means" would have any teeth until there was a body of substantive and procedural law that established the legal rights of members of the protected classes and the scope of the obligations imposed on employers and unions. Because Congress gave the federal courts the final responsibility for the enforcement of Title VII and authorized private enforcement, the employment discrimination litigation campaign became a major part of the LDF's work.

THE EDUCATIONAL AND OUTREACH PHASE

The initial phase of the litigation campaign was a massive education and outreach program launched in late June 1965, even before the EEOC first officially opened its doors for business. The purposes of the LDF's education and outreach phase were to inform African American applicants and employees of their newly created rights under Title VII; to assist them in filing charges of unlawful employment discrimination with the EEOC; and to encourage individuals and organizations in the African American communities in southern states to become activists in the enforcement of Title VII.

Since the South has historically been one of the testing grounds for the development of civil rights law, ten southern states were targeted. Private employers' racially discriminatory practices were easier to document in southern states because the discrimination was rather blatant, as seen through official acts and long-standing customs and practices. The LDF hired eight African American law students as fieldworkers for the summer of 1965 to work in eight of the ten states under the supervision of Ruth Abram, a seventeen-year-old Sarah Lawrence College student whom Greenberg had hired to coordinate the education and charge-gathering phase;[19] she worked out of the LDF's headquarters in New York. The eight students were Delbert Spurlock (Tennessee); Richard Hopkins (Virginia); Beverly Whatley (Georgia); Marvin E. Maynor (South Carolina); Isaiah Madison (Alabama); Ira T. Simmons (Florida); D'Army Bailey (Louisiana); and Earl Harris (Mississippi). With no one assigned to North Carolina and Arkansas, the Reverend Cecil A. Cone worked with the project in Arkansas, and another fieldworker, Adam Stein, then a student at George Washington Law School, participated in the summer project in Charlotte, North Carolina, under the auspices of the Law Students Civil Rights Research Council (LSCRRC) as a summer intern with civil rights attorney Julius L. Chambers.[20] The LSCRRC was a child of the civil rights movement of the 1960s. It initially began in 1963, largely in an effort to provide research by white, liberal northern law students, a number of whom were Jewish, to civil rights practitioners handling cases in the South, and it later developed an internship program in which law students were placed with civil rights practitioners in summer jobs. The LSCRRC became a bridge for law students between law school and entry into a civil rights practice.[21] Stein drafted an EEOC charge filing form because the EEOC had not prepared one by the time it opened its doors.[22] Stein later became a founding partner of one of the first racially integrated law firms in the south in Charlotte, North Carolina: Chambers, Stein, Ferguson & Lanning—the firm that I joined after leaving the LDF.

Before leaving for their assignments, the students were briefed on Title VII by the LDF attorneys and given written guidelines on assisting individuals in filing discrimination charges with the EEOC. The students then went to their assigned states, where they met with local leaders; made presentations to African American churches and business groups; worked with civil rights and social groups to establish community-based fair employment committees; set up speaking engagements; contacted newspapers to do articles on their activities;[23] held press conferences; conducted workshops on Title VII;[24] identified industries that warranted study by the EEOC; contacted and worked with other civil rights groups such as the NAACP, the Congress of Racial Equality (CORE), and the Southern Christian Leadership Conference (SCLC); reviewed help-wanted ads in newspapers for race-designated employment opportunities; used African American and white testers to audit employers' compliance with Title VII; made use of television and radio to explain the LDF's program; undertook publicity campaigns to spread the word about Title VII; and distributed flyers about Title VII in African American communities. The students also took steps to stimulate and train local leaders to continue the educational and charge preparation work after they returned to their colleges and universities at the end of the summer. Notably, one of the major problems students encountered was the reluctance of some African Americans to fill out charges of discrimination for fear of losing their job if their names were disclosed.

The students sent all employment discrimination charges to Abram, who then bundled the charges to be filed with the EEOC. Working with Herbert Hill, National Labor Secretary for the NAACP, the LDF and the NAACP submitted 475 charges of racial discrimination to the EEOC shortly after the EEOC officially opened for business. Another 374 racial discrimination charges arising out the summer project were filed with the EEOC soon thereafter.[25] The initial phase of the litigation campaign was very successful because the LDF and the NAACP assisted African Americans in filing 1,800 charges with the EEOC during the agency's first eighteen months of existence.[26] The EEOC expected no more than 2,000 charges during its first year of operation, and its initial budget of $3.25 million and staffing requirements had been geared to that expectation. The agency, however, received 8,854 charges during its first fiscal year, most of which were claims of race discrimination and a substantial number of which were filed as a result of the joint effort between the LDF and the NAACP. Eleven southern states accounted for almost half of the charges filed with the EEOC during its first fiscal year, with the most coming from North Carolina, Alabama, and Tennessee, which were three of the states to which the LDF summer interns had been assigned.[27] In many instances, parallel charges of racial discrimination in employment were filed with the Department of Justice and other federal agencies, such as the National Labor Relations Board, the Office of Federal Contract Compliance, and the Department of Labor, which has administrative responsibility to enforce the presidential Executive Orders on employment discrimination against employers who hold contracts with the U.S. government.

In the fall of 1965, Greenberg created the LDF Division of Legal Information and Community. He hired Jean Fairfax, an African American female, as its director of community services. Fairfax, who graduated from the University of Michigan and then earned a master's degree in comparative religion at Union Theological Seminar, had a long and distinguished career as an educator, civil rights activist, and philanthropist. For the two decades she worked for the LDF, Fairfax played an important role in forging a link between the LDF and local African American communities by organizing community participation in school desegregation and working on projects for the employment discrimination litigation campaign. In addition, she published influential pamphlets dealing with, among other matters, racial discrimination in employment. Fairfax became the single most influential staff member in determining the direction the LDF took on issues such as the integration of black colleges and identifying industries to target in the employment discrimination litigation campaign. She and her fieldworkers, most notably Allen Black and Bob Valder, were instrumental in identifying major industries, such as steel, railroads, tobacco, trucking, pulp and paper, shipbuilding, and southern textiles, that generated a substantial number of charges of racial discrimination filed with the EEOC.[28] Many of the charges involving these industries ultimately became cases in the litigation campaign out of which some of the most important LDF landmark employment discrimination decisions arose.

THE LITIGATION TEAM

Michael Meltsner and Leroy Clark were the two LDF attorneys who had the initial responsibility in the very early stages of the campaign. Meltsner, a 1960 Yale Law School graduate, was one of the Jewish liberals who went to work for the LDF or worked with it; he served as its first assistant counsel from 1961 to 1970.[29] He also played a major role in the Fund's litigation campaign to have the Supreme Court declare the death penalty to be cruel and unusual punishment. After leaving the LDF, Meltsner joined the faculties first at Columbia University Law School and then at Northeastern University Law School, where he served as dean. Clark, who is African American, graduated from Columbia University Law School in 1961 and served as first assistant counsel with the LDF from 1962 to 1968. He later became a law professor at New York University Law School and then joined the faculty at Columbus School of Law at the Catholic University of America after serving as general counsel of the EEOC from 1979 to 1981.

The second phase of the campaign, which overlapped with the first, involved the assignment by Greenberg of the LDF attorneys who would have the major responsibility for the litigation campaign. Clark became my immediate supervisor upon my joining the LDF in December 1965. By this time, Clark had assumed most of the responsibility for the campaign while Meltsner focused on other civil rights litigation projects. Almost from my first day on the job, I became heavily involved in the employment litigation campaign even though I also had initial responsibility for some of the school desegregation cases, most of which were in South Carolina.[30]

Upon joining the LDF, my secret aspiration was to be a part of the team that had launched or was about to launch the campaign to have the Supreme Court declare the death penalty to be cruel and unusual punishment, but that was not to be. When I first joined the LDF, Clark and Al Feinberg were the two attorneys doing most of the work on the employment discrimination project. Clark had major supervisory responsibility, but Feinberg, who had worked for a short period with Clark and Meltsner on the project in its very early stages, did most of the day-to-day work such as interaction with

Fairfax, the cooperating attorneys, the NAACP, and the EEOC. Shortly after it became clear that Feinberg would be leaving, Clark assigned most of the day-to-day work on the project to me because of his heavy involvement in other LDF projects and initiatives. Around March 1966, Clark recommended to Greenberg that I should be assigned the lead role in the litigation campaign because, based on the short period I had worked under his supervision, he had the confidence that I could handle the responsibility even though I had only recently graduated from law school.[31] While I still had aspirations to work on the death penalty campaign, in retrospect the opportunity to play a major role in the employment discrimination litigation campaign and with *the* leading civil rights public interest legal organization in the United States turned out to be unparalleled for the career of a young lawyer. Such a chance is one that only a few lawyers get during their entire careers, and in a big law firm, if it ever happened, it might be the capstone of a career. This unique opportunity, the fulfillment of a long-held aspiration of devoting my professional life to public interest and civil rights, allowed me to play a major role in transforming Title VII into a "potential tool for equalization of employment opportunity."[32] I had a front-row seat for many of the cases covered in this book because I served as one of the lead attorneys for the plaintiffs in *Griggs* and many other landmark employment discrimination cases.

As an African American, I personally had experienced racial discrimination in all of its manifestations. I was born and raised in High Point, North Carolina, the fourth oldest of eighteen children of Daniel and Mary Lendon Belton. I grew up in the segregated South. Racial segregation was the order of the day in all aspects of my life growing up in High Point, not only in public education but also in access to restaurants, hotels, theaters, employment, parks, cemeteries, buses, trains, drinking fountains, hospitals, lunch counters, retail stores, recreational and sporting events, barber shops, churches, restrooms, housing, and transportation. I graduated from the state law–mandated racially segregated William Penn High School in 1953, a year before the Supreme Court's May 1954 decision in *Brown v. Board of Education*. Many of my high school teachers, all of whom were African Americans, had Ph.D.s and some were unable to pursue their career aspirations to teach on a college level because racially discriminatory hiring practices prevented them from even entering the applicant pool of those seeking appointments at historically white colleges and universities and because there were a limited number of jobs as professors at historically African American colleges and universities.

I still have vivid recollections of African American men and women, including my father, who, if hired at all, were employed only in low-paying, physically demanding, dirty, and dead-end jobs in many of the furniture manufacturing businesses in High Point, a city that is known as the "Furniture Capital of the World." I also recall the help-wanted ads in the local newspapers under the heading of "Help Wanted—Colored," "Help Wanted—White," or "jobs for colored man," "colored boy," or "colored woman."[33] Many of these African American workers rode to work in the back of segregated buses, as I did, operated by Duke Power Company, the same Duke Power Company that was the defendant in *Griggs*. I witnessed firsthand the discrimination my father endured on his job because of his race, and on two occasions my oldest brother, Dan, and I were with him when his life was threatened by mobs of angry white men. My firsthand, day-to-day experience with racial segregation and particularly the two episodes with my father were major factors that ultimately informed my decision to be a civil rights lawyer. Another factor that shaped my decision was the opportunity to study, during Negro History Week (now Black History Month), the contributions that African Americans such as Charles Hamilton Houston and Thurgood Marshall had made in the field of civil rights and the history of the long struggle to gain equality for African Americans.

My civil rights activism began when I was in undergraduate school at the University of Connecticut (UConn), where, among other things, I was a founding member of the campus chapter of the NAACP. There were only a few African American students at UConn at that time in the middle and late 1950s. On one occasion while attending UConn, I made a trip by car from Connecticut to North Carolina with a white female professor to visit with my family. Because of racial segregation, I sat in the backseat of the car from Washington, D.C., to North Carolina to avoid the risk of harm to either of us at the hands of whites because I was driving with a sole white female through the South. That leg of the trip was a harrowing experience, and I decided to return to UConn by a different mode of transportation. After receiving my undergraduate degree from UConn in 1961, I continued my activism by joining the New York City chapter of the Congress of Racial Equality (CORE). During this time, I was arrested and jailed for participating in CORE-sponsored sit-in demonstrations protesting racially discriminatory rental referral practices. Later, I entered Boston University Law School with the intent of devoting my legal career to public interest and civil rights. After graduating in 1965, I began working at the LDF in December 1965, and in 1970 I joined the racially integrated law firm Chambers, Stein, Ferguson & Lanning in Charlotte, North Carolina. Although I left the New York office of the LDF in late 1969, pursuant to an arrangement with Greenberg I remained on the LDF payroll in order to litigate a number of employment discrimination cases in which I served as counsel for plaintiffs while engaged in the process for admission to the North Carolina bar. I left private practice in 1975 to join the faculty at Vanderbilt University Law School, where I eventually became the first tenured African American law professor in its history and was the only person of color on its full-time tenured faculty for twenty-seven years until another African American earned tenure there.[34] There were other tenured African American professors on the law faculty during this time, but they earned tenure at other law schools and thus came with tenure when hired. During my first several years at Vanderbilt, I conducted an employment discrimination law clinic under a grant from the EEOC.

The two other persons who formed the core of the LDF's employment discrimination litigation team were Gabrielle Kirk McDonald (Gaby) and Albert J. Rosenthal (Al). Gaby, an African American female, joined the LDF in June 1966.[35] She and I were the key LDF staff attorneys who, under the leadership of Greenberg, had the day-to-day responsibility for the execution and administration of the litigation campaign during its early years. Born in St. Paul, Minnesota, Gaby was raised by her mother in New York City. She, like me, had firsthand experience with racial discrimination while living in New York and Teaneck, New Jersey. She attended Boston University and Hunter College and then, without earning her undergraduate degree, enrolled in Howard University Law School. Howard Law School, a historically African American school, trained many of the most important and influential civil rights lawyers, including Thurgood Marshall, and many of the lawyers who would later become cooperating attorneys in southern states in the employment discrimination litigation campaign and other civil rights cases on the LDF's docket. Gaby never wanted to be *just* a lawyer; she wanted to be a civil rights lawyer, and for this reason applied only to Howard because it had been one of the cradles of the legal arm of the civil rights movement. She graduated first in her class at Howard and was a member of the *Howard Law Journal*.

Gaby's employment with the LDF was only the beginning of a very distinguished career. After leaving the LDF in 1969, Gaby went into private practice in Houston, Texas, and continued to specialize in employment discrimination cases. One of her biggest victories while in private practice in Texas was a $1.2

million settlement for about 400 black employees of the Lone Star Steel Company.[36] Upon the recommendation of U.S. Senator Lloyd Bentsen of Texas and the nomination of President Jimmy Carter, Gaby became a judge for the U.S. District Court for the Southern District of Texas in 1979.[37] She was the first African American to be appointed to the federal bench in Texas and only the third African American female federal judge in the United States. Race became an issue in several high-profile cases she handled as a federal judge, when one of the parties asked her to recuse herself on the grounds that she could not be an impartial judge in cases involving minority parties. She refused to do so.[38] She resigned from the federal bench in 1988 and once again entered the private practice of law and taught at several law schools. She returned to the bench in 1993 but this time as a judge on a new court, the International Criminal Tribunal for the former Yugoslavia (ICTY), created by the United Nations to try war crimes arising out of the atrocities in the former Yugoslavia. Gaby was the sole American and one of two women on that court. Between 1997 and 1999, she was the president of ICTY, with the additional duties of overseeing the trials in the genocide cases that occurred in Rwanda, Africa.

Greenberg enlisted Al Rosenthal to be a consultant to the employment discrimination litigation campaign. Al served in this role for about ten years, from 1966 to 1976. He graduated from Harvard Law School, where he was the president of the *Harvard Law Review*. After clerking for several federal judges, including Supreme Court Justice Felix Frankfurter, Al worked in government and private practice before joining the Columbia Law School faculty in 1964. Greenberg hired Al because he was a superb "combination scholar and litigator" who would be a good fit for the employment discrimination litigation project.[39] In addition to serving as counsel in a number of landmark employment discrimination cases on the LDF's docket, including *Griggs,* Al brought together a consultative group of distinguished labor law practitioners and scholars, as well as labor economists, to meet periodically with members of the employment discrimination litigation team to discuss critically some of the thorny substantive and procedural issues that had to be litigated. Al also recruited an amazing and energetic group of bright young lawyers to assist pro bono in legal research, drafting pleadings and discovery documents and writing briefs and other legal memoranda on new or novel issues. Many of these young lawyers were recent law school graduates and were employed at major law firms in New York City.

Al wrote superb briefs and memoranda in a number of cases. Some of the law professors he recruited also wrote briefs, particularly appellate briefs, involving novel substantive and procedural issues arising under Title VII. Professor George Cooper of Columbia Law School, for example, drafted the court of appeals brief in *Griggs* and also wrote the petition for certiorari and the plaintiffs' briefs the LDF filed in the Supreme Court in the case. Another professor, Sandy J. Rosen, then at the University of Maryland Law School, took a lead role with the LDF's consultative group of lawyers and professors to develop litigation strategies in the Fund's seniority discrimination cases. Other law professors served as "sounding boards" on procedural and substantive issues that we expected to be raised or supervised law students who researched novel issues or drafted legal memoranda or discovery demands. The LDF's use of academics in its employment discrimination litigation campaign was similar to the assistance it received from academics in some of its other major litigation campaigns, including *Brown v. Board of Education* and the death penalty project.

Gaby, Al, and I worked closely together, developing and implementing the various litigation strategies for the campaign. We compiled an extensive bank of complaints, legal memoranda, discovery documents such as interrogatories, and briefs on many issues that provided a ready resource for other LDF attorneys who handled a few employment discrimination cases, cooperating attorneys, and other attorneys in private practice who represented plaintiffs in employment discrimination cases. These litigation documents served as a model for many years not only for the LDF and its cooperating attorneys but also for other lawyers. We also had the first line of responsibility for evaluating cases to be litigated, and we requested Greenberg's input about any cases in which there was any doubt as to whether we should proceed. I cannot recall any instance in which he rejected our litigation recommendations, but it was rare indeed for us not to recommend assistance for cooperating attorneys, particularly with respect to charges that had been filed with the EEOC with some assistance from the LDF.

THE ROLE OF THE COOPERATING ATTORNEYS

Although the core LDF litigation team consisted of Gaby, Al, and me, it is important to note that my reference to the litigation team of necessity in particular cases includes cooperating attorneys, although for many cases the local attorney may not be specifically identified. The success the LDF had in its employment discrimination litigation campaign could not have been achieved without their participation; the staff worked with about 200 of them.[40] Most of the LDF's cooperating attorneys in the early years of the employment discrimination litigation campaign were African Americans, many of whom practiced law in southern states and had graduated from historically black law schools, such as Howard University, Northern Carolina Central, Southern University, Florida A&M, and Texas Southern.

Many of the cooperating attorneys assisted African Americans with the filing of charges with the EEOC, with charges often becoming the basis of lawsuits on the LDF docket. Cooperating attorneys, as used in public interest litigation, generally are lawyers in private practice who represent plaintiffs on either a pro bono basis or for a significantly lower attorney's fee.[41] However, the "significantly lower fee" standard is inapplicable in civil rights cases in which Congress provides for a statutory award of attorney's fees. For example, Title VII provides for reasonable attorney's fees for successful plaintiffs, but what is a reasonable fee under fee-shifting statutes became a major issue in civil rights cases.

The LDF established a Civil Rights Institute to provide a form of continuing legal education on civil rights developments and to provide the opportunity for the cooperating attorneys and staff attorneys to have a bit of respite from the trench warfare of civil rights litigation. As Meltsner described it:

> The Fund had an enormous interest in keeping the Southern black lawyers who were a source of its cases, and ultimately its power, well informed of the dizzying developments in civil rights, a legal specialty with its own technicalities, as complex as tax or copyrights law. One means of doing this was periodic Civil Rights Institutes, held at Howard Law School in Washington. The front-line troops, most of them Howard graduates, were invited from the battle zone to hear three days of lectures and not incidentally, to bivouac in the District's watering places. By 1963 these conferences had acquired a prestige as the birthplace of many a civil rights strategy, but the assorted pleasures of liberty were a constant distraction, and so they were moved first to New Orleans, then to Atlanta, and finally to Airlie House, a pleasant and relatively isolated conference center in the Virginia hunt country.[42]

The Airlie House, located in Warrenton, Virginia, was one of the only conference centers in the South before 1964. The LDF Airlie House Civil Rights Institute and its previous iterations had become an integral part of the culture of civil rights and related educational mission of the LDF when I joined in 1965. After the employment discrimination litigation campaign was initiated, developments in employment discrimination law, legal theory, trial strategy, and remedies became an important part of the curriculum. Representatives from other civil rights groups and the EEOC often attended the Airlie House conferences as either speakers or participants, and the litigation team maintained regular communication with other organizations, such as the NAACP, that were engaged in the Title VII enforcement process in order to coordinate the various strategies of enforcement when advisable.

The employment litigation campaign also benefited from other LDF initiatives. Beginning in 1962, the Field Foundation provided funding for what later became the Earl Warren Legal Training Program. Its purpose was to alleviate the shortage of African American lawyers in southern states. Pursuant to this funding initiative, some recent African American law school graduates participated in a postgraduate fellowship program that included a year of internship with the LDF at its headquarters in New York or in the office of one of the LDF's cooperating attorneys. After the year, the fellows began to practice law in a mutually agreed upon location, primarily in the South, where few or no black lawyers were available to serve black citizens. They were paid a diminishing subsidy for three years, and one of the most important benefits of this subsidy served to help these new lawyers establish a law library for their newly opened offices.[43] Some white law graduates were also beneficiaries of the Legal Training Program, and the inclusion of white law graduates led to some of the first integrated law firms in the South.

A number of the cooperating lawyers who were the beneficiaries of the training program carried a substantial load of employment discrimination cases. This new cadre of lawyers had the opportunity to become the current civil rights trailblazers in establishing new laws under the Civil Rights Act of 1964, including Title VII, that were unavailable to a number of pioneering civil rights lawyers who had preceded them.[44] One of the first beneficiaries of the fellowship program, Julius Chambers, returned to his native state of North Carolina and opened one of the first integrated law firms in Charlotte. Chambers and I were the lead attorneys in *Griggs.*

THE LITIGATION CHALLENGE

Because Title VII was brand-new law that had more bones than flesh, it had to be interpreted in numerous lawsuits before the groups and individuals it sought to protect would know what impact it would have on their working lives. The most challenging problem the litigation team faced was selecting cases that would best provide the opportunity for the orderly and positive development of favorable precedent-setting legal principles. Without a doubt, the most important issue in Title VII at the time it was enacted was (and still is) the meaning of the term *discrimination*. At a news conference the day before Title VII's effective date, Meltsner and Clark specifically noted that Congress had not defined the critical concept of discrimination in Title VII and that this issue would be a major one that had to be addressed by the EEOC and by the courts.[45]

Although Title VII speaks in grand and majestic language in prohibiting discrimination because of race, color, religion, sex, and national origin, the statute does not define key terms such as *to discriminate, intended,* and *intentionally,* which are used repeatedly throughout the Act. There is no real dispute that Congress intended to prohibit blatant, overt, or intentional racially discriminatory employment practices.[46] This view of the meaning of *discrimination* is now firmly embraced in the disparate treatment theory of discrimination, which requires proof of intentional discrimination. Had Congress clearly wanted to prohibit only intentional discrimination, it easily could have accomplished that goal by including only Section 703(a)(1), which provides that it is an unlawful employment practice for an employer "to fail or refuse to hire or discharge any individual or otherwise to discriminate against any individual with respect to his compensation, terms, conditions, or privileges of employment because of such individual's race, color, religion, sex, or national origin." But Congress added another provision, Section 703(a)(2), which provides:

> It shall be an unlawful employment practice for an employer—
>   (2) to limit, segregate, or classify his employees or applicants for employment in any way which would deprive or tend to deprive any individual of employment opportunities or otherwise adversely affect his status as an employee, because of such individual's race, color, religion, sex, or national origin.[47]

Section 703(a)(2) does not include either the term *intent* or *discriminate.* The inclusion of Section 703(a)(2) in the Act raised the critical issue of whether Congress intended to prohibit more than intentional or disparate treatment discrimination. The legislative history of Title VII, as originally enacted and as amended a number of times since 1964, is silent on the issue even though

Congress in the original Act and in later amendments included statutory definitions of some other terms, and there is legislative support for the *Griggs* disparate impact theory in the legislative history of the 1972 amendments to Title VII even before Congress legislatively endorsed the theory in the Civil Rights Act of 1991, with the *Griggs* theory directly referenced there. The Supreme Court made specific reference to this legislative history when it stated in *Connecticut v. Teal* that this legislative "history demonstrates that Congress recognized and endorsed the disparate-impact analysis employed by this Court in *Griggs*."[48]

Concerning the terms used in the statute, Congress provides a statutory definition of *employer* in the original version of Title VII. *Religion* was statutorily defined in the 1972 amendment to Title VII. *Because of sex* was defined in the 1978 amendment to Title VII. Other terms, such as *complaining party* and *demonstrate* to explain the meaning on the allocations of the burdens of proof, are statutorily defined in the Title VII amendments of the Civil Rights Act of 1991. Congress also defined *discriminate* in the later-enacted Americans with Disabilities Act (ADA) of 1990. The ADA definition of *discrimination* includes all of the theories of discrimination, i.e., present effects of past discrimination, disparate impact, and disparate treatment developed in the context of the enforcement of Title VII.

There are several possible reasons Congress did not provide a statutory definition of *discriminate* or *discrimination*. The first is that racial discrimination even in 1964 was so blatant; made so ugly, visible, revolting, and repulsive by the civil rights demonstrations of the 1960s; and legitimated by positive law in so many instances, that Congress deemed it unnecessary to define the term. Second, the civil rights coalition that rallied in support of the Civil Rights Act of 1964 might have deemed it unnecessary to push for a definition of *discrimination* or critically explore the concept of equality based on the assumption that all constituents of the coalition subscribed to the same concept. Third, the argument has been made that many of the critical issues and terms, including *discriminate*, were glossed over so that the supporters of the bill could keep the support of Senator Everett M. Dirksen, who held the sixty-seventh vote that was needed to break the filibuster of the Southern Democrats.[49] Even today, there is still an often contentious debate about the meaning of *unlawful discrimination*, and the *Griggs* disparate impact theory has added a new dimension to that debate.

The issues of defining *discrimination* and the kind of evidence relevant to proving unlawful employment discrimination have been an ongoing national problem since the establishment of the first federal Fair Employment Practices Committee pursuant to President Roosevelt's Executive Order in 1941. For example, the following are some of the guidelines the first FEPC developed to determine the validity of a discrimination complaint:

- Facts showing that it was the policy or practice of an employer to hire members of a minority group as laborers or custodial workers without regard to qualification
- Recruiting a substantial group of skilled workers from a technical school that blacks or Jews attended, but hiring no blacks and only a small number of Jews
- Placing racial or religious limitations in job advertisements
- Discharging an employee for failing to salute the flag because of religious conviction
- Requiring black applicants to obtain a permit from a union known to discriminate
- Quota hiring to restrict the number of blacks in the workforce

The mere fact that an employer had no blacks or only a small number in its employment was insufficient for a finding of discrimination unless coupled with two other conditions: the plant guard turned black applicants away, and the employer contended that certain skills were concentrated in certain nationalities.[50] The records of the first FEPC seem to make clear that its view of unlawful employment discrimination required a finding of motive or intent, yet its method of proving unlawful discrimination under this test of discrimination would inevitably provide a remedy for class, rather than individual, discrimination.[51]

In addition to the problem of defining *discrimination* or fleshing out a theory or theories of discrimination, other questions that had to be resolved included the following:

- What kind of proof is relevant to prove unlawful employment discrimination because of race, color, sex, national origin, or religion in light of the fact that practically all employers, labor unions, and employment agencies would likely claim that their employment policies have been in compliance with Title VII since July 2, 1965, even if they openly discriminated against those protected by the law before July 2, 1965?

- What kinds of practices beyond "white only" or "men only" policies and practices are unlawful?
- Does Title VII reach present effects of past overt discriminatory policies and practices even when such practices may have been lawful before Title VII or may have been eliminated prior to the effective date of the statute?
- How should the rights of white employees be reconciled with the rights of those protected under the statute who accrued little or no seniority rights to jobs historically reserved for white or male employees because of pre–Title VII discriminatory policies and practices of employers and unions?
- Under what circumstances, if any, do seniority provisions and "last-hired, first-fired" provisions in collective bargaining agreements in the unionized sector of the workplace constitute unlawful employment discrimination if they have the effect of perpetuating or "locking in" the effects of past discriminatory practices in the post–Title VII period in light of the statutory protection provided for "bona fide seniority and merit systems," and the legislative history on protection of "vested rights of seniority"?
- If seniority systems facilitate some form of discrimination, under what circumstances would the system be unlawful under Title VII?
- Under what circumstances may an employer administer pre- and postemployment tests in view of the fact that the statute provides that it is not unlawful for employers to "give or act upon the results of any professionally developed ability test provided its administration or action upon the results is not designed, intended, or used to discriminate because of race, color, religion, sex or national origin"?
- May plaintiffs pursue class actions under Title VII in light of the fact that the statutory language tends to speak in terms of individual rather than group rights?
- Are defendants entitled to a jury trial in light of the fact that Title VII provides for damages in the form of back pay for individuals who have suffered economically because of unlawful discrimination?
- Assuming that a plaintiff is successful in proving unlawful discrimination, what kind of relief should be awarded?
- How should the rights of long-term employees be reconciled with the rights of those protected by the statute who accrued little or no

seniority rights in "white only" jobs because of pre-Act discriminatory hiring and promotion practices of employers and unions?

These are some of the same or similar questions that had been identified years earlier by the first FEPC set up by President Roosevelt's Executive Order.[52]

Employers and unions, like the LDF, were also concerned about the many unanswered questions raised by Title VII. For example, in September 1964, the National Association of Manufacturers (NAM) conducted a nationwide series of seminars in twenty-two cities to acquaint businessmen with their rights and obligations under the law. Among the questions NAM deemed to be most frequently asked and discussed in these seminars were the following:

- Does Title VII require affirmative action?
- Is preferential treatment for those protected by the Act required?
- Are employers protected from multiple lawsuits before state and federal courts and agencies?
- Does the Act have any effect on tests used by employers to make employment decisions?
- May employers deny black applicants jobs if they are not capable of or qualified for vacancies?
- How best may employers defend against employment discrimination lawsuits?
- Is an employer required or permitted to maintain a certain percentage (quota) of minorities?[53]

A major issue of concern for unions was the effect, if any, Title VII would have on the seniority rights of white union members who had obtained superior seniority rights in a segregated workplace and segregated bargaining units.[54]

A LITIGATION STRATEGY EMERGES: REPRESENTING PRIVATE ATTORNEYS GENERAL

In order for the courts to decide these and other issues, they had to be raised by one of the other two instrumentalities Congress had authorized to seek judicial enforcement—the Department of Justice, under its authority to litigate "pattern and practice" cases, or individually aggrieved "private attorneys general," through private litigation. The private plaintiffs the LDF represented in its litigation campaign were "private attorneys general." The private attorney general philosophy is based on the view that private individuals have important roles to play in vindicating the public policy of civil rights legislation because the goals of civil rights legislation cannot be achieved solely by enforcement initiatives undertaken by the Attorney General and the Department of Justice. In *Newman v. Piggie Park Enterprises, Inc.*, an early 1968 LDF case that arose under the public accommodations provision of the Civil Rights Act of 1964 (Title II) and in which LDF had advanced the private attorney general theory in its brief, the Supreme Court endorsed the view that Congress, by allowing private suits under the Civil Rights Act of 1964, had empowered private individuals to become private attorneys general to vindicate the civil rights policy objectives of the statute:

> When the Civil Rights Act of 1964 was passed, it was evident that enforcement would prove difficult and that the Nation would have to rely in part upon private litigation as a means of securing broad compliance with the law. A . . . suit [under the Civil Rights Act of 1964] is private in form only. When a plaintiff brings an action under that [Act], he cannot recover damages. If he obtains an injunction, he does so not for himself alone but also as a "private attorney general," vindicating a policy that Congress considered of the highest priority.

The Court went on to say that Congress had provided for attorney's fees "not simply to penalize litigants who deliberately advance arguments they know to be untenable but, more broadly, to encourage individuals injured by racial discrimination to seek judicial relief under [the Act]."[55]

As the first steps in devising its litigation strategy in the fall and winter of 1965, the LDF litigation team analyzed and tabulated the large number of charges it and the NAACP had helped African Americans file with the EEOC. The analysis also showed that seniority systems and pen-and-paper tests that seemed neutral on their face were among the most discriminatory practices engaged in by employers and labor unions. These findings from the analysis about the discriminatory effects of seemingly neutral practices were shared with a number of historians, sociologists, and labor law and civil rights professors, who generally confirmed the LDF's preliminary analyses. The analysis of the charges also identified several industries that should be examined closely as targets of litigation. The litigation team targeted industries where African American unemployment and economic growth were high and focused on semiskilled and skilled blue-collar jobs, which paid well but did not require much formal education.[56] These industries included railroads,[57] pulp and paper,[58] steel,[59] tobacco,[60] textile,[61] trucking,[62] and public utilities.[63] Many of the employers in these industries used tests in making employment decisions, and practically all of them were unionized and had a history of using facially neutral seniority practices to make employment decisions that adversely affected the employment opportunities of African Americans because of race. The railroad industry, for example, had a long history of excluding blacks from jobs that paid well or blatantly segregating them into all-black seniority units. This blatant segregation by employers and unions in highly visible and closely related jobs, such as porters and conductors, made the railroad industry such a symbol of discrimination that its inclusion as a target was required despite its general economic decline. A positive aspect of focusing on the railroad industry was that there were a large number of black employees who were willing to assert their rights and had done so historically while the segregated black unions gave them an organizational base for support. The paper industry, meanwhile, was a high-paying growth industry with plants located throughout the southeastern part of the United States, where a large number of blacks were available for work and the plants were often a primary employer in the community. Blacks in the paper industry were relegated to menial, lower-paying jobs, and pen-and-paper tests were used to screen applicants for jobs traditionally reserved for whites. More often than not, many of the big unions were named as defendants because the seniority agreements in the LDF's seniority discrimination cases were the product of collective bargaining between unions and employers. As with the railroad industry, international unions had sanctioned and charted separate racially segregated unions. The EEOC conducted its first-ever hearings on January 12 and 13, 1967, in Charlotte, North Carolina, and focused on racial discrimination in employment in the textile industry.[64] The textile industry in the South then became another potential target of opportunity in the campaign.

One of the major problems in deciding upon a litigation strategy was that employment discrimination litigation did not fit neatly into the traditional civil rights law reform model that the LDF honed to a fine art in the campaign leading to *Brown v. Board of Education*. Under the *Brown* model, organizational control over the sequence and pace of the litigation was the cornerstone of the successful implementation of the LDF's goals.[65] Leroy Clark, who participated in the early phase of the employment discrimination litigation strategies, described the differences in the two classes of cases:

The difficulties of litigation as a remedial tool without the black community independently generating its pressure are readily apparent. First, persons must know how to make a complaint and, at least initially, they may risk discharge from employment. The attorney must have sufficient facts about the internal operation of the plant in order to judge whether a violation of [Title VII] has occurred. Such information is difficult to ascertain; whereas in school desegregation suits the discriminatory pattern in one school district resembled the pattern in another, employment discrimination patterns differ from industry to industry. Also, the typical voting rights suit involved a Southern state agency with mediocre attorneys; the defendants in employment cases were the largest companies in the country, retaining highly paid, competent counsel who offered vigorous opposition and were extremely adept at delay. With the added ingredient of a hostile federal Southern judiciary, a single suit could last two years or more. In the interim, the plaintiffs may have lost faith in the efficacy of litigation, moved to other jobs, or accepted inadequate settlements. It is in this kind of trench warfare, with limited staff, limited financial resources, and the inherent capacity in the law for delay, that civil rights attorneys will face serious difficulties in having a major impact on employment discrimination.[66]

Another problem in thinking about a litigation strategy was that employment discrimination litigation prior to Title VII presented easy and obvious targets, such as explicit policies or union contracts excluding African Americans from desirable jobs,[67] segregated departments and facilities,[68] or discriminatory pay scales.[69] Much of the more blatant and overt racial discrimination was eliminated by the Plans for Progress and state FEPC activities. After July 1, 1965, overt discrimination on the basis of race became unlawful, and employers and unions began to abandon obvious and blatant racially discriminatory policies and practices. However, the effects of those earlier obvious and blatant racially discriminatory policies and practices were carried forward into the post–July 2, 1965, period. Discriminatory employment practices became more subtle. Major employers and unions began to adopt testing and educational devices and seniority systems that appeared facially neutral or colorblind but that operated to perpetuate the effects of past and societal discrimination.

With many of the overt incidents of racial discrimination abandoned or about to be abandoned by employers and unions, what was left was systemic and institutional discrimination embedded in basic personnel policies or organizational structures of companies and unions. Unlike racial discrimination, many overt manifestations of sex discrimination continued after 1965 because employers believed that the "bona fide occupational qualification" exception exempted some sex-based employment practices from the prohibitions of

Title VII. This more subtle brand of racial discrimination did not constitute the easiest target for an effective litigation campaign to eradicate job discrimination. Consequently, it soon became obvious that Title VII litigation would require substantial manpower in pretrial preparation, including an analysis of voluminous records and extremely technical factual and legal questions. Proving the existence of discrimination in hiring, testing, seniority, and promotion practices would be demanding.[70] One can see this from the fact that over 1,000 lawyer hours were devoted to litigating *Griggs* through the Supreme Court, and *Griggs* was a relatively easy case to prepare for trial compared with most cases tried during the early stages of Title VII enforcement. The great effort required to litigate a class action Title VII case would severely strain the limited resources of the private plaintiffs' bar, while defendants would be able to bear the demands and costs of litigation with less difficulty, leaving a "David-Goliath confrontation."[71]

While some federal and state case law on employment discrimination existed at the time of Title VII's enactment, a coherent body of law on the subject did not exist.[72] Moreover, much federal employment discrimination case law was premised on the Constitution because discrimination in the private sector was not generally subject to legal restraints. The existing case law did not become useful until efforts were devoted to the development of legal concepts of discrimination that could be applied to private employers. There were, however, three overarching simply stated but difficult issues that informed the LDF's litigation campaign. The first and most critically important issue was defining a theory or theories of discrimination. The second was deciding what kind of evidence would be relevant to proving a claim of unlawful discrimination in light of the fact that no defendant was likely to readily admit that it practiced racial discrimination. As one court once observed, "[d]efendants of even minimal sophistication will neither admit discriminatory animus; and because most employment practices involve an element of discretion, alternative hypotheses (including that of simple mistake) will always be possible and often plausible."[73] The third issue was determining the specific kinds of relief that would be appropriate to remedy proven claims of unlawful employment discrimination.

For several reasons, a litigation strategy patterned primarily on the *Brown* campaign to develop a body of employment discrimination law on these simply stated but difficult issues would not have been feasible. First, the LDF could not ethically put some cases on the back burner while more forcefully pressing other and perhaps more favorable cases. Second, unlike in the *Brown* campaign, where there was some possibility of controlling the manner in which issues should be raised and the kinds of cases that would be most helpful in raising them, it was literally impossible to exercise control over issues and cases in the employment discrimination litigation campaign because other entities such as the Department of Justice and other law reform organizations also had an interest in developing the law under Title VII. Third, the *Brown* paradigm was ill-suited for the more subtle discriminatory tactics that had replaced the earlier more blatant forms of discrimination. In most of the pre- and early post-*Brown* cases, the real issue was not so much whether a school board had, in fact, engaged in racial discrimination but rather what the remedy should be. Overt racial discrimination in employment was less prevalent in 1965 than in earlier years, but the effects of the pre-1965 overt discrimination continued pervasively. Fourth, the requirement of exhaustion of administrative remedies before the EEOC made it a possibility that ideal "test cases" would be settled or conciliated in an unsatisfactory way, and conciliation is not a process for establishing judicial precedents.[74] Finally, Title VII presented procedural technicalities to private enforcement that required judicial clarification before substantive interpretations could be reached. Because the LDF staff was too small to handle the anticipated volume of cases, a project to develop standards for the appointment of counsel was considered.[75] This strategy, however, was assigned a low priority because of the need first to develop the legal concepts of employment discrimination.

Lawyering skills and law development techniques could have been devoted to trying to make the EEOC administrative process a more responsive conflict resolution device for employment discrimination claims, but the experience under older administrative enforcement procedures and the uncertain start of the EEOC suggested that the limited private resources could better be used in the judicial enforcement process. A major factor that ultimately determined the LDF's strategy in the litigation phase was the reality of the difficulty in identifying the constellation of facts that would best raise the issues considered critical to programmatic law development. Because of the difficulty of making an informed decision about which issues should be raised first and in what kinds of factual paradigms, the LDF finally settled upon an initial litigation strategy that involved filing suit in any and all cases in which cooperating attorneys had been retained and the attorneys had requested the assistance of the LDF and dealing with substantive and procedural issues as they arose.

Specific industries were targeted later, but two of the most important categories of cases that bubbled to the surface early were seniority discrimination and testing cases.

On October 18, 1965, just over three months after the effective date of Title VII, Julius Chambers, then a cooperating attorney, and I filed the first-ever complaint in federal court on behalf of private plaintiffs under Title VII.[76] The litigation phase of the campaign had begun.

4. The Litigation Phase Begins

The litigation phase began when the LDF filed the case of *Brinkley v. The Great Atlantic & Pacific Tea Company* (A&P)[1] in the United States District Court for the Eastern District of North Carolina in Wilmington, on October 18, 1965. *Brinkley* was the first case ever filed under Title VII and was filed just over three months after the effective date of Title VII. The plaintiff, Annie Brinkley, an African American female, had applied for jobs as a cashier at two of the A&P's food stores in Wilmington on July 20, 1965. She was not offered employment at either. The employees at one store told her that the manager was out and could not be located. The manager at the other store told her that no jobs were available and that applications for employment at later dates would not be accepted. With the assistance from an LDF summer intern, Brinkley filed a charge of racial discrimination with the EEOC on July 29, 1965. The EEOC found reasonable cause to believe that Brinkley had been the victim of unlawful employment discrimination and issued her a notice of right to sue in September 1965. The parties reached a settlement in January 1966, pursuant to which A&P hired ninety-one African Americans in North and South Carolina. Of those hired by October 1966, forty-two were cashiers. A&P hired the lead plaintiff, Annie Brinkley, as a cashier and paid her at the highest salary for a beginning employee.

Despite the settlement and the fact that the district court did not discuss any of the three generations of procedural issues soon to be addressed, the case was nonetheless significant for the complaint in the case, which Michael Meltsner drafted. There were several reasons for its significance. First, it served as a model for practically all the complaints that the LDF, its cooperating attorneys, and many other attorneys and civil rights organizations filed in employment discrimination cases. Second, a number of the allegations made in the complaint raised some important issues, most of which the courts eventually resolved in favor of plaintiffs. In *Brinkley*, Meltsner alleged that the case was brought as a class action on behalf of Brinkley and other similarly situated African Americans. The relief requested included a claim for back pay for Brinkley for the economic damages she had suffered because of the unlawful denial of employment, costs, and reasonable attorney's fees. Title VII specifically provides that a court may award back pay and attorney's fees. Meltsner also included a claim for relief under 42 U.S.C. § 1981, a civil rights statute enacted during the Reconstruction era after the Civil War.[2] Each of these allegations—class action, back pay, and the Section 1981 claim—led to some important legal developments that took on added significance after *Griggs*.

Broadly speaking, the first decade of litigation under Title VII spawned three overlapping generations of issues. The first-generation issues were primarily procedural, involving, for example, the scope of the obligations imposed on private plaintiffs to exhaust the administrative proceedings of the EEOC before seeking judicial relief. The second-generation issues concerned the merits of claims of unlawful employment discrimination and focused on theories of liability, defenses, the order and allocation of burdens of proof, and the type and quantum of evidence relevant to prove or disprove claims of unlawful employment discrimination. A critical second-generation issue involved the development of theories of discrimination because Congress had not provided a statutory definition of *discrimination* in Title VII. The third-generation issues involved the task of formulating effective remedies, such as injunctive relief, back pay, other monetary awards, costs, and attorney's fees.[3] These three generations of issues frequently appear in single cases even today. In exploring *Griggs*, this book focuses primarily on second- and third-generation issues. However, a brief examination of how the courts approached first-generation issues provides great insight into how they handled the later generations.

The courts adopted a liberal approach in deciding first-generation issues, and that liberal approach carried over to second- and third-generation issues as well, at least during the first decade of the litigation campaign. The arrangement Congress established for the exhaustion of administrative remedies before the EEOC[4] was, and still is, fraught with uncertainty, technicalities, and potential procedural traps. As one court correctly observed, Title VII is "rife with procedural requirements which are sufficiently labyrinthine to baffle the most experienced lawyer, yet its enforcement mechanisms are usually triggered by laymen."[5] This exhaustion labyrinth exists because Title VII went through extensive revisions in Congress. On the one hand, the congressional compromise spoke in lofty terms about ending discrimination in employment. On the other hand, some senators believed that if the process for seeking judicial relief became so administratively encumbered, many individuals who believed they were the victims of unlawful employment discrimination would forfeit their right to seek judicial relief.[6]

In the early years of the campaign, I argued some of the more important early Title VII cases involving first-generation issues in the district courts and the Courts of Appeals for the Fourth and Fifth Circuits.[7] The litigation team spent a substantial amount of time defending against a constant barrage of procedural and technical defenses raising exhaustion of administrative remedies questions. Defendants raised every defense imaginable, technical and otherwise, and attempted to take advantage of every ambiguity in Title VII to block, deny, or delay the opportunity for plaintiffs to seek judicial relief.[8] Generally, the courts liberally construed the administrative exhaustion requirements in favor of the plaintiffs on the theory that, as one court said in an early LDF case, the congressional purpose in requiring aggrieved individuals to first resort to the EEOC was to give defendants the opportunity to respond to persuasion rather than judicial coercion.[9] Another court said in an LDF case that "the procedures of Title VII were [not] intended to serve as a stumbling block to the accomplishment of the statutory objective."[10]

One of the favorite procedural defenses asserted by employers and unions in almost every case during the early years of litigation was that Title VII imposed a mandatory statutory obligation on the EEOC to attempt to conciliate a charge, and its failure to do so was a jurisdictional bar to the filing of a civil action. Lower courts routinely rejected this defense. In 1973, in a case in which the LDF served as cocounsel for the plaintiff, the Supreme Court settled the issue when it ruled that the jurisdictional prerequisites for filing a judicial complaint are satisfied when a plaintiff files a timely charge with the EEOC and, after receipt of a notice of right to sue from the EEOC, files a timely complaint in the district court.[11] The courts thus refused to hold the plaintiffs hostage to the omission of acts by the EEOC as long as those two requirements were satisfied.

Almost all of the major administrative exhaustion issues were decided in favor of the plaintiffs, but often only at the appellate level. The courts also took a liberal view of the scope of the claims that could be raised in the judicial complaint based upon the allegations made in the charge to the EEOC, even though some of the claims alleged in the complaint were not specifically alleged in the charges filed with the EEOC. The courts did so based on the theory that Congress intended the courts to be the final arbiter of claims arising under Title VII.[12] Some courts were sympathetic to plaintiffs who were unable to find an attorney to represent them after they received a notice of right to sue from the EEOC. Receipt of the right-to-sue notice triggers the time frame within which a plaintiff must file a complaint in court, and failure to file the complaint within that period results in a forfeiture of the claim. These courts allowed potential plaintiffs to file the EEOC's notice-of-right-to-sue letter with the clerk of court to toll the limitations period for filing a judicial complaint while they continued to search for an attorney willing to take the case. The Supreme Court put a halt to this practice in 1984 in *Baldwin County Welcome Center v. Brown* when it held that only a complaint that complies with the requirements of Federal Rules of Civil Procedure tolls the complaint-filing period.

Some defendants attempted to get cases dismissed on the grounds that they were not brought in good faith. For example, in an LDF case filed in North Carolina in 1966, *Lea v. Cone Mills,* the employer argued that the case was not brought to remedy unlawful employment discrimination but instead was brought "on the part of persons, organizations or associations whose identity is presently unknown . . . to solicit, excite, and stir up a large number of claims against the employer."[13] This argument was essentially a veiled attempt to get the court to throw out the case on the grounds that the LDF was simply trying to stir up Title VII employment discrimination litigation. The plaintiffs in *Lea* had been assisted in filing charges of violation of Title VII through the LDF's summer project, and that project had been broadly announced in the geographical area in North Carolina out of which the case arose. The district court rejected the argument, ruled for the plaintiffs on the merits, and entered an injunction against Cone Mills. However, the court denied back pay to the plaintiffs, reasoning that, because the plaintiffs were testers—that is, simply trying to show discrimination without actually seeking employment—they had suffered no economic loss. This lack-of-good-faith argument was not isolated and was even endorsed by some courts. Judge William Brevard Hand of the Southern District of Alabama, not a friend of civil rights lawyers and activists, complained that the LDF was using the courts to establish its "pet theories" of discrimination by employing runners, i.e., summer interns, to drum up plaintiffs for that purpose.[14]

Class Actions

The filing of complaints as class actions in the employment litigation campaign was not unusual; most of the civil rights cases filed by the LDF, including *Brown v. Board of Education,* had been brought as class actions. Meltsner was simply following that tradition in *Brinkley*.[15] The litigation team assigned a high priority to developing the law to allow class actions in Title VII cases.[16] It was not at all clear that class actions would be allowed, because Title VII requires that persons claiming to be victims of unlawful employment discrimination first file a charge with the EEOC, and the overwhelming number of class members on whose behalf the cases were brought had not done so. Another potential legal obstacle to class action claims under Title VII was the difference between the *Brown* school desegregation cases and Title VII cases. Monetary damages were not sought for class members in the school desegregation cases. On the other hand, Title VII has always provided for monetary damages, first in the form of back pay and then later compensatory and punitive damages. As to the difference between school desegregation and Title VII class action cases, Greenberg testified:

> The civil class action for back pay and damages, coupled with attorney fees, is one of the most effective ways of enforcing [Title VII] as it exists today. The potential of a class action means essentially that the meter is running, that an employer who is discriminating cannot expect to discriminate with the expectation that he will keep doing it until he is caught, and then when caught, an order will be entered against him and he will have to stop. He will have to pay back pay. . . . It is not like a school desegregation order, where the school board can sit back and be sued and if it is sued after the complainant graduates from school, then it has nothing to do. The class action, with the accompanying back pay provision, means the meter is running and the employer has an incentive to end discrimination in his employment, and the labor union has an incentive to end discrimination in its bargaining unit as soon as possible.[17]

This view of the role of back pay in employment discrimination law was essentially endorsed by the Supreme Court later in another landmark LDF case, *Albemarle Paper Co. v. Moody.*

One of the notions driving the litigation team's effort to push for class actions under Title VII was that such suits would provide an enforcement technique that was substantially similar to the pattern-or-practice suits that Congress authorized the Department of Justice (and later the EEOC) to litigate. While law development can occur in individual cases, litigating many separate cases would require a significant amount of time and resources. The class action device, on the other hand, would allow the LDF to use its limited resources to obtain as much relief as possible for large numbers of African Americans in a single lawsuit. In addition to the benefits of efficiency and economy, the ability to pursue class actions also would enhance settlement possibilities. If the courts denied the option for the LDF to pursue class actions under Title VII, it certainly would have placed the named plaintiffs into a weaker bargaining position in either litigation or settlement possibilities.

A favorable ruling that Title VII cases could be brought as class actions was one of the first major victories the LDF obtained in its litigation campaign. This ruling was handed down by U.S. District Judge Frank Gray, Jr., of the Middle District of Tennessee in March 1966 in *Hall v. Werthan Bag Corporation.* Involving a company later made famous in the movie *Driving Miss Daisy, Werthan Bag,* like *Brinkley,* was among the first round of cases the LDF filed in the litigation campaign; was the first Title VII case to be officially reported; and was the first case in which a court upheld the right of a single plaintiff to bring a class action on behalf of similarly situated African Americans. The case was filed as a class action on December 16, 1965, before the effective date of the 1966 amendments to the Federal Rules of Civil Procedure that specifically endorsed class actions in civil rights cases. The complaint alleged that the case was brought on behalf not only of Robert Hall but also of "all other Negroes who are similarly situated" to Hall and who were adversely affected by the racially discriminatory employment practices of Werthan Bag.[18] The phrase "similarly situated" became a term of art in employment discrimination litigation to identify members of a statutorily protected class who were deemed to have been subjected to the same or similar discriminatory terms and conditions of employment as the plaintiff.

The issue of whether class actions could be brought under Title VII arose in connection with a motion filed on behalf of another African American employee, Ray Tate, to intervene in the case. Tate, unlike Hall, had not filed his own individual charge of discrimination with the EEOC. The district court asked the parties to file briefs addressing two issues: (1) whether Hall was entitled to bring a class action under Title VII and (2) whether a member of a class in a Title VII suit may intervene in the case even though he had not filed his own charge of discrimination with the EEOC. Fred Wallace, an African American who had graduated from Harvard Law School, was the LDF attorney who briefed and prepared the plaintiff's response to the judge's questions. While working with civil rights attorneys in Virginia during the summer of 1963 between his second and third years of law school, Fred was arrested and convicted of an assault on a sheriff during a voting rights demonstration. His arrest and conviction posed a potential problem when he sought admission to the New York bar, but he was eventually admitted to the bar based on an affidavit submitted by Greenberg stating that he believed that Fred's conviction was illegal.[19]

Fred made essentially three arguments in response to Judge Gray's questions: the first was that class actions had long been allowed in race discrimination cases brought under the Equal Protection Clause of the Fourteenth Amendment. The second was that use of class actions was appropriate because by definition, race discrimination is class discrimination. The third was that the Fifth Circuit had recently ruled in a case arising under the public accommodations provision of the Civil Rights Act of 1964 (Title II), in which LDF attorneys were cocounsel, that private class actions could be maintained even though the attorney general also could seek relief for a class under its pattern-or-practice litigation authority.[20] Werthan Bag argued that Congress intended to allow only individual and not class relief and that, to the extent class relief was available, it should be limited to Title VII claims brought by the Attorney General under the Department of Justice's pattern-or-practice authority.[21]

Judge Gray ruled in favor of the litigation team when he held that class actions could be brought under Title VII on the theory that

> [r]acial discrimination is by definition class discrimination. If it exists, it applies throughout the class. This does not mean, however, that the effects of the discrimination will always be felt equally by all the members of the racial class. For example, if an employer's racially discriminatory preferences are merely one of several factors which enter into employment decisions, the unlawful preferences may or may not be controlling in regard to the hiring or promotion of a particular member of the racial class. But although the actual effects of a discriminatory policy may thus vary throughout the class, the existence of the discriminatory policy threatens the entire class. And whether the Damoclean threat of a racially discriminatory policy hangs over the racial class is a question of fact common to all the members of the class.[22]

In reaching his decision, Judge Gray found it necessary to harmonize the applicability of the class action rules of the Federal Rules of Civil Procedure with the enforcement procedures of Title VII. Noting that the version of Title VII that passed in Congress had stripped the EEOC of both its authority to seek judicial enforcement and cease-and-desist authority, Judge Gray concluded that Congress, at first blush, had rejected a public interest enforcement model and instead shifted the emphasis to a private interest enforcement model. But even as Title VII metamorphosed from a public interest to a private interest enforcement model, Judge Gray concluded, a significant aspect of the public law enforcement model remained because Congress gave the EEOC the authority to bring judicial actions to enforce an injunction obtained in a case initially brought by a private party, thus emphasizing the broader public interest.[23] Judge Gray's reasoning was consistent with the observation one commentator made shortly after the enactment of Title VII, that Congress had not fully understood the broader issue of whether employment discrimination is a public or private wrong and that if Title VII class actions were allowed, then doing so would be to view employment discrimination as a public wrong.[24]

After holding that class actions could be brought under Title VII, Judge Gray then turned to Werthan Bag's argument that Tate was precluded from intervening because he had not filed his own individual charge with the EEOC. Again, relying on the legislative history of Title VII, Judge Gray held that the primary purpose for the charge-filing requirement was to give "a discriminator opportunity to respond to persuasion rather than coercion, to soft words rather than the big stick of injunction," and that the charge-filing requirement was designed to prevent frivolous complaints from reaching the courts. Judge Gray faced potentially "vexing possibilities of collateral estoppel" if each individual in the plaintiff's class was required to file separate charges with the EEOC seeking relief from the same allegedly racially discriminatory employment practice. To avoid that difficulty, he held that class relief would be limited to injunctive relief. However, class members, including Tate, who had not filed charges with the EEOC, would not be entitled to back pay. The court further held that Tate would be allowed to intervene upon the service of a verified complaint of intervention. Judge Gray refused Werthan Bag's motion to certify that his two rulings involved controlling questions of law as to whether there were substantial grounds for differences of opinion. Such a certification would have allowed Werthan Bag to take an immediate appeal to the courts of appeals. *Werthan Bag* established an important precedent and a theoretical foundation that courts generally followed in upholding the right of plaintiffs to bring broad-based class actions under Title VII.[25]

Fred's victory in *Werthan Bag* provided a significant boost for the employment litigation campaign and the occasion for a small informal celebration in the LDF's headquarters in New York. Fred had devoted a substantial amount of time researching and writing the litigation team's responses to Judge Gray's questions, and periodically we had gently chided Fred because of his extreme optimism that Judge Gray would rule in the plaintiff's favor. I remember Fred walking around the office after he received a copy of Judge Gray's opinion, excitedly waving it over his head, and repeatedly saying, "We won, we won, I told you we would win." One argument Fred made in the *Werthan Bag* memorandum that proved problematic later on but which was ultimately resolved in favor of the plaintiffs was that no back pay is sought by any class member not actually before the court.

One strategy employers used in an effort to thwart plaintiffs' efforts to bring class action employment discrimination claims was to award the named plaintiffs the jobs they claimed had been denied to them because of race. However, the employers did so only after the plaintiffs had filed a complaint in federal court. The U.S. Court of Appeals for the Fifth Circuit soundly rejected this strategy in another early LDF case, *Jenkins v. United Gas Corporation,* in which the employer had denied Thomas Jenkins, an African American serviceman helper, a promotion to a serviceman's vacancy and awarded it instead to a less-qualified white employee. The litigation team filed suit on behalf of Jenkins and moved for class certification. A few weeks after the complaint was filed, United Gas offered a serviceman's position to Jenkins and, when he accepted, moved to have the case dismissed because of mootness. The employer argued that the filing of a charge of unlawful discrimination with the EEOC is the "key" to the courthouse and that the "door" to the courthouse "slams shut" once the job claimed to have been denied because of race has been offered to and accepted by the employee who has made the charge. The district court accepted the employer's argument, but the court of appeals reversed. Al Rosenthal and Thomas Woodhouse, a Harvard Law alumnus and one of the recent graduates recruited by Al to do pro bono work with the litigation team, wrote the appellate brief. Greenberg argued the case on appeal.

Relying in substantial part on the reasoning in *Werthan Bag,* the Fifth Circuit articulated additional reasons for allowing class actions in employment discrimination cases. First, the court held that if class-wide relief were not expressly included in any injunctive or declaratory relief awarded to the named plaintiffs, then the "result would be the incongruous one for a court—a Federal Court no less—being an instrument of racial discrimination."[26] Second, the court endorsed the idea of Title VII plaintiffs as private attorneys general. In an earlier non-LDF case, *Oatis v. Crown Zellerbach Corporation,*[27] the Fifth Circuit had adopted the private attorney general rule in upholding class actions in employment discrimination cases. The LDF had first advanced the private attorney general theory in support of its argument before the Supreme

Court in *Newman v. Piggie Park Enterprises, Inc.* The Fifth Circuit supported this theory again in *Jenkins,* holding that in Title VII cases, the plaintiffs act as private attorneys general to defend the civil rights policy objectives of the statute. For this reason, the court found, class actions are proper.[28]

The class action device, which originated in order to circumvent the stringency of common-law joinder requirements, permits a lawsuit to be brought by a representative of a class who asserts not only his own claim but also the rights of the class as a whole.[29] One of the problems in pursuing class action litigation in civil rights cases before the federal class action rules were revised in 1966 was that of trying to fit civil rights cases into one of three categories under the old equity practice: true class action, hybrid class action, or spurious class action. These old categories proved to be a source of confusion.[30] This problem was eliminated when the Supreme Court adopted an amended Rule 23 of the Federal Rules of Civil Procedure on class actions, replacing old class action rules that had been in effect since 1938. The Advisory Committee Notes to Rule 23(b)(2) of the 1966 revisions stated that this new section was specifically included and designed for civil rights actions where the "party opposing the class has acted or refused to act on grounds generally applicable to the class," thereby making relief appropriate for the "class as a whole," specifically adding that civil rights cases fall within that provision.[31] Albert Sacks, a Harvard Law School professor as well as the associate reporter for the 1966 amendments to the Federal Rules of Civil Procedure and a frequent lecturer at the LDF's Airlie House civil rights lawyers' training programs, wrote that the revised rules made it easier to bring class actions in civil rights cases.[32] The decisions in *Werthan Bag, Jenkins,* and *Piggie Park* and the new Rule 23(b) (2) set the stage for the development of the class action device as an effective enforcement strategy in the litigation campaign that embraced the public interest law enforcement model. In an important article, Harvard Law Professor Abram Chayes described class action employment discrimination litigation, like the campaign conducted by the LDF, as one of the "avatars" of the emerging model of public law litigation.[33]

Over time, the courts recognized the right of private plaintiffs to bring broad-based class actions based upon three interrelated theories. The first is the *Piggie Park* private attorneys general theory, which holds that a private civil rights action is more than a private claim by a single individual seeking to vindicate purely private rights because, whether in name or not, the suit is perforce a sort of class action for fellow employees similarly situated. Second, beginning with the LDF case of *Johnson v. Georgia Highway Express, Inc.*, decided in 1969, the courts adopted an "across-the-board" theory under which plaintiffs or a representative group of plaintiffs were permitted to challenge an employer's entire range of employment practices. The across-the-board theory was a major judicial victory in the litigation campaign. Under this theory, the LDF and others could bring class action cases attacking broad racially discriminatory employment practices, even though the charge filed with the EEOC had complained only about a limited number of practices of the defendants. Pursuant to the across-the-board theory, the class in a single case could include African American employees who held different jobs or worked in different organizational units of the employer; applicants; deterred applicants; future employees, and/or former employees; and employees with failure to promote or hire or demotions claims. As long as the members of the class were of the same race, such allegations were deemed sufficient to satisfy the requirements of Rule 23 of the Federal Rules of Civil Procedure that questions be common to the class and plaintiffs be typical of the class.[34] The rationale for the across-the-board class actions is that despite the different factual questions with regard to different employees, the threat of a racially discriminatory policy, as first characterized by Judge Gray in *Werthan Bag,* hangs over the head of every member of the racial class and is a question of fact common to all members of the class.[35] Third, the courts held that class actions were appropriate as a matter of policy because this mode of adjudication promotes judicial economy, eliminates the possibility of inconsistent and varying outcomes, and protects the employers from the possible burden of defending multiple lawsuits challenging the same employment practice.[36]

In addition to the broad-based attack on plaintiffs' entitlement to class actions in employment discrimination cases, defendants also relied on more technical arguments, for example, that even if class actions were allowed, the plaintiffs nevertheless had not satisfied the requirements of the federal class action procedural rules. The arguments were made singly or in combination, that the class did not satisfy the numerosity requirement; there was no sufficient community of interest between the plaintiffs and the putative class members; the claims at issue were peculiar to the particular plaintiffs; plaintiffs who had never worked for the employer or were not members of the defendant union could not represent a class of incumbent employees; and the plaintiffs lacked standing because they were not interested in employment with the employer.[37] The LDF attorneys responded forcefully to these arguments, and the courts in most of the early cases agreed with the LDF's argument.[38]

One of the problems in seeking class certification was whether back pay or monetary relief could be awarded to individuals who were not named plaintiffs or who had not filed a charge of discrimination with the EEOC. This was a particularly troubling issue for the litigation team, so the initial decision was to argue that the class action part of the case was limited to injunctive relief only and that back pay was sought only for the named plaintiffs but not for the class.[39] However, the litigation team did not abandon its goal of developing the law on the remedy of class-wide back pay. Rather than pressing the issue of the appropriateness of class-wide back pay during the very early stages of the campaign, the litigation team decided that it was advisable to focus first on clearing out the procedural underbrush, which required a substantial amount of time, and on developing theories of discrimination other than disparate treatment. In addition, the issue of the appropriateness of class-wide back pay was intertwined with the critically important issue of whether there was right to a jury trial in Title VII cases.

Developing the law on the availability of class actions turned out to be one of the most important procedural tools in eradicating unlawful discrimination in the workplace. Without the efficiency and economy of this procedural tool, it is highly likely that the employment discrimination claims of many, many thousands of African Americans would not have been redressed because there simply were not enough attorneys willing to represent them. Although the Supreme Court in 1982 affirmed the recognition by Judge Gray in *Hall* that racial discrimination is by definition class discrimination, beginning in 1977, it handed down decisions that now make it more difficult to bring class actions in the post-*Griggs* era.[40] Also, more recent revisions in the class rules themselves have made it more difficult, but not impossible, to bring class action employment discrimination.[41]

JURY TRIALS UNDER TITLE VII

One of the most important developments accomplished by the litigation team was convincing the courts that Title VII claims were to be tried before a judge sitting without a jury. The jury trial issue arose because Title VII specifically provides for awards of back pay to compensate victims for the economic loss suffered as a result of unlawful employment discrimination,[42] but back pay demands immediately raised the issue of whether either plaintiffs or defendants were entitled to a jury trial. In its answer to the complaint in *Brinkley,* the very first case filed by the litigation team under Title VII,[43] the employer demanded a jury trial, and demands for jury trials in every case soon became the standard practice for attorneys representing employers and unions.[44] However, although *Griggs* was among the first the litigation team filed under Title VII, Duke Power did not request a jury trial.

Meltsner was well aware that the back pay claim would likely raise the jury trial issue. But he also thought a good argument could be made that back pay is purely a statutory remedy that should be deemed a part of equitable relief, and therefore no right to a jury trial existed in these cases. At a purely strategic level, he concluded that if the jury trial issue was going to cause problems, the prudent thing to do would be to amend the complaints later to drop the back pay claims to avoid the possibility of making bad law.[45]

The jury trial issue raised several significantly interrelated concerns for the litigation team. First, the litigation team recognized that it would be difficult, if not impossible, to establish a coherent and uniform body of law if Title VII cases were to be tried before juries. At a strategic level, the LDF wanted these cases to be tried before judges without a jury—particularly so because some of the more liberal federal judges in the South were on the front line in the implementation of *Brown v. Board of Education,* ordering innovative remedial orders to compel compliance.[46] The litigation team believed that these judges would be receptive to a liberal construction of Title VII.[47] Furthermore, it would be much easier to appeal a trial judge's decision on the merits than it would be if the jury had decided the case on its merits.

Second, the frightening prospect that the merits of its race discrimination cases would be decided by all-white or mostly white juries powerfully informed the employment litigation team's thinking about fashioning a theory of discrimination not based on intent. If the sole theory of discrimination required a finding of intent to discriminate in order to establish a violation of Title VII, there was a strong possibility that African American plaintiffs would lose on the merits because of their race before all-white juries. Attorneys for defendants probably made demands for a jury trial knowing full well that all the jurors would likely be white and less sympathetic to African American plaintiffs out of fear that one day they may be in competition with African

Americans for jobs. It was highly likely that white jurors would be less sympathetic to African American plaintiffs than federal judges who had lifetime appointments.

The litigation team had little faith that white jurors would be willing to put aside any racial prejudices they might have in deciding whether an employer had intentionally discriminated against African American plaintiffs because of race. The team's healthy suspicion that white southern juries would be unsympathetic to the claims of African American plaintiffs was not unfounded. Although there have been some studies on racial bias in civil jury trials, none of them seems to have focused primarily on civil trials in southern states. However, in a frequently cited and often-criticized study of over 9,000 civil trials in Cook County, Illinois, between 1959 and 1979, the authors found that the race of the parties affected the outcomes. The authors reported that, for example: "On average, [African American] plaintiffs received only three-fourths as much compensation as whites who had the same injury, lost income, and type of legal claims." Typically, African Americans received about $2,000 less than whites for the modest injuries that predominated in trials in Cook County. For example, a white plaintiff received an estimated median award of $6,300 for a slip-and-fall injury of moderate severity, when suing a white defendant. In a similar case an African American received only $4,600.[48] Although in the last fifty years, the number of white Americans who openly espouse racial discrimination has declined, numerous studies show that many whites still harbor significant levels of covert prejudice against racial minorities. As recently as 1990, over half of white Americans surveyed rated African Americans and Latinos as less intelligent than whites, and 36 percent rated Asians as less intelligent than whites. Sixty-two percent rated African Americans as less hardworking than whites, 54 percent rated Latinos as less hardworking, and 34 percent rated Asians as less hardworking.[49]

Legislative history shows that some members of Congress were very much concerned about whether African Americans would be treated fairly in civil rights cases by southern white juries. The LDF relied upon such legislative history in its argument before the Supreme Court in a housing discrimination case, *Curtis v. Loether,* brought under Title VIII of the Civil Rights Act of 1968:[50] "Congressional proponents of civil rights legislation have consistently opposed jury trials in actions to enforce such statutes on the ground that hostile juries would nullify the proposed law."[51] The Supreme Court nevertheless upheld the right to a jury trial in a statutory housing discrimination case.

Because of the adverse impact on law development that would likely flow from trying cases of employment discrimination against African Americans before hostile white southern jurors, the litigation team assigned a high priority early in the campaign to opposing jury trials in Title VII cases and filed motions to strike the demand in every case in which the demand was made. The resolution of the issue turned on whether, as a constitutional matter, the claim was to be characterized as a legal or equitable issue. The Seventh Amendment to the Constitution, which provides that in "[s]uits at common law, where the value in controversy shall exceed twenty dollars, the right to a jury trial shall be preserved," guarantees a right to a jury trial only if a statute creates legal rights enforceable in the ordinary courts of law. Practically all of the back pay claims in employment discrimination cases, whether in an individual case or in a class action, involve more than twenty dollars. The Supreme Court has held that the Seventh Amendment guarantees the right to a jury trial, as a general rule, on legal claims and that claims seeking monetary damages are presumptively legal claims. If, however, the claims are seeking only equitable or injunctive relief, then there is no constitutional right to a jury trial.

In addition to their argument that they were entitled to a jury trial in Title VII cases in which back pay was sought (on behalf of an individual or for a class), defendants relied heavily upon two leading Supreme Court cases on the right to a jury trial. The first was a 1959 decision in *Beacon Theatres, Inc. v. Westover,* in which the Court held that where legal and equitable claims are involved in the same case, the legal claim must be tried first before a jury. The second case was *Dairy Queen v. Woods,* in which the Court held in 1962 that the mere characterization of a legal claim as incidental to equitable claims is insufficient as a matter of fact and law to deny the right to a jury trial. To prevail on the jury trial issue, the litigation team had to convince the courts that Title VII claims were equitable claims even in cases in which back pay was sought. The team basically relied upon three interrelated arguments. First, Congress had not provided for the right to a trial by jury in Title VII cases, and on numerous occasions Congress had considered and rejected proposed amendments to grant the parties the right to a jury trial out of fear that jury bias, especially in the South, might frustrate the remedial purposes of Title VII.[52] There was even some evidence that this congressional fear was not completely unfounded.[53] Second, the demand for back pay is not in the nature of a legal claim for damages but rather is an integral part of the statutory remedial scheme that is committed to the exercise of a court equitable discretion to award injunctive relief. The litigation team found support for this argument in *NLRB v. Jones & Laughlin Steel Co.*, in which the Supreme Court had held in 1937 that there is no right to a jury trial in an action brought by the NLRB in which the Board sought back pay for union employees who lost income because of an unfair labor practice committed by an employer. The third argument was that *Beacon Theatres* and *Dairy Queen,* the cases defendants often cited to support entitlement to jury trials, were inapplicable because they involved a joinder of several claims, some legal, some equitable, and thus were not like Title VII claims, which are single claims and must be characterized as either legal or equitable, but not both.

Practically all of the courts granted plaintiffs' motion to strike demands for a jury trial on either one or more of the arguments the team advanced and held that neither party was entitled to a jury trial in a Title VII case even though back pay was sought.[54] The litigation team participated in the first court of appeals case on this issue in *Johnson v. Georgia Highway Express, Inc.,* which became a leading case holding that there is no right to a jury trial in Title VII cases. Every court of appeals deciding the issue followed *Johnson.*[55] The issue of a right to a jury trial eventually became moot in disparate impact cases in light of *Albemarle Paper Co v. Moody,* where the Supreme Court held in 1975 that back pay claims were an integral part of the injunctive relief to be awarded by a court and not by a jury. However, under the amendments to Title VII in the Civil Rights Act of 1991, Congress has now provided for a right to a jury trial in disparate treatment cases, but only in such cases in which a plaintiff seeks compensatory and punitive damages. The law remains intact that there is no right to a jury trial in the *Griggs* disparate impact cases in which class-wide back pay is an appropriate remedy. In some cases, courts have empanelled advisory juries in Title VII cases under Rule 39(c) of the Federal Rules of Civil Procedure, so long as the trial court itself ultimately makes the findings of fact on whether discrimination is proven.[56]

Section 1981

Meltsner included a claim for relief under 42 U.S.C. § 1981, in addition to the Title VII claim, in the *Brinkley* complaint. Section 1981 provides that "[a]ll persons within the jurisdiction of the United States shall have the same rights . . . to make and enforce contracts, to sue, be parties, give evidence, and the full and equal benefits of all laws and proceedings for the security of persons and property as is enjoyed by white citizens." The origin of Section 1981 is the Civil Rights Act of 1866, which Congress enacted pursuant to its authority under the Thirteenth Amendment. The Thirteenth Amendment prohibits slavery and involuntary servitude. A major reason Congress enacted the 1866 Act was to remedy the racially discriminatory labor system in the South because its supporters believed that the freedoms adopted in the Thirteenth Amendment would be meaningless to the recently freed slaves unless they had an equal opportunity to bargain for their labors.[57] However, there was uncertainty as to whether the Thirteenth Amendment was an adequate constitutional basis to support the 1866 Civil Rights Act. Thus, once the Fourteenth Amendment was adopted, Congress enacted the Civil Rights Act of 1870, which embodies the aims of the 1866 law under the newer amendment's enforcement power.[58]

On its face, Section 1981 makes no distinction between public and private employers, but the Supreme Court narrowly construed the reach of much of the Reconstruction civil rights legislation by holding that Congress did not have the power under the Fourteenth Amendment to prohibit wholly private acts of discrimination.[59] For example, in a case decided in 1948, *Hurd v. Hodge,* the Supreme Court held that "governmental action," or state action, was required in cases based on the post–Civil War civil rights legislation, including Section 1981.[60] Why, then, in light of *Hurd,* did Meltsner include a claim for relief under Section 1981 in the *Brinkley* complaint when the law seemed well settled that a claim under that section could not be brought against a private employer? The reason, according to Meltsner, was to test whether *Hurd* and its progeny were still good law in the 1960s and to see that the decision to do so was consistent with the LDF's historic mission of engaging in cutting-edge litigation to eliminate racial discrimination in the public and private sectors. He believed that the time had come to test the continued viability of *Hurd* because in 1961 the Supreme Court, in *Monroe v. Pape,* had broadly construed the state action doctrine to allow citizens to sue individual employees of government units in addition to the appropriate governmental unit.[61]

The district court judges reached opposite results in some of the earlier cases in which African Americans sued private employers for racial discrimination under Section 1981 (in addition to Title VII). Some courts allowed the Section 1981 claims to go forward.[62] Others did not, relying essentially on the state action doctrine.[63] Beginning with *Waters v. Wisconsin Steel Works,* decided in 1970, the courts of appeals uniformly began to construe Section 1981 to allow African Americans to sue private employers for racial discrimination in employment. The issue of whether Section 1981 provided a legal basis to remedy racial discrimination in employment by private employers was ultimately resolved only after the Supreme Court decided *Jones v. Alfred H. Mayer Co.* in 1968. In this case, the plaintiffs, an African American couple, claimed that the private defendants had refused to sell them a house in a white neighborhood solely because of their race. They sued under 42 U.S.C. § 1982 which, like Section 1981, was part of the post–Civil War civil rights statutory legislative package and provided that all citizens shall have the same rights as white citizens to inherit, purchase, lease, sell, hold, and convey real and personal property. After critically reviewing its earlier decisions on the reach of Section 1982 and the legislative history of the post–Civil War Reconstruction civil rights legislation, the Supreme Court held that purely private acts of discrimination were covered by Section 1982. The Court agreed with the Attorney General of the United States, who in oral argument asserted that "[t]he fact that the statute lay partially dormant for many years cannot be held to diminish its force today."[64] The Court also expressly overruled its 1906 decision in *Hodges v. United States,* which suggested that Section 1981 was inapplicable to employment discrimination in the absence of state action.

Following *Jones v. Mayer,* the LDF continued its practice of including a claim for relief under Section 1981 in all of its employment discrimination complaints, and it became a regular practice of other plaintiffs and legal organizations to do likewise. Defendants regularly moved to dismiss these claims on a number of grounds, for example, arguing that claims under Section 1981 require state action and that Title VII constitutes an implied repeal of any remedy for racial discrimination under Section 1981. Defendants had some success with these arguments in the lower courts,[65] but beginning with the Seventh Circuit's decision in *Waters v. Wisconsin Steel,* every court of appeals deciding the issue before 1975 held, relying on *Jones v. Mayer,* that Section 1981 provides a federal remedy against private acts of discrimination in employment.[66]

The Supreme Court finally resolved the issue in the landmark case of *Johnson v. Railway Express, Inc.* in 1975. The issue on which the Court granted certiorari was whether the timely filing of a charge of employment discrimination with the EEOC tolls the running of the statute of limitations applicable to an action based on the same facts under Section 1981. Deborah Greenberg, Jack Greenberg's wife, argued *Johnson* in the Supreme Court for the LDF. In the course of addressing the issue posed by the case, the Court concluded that "[i]t is well settled among the federal courts of appeals—and we now join them—that § 1981 affords a federal remedy against discrimination in private employment on the basis of race."[67] The Court in *Johnson* specifically stressed the point that Title VII and Section 1981 were two independent statutory provisions in terms of coverage, jurisdictional requirements, and the different kinds of relief available under both. For example, whereas Title VII applies to fifteen or more employees, Section 1981 does not have a statutory minimum of employees so it can, in effect, reach racially discriminatory practices of every mom-and-pop business. Also, compensatory and punitive damages were, and still are, recoverable under Section 1981, but similar kinds of damages were not made available under Title VII until the enactment of the Civil Rights Act of 1991, but only then in disparate treatment and not disparate impact cases. In a later case, *St. Francis College v. Al-Khazraji,* in 1985 the Supreme Court broadly defined the meaning of race in terms of ethnic groups that included, for example, Jews, Arabs, Norwegians, Finns, and Italians. In a case I argued in the U.S. Court of Appeals for the Fourth Circuit, in which that court held that plaintiffs are entitled to sue private employers for racial discrimination in employment under Section 1981, the dissenting judge referred to Section 1981 as "this 'quickening of the statutory Lazarus'" because it had laid dormant for so many years,[68] but the courts were beginning to adopt a uniform view in allowing such claims.

The victories the litigation achieved on class action, jury trials, and Section 1981 were critical developments in building a legal edifice that would help to make the *Griggs* disparate impact theory a revolutionary theory of equality.

5. *Quarles* and the Present Effects Theory: A Prelude to *Griggs*

A case that is rarely discussed and is too often overlooked in the history of the development of the *Griggs* disparate impact theory is *Quarles v. Philip Morris*. *Quarles* was a precedent-setting decision in the litigation campaign because the court deciding it endorsed a theory of discrimination advocated by the LDF that did not rest solely on proof of discriminatory intent. In *Quarles,* the court endorsed the present effects of past discrimination theory. Victims of unlawful employment discrimination were entitled to relief under this theory even though the defendants might have abandoned overt policies of intentional discrimination before or after the effective date of Title VII. The present effects of past discrimination theory was the most important new theory of discrimination in civil rights law until it was overshadowed by *Griggs*. While the Supreme Court eventually rejected the *Quarles* theory about ten years later in *Teamsters v. United States,* it candidly acknowledged the fact that the *Quarles*'s present effects of past discrimination theory had "enjoyed wholesale adoption in the Courts of Appeals."[1] Also, the *Quarles* theory explains in substantial part the high success rate the litigation team achieved over the next decade in opening up new employment opportunities, not only for African Americans but also for other groups protected under Title VII. The LDF's reputation as a major leader in using the courts to bring about social change also "took an even sharper turn upward in the civil rights community" as a result of *Quarles*.[2]

Quarles was a seniority discrimination case. The seniority discrimination cases, like the testing and educational requirement cases, soon surfaced as litigation priorities as a result of the analysis of the EEOC charges undertaken by the LDF in the fall of 1965.[3] The seniority discrimination cases challenged one of the most widespread practices in the unionized sector of the workplace, namely, facially neutral seniority systems to determine future job advancement and opportunities.

Fundamentally, a seniority system is a set of rules for allocating employment opportunities including promotions, transfers, demotions, layoffs, and recalls in an employment unit. The most senior employee among competing employees is preferred, provided that he is qualified to fill the job in question and eligible to bid for that job.[4] As the Supreme Court explained, a seniority system is

[a] scheme that, alone or in tandem with non-"seniority" criteria, allots to employees ever improving employment rights and benefits as their relative lengths of pertinent employment increase. Unlike other methods of allocating employment benefits and opportunities, such as subjective evaluations or educational requirements, the principal feature of any and every "seniority system" is that preferential treatment is dispensed on the basis of some measure of time served in employment.[5]

There are generally two types of seniority that serve different purposes. *Benefit seniority* determines an employee's terms and conditions of employment with respect to pensions, vacation pay, sick leave, parking-lot privileges, and other fringe benefits. *Competitive seniority* determines an employee's employment opportunities with respect to promotions and transfer opportunities and the order of layoffs and recalls.[6] Most of the important early seniority discrimination cases arising under Title VII involved competitive seniority. An employee's competitive seniority status may be computed by total length of employment with the employer (company, employment, mill, or plant seniority), length of service within a particular department (departmental seniority), or length of service in a line of progression (job seniority). Seniority systems are commonly accompanied by lines of progression, promotion, and demotion, along with layoff ladders. The variations and combinations of seniority principles are numerous, but in all cases the basic measure is length of service, with preference given to the most senior employee.[7] Because seniority is a system of employment preferences based on length of service, employees with the longest service are given the greatest job security and the best opportunities for advancement.

Union members tend to consider their seniority status as a vested fundamental right.[8] As one court observed in a Title VII case, the one hard fact upon which every union member agreed was that "seniority was the most important benefit he had next to God and family."[9] Unions historically and traditionally have fought for the allocation of employment opportunities on the basis of seniority in an effort to eliminate arbitrary employment decisions by employers.[10] On the other hand, employers have been willing to accept seniority systems not because they are necessarily helpful in making employment decisions but because of the bargaining strength of unions.[11]

The historical backdrop against which *Quarles* and the other seniority discrimination cases arose was the long history of racially discriminatory hiring practices by employers combined with an equally long history of racial discrimination by unions in excluding African American employees from union membership or by chartering racially segregated unions.[12] White unions had exclusive jurisdiction over jobs reserved for whites, and African American unions had exclusive jurisdiction over jobs reserved for African Americans. Employers limited employment of African Americans to the least desirable and poorest-paying jobs. These racially segregated jobs were, in turn, organized into racially segregated lines of progression that resulted in white lines of progression and African American lines of progression. Job promotions were based on seniority, such as departmental or plant seniority, within these segregated lines of progression.[13] In many instances, employers and unions had a no-transfer policy between racially segregated departments and seniority units. A combination of racially discriminatory hiring, segregated lines of progression, and no-transfer policies had the effect of locking in pre-Act racially discriminatory employment policies after the effective date of Title VII.

Prior to the enactment of Title VII, some efforts were made to eliminate racial discrimination in seniority discrimination through government intervention pursuant to actions by the federal FEPCs under presidential Executive Orders. The pre–Title VII remedies in many cases consisted of abolishing the racially separate unions and their accompanying bargaining arrangements and tacking the African American lines of progression onto the bottom of the white lines of progression for seniority purposes. Under the "tack-on" remedy, if seniority within a line of progression were to continue to be the only criterion for advancement up the line, African Americans with years of company or employment seniority would continue to be behind many white employees junior to them in terms of seniority for the sole reason that African Americans had earlier been denied the opportunity to work in white jobs and lines of progression because of their race.

It quickly became obvious to the litigation team that facially neutral seniority systems imposed significant impediments to making Title VII an effective remedy for racial discrimination in the workplace. The seniority discrimination cases thus raised one of the thorniest issues the team encountered early in the litigation campaign. On the one hand, white employees with the support of unions were determined to hold on to the better-paying and more attractive jobs they had obtained because of racially discriminatory hiring practices by employers and secured to them by the facially neutral seniority arrangements. On the other hand, African American employees who were also union members complained that the seniority arrangements limited their opportunities for jobs traditionally awarded to white employees and looked to Title VII for a remedy. Congress had not definitively addressed the issue of how the courts should analyze claims in the seniority discrimination cases. In addition, a pre–Title VII case from 1959, *Whitfield v. United Steelworkers Local 2708*, offered strong support for the employers' and unions' position that the present effects of past discrimination theory is inapplicable to invalidate facially neutral seniority systems even if such systems "lock" the effects of pre-Act overt discrimination into the post-Act period. The opinion in *Whitfield*, written by Judge John Minor Wisdom, one of the most pro–civil rights judges on the U.S. Court of Appeals for the Fifth Circuit,[14] was a potential weighty precedent that offered strong support for the employers and unions.

The facts in *Whitfield* bore a strong resemblance to the basic factual paradigm of the Title VII seniority discrimination cases. From its opening in 1942 until 1956, the Houston, Texas, operation of Armco Steel Corporation had been divided into two lines of progression comprising separate seniority units. Armco hired only whites for Line 1, the line of progression for the more skilled jobs, and hired only African Americans for Line 2, the line of progression for the unskilled jobs. Each line of progression encompassed a distinct operation and was composed of a series of interrelated jobs. The entry-level jobs started with the easiest in terms of skill, experience, and potential ability and progressed step-by-step to the top of the line. The knowledge acquired in the preceding job was necessary for the efficient handling of the next job in the progression. White employees were hired into the bottommost job in Line l, after close screening by management, followed by a strict probationary period. African Americans were not subject to the rigorous screening process but were instead hired into a labor pool from which they could bid into a starting job in Line 2. The Steelworkers represented the employees in both lines, and its membership had always been racially integrated. In 1956, after African American employees in Line 2 complained about being excluded from the skilled jobs in Line 1 because of their race, Armco and the United Steelworkers of America entered into a new collective bargaining agreement. Pursuant to the new agreement, African Americans were permitted to bid for jobs in Line 1 but had to take a test rather than go through a screening process; bid only on the lowest job in Line 1; and then proceed up the progression ladder job by job. This meant that African Americans who wanted to bid for a job in Line 1 had to take a pay cut if the starting job in Line 1 paid a lower rate than the job they had in Line 2 and that they would suffer a loss of seniority previously accrued in Line 2 no matter how long they had been employed by Armco.

The plaintiffs brought a class action against the Steelworkers and Armco, seeking relief based on the theory that the union had breached its duty of fair representation by entering into the new agreement that preserved the old racially discriminatory employment system, as racial discrimination by a union is an obvious breach of a union duty of fair representation. Essentially, the plaintiffs' theory was that the new agreement perpetuated into the post-1959 period the effects of a long history of racial discrimination by the employer and the union. Neither Armco nor the Steelworkers questioned the theory on which the plaintiffs relied. They defended their actions on the ground that the 1956 modification of the seniority arrangement was fair and nondiscriminatory and that the requirement that African Americans start at the bottom of Line 1 was based on business necessity rather than racial discrimination. The district court ruled in favor of the Steelworkers and Armco.

The court of appeals affirmed. In his opinion for the court, Judge Wisdom candidly acknowledged that was "it is undeniable that negroes in Line [2], ambitious to advance themselves in skilled jobs, are at disadvantage compared with white incumbents in Line [1]. This is a product of the past." However, he wrote, "We cannot turn back the clock. Unfair treatment to their detriment in the past gives the plaintiffs no claim now to be paid back by unfair treatment in their favor." Then he concluded his opinion with broad generalizations that, if followed, potentially sounded the death knell for the litigation team's effort to use Title VII to remedy the present effects of past discriminatory conduct in its seniority discrimination cases:

> The problem before us is not unique. It is bound to come up every time a
> large company substitutes a program of equal job opportunity for previous
> discriminatory practices. In such cases it is impossible to place negro incumbents
> holding certain jobs, especially unskilled jobs, on an absolutely equal footing with
> white incumbents in skilled jobs. In this situation time and tolerance, patience and
> forbearance, compromise and accommodation are needed in solving a problem
> deeply rooted in custom.
>
>   We attach particular importance to the good faith of the parties in working
> toward a fair solution. It seems to us that the Union and Company, with
> candor and honesty, acknowledge that in the past negroes were treated unfairly
> in not having the opportunity to qualify for skilled jobs. They balanced the

interest of negroes starting in Line 1 against the interest of [white] employees who have worked previously in Line 1 jobs, in light of fairness and efficient operation. . . . Courts, when called upon to eye such arrangements, should not be quick to substitute their judgment for that of a bargaining agency on the reasonableness of the modification.

He ended by saying, "The Union and Company made a fresh start for the future" and "Angels could do no more."[15]

The complexity of resolving the problem in the seniority discrimination cases produced a great deal of activity in the early stages of the enforcement of Title VII on the part of the LDF, unions, and employers. Also, the EEOC realized very early during its first year of operation that the seniority discrimination cases raised difficult legal and remedial problems.[16] Efforts by the EEOC to resolve literally hundreds of seniority discrimination charges through conciliation during its first year of operation were strongly resisted by unions. The unions relied in substantial part on *Whitfield* in their opposition.[17] In May 1966, the AFL-CIO and several other major unions attempted to obtain a commitment from the EEOC that it would not assert jurisdiction over charges involving violations of Title VII because of union seniority systems.[18] Then, in the spring of 1966, the EEOC engaged William B. Gould IV as a consultant to advise on the position it should take in the seniority discrimination cases, including whether it should issue substantive guidelines on the subject.[19] At the time, Gould was in private practice with a law firm that represented management in labor law matters. He later became a distinguished and well-respected labor law scholar and served as chairman of the National Labor Relations Board during the Clinton administration from 1994 to 1998. Gould, who participated in the EEOC meetings with union leaders, later wrote that the Steelworkers "played a leading role in the 1966 meeting with representatives of EEOC," that "the AFL-CIO [took a] rigid stance against any modification of seniority systems which would improve the lot of black employees," and that the trade unions' reactions to changing seniority systems were uniformly negative.[20] Gould concluded that most seniority arrangements were unlawful under Title VII and recommended that the EEOC issue guidelines for the seniority discrimination cases in the report he submitted to the EEOC in fall 1966.[21]

The EEOC solicited comments from the LDF on the Gould report because the LDF was carrying the major burden of enforcing Title VII and had filed a significant number of seniority discrimination cases in the federal courts, primarily in the South. To prepare the LDF's response to Gould's report and proposal, Al Rosenthal pulled together a list of distinguished labor law and economics professors, as well as labor law and civil rights practitioners, to form a consultative task force to assist the litigation team in deciding what position, if any, the LDF should take. During November and December 1966, Al extended invitations to join the task force. The task force met on three occasions in 1967. The members of the litigation team—Greenberg, Gaby, Al, and I—met regularly with the task force, and I served as the liaison between the task force and the litigation team. A subgroup of members of the task force was sent the complete files from the seniority discrimination cases then being litigated by the LDF and asked to analyze the cases through the lens of the following questions: (1) What constitutes proof of discrimination? (2) What is an illegal discriminatory seniority system, given the fact that by nature they exist to facilitate some form of discrimination? (3) Assuming a seniority system is discriminatory, what would be appropriate remedies? (4) How can the LDF get around July 2, 1965—the effective date of Title VII—in challenging seniority systems that are facially neutral but continue the effects of overt discriminatory hiring practices that may have ended prior to the effective date of Title VII?

The written case memoranda submitted by the members of the task force were outstanding, but, after a rather robust discussion, no consensus emerged on the specific issues the members were asked to address. There was also a rather lengthy discussion of theories of discrimination that could be advanced in the seniority discrimination cases. The potential theories ranged from a pure intent or disparate treatment theory to the present effect of past discrimination of a facially neutral seniority provision. The task force also looked to legal norms from areas of the law, such as constitutional law and labor relations law, in which the federal courts and the National Labor Relations Board had confronted the problem of conceptualizing theories of discrimination. For example, many years ago the Supreme Court had announced the principle that a law nondiscriminatory on its face, i.e., facially neutral, may be grossly discriminatory in operation,[22] and that constitutional theory of discrimination was applied with special vigor in determining the validity of acts that may result in the denial of voting rights to African Americans.[23] The task force also considered the fact that the Supreme Court had endorsed two conceptions of discriminatory animus in deciding claims of unfair labor practices that are prohibited by the National Labor Relations Act and are administratively enforced by the National Labor Relations Board because Congress had patterned some provisions of Title VII after the NLRA. For this reason, the task force spent some time discussing the relevance of these conceptions of discrimination to the Title VII seniority discrimination cases. The task force recognized that *Whitfield* was a "hoary beast" that had to be confronted because it stood as a potential major legal impediment to proving unlawful discrimination in the seniority discrimination cases. The task force reached a general consensus that the LDF should press the EEOC not to publish guidelines or standards on seniority discrimination. This recommendation was based on the generally held belief that the LDF and government enforcement agencies—the EEOC, the Department of Justice, the OFCC, and the NLRB—would probably be able to obtain more effective remedies in this class of cases through conciliation and negotiation and that more could be accomplished through litigation rather than a fixed set of EEOC seniority discrimination guidelines. Unlike their treatment of the substantive rulings of the NLRB, courts may defer to the substantive interpretations of Title VII by the EEOC but are not obligated to do so.[24]

Before the seniority discrimination consultative task force finished its work, several significant events occurred that mooted the purpose for which it was assembled, and so its work came to an end. The most significant of these events was that several months after the last meeting of the task force in October 1967, Judge John Butzner issued his decision in *Quarles* on January 4, 1968. Then, about six months after *Quarles,* another district court in Louisiana handed down the seniority discrimination decision, *United States v. Local 189 Papermakers and Paperworkers* (hereafter *Local 189*), which had been brought by the Civil Rights Division of the Department of Justice. The other events included the publication of two relevant law review articles in the *Harvard Law Review.* The first was a student Note on seniority discrimination that was published in 1967,[25] which substantially influenced the development of remedies in the seniority discrimination cases, and Judge Butzner relied heavily upon it in *Quarles.* The second was an article by George Cooper and Richard Sobol that was published in 1968.[26] The Cooper and Sobol article specifically focused on both the seniority discrimination cases and the testing and educational requirement cases in advocating that facially neutral policies that have an adverse effect or disparate impact on the employment opportunities of members of classes protected under Title VII constitute unlawful discrimination even absent evidence of discriminatory intent. Cooper and Sobol were also involved at that time in several significant seniority and testing employment discrimination cases that were brought under the auspices of the Lawyers Constitutional Defense Committee.[27] Although the Cooper and Sobol article had not been published before Judge Butzner decided *Quarles,* they had shared page proofs of the article with the litigation team before the decision was handed down, and their analysis helped shape the LDF's legal arguments on behalf of the plaintiffs in *Quarles* and later in *Griggs.*

Quarles was one of the first Title VII cases that the litigation team tried on the merits and that raised issues of first impression involving seniority discrimination and, more broadly, the theory of discrimination under Title VII. The case was brought as a class action against Philip Morris and Local 203 of the Tobacco Workers International Union,[28] which represented the bargaining unit employees at Philip Morris's cigarette and tobacco manufacturing facility in Richmond, Virginia. The complaint requested injunctive relief for the class and sought back pay only for Douglas Quarles and several other individual members of the class. The Richmond facility was divided into four general departments: (1) green leaf stemmery, a seasonal operation;[29] (2) prefabrication; (3) fabrication; and (4) warehouse, shipping, and receiving. The employees in prefabrication processed the tobacco, and the processed tobacco was sent to fabrication, where employees made and packed cigarettes and other smoking products. The employees in warehouse, receiving, and shipping handled the inventory of the finished products.

The overwhelming number of jobs in the white departments were not highly skilled ones, and the employees learned to perform them through on-the-job training. The jobs in the prefabrication department were generally lower paying and less desirable than jobs in other departments. Even the few African Americans who worked in warehouse, receiving, and shipping were generally paid less than similarly situated white employees. From the opening of its Richmond facility in 1929 until 1955, Philip Morris openly engaged in racially discriminatory hiring practices. It employed only African Americans to work in the prefabrication department. All janitors working in both prefabrication and fabrication were assigned to the prefabrication department, and employees who did not work on cigarette-making machines, such as painters, air conditioner repair employees, factory clerks, and watchmen, were assigned to fabrication regardless of where the work was done. Each department had its own separate seniority provisions and lines of progression, and Philip Morris usually hired employees for entry-level jobs in a department, filling the higher-paying jobs by advancement based on departmental seniority.

Philip Morris made a few minor changes in its employment practices before the effective date of Title VII. For example, in 1955, as a result of President Eisenhower's Executive Order 10599, it moved thirteen African Americans to the fabrication department. Then, in May 1961, again to comply with the Executive Order requiring employment and promotion without regard to race, Philip Morris adopted a policy pursuant to which it employed a token number of African Americans in the fabrication and warehouse, receiving, and shipping departments. Philip Morris also prohibited interdepartmental transfers until 1961, when the collective bargaining agreement was changed to permit a few transfers every six months. Transferring employees were allowed to take with them the departmental seniority they had earned from the date of their initial employment. The effect of the discriminatory hiring policy, the departmental seniority agreement, and the nontransfer rule was to "lock" African American employees in the less desirable jobs while white employees with no seniority were hired off the street into better-paying jobs.

Until 1963, the employees of Philip Morris were represented by racially segregated local unions. The African American union, Local 209, had exclusive jurisdiction over jobs in prefabrication; Local 203, the white union, had exclusive jurisdiction over jobs in the white departments. The racially segregated local unions were merged in 1963 to comply with the Executive Order. After the merger, Local 203 became the bargaining representative for all bargaining unit employees, and although African American employees were permitted to serve on the bargaining committees, they were not allowed to serve as officers in them.

When Title VII became effective, Philip Morris did not immediately change its race-based hiring practices significantly, but Judge Butzner found that the racially discriminatory hiring practices ceased on January 1, 1966. Philip Morris, unlike Duke Power in *Griggs* and most of the employers and unions in other cases, admitted that for most of its existence it had engaged in racially discriminatory hiring practices.

Quarles began when the lead plaintiff, Douglas Quarles, an African American, filed a charge with the EEOC in October 1965 claiming that he had been discriminated against because of his race when Philip Morris denied his request to transfer from the prefabrication department to a truck-driving position in the shipping department. He had been employed by Philip Morris for nine years at that time, and, although classified as a laborer, he had worked elsewhere as a truck driver and in a warehouse job prior to his employment with Philip Morris. Philip Morris did not permit transfers from prefabrication to shipping at the time Quarles filed his charge of discrimination with the EEOC. The litigation team filed a Title VII class action on his behalf on November 5, 1965, after exhausting his EEOC administrative remedies challenging the "lock-in" effect of the racially discriminatory hiring practices of Philip Morris combined with the facially neutral seniority arrangements.[30]

Gaby, whose name does not appear in the credits of the published opinion but who was a lead attorney in the case, Al, and cooperating attorneys Henry L. Marsh and Oliver Hill of Richmond, Virginia, did the yeoman's work on behalf of the plaintiffs in *Quarles*. Leroy Clark, first assistant counsel at the LDF, also joined the team when it came to trial. Marsh, an African American, was born in Richmond. As a child he walked five miles each way to a one-room school for African Americans, where a single teacher taught seventy students, while whites traveled by bus to a large modern school. His childhood experience with racial discrimination and his admiration of and inspiration from his civil rights heroes such as Thurgood Marshall and Oliver Hill influenced his decision to join in the struggle for racial justice. Marsh graduated from historically black Virginia Union, did a stint in the army, and received his law degree from the historically black law school at Howard University. He began practicing law in Richmond when he joined the firm that later became Hill, Tucker & Marsh. In 1977, Marsh was elected the first African American mayor of Richmond, and he was later elected to the Senate of Virginia.[31]

Hill, also African American, was one of this nation's foremost civil rights attorneys over the course of a career that spanned six decades. He graduated from Howard Law School and was second academically in his graduating class only to his friend Thurgood Marshall. Hill was one of the plaintiffs' attorneys in the 1952 school desegregation case, *Davis v. County School Board of Prince Edwards County*, which was consolidated with and decided under *Brown v. Board of Education*. Hill played a major role in developing the legal strategy in response to the "massive resistance" by whites to *Brown* when white officials in Virginia chose to close historically white public schools rather than admit African Americans. During the 1950s, a cross was burned on the lawn of Hill's home, and he and his family were recipients of constant threats because of his involvement in civil rights litigation. The Hill, Tucker & Marsh law firm played a substantial role in the post-*Brown* school desegregation litigation involving the Richmond public school system.

The *Quarles* case was tried in May 1967 before federal judge John D. Butzner, Jr. Judge Butzner was born in Scranton, Pennsylvania, and graduated from the University of Virginia Law School in 1941. President Kennedy appointed him to the district court in 1962, and President Johnson appointed him to the U.S. Court of Appeals for the Fourth Circuit in June 1967. During his tenure as a federal judge at the district court and court of appeals levels, Butzner became a highly respected judge who participated in some important civil rights and Title VII cases in addition to *Quarles*.[32] The judge's appointment to the court of appeals occurred after the trial in *Quarles* and, because he had conducted the trial, he was asked to sit by designation on the district court to render the decision in the case. After the parties' first round of posttrial submissions (proposed findings of fact and posttrial briefs), Judge Butzner, joined by counsel for the parties, toured the Richmond facility of Philip Morris before hearing posttrial arguments.

The case raised an issue of first impression. No other court had decided the precise issue of whether pre-Act intentional racial discrimination that arguably ended after the effective date of Title VII but the consequences of which continued to adversely affect the employment opportunities of African Americans after the effective date of Title VII was unlawful employment discrimination under Title VII. The litigation team framed the seniority issue as follows:

> In view of the conceded past history of discrimination at Philip Morris, resulting in a concentration of the more attractive jobs in the department reserved for white employees, with [African Americans] relegated to the department with poorer paying jobs, does the continuation of restrictions on transfer from the previously [African American] department to the previously white departments, and the use of departmental seniority in determining priorities for promotion, constitute a violation of the Civil Rights Act of 1964?[33]

More particularly, the issue, as framed, was designed to have Judge Butzner address the much larger issue of whether the term *discrimination,* as used in Title VII, lends itself to more than one theory of discrimination. The issue of the meaning of *discrimination* under Title VII had been the subject of numerous robust discussions among the attorneys at the LDF, with the LDF's consultants, including the seniority discrimination task force, with the EEOC, with cooperating attorneys, and at conferences on Title VII conducted by the LDF at its Airlie House conferences.

The litigation team's response to the issue, as it framed it in *Quarles,* established the core foundations for the present effects of past discrimination theory and was an innovative statutory construction approach. The theory was based on several key provisions of Title VII. First, Section 703(a)(1) makes it an unlawful employment practice for an employer "to discriminate against any individual with respect to his [terms of employment] . . . because of such individual's race." Second, Section 703(a)(2) makes it an unlawful employment practice for an employer "to limit, segregate, or classify his employees . . . in any way which would deprive or tend to deprive any individual of employment opportunities or otherwise adversely affect his status as an employee because of such individual's race." Third, Sections 703(c)(1) and 703(c)(2) impose similar obligations on unions. Fourth, Section 703(c)(3) makes it an unlawful employment practice for a union "to cause or attempt to cause an employer to discriminate against an individual" in violation of the duty imposed on unions by Title VII. None of these sections uses the term *intent,* but two other sections do. Section 703(h) provides that "it shall not be an unlawful employment practice for an employer to apply different [employment] standards . . . pursuant to a bona fide seniority or merit system . . . provided that such differences are not the result of an *intention* to discriminate because of race." And Section 706(g) provides that a court may award injunctive relief "[i]f the court finds that [an employer or union or both have] *intentionally* engaged in or is *intentionally engaging in*" a discriminatory practice prohibited by Title VII.

The litigation team recognized that a pure statutory argument could be made that, even though Sections 703(a)(1) and 703(a)(2) did not contain the term *intent,* by including the phrase "not the result of intention" in Section 703(h) and the phrase "intentionally engaged in or is intentionally engaging in" in Section 703(g), Congress wanted to endorse a pure intent standard as the theory of liability under Title VII. Alternatively, a powerful statutory construction argument could be made that Section 703(a)(2), which contains neither the term *intent* nor *discrimination* but speaks broadly in terms of "limit[ing] . . . in any way which tends to *deprive* any individual of employment opportunities or otherwise *adversely affect*" employment opportunities because of race, embraces an effects, or the disparate impact, theory of discrimination. Rather than try to distinguish the potentially different statutory approaches to the meaning of the terms *discrimination* and *discriminate,* the approach taken by the LDF was essentially to harmonize the two in advancing the present effects of past discrimination theory. Thus, the LDF argued in its *Quarles* posttrial brief that

> [b]ecause of their race, . . . [Philip Morris] and [Local 203] are both discriminating against [African American] employees in the "terms, conditions [and] privileges of employment" by making it impossible as a practical matter for more than a token few of the senior [African American] employees ever to have a chance to compete for the more attractive jobs in the Fabrication Department [because of a history of intentional racial discrimination]; for the same reason, they are limiting, segregating and classifying their employees in a way which would deprive them of employment opportunities; and they are discriminating against them in the on-the-job training which is given as a matter of course to employees promoted from within the Fabrication Department to better jobs in that department. The only way the court could avoid finding the challenged employment practices violate both Sections [703(a)(1) and 703(a)(2)] is to ignore the entire history of racial discrimination imposed by Philip Morris and the union, and to ignore the way in which the present restrictions perpetuate in the present and into the future the discrimination of the past.[34]

The present effects strand of the theory rests on the statutory provisions that speak in terms of "adverse effects" in Sections 703(a)(2) and 703(c)(2), and the past discrimination strand of the theory rests on the two provisions that specifically speak in terms of intent: Sections 703(h) and 706(g).[35] The past discrimination strand theory would require proof of intentional discrimination. Evidence in support of this strand of the theory was easily satisfied in *Quarles* by Philip Morris's admission of overt pre-Act racially discriminatory hiring policies and the racial chartering of unions by Local 203. The "present effects" strand of the theory focused on the fact that the facially neutral seniority system telescoped the effects of that prior overt discrimination into the post-Act period. The litigation team presented evidence of the present effects of pre-Act intentional discrimination through statistics showing that a large percentage of African American employees were "locked" into or essentially frozen in the prefabrication department because of the departmental seniority rule and the limitation placed on transferring out of that department under the notice-of-transfer policy. An alternative theory of discrimination based solely on a pure intent standard, and one advocated in the *Harvard Law Review* Note, was that it is reasonable to impute discriminatory intent to all subsequent actions based on a seniority system if that employer had entered into a binding collective bargaining agreement provision designed to discriminate against African Americans.[36] The litigation team declined to advance the

Harvard Law Review theory of discrimination in *Quarles* even though it did rely on the article in addressing the issue of appropriate relief should Judge Butzner rule in favor of the plaintiffs on the liability issue.

The EEOC filed an amicus brief. It did so because the agency was particularly interested in advising the courts of its views on both the theory or theories of discrimination that should apply in Title VII cases and the appropriate remedies courts should award in the seniority discrimination cases. The EEOC was well aware of the fact that Judge Butzner would probably be the first federal judge to address these issues and that his decision would also have important consequences for the EEOC in administratively enforcing Title VII. However, prior to 1972, the EEOC, with only limited authority to seek judicial enforcement of Title VII, had to be represented in judicial enforcement proceedings by the Department of Justice. Yet, according to David Cashdan, an attorney whom the EEOC hired in its Office of General Counsel in 1965, the Department of Justice had not decided what position it should take in the seniority discrimination cases by the time posttrial briefs were due. Cashdan took the position that the EEOC should nevertheless file an amicus brief because of the importance of the issues that would be decided by a dynamic district court judge. After he consulted with the then-chair of the EEOC, Clifford Alexander, and obtained his approval, the amicus brief in *Quarles* was filed by the agency. It was the first time the EEOC filed its amicus brief on substantive Title VII issues in its own name without the usual protocol of having the Department of Justice also sign the brief.[37] Cashdan had major responsibility for writing the EEOC's brief.

The theory of discrimination advanced by the EEOC was that proof of specific intent was not always required to establish a violation of Title VII. The EEOC relied upon two lines of cases in making its argument.[38] The first was Supreme Court constitutional law cases going back to 1931 that held that the validity of an act must be "tested by its operation and effect."[39] For example, in *Griffin v. Illinois*,[40] the Supreme Court had stated, "A law [or as here, a seniority system] non-discriminatory on its face, may be grossly discriminatory in its operation." This principle had been applied by the Court with special vigor in determining the validity of acts that result in the denial of equal rights to Negroes. The second line of cases encompassed administrative and judicial decisions under the National Labor Relations Act holding that an employer's conduct speaks for itself and is discriminatory if it discourages union membership and has unavoidable consequences that the employer not only foresaw but must have intended.

Philip Morris and the Tobacco Workers, relying on the term *intentional* in Section 706(g), urged Judge Butzner to endorse a pure intent standard—the disparate treatment theory—as the only theory of discrimination under Title VII. They made this argument primarily in response to the amicus brief filed by the EEOC. Philip Morris, in responding to the EEOC's argument, relied upon not only the specific instances in Title VII where the term *intent* or *intentionally* was used but also the legislative history of Title VII in support of its argument that a plaintiff must prove intentional discrimination.[41] During the congressional debate, opponents of Title VII argued that the concept of discrimination was so ill-defined and vague that the EEOC would be at liberty to interpret the term *discriminate* to require racial balancing or preferential treatment of members of protected groups. In response to this argument, the floor managers of Title VII entered a memorandum in the legislative record that included the following:

> It has been suggested that the concept of discrimination is vague. In fact it is clear and simple and has no hidden meaning. To discriminate is to make distinctions, to make a difference in treatment or favor, and those distinctions or differences in treatment or favor which are prohibited by Section 704 are those which are based on any five of the forbidden: race, color, religion, sex, and national origin.[42]

Senator Hubert H. Humphrey, one of the supporters of Title VII, also stated in response to the concern about the lack of a definitive definition of discrimination that the inclusion of the term *intentional* in Section 706(g) was "a clarifying change" because "the Title bars only discrimination because of race, color, religion, sex, or national origin it would seem already to require intent, and thus the proposed change does not involve any substantive change in the title."[43] The union responded to the EEOC's brief by reiterating its earlier argument that only proof of intentional discrimination violates Title VII.[44]

Section 706(h) also presented an additional statutory hurdle that the litigation team had to address in order to prevail on the merits. That section provided a safe harbor for bona fide seniority systems that were not the result of an intention to discriminate. Title VII, as originally introduced, made no specific reference to its effect, if any, on seniority systems, and it did not even mention seniority. That section was added in response to a major concern of some members of Congress and union defenders of seniority that Title VII could possibly result in the wholesale destruction or revision of seniority practices by requiring employers to achieve a racially balanced workforce notwithstanding seniority provisions in collective bargaining agreements or by compelling employers and unions to revise their seniority provisions.[45] The concern of unions could be described as their fear that if Title VII provided a remedy for presumptively facially neutral seniority rules it would amount to a kind of Sadie Hawkins Day[46] or "freedom now"[47] seniority remedy that would allow qualified African Americans with greater seniority to immediately displace white employees with less seniority who held better-paying and more desirable jobs. The debate over the potential adverse impact of Title VII on seniority prompted Senators Joseph Clark and Clifford Case to insert an interpretive memorandum in the *Congressional Record*. It stated, in part:

> Title VII would have no effect on established seniority rights. Its effect is prospective and not retrospective. Thus, for example, if a business has been discriminating in the past and as a result has an all-white working force, when the title comes into effect the employer's obligation would be simply to fill future vacancies on a non-discriminatory basis. He would not be obligated—or indeed, permitted—to fire whites in order to hire Negroes, or to prefer Negroes for future vacancies, or, once Negroes are hired, to give them special seniority rights at the expense of white workers hired earlier.[48]

The Clark-Case memorandum had been prepared by the Department of Justice and included a statement that it was incorrect to assert that Title VII would undermine vested seniority rights. Both statements were made before Section 703(h) had been proposed and adopted. In addition, Senator Clark introduced written answers to questions propounded by Senator Dirksen, which included the statement that "[s]eniority rights are in no way affected by [Title VII]."[49]

Aware of the legislative debate surrounding the inclusion of Section 703(h) with respect to seniority, the litigation team unequivocally stated in its post-trial brief in *Quarles* that the plaintiffs were "not asking that white employees who received jobs or promotions because of racial discrimination now be made to give them up." However, the LDF argued that Title VII should be construed so "that as future opportunities for transfer or promotion arise, [African American] employees already working for Philip Morris not be subjected to further, additional, future disadvantages because of discrimination in the past."[50] The LDF, in support of this argument, relied upon a line of Supreme Court precedents holding that potential opportunities for future vacancies based on seniority are expectancies rather than vested rights.[51] Addressing the limitations, if any, of Section 703(h) on the issue of liability, the LDF made a short, simply stated statutory argument: Section 703(h) provides a safe harbor only for seniority systems that are not the result of an intention to discriminate because of race, and a seniority system that perpetuates discrimination and that will continue to do so in the future in favor of whites with less seniority than more senior African Americans "can scarcely be called 'bona fide.'"[52] This was essentially the same argument that had been advanced in the *Harvard Law Review* student Note on seniority.

Philip Morris and the union relied heavily on *Whitfield*.[53] They advanced four reasons Judge Butzner should rule in their favor in light of that case. First, they argued that the facts of *Quarles* and *Whitfield* were similar in that the employers in both cases had put in place before the effective date of Title VII an employment policy to allow African Americans to bid for the more-skilled and better-paying jobs in the white departments. Second, they argued that the test of discrimination in both cases was the same even though the claims were brought under different statutes. Third, as a practical matter, they argued that the court in *Whitfield* recognized that it could not turn back the clock but could only look to the future. Fourth, they argued that the *Whitfield* test of "reasonableness and good faith" should be equally applicable in *Quarles*. The LDF briefly addressed *Whitfield* in its reply brief with two simply stated responses. First, the two cases were factually distinguishable in that *Whitfield*, unlike *Quarles*, dealt with skilled and unskilled lines of progression, and, second, the two claims arose under different statutes.

Judge Butzner decided *Quarles* on January 4, 1968. He deemed the critical issue to be the one as framed by the litigation team, namely, whether "present consequences of past discrimination [are] covered by" Title VII. Acknowledging his debt in deciding the case to "[a] perceptive analysis of the problem [in the seniority discrimination cases] and its solution" found in the *Harvard Law Review* student Note, Judge Butzner carefully reviewed the facts of the case and the legislative history of Title VII. He then totally rejected the defendants' statutory and legislative history arguments. He held that although Congress did not intend to require reverse discrimination or that African Americans be preferred over white employees who possess employment seniority, it was equally clear that Congress "did not intend to freeze an entire generation into discriminatory patterns that existed before" the enactment of Title VII.[54] He made a factual ruling that the present differences in the departmental seniority of African American and white employees were because of Philip Morris's intentional, racially discriminatory hiring policy before Title VII that could not be afforded the protection of Section 706(h). The critical development in *Quarles* was that Judge Butzner thus specifically endorsed the LDF's present effects of past discrimination theory.

> While no case on point appears to have been decided, the governing principles are not new. Present discrimination may be found in contractual provisions that appear fair upon their face, but which operate unfairly because of the historical discrimination that undergirds them. . . . Departmental seniority rooted in decades of racially segregated departments can neither mask the duty of a union to fairly represent its members nor shield the employer who is privy to the union's derelictions.[55]

Ruling that the defendants "intentionally engaged in unlawful employment practices by discriminating on the ground of race," Judge Butzner found that the discrimination was embedded in seniority and transfer provision of collective bargaining agreements and that it "adversely affects the conditions of employment, and opportunities for advancement of the class."[56] He specifically rejected the defendants' statutory and legislative history arguments that only intentional discrimination violated Title VII and that the present effects of a racially discriminatory hiring policy that was abandoned before the effective date of Title VII were beyond the reach of the act. On this point, he concluded that "[t]he plain language of [Title VII] condemns as an unfair practice all racial discrimination affecting employment without excluding present discrimination that originated in seniority systems devised before the effective date of the Act."[57]

Judge Butzner, like the parties themselves, made no attempt to ground his decision solely in one or the other of the two substantive provisions of Title VII, i.e., Section 703(a)(1) or 703(a)(2). Like the parties in *Quarles* and the parties in the overwhelming majority of other cases decided before *Griggs,* he relied upon both provisions in his opinion. He seemed to ground his version of the past discrimination component of the theory in Section 706(h), which uses the term *intent.* For example, he concluded that "[t]he differences between the terms and conditions of employment for whites and Negroes about which plaintiffs complain are the result of an intention to discriminate in hiring policies on the basis of race before January 1, 1968. . . . The act does not condone present differences before the effective date of the act although such a provision could have been included in the act had Congress so intended."[58] He also did not specifically address or accept the EEOC's major argument that intent need not be shown to establish a violation of Title VII. The fact that Judge Butzner did not clearly identify the provision of Title VII on which he grounded his acceptance of the present effects of past discrimination theory is not unusual because Congress gave no clear indication about whether Title VII would allow more than one theory of discrimination. This problem was not clarified until the Supreme Court decided *Connecticut v. Teal* in 1982, which held that the disparate impact theory was based on a construction of Section 703(a)(2).

Judge Butzner had little difficulty in disposing of the defendants' arguments based on Section 703(h) and *Whitfield*. With respect to 703(h), he accepted the LDF's argument that a departmental seniority system that had its genesis in racial discrimination was not a bona fide seniority system. He distinguished *Whitfield*, saying that it

> does not stand for the proposition that present discrimination can be justified simply because it was caused by conditions in the past. Present discrimination was allowed in *Whitfield* only because it was rooted in the Negro employees' lack of ability and training to take skilled jobs on the same basis as white employees. The fact that white employees received their skills training in a discriminatory progression line denied to the Negroes did not outweigh the fact that the Negroes were unskilled and untrained. *Business necessity, not racial discrimination, dictated the limited transfer privileges under the contract.*[59]

The business necessity defense, now a major statutory defense in the *Griggs* disparate impact cases as a result of the 1991 amendments to Title VII, was first introduced in employment discrimination jurisprudence by defendants' reliance on *Whitfield* to exclude seniority discrimination cases completely from coverage of the Act. The courts did not begin to flesh out the business necessity defense until after the Supreme Court decided *Griggs*.

On the issue of appropriate relief, Judge Butzner declined the invitation of the LDF and the EEOC to, in his view, abolish the departmental structure and merge the seniority rosters of the respective departments according to seniority. This would have been what I earlier identified as the Sadie Hawkins remedy. He also declined the defendants' proposal that would continue to subordinate the employment opportunities of African Americans to white employees regardless of seniority. Although recognizing that he had the power to issue a far-reaching decree to invalidate the separate lines of progression and affirmatively require the company and union to grant the same seniority rights, training privileges, assignments, and opportunities to African

American employees as they do to white persons with the same continuous service date, Judge Butzner opted for a more modest decree. He thus decided that the remedy should permit African American employees in plaintiffs' class, i.e., those employed before January 1, 1966, to train and advance on the same basis as white employees with comparable ability and employment seniority. This approach was designed to disturb as little as possible the efficiencies of Philip Morris's department structure. Taking a lead from the defendants' own agreement modifying and loosening interdepartmental transfers, Judge Butzner issued a fairly intricate and detailed decree to unlock African Americans from the formerly racially discriminatory and less desirable department.

The decision in *Quarles* was occasion to celebrate the victory Gaby, Al, Henry, and Oliver Hill had obtained. Gaby, like Fred Wallace when he prevailed on the class action issue in *Hall v. Werthan Bag,* walked around the office waving the *Quarles* decision over her head after she received a copy. She jokingly reminded me then and on a few other occasions that *Quarles* was one of the "dog cases," meaning weak and unwinnable, I had assigned to her when she joined the litigation team.[60]

The defendants did not appeal *Quarles* to the court of appeals, and soon other courts adopted the present effects of past discrimination theory. Less than three months after *Quarles,* the district court in *Local 189, Papermakers and Paperworkers v. United States* specifically adopted the *Quarles* present effects theory in a seniority discrimination case.[61] The facts in *Local 189* mirrored in significant respects the facts of *Quarles.* The Department of Justice filed the complaint in *Local 189* against the paper manufacturing facility of Crown Zellerbach, located in Bogulusa, Louisiana, and the Papermakers and Paperworkers union on January 30, 1968, in the same month Judge Butzner decided *Quarles.* The case was brought pursuant to the Department of Justice's pattern or practice authority under Title VII and to enforce Crown Zellerbach's obligation under presidential Executive Order 11246, which required nondiscrimination assurances from all employers who contracted with the federal government. Prior to filing the complaint, the federal government had worked out a compromise with Crown Zellerbach to change the segregated seniority system. However, the union not only refused to agree to the compromise but also threatened a strike if the employer unilaterally implemented the compromise. The Department of Justice then filed its lawsuit to enjoin the strike on the grounds that the union would be using the strike to preserve a seniority system that discriminated against African Americans. In addition, the

Department of Justice abandoned any interest in a compromise and sought instead the abolition of the seniority system that preserved the more desirable jobs for whites and gave the undesirable and lower-paying "left over" jobs[62] to African Americans.

The U.S. Court of Appeals for the Fifth Circuit affirmed the decision of the district court in *Local 189* in an opinion written by Judge John Minor Wisdom. Judge Wisdom is considered one of the civil rights activists' judicial heroes.[63] President Eisenhower appointed him in 1957 to the court of appeals, where he sat during the era of the implementation of *Brown* and the early enforcement of the Civil Rights Act of 1964. Greenberg has stated that

> John Minor Wisdom came from a traditional, well-connected New Orleans background, belonged to—and continued to after he went on the bench—the "right" clubs, even those that excluded blacks and Jews. He was outspoken, however, in his belief in absolute racial equality. One of his grandfathers, Wisdom proudly observed, came from a Jewish, French background. He went to Tulane Law School and to Harvard as a graduate student. Wisdom returned to New Orleans [after service in the Second World War] to build a highly successful practice and developed a national nonracial perspective.[64]

In an important civil rights case involving a claim of racial discrimination in voting, *Gomillion v. Lightfoot,* the Fifth Circuit upheld a redistricting plan because the plan made no explicit reference to race even though the evidence showed that it had a devastating discriminatory effect on the voting rights of the African Americans. The Fifth Circuit rejected the plaintiffs' argument that the exclusionary effect of the redistricting plan on African Americans on whose behalf the case was brought was unconstitutional. Judge Wisdom joined fully in the majority opinion, but he also wrote a separate concurring opinion in which he said that the Supreme Court's rulings refusing to intervene in redistricting issues controlled this case, and he objected to the "intrusion of national courts in the policy of a state." He went on to say, "I see no difference between partially disfranchising negroes and partially disfranchising Republicans, Democrats, Italians, Poles."[65] Later, after the Supreme Court overturned the Fifth Circuit's decision in *Gomillion* and held that a statute's discriminatory effect could be the basis for a finding of discriminatory intent, Judge Wisdom referred to his view to the contrary in *Gomillion* as the "most painful memory of his judicial service," because "he had overreacted to a skepticism that he developed in law school over judicial intermeddling into purely 'political matters' better left to the legislative or executive branches."[66]

Judge Wisdom's honesty in recognizing that he had failed to realize that a discriminatory effect can be evidence of discriminatory intent factored into views on the early landmark Title VII employment discrimination cases, *Local 189* and *Whitfield*.[67] In *Local 189*, he began his decision by stating that the case presents "one of the most perplexing issues troubling the courts under Title VII: how to reconcile equal employment opportunity today with seniority expectations based on *yesterday's* built-in racial discrimination. May an employer continue to award formerly white jobs on the basis of seniority attained in other formerly white jobs, or must the employer consider the employee's experience in formerly Negro jobs as an equivalent measure of seniority?"[68] As to the first question, relying heavily on *Quarles* and the same *Harvard Law Review* student Note on seniority as did Judge Butzner and also reviewing the same legislative history as did Judge Butzner, Judge Wisdom endorsed both the present effects of past discrimination theory and the reasoning on which Judge Butzner based that theory. He found the legislative history on the seniority issue "singularly uninstructive."[69] Judge Wisdom clearly articulated the theory of present effects of past discrimination, more so than Judge Butzner had done in *Quarles*, when he stated that "[w]e hold that . . . [a] job seniority system [that was in effect prior to the elimination of intentional racial discrimination] was unlawful because by carrying forward the effect of former discriminatory practices the system results in present and future discrimination. When [an] African American applicant has the qualifications to handle a particular job, [Title VII] requires that [African American] seniority be equated with white seniority."[70]

Judge Wisdom gave more careful attention than Judge Butzner to the issue of the appropriate remedy. He stated the crux of the remedy issue as posing the problem of how far the employer must go to undo the present effects of past discrimination. On this issue, he found the *Harvard Law Review* student Note on seniority quite helpful. That article had articulated three potential remedial schemes. The first was the "freedom now," or Sadie Hawkins, approach that would be a complete purge of the "but-for" effect of pre-Act discrimination by allowing African American employees to displace incumbent white employees who had less employment seniority. The second, the "status quo" theory advocated by the defendants, would continue the effects of past racial discrimination so long as the defendant had adopted policies and practices that ended explicit racial discrimination. The third theory, the "rightful place"—which stands between "freedom now" and "status quo"—would provide African American workers the right to bid for future vacancies based on plant or employment seniority rather than a seniority arrangement that "locks in" past discrimination. Judge Wisdom endorsed the "rightful place" theory because he believed that it would be in accordance with the history and purpose of Title VII. His reasoning for adopting the rightful place theory was based on his view that Title VII should be construed to prohibit the future awarding of vacancies on the basis of a seniority system that "locks in" prior racial discrimination, that white employees should not be bumped out of their present positions by the African Americans who were discriminated against, and that plant or company seniority should govern new job openings.

The defendants in *Local 189*, like the defendants in *Quarles*, argued that *Whitfield* supported a decision in their favor. Judge Wisdom rejected the defendants' reliance on *Whitfield* for essentially the same reason relied on by Judge Butzner in *Quarles* that the opposite outcome in *Whitfield* would be the result of business necessity rather than racial discrimination for upholding the seniority system with its present lock-in effects of past discrimination. The relevancy of *Whitfield* to seniority discrimination claims arising under Title VII was finally put to rest by Judge Wisdom, the author of *Whitfield*, in a later case in 1970, *Taylor v. Armco Steel Corporation*. *Taylor* involved the same employer and union as in *Whitfield*. In *Taylor*, decided less than a year after *Local 189*, Judge Wisdom held that although *Whitfield* was still defensible within the context of the NLRA, it was indefensible under Title VII in light of *Local 189*. Al and Gaby, who was then in private practice in Houston, Texas, served as cocounsel in *Taylor*, and Gaby argued the case in the Fifth Circuit.[71]

Although neither the LDF, the EEOC, the defendants, nor the courts specifically addressed the issue of whether Title VII embraced two different theories of discrimination in the early cases, the success of the LDF in *Quarles* was significant in several respects because it established important doctrinal foundations for legal principles on which the *Griggs* disparate impact theory was based. Although *Quarles* and *Local 189* were grounded in the view that proof of intent was necessary to establish a violation of Title VII, the foundations for the disparate impact, or effects, test were laid down. The courts did not clearly uncouple intentional discrimination (the disparate treatment theory) from the effects of discrimination not grounded in intentional discrimination (the disparate impact theory) until the Supreme Court decided *Griggs*.

In *Quarles* and *Local 189*, the courts for the first time in American jurisprudence judicially reformed seniority systems to provide employment opportunities to African American workers that are equal to those of whites.[72] The acceptance by Judge Butzner of the LDF's present effects of past discrimination theory in *Quarles*, fleshed out more fully in *Local 189* and later cases, was a critical development that contributed to much of the success that not only African Americans, but also women, Asian Americans, and other protected groups have experienced in the workplace. Thus, for almost a decade, the present effects of past discrimination theory provided a remedy for meaningful employment opportunities to African Americans who, for decades before the effective date of Title VII, had been locked into segregated and low-paying jobs because of their race. As one official said, "[o]nce the concept of 'present effect of past discrimination' began to develop, every middle-to-large employer found itself guilty based simply on the constitution of its work force as of January 1, 1965," because "[o]bviously they could not obliterate their existing work forces and start anew" and "neither could they completely restructure the existing work forces with substantial sacrifices of safety, efficiency and employee morale."[73]

6. *Griggs*: The Factual Setting

Griggs, like *Quarles*, arose against the background of decades of widespread overt racial discrimination against African Americans in the South in all facets of public and private activities: employment, education, places of public accommodation, transportation, and voting. Whereas *Quarles* involved the legality of facially neutral seniority systems under Title VII, *Griggs* involved the legality of racially neutral educational and testing practices. In 1990, it was reported that, for more than 100 years, employers had been requiring more and more education of applicants for more and more jobs.[1] And a 1963 study, published the year before the enactment of Title VII, reported that although the evidence was fragmentary, it was fairly clear that a large number of industrial firms in the United States used standardized tests in selecting, promoting, and transferring personnel.[2]

Testing and educational requirements are only part of a larger phenomenon in American life: a preoccupation with objective measurements of ability to implement the meritocracy principle. Selection of the best-qualified employees to fill job vacancies based on objective criteria, such as tests and educational requirements, is believed to improve productivity and to provide security from claims of unlawful employment discrimination. Making employment decisions on that basis reduces, if not entirely eliminates, discriminatory decision making.[3] On the other hand, economic considerations are also factors that employers take into account when they adopt testing and educational requirements: it is less costly to screen applicants and employees with testing and educational requirements than other selection procedures such as interviews, background checks, and recommendations.[4] Industrial psychology as a discipline developed with the use of employment testing and the trend toward more objective and scientific selection of employees.[5]

The discriminatory effects of testing on the employment opportunities of African Americans became a highly controversial issue during the congressional deliberations on Title VII in 1964 as the result of a case, *Myart v. Motorola*, decided by an Illinois FEPC hearing officer during that time. In *Myart*, an African American man applied for a job with Motorola on a production line that involved testing and adjusting television sets. Motorola gave Myart a five-minute written test of verbal and numerical abilities and interviewed him briefly. After hearing nothing from Motorola for several weeks, Myart filed a racial discrimination complaint with the Illinois FEPC alleging that he had passed the test but had not been offered a job because of his race. The FEPC hearing examiner ruled in Myart's favor on the grounds, among others, that Motorola's use of the test did not lend itself to equal opportunity for culturally deprived and disadvantaged groups and that proof of intent to discriminate need not be shown if a test is culturally biased in favor of whites. The hearing examiner ordered Motorola to replace the test with one that was not culturally biased against disadvantaged and culturally deprived groups. (In 1966, after the enactment of Title VII, the Illinois Supreme Court rejected the hearing examiner's factual determinations as unreasonable.)[6]

Myart caused a great deal of unease and shock among employers and others involved in the testing business and focused national attention on the use of employment tests, deliberately or inadvertently, as instruments of racial discrimination that adversely affected the employment opportunities of African Americans. As one commentator described the reaction, the decision "caught personnel psychologists and businessmen flat-footed." Many employers were shocked to learn that employment testing, a generally accepted management prerogative, was being challenged on the grounds of racial discrimination because, during the 1950s and early 1960s employment testing had increased to unprecedented levels.[7] The Supreme Court, in *Griggs*, specifically noted the controversy that *Motorola* caused when it stated that the case suggested employers could not use standardized tests on which whites performed better than African Americans, even if the tests could be justified by the business needs of employers.[8]

Congressional opponents of Title VII unsuccessfully advocated for the inclusion of specific language in the bill to assure that the *Motorola* decision would not be relied upon by the EEOC and courts as precedent. Instead, Section 703(h) emerged as a compromise measure. Section 703(h) is often referred to as the Tower Amendment because Senator John Tower (R-Texas), who strongly opposed Title VII, introduced an amendment authorizing "professionally developed ability tests." Section 703(h), as finally enacted, provides that it shall not be a violation of Title VII for an "employer to give and act upon the results of any professionally developed ability test provided that such test, its administration or action upon the results is not designed, intended or used to discriminate on the basis of race, color, religion, sex or national origin."[9] However, because Congress failed to provide definitions or guidelines for phrases such as "professionally developed," "ability test," or "designed, intended or used to discriminate," Section 703(h) was necessarily ambiguous about congressional intent and had to be fleshed out in litigation either in cases brought by the Department of Justice or by private parties in their roles as private attorneys general.

Employment tests run the gamut from skill tests—such as sewing, typing, and welding—which approximate job tasks, to highly abstract and academic tests of general intelligence.[10] Social scientists have long been aware of the potential for racial discrimination in the use of standardized pen-and-paper tests to screen job applicants because African Americans generally do not perform as well as whites on them.[11] In light of this, the limits, if any, that courts would place on a Section 703(h) statutory defense were critical.

The EEOC, through its Office of Research and Reports, undertook a study of the "professionally developed ability" testing issue. The study was done under the supervision of Dr. Phyllis A. Wallace, the first African American woman to receive a Ph.D. in economics from Yale University, who became the chief of technical studies at the EEOC in 1965. The participants in the study framed the question to be explored as "whether many 'professionally developed ability tests' used by employers to select qualified employees do in fact discriminate *inadvertently*."[12] The report specifically stated that the study did not focus on the willful or intentional misuse of tests to discriminate in employment, such as administering tests to African Americans but not to whites or requiring African Americans to achieve a higher score than whites. The study involved an intensive review of the scholarly literature on testing and a review of data collected by some of the leading scholars on personnel testing who had made suggestions for mitigating the effects of unintentional types of discrimination against minorities. Dr. Wallace's team submitted its report to the EEOC in March 1966. The report concluded that

[i]ndividuals from culturally disadvantaged backgrounds perform less well on [general intelligence] tests on the average than do applicants from middle class environments and consequently may be screened out of training programs and/or excluded from jobs; that differences in culture, in opportunity, and in experience can have a devastating effect on test performance; and that since many [African Americans], Mexican Americans, Indians, and lower-class whites have not shared the middle class culture, they may perform in an inferior manner on tests of general intelligence, particularly paper and pencil, but not necessarily on performance for which these tests are supposed to be predictive.[13]

The recommendations made in the Wallace report and by a panel of psychologists it had commissioned for advice on the use of aptitude and/or ability testing in industrial settings were the basis for the EEOC's first Guidelines on Employment Testing Procedures, which it issued on August 24, 1966.[14] EEOC officials had concluded that many employers had introduced standardized testing in making employment decisions in the 1950s and early 1960s after realizing that they could no longer discriminate against African Americans because of their race and that testing posed a major barrier to the formulation of effective remedial action to eliminate racial discrimination in employment, and those conclusions were the basis of the publication of the guidelines.[15] These guidelines were not published in the *Federal Register,* the official publication for rules, proposed rules, and notices of federal agencies, but in pamphlet form only. The original guidelines put the EEOC on record as interpreting the phrase "professionally developed ability test," as used in Section 703(h), to mean a test that fairly measures the knowledge or skill required by the particular job or class of jobs that the applicant seeks, or that fairly affords the employer a chance to measure the applicant's ability to perform a particular job or class of jobs. Under the guidelines, the fact that a test was prepared by an individual or organization claiming expertise in test preparation did not in and of itself legitimate use of the test. The first and later testing guidelines adopted the requirement of validation for determining whether a test was "professionally developed." Simply stated, validation is a procedure by which it can be determined whether applicants or employees who achieve high scores on tests perform better on the job than applicants and employees who receive lower scores.[16]

The EEOC guidelines did not explicitly articulate the disparate impact theory of discrimination but did implicitly suggest it when they stated that "[e]mployers have discovered they may inadvertently exclude qualified minority applicants through inappropriate testing procedures" because "such testing procedures may discriminate in employment and promotion as effectively as the once common 'white only' or 'Anglo only' signs."[17] The use by both the Wallace report and the 1966 EEOC guidelines of the terms "inadvertently" and "unintentionally" formed the foundational legal building blocks upon which the *Griggs* disparate impact theory rests. The 1966 testing guidelines were superseded and enlarged upon in the EEOC's Guidelines on Employment Selection Procedures, which became effective upon publication on August 1, 1970.[18] The 1970 testing guidelines were published after the decisions by the district court and the court of appeals and after the Supreme Court granted the LDF's petition for certiorari in *Griggs* on June 29, 1970,[19] but before the Court decided *Griggs*.

George Cooper and Richard Sobol became involved in employment discrimination litigation about a year after the effective date of Title VII through working with the Lawyers Constitutional Defense Committee.[20] Cooper drafted the Supreme Court briefs for the LDF in *Griggs* and another landmark case that came out of the litigation campaign, *Albemarle Paper Co. v. Moody*. He attended racially segregated public schools in Baltimore, Maryland. He received his law degree from Harvard Law School in 1961 after completing his undergraduate studies at the University of Pennsylvania. After a stint of several years of military service, Cooper worked as an attorney with a major law firm in Washington, D.C., from 1963 through 1966 and then as a professor of law at Columbia Law School from 1966 through 1985. In 1971, Cooper and fellow Columbia professor Harriet Rabb started a special clinical law program for Columbia students that was devoted exclusively to employment discrimination law, and they published a loose-leaf casebook on employment discrimination law and litigation that was funded by the EEOC and the New York City Commission for Human Rights.[21] Most of the early cases on which the clinical students worked were LDF employment discrimination cases, but the number of those cases declined over time because George and Harriet became involved in local cases arising in New York City.[22]

Richard Sobol received his undergraduate degree from Union College in 1958 and his law degree from Columbia University in 1961. Before becoming chief state counsel for the Lawyers Constitutional Defense Committee in New Orleans in 1966, he served as a clerk for a federal judge and then worked as an attorney with a major law firm, also in Washington, D.C. Cooper and Sobol became friends when both were working in Washington. Cooper joined Sobol to serve as cocounsel on some civil rights cases under the auspices of the Lawyers Constitutional Defense Committee. Sobol also was a professor of law for several years at the University of Michigan Law School. Both men had an interest in doing civil rights litigation on behalf of African Americans and eventually decided to focus on Title VII to help shape how the new law should be interpreted and enforced. Cooper and Sobol, like the LDF litigation team and the EEOC, began to focus critically on a theory, or theories, of discrimination that would offer the prospect of making Title VII a more effective legal remedy for unlawful discrimination than had been the case prior to Title VII. Based on their experience in litigating Title VII seniority discrimination and testing employment discrimination cases,[23] they eventually coauthored an influential and widely cited article that the *Harvard Law Review* published in June 1969.[24] The central thesis of the article was an argument for the adoption of an "effects-oriented" (disparate impact) theory of discrimination rather than the "intent-oriented" (disparate treatment) theory followed in earlier laws. The central thesis of the article was based on three propositions. The first was that discrimination was class-based. The second was that subjective decision making in allocating employment opportunities had to be replaced by objective evaluations. The third was that objective employee screening evaluations had to relate to actual job needs.[25]

The Cooper and Sobol article was the first to articulate the theoretical foundations for the disparate impact theory involving facially neutral policies or practices that have an adverse effect on the employment opportunities of African Americans, even absent proof that the employer or union adopted the policy or practice without the intent to discriminate. Based on an in-depth analysis of the facially neutral seniority and testing practices and cases, they set out their theoretical approach. They concluded

> that seniority and testing violate fair employment laws in situations where an adverse racial impact is not adequately justified, without regards to the motive of the employer in adopting the practice. This shift away from a restrictive focus on the state of mind of the employer is essential to the effective enforcement of fair employment law, not merely because specific intent is difficult to prove, but because there is frequently no discriminatory intent underlying the adoption of seniority and testing practices, or a wide variety of other objectives and apparently neutral conditions to hire or promote. These conditions are possibly the most important contemporary obstacles to the employment and promotion of qualified black workers. In recognizing this fact and interpreting fair employment laws to bar the imposition of an unnecessary disadvantage to black workers, whether or not it is imposed because of racial bias, such cases as *Quarles* and *Local 189* and the orders of various agencies regarding testing suggest the outline of a generally effects-oriented approach to objective criteria.
>
> There are two steps to this approach: first a determination of a racial impact of the practice, and second, a determination whether any significant racial impact that exists can be adequately justified by non-racial considerations. The first step is to assure that a practice is not found to be discriminatory merely because it disadvantages an individual black in some isolated situation. A practice should be found discriminatory only where it consistently and systematically prefers whites over blacks. . . .

The second determination a court should make is one of policy: whether the nonracial justification for the practice is sufficient to support its racial impact.... In *Quarles* and *Local 189*, it was held that the seniority expectations of incumbent white employees are not sufficient to justify the prejudicial impact of seniority rules on blacks, at least where those expectations derived from the prior exclusion of black workers from the seniority unit. These cases also indicate that even a bona-fide business justification will not serve to justify a practice adversely affecting blacks if the same interest can be served by alternative procedures that would be less prejudicial.... On the other hand, practices having adverse racial impact should be permitted when they serve a significant business purpose that cannot be adequately served by a less prejudicial practice.[26]

The *Griggs* case arose in context of the reality of the difficulty of effective enforcement of Title VII based solely on the disparate treatment theory, which requires proof of intent to discriminate; the LDF's concern about trying disparate treatment cases before all-white juries; and the effort by the LDF litigation team, the EEOC, and Cooper and Sobol to articulate a theory of discrimination that was not based solely on discriminatory intent and to find a remedy that would substantially expand the employment opportunities of African Americans. The employer in *Griggs*, Duke Power Company, was a public utility corporation that was engaged in the generation, transmission, distribution, and sale of electric power to the general public in North Carolina and South Carolina.[27] Duke Power also supplied electric power to federal government agencies and, for that reason, was subject to the Executive Order that prohibited discrimination in employment.[28]

The plaintiffs were Willie Griggs, James Tucker, Herman Martin, William Purcell, Clarence Jackson, Robert Jumper, Lewis Hairston, Jr., Willie Boyd, Junior Blackstock, John Hatchett, Clarence Purcell, Eddie Galloway, and Eddie Broadnax. All of the plaintiffs were employed and classified as laborers or semiskilled laborers at Duke's Dan River Steam Station, a steam-generating facility in Eden, Rockingham County, North Carolina.[29] The Dan River facility converted the energy in coal into electric energy that Duke Power sold to its customers. The process of converting coal into electric energy involves receiving large quantities of coal brought to the facility from mines, the weighing of coal shipments, and the sampling, unloading, and distributing of the coal to storage bunkers. The coal is fed from the bunkers through pulverizing mills into boilers. From the boilers, the energy from the coal is turned into heat energy by burning, and this heat energy forms steam. The steam is sent to turbine generators, where the heat energy is turned into mechanical energy, and the end result is electrical energy. The electrical energy is sent to substations and from there to customers.

At the time the LDF began to represent the plaintiffs, Duke Power owned and operated approximately 120 offices, branches, district offices, and power-generating plants throughout the two states. Duke Power employed more than 5,600 persons in all of its facilities.[30] The overwhelming majority of its African American employees were employed throughout all of its operations in semi-skilled, unskilled, or service worker jobs, with African Americans filling 562 out of 600 such jobs.[31] Duke Power employed ninety-five employees at the Dan River Station; of these ninety-five, fourteen were African American and eighty-one were white. The Dan River Station went into operation in late 1949. Some of the plaintiffs, for example, Willie Boyd, the principal spokesperson for the plaintiffs, and William Purcell, had earlier worked as laborers in the construction of the Dan River facility; they became full-time employees after the facility became operational.[32] Employees were not represented by a union.

The Dan River Station was divided for operational purposes into five departments: (1) operations, (2) maintenance, (3) laboratory and testing, (4) coal handling, and (5) labor. The jobs of watchman, clerk, and storekeeper were in a miscellaneous category. There were approximately thirty-six job titles used at Dan River, but Duke Power had never prepared written job descriptions for any of them. Employees in the coal-handling department weighed, sampled, and unloaded coal and did so with equipment such as bulldozers and coal crushers. The employees in the operating department then took over and operated or monitored equipment such as boilers, turbines, and auxiliary control equipment. The maintenance department had the responsibility for all mechanical and electrical maintenance throughout the Dan River facility. Employees in the laboratory department analyzed materials such as coal, boiler water, and other fluids and liquids used in the operation of the station. The duties performed by employees in each category were determined by practice and tradition and an understanding between the supervisor and the employee in the particular job category. Employees in all of the departments, except coal handling and labor, worked inside the plant, or in the "inside" departments. The employees who worked coal handling and labor generally worked outside, or in the "outside" departments. The "inside" positions were reserved for white employees while both African Americans and whites held "outside" positions.

The plaintiffs, who were laborers, held the least desirable and lowest-paid positions, which involved, among other things, janitorial duties throughout the Dan River facility and other menial and manual tasks, such as driving trucks or cleaning equipment and machines. The maximum wage earned by any of the plaintiffs, including some who had almost twenty years of service, was $1.645 per hour, whether or not they had a high school education. This maximum was lower than the minimum wage of $1.875 per hour Duke Power paid to any white employee, many of whom also did not have a high school education. Of the eighty-one white employees, only thirty-three, or 40 percent, had finished high school. Of the fourteen African American employees, three, or 21 percent, had finished high school.[33] The wages earned by the plaintiffs were drastically lower than the wages paid to white employees with comparable seniority in the "inside" departments, where the top pay was $3.18 per hour or more.[34] After the effective date of Title VII, Duke Power also created a new job classification: auxiliary service man. This new job was established primarily for African American employees in the labor department who "exhibited . . . extraordinary skills" such as being able to "do a little bit of rough carpentry work or some brick work or something like that . . . or other special skills [over and above what is required to do janitorial duties] that warranted a little bit more money even though he could not be promoted due to a lack of a high school education."[35] No one held that position at the time of trial in 1968.

An unofficial "line of progression" existed within each department, but the notion of "line of progression" was synonymous with "department."[36] Duke Power's promotion practices allowed employees to advance from a lower-paid job to a higher-paid job based on departmental seniority. There were no formal job training programs for any of the employees at the Dan River plant. All employees, except supervisors, entering new jobs for the first time received informal on-the-job training either in the new job or in a job to which they were aspiring. Employees seeking promotions to higher-paying jobs could request promotions to vacancies, and Duke Power did not have a policy barring white employees from transferring from one department to another, nor a strict policy that required a transferring employee to start at the bottommost job upon transfer to a new department.

Not only were jobs rigidly segregated by race, but Duke Power also maintained racially segregated facilities such as locker rooms, showers, toilet facilities, and drinking fountains at the Dan River Station. The EEOC concluded in its investigation that the segregated facilities for African American employees were located in a crowded, filthy brick building by the railroad tracks at the base of the soft coal stockpile. Locker rooms, drinking fountains, and showers for white employees, including those working in the coal-handling department, were located inside the main building.[37] Duke Power made no effort to eliminate its racially segregated facilities until after the plaintiffs had filed their charge of unlawful employment discrimination with the EEOC. The plaintiffs filed their charges against Duke Power with the EEOC on March 15, 1966. The EEOC's investigation team visited the Dan River facility on April 21, 1966, to begin its work. Several days after the visit by the investigation team, Duke Power advised the EEOC that on April 28, 1966, all employees were assigned to the same locker room.

About ten years before the effective date of Title VII, or around 1955, Duke Power instituted an employment policy of requiring that all new applicants for jobs historically reserved for the white "inside" departments have a high school education. The new policy did not bar white employees already in lines of progression in the inside departments who did not have a high school education from promotions to higher-paying jobs.[38] Many white employees in lines of progression in the inside departments who did not have a high school education were often promoted to better jobs. For example, a white employee with only a seventh-grade education who had started as a laborer eventually became the foreman of the plaintiffs even though there were several plaintiffs who had a high school education. Another white employee with only a tenth-grade education started as a water boy and eventually became a control operator. Another white employee with only an eighth-grade education started as a watchman and progressed to become a welder. Yet another white employee with only a ninth-grade education started out as a truck driver and eventually became a control operator.[39]

On July 2, 1965, the same date that Title VII became effective, Duke Power added a new requirement that all applicants for jobs in the inside departments had to satisfy, in addition to the high school education requirement. The new requirement was that the applicants must successfully pass a written test battery. Duke Power stated that it added the test battery to the high school education requirement because its experience was that some of its employees who did not have a high school education had insufficient ability to be promoted to top-level jobs as the complexity of its operations grew.

> The nature of our business is becoming more complex all the time. We have got seven or eight computers on order. We are rapidly moving into the nuclear power area with [one of our stations]. We use our existing Power Stations as nucleus

pools from which to draw man power with the skills required to move into new [stations]—new locations, and they form the nucleus of the experienced people, into moving into these more complex areas. Many years ago, we found that we had people who, due to their inability to grasp situations, to read, to reason, to have a general intelligence level high enough to be able to progress in jobs—that we were—getting some road blocks in our classifications in our Power Stations, and this is why we embraced the High School education as a requirement. There is nothing magic about it, and it doesn't work all the time, because you can have a man who graduated from High School, who is certainly incompetent to go on up, but we felt this was a reasonable requirement that would have a good chance of success in getting us the type of people that are required to operate the more complex things that we are faced with all the time.[40]

Another reason Duke Power added the test battery was that other public utilities companies had done so. For example, as to this second reason, one Duke Power official testified that the Virginia Electric and Power Company (VEPCO), which has its principal office in Richmond, Virginia, was one of the public utilities it was attempting to follow in screening new employees. VEPCO had adopted a high school education requirement in 1958 for certain jobs historically filled only by whites, and then it added a testing program for certain bargaining jobs in 1961. (In *United States v. Virginia Electric and Power Co.*, the court, relying in substantial part on the Fourth Circuit's decision in *Griggs*, the Fifth Circuit's decision in *Local 189*, and Judge Butzner's decision in *Quarles*, held that VEPCO's high school and testing requirements were unlawful under Title VII because they constituted racial discrimination against African Americans.)[41]

Even though Duke Power had at least a year to take appropriate measures to bring its employment into compliance with the mandate of Title VII, it did substantially nothing until it actually became subject to the mandate of the Act on July 2, 1965. It seemed ironic to the litigation team that Duke Power instituted its test battery on the same date Title VII became effective. Before implementing its test battery, Duke hired Dr. Dannie Moffie, a professor of business administration at the University of North Carolina, Chapel Hill, and a management consultant, as a consultant on which tests it should adopt in order to pass muster under the safe harbor "professionally developed ability" provision of Section 703(h). Dr. Moffie conferred with officials of Duke Power at its headquarters in Charlotte, North Carolina, on July 2, 1965.[42] Dr. Moffie also recommended the test battery based on the fact that other public utility companies, like VEPCO, were using them.[43]

The tests Duke Power selected, after consultations Dr. Moffie, were the Wonderlic Personnel Test-Form 1, the Revised Beta Examination, and the Bennett Mechanical Comprehension Test, Forms AA and BB.[44] The Wonderlic is a general intelligence test consisting of fifty multiple-choice and short-answer questions that include verbal, mathematical, analytical, and pictorial items, and it is administered using a twelve-minute time limit. It is doubtful that even one of the questions on this test was relevant to some of the white jobs the plaintiffs sought.[45] The Revised Beta Examination is also a general intelligence test and is designed to measure the general intellectual ability of persons who are relatively illiterate or non–English speaking. The Bennett Mechanical examines the takers' level of mechanical information, spatial visualization, and mechanical reasoning.

After the July 2, 1965, Charlotte conference, Dr. Moffie sent a letter, dated July 7, 1965, to Duke Power in which he informed the company that "[t]he psychological tests which you plan to use in your employment process have been 'professionally' developed and accordingly should meet the requirements of Title VII" and that "based on national norms, the percentage of rejection of your application population should be approximately 40% for the Beta, 50% for the Wonderlic, 55% for the Bennett AA, [and] 85% for the Bennett BB."[46] He further advised that the passing scores for each of the tests were essentially the same as those established by VEPCO, which had been using these passing scores for a year and half. Dr. Moffie further advised Duke Power that it could not "indefinitely" postpone efforts to validate the tests for the jobs for which they were used and "still comply with Title VII,"[47] and that validation of tests "is not easily done nor can these evaluations be done over-night." To underscore the point that validation is not easily done, he pointed out that "[i]n the looping and knitting departments [of textile mills], almost five years of test validation research was necessary before we were able to establish reliable employment standards at Hanes." Dr. Moffie also recommended that Duke Power begin its validation studies in the technical group first, followed by studies in the clerical groups, before undertaking validation studies for unskilled and semiskilled jobs.

Duke Power knew, or should have known, that the passing scores on the tests were stringent standards because they would eliminate about half of all high school graduates in the United States. Dr. Moffie put Duke Power on notice of this fact in his July 7, 1965, letter, first calling attention to the passing scores for each test:[48]

(a)   Revised Beta   57

(b)   Wonderlic-Form 1   20

(c)   Bennett Mechanical Comprehension (Form AA)   39

(d)   General Clerical (Total Score)   140

(e)   Bennett Mechanical Comprehension (Form BB)   27

He then noted:

> In my opinion, if you are unable to meet your hiring quota at any given period of time because your standards are too high, you can lower your standards and still comply with the law providing all people applying for a job during that period of time are considered for employment based on the then existing standards. This standard will need to be fully documented.[49]

Several months after the effective date of Title VII, Duke Power adopted yet another policy, which applied only to employees who did not have a high school education. This policy was adopted in response to complaints from white employees in the coal-handling department who wanted to be promoted to inside jobs but did not have a high school education. The policy, adopted on September 10, 1965, provided that employees without high school diplomas who worked in coal handling, as watchmen, or as laborers and who were hired prior to September 1, 1965, could become eligible for promotion to inside jobs if they took both the Wonderlic and the Bennett Mechanical Comprehension Test and scored 39 on the Bennett Mechanical and 20 on the Wonderlic. If they made these scores, then they would be deemed to have the equivalent of a high school education. However, Duke Power indicated that its new policy was flexible, for example, an employee without a high school diploma in one of the covered departments would be considered as having passed the test battery if he scored 19 on the Wonderlic and 40 on the Bennett Mechanical and vice versa.[50] No one had been promoted under this policy at the time of trial in 1968. The high school diploma and tests were not required for maintaining an employee's present position or for securing promotion to jobs paying $3.18 per hour or more.

As an example, Clarence M. Jackson, a black employee with a seventh-grade education, was hired in 1951 as a laborer, remained a laborer in 1967 (with a salary of $1.645 per hour), and was unable to transfer to a better job, while three white employees provide a contrast. Jack O'Dell, who had a fifth-grade education, was hired in 1951 as a helper and had been promoted to coal-handling operator by 1967 (with a salary of $2.79 per hour); Jady Martin, who had a seventh-grade education, was hired in 1956 as a helper, had worked his way to Mechanic B in 1965, and was promoted to Mechanic A in 1966; and C. R. Rollins, who had an eighth-grade education, was hired by Duke as a laborer in 1942, became the labor foreman of the plaintiffs in 1966, and, in that position, supervised three of the plaintiffs who had a high school education. Neither O'Dell, Martin, nor Rollins was ever called upon to take the tests, even though Duke adopted the test battery on July 2, 1965.[51]

Willie Boyd was the plaintiff in *Griggs* who played the leading role in initiating action to challenge Duke Power's employment practices under Title VII. Boyd, Junior Blackstock, and James S. Tucker started work with Duke Power in 1948. William C. Purcell, Clarence Jackson, Eddie Galloway, and Lewis Hairston, Jr., had been employed in the early 1950s. Robert Jumper, Jesse C. Martin, and his brother, Herman E. Martin, were hired in 1959. Eddie Broadnax, Willie Griggs, and W. Clarence Purcell had been hired in the 1960s. Jumper, Herman Martin, and Jesse Martin were three African Americans who had completed high school before their employment at the Dan River Steam Station. Jumper was hired in 1954 and had completed high school in 1947. Herman Martin was hired in 1957 and had completed high school in 1941, and in 1970, Jesse Martin had completed high school and Clarence Purcell obtained a GED.

The circumstances that eventually led the plaintiffs to file a charge of racial discrimination with the EEOC against Duke Power were powerfully captured in a 1991 *Los Angeles Times* article based on an interview with Boyd:

> [The Dan River Station's] 81 white employees were supervisors, machine operators and technicians. They monitored shiny dials and gauges that operated the massive boilers. Each job could lead to one better. [African American employees] on the other hand were all janitors, and that is what they could expect to do for the rest of their life.
>
> Trains would haul in huge loads of Appalachian coal, rolling along tracks beside the slow, brown-green waters of the Dan [River]. White workers would mechanically transfer the freight, adding it to the plant's coal pile that rose higher than any building in this part of the Carolina upland.
>
> Sometimes dust and grime would clog the iron claws as they scooped up the lumpy fuel. The janitors were then summoned to help with the filthy work of unclogging the machinery. Only whites, however, were allowed the job title of "coal handler," and only they earned the extra pay.
>
> Willie Boyd was one of the [African American employees]. Son of a sharecropper, he had dropped out of high school in 1938 after his father took

ill. Someone had to help the family meet the landowner's quota of tobacco production.

Like millions of other Southern black men, Boyd escaped the farm in the post-war boom. Factories were springing up all around the Piedmont [area in North Carolina]. And with them came a demand for power—and more generating stations.

Boyd's job at Duke Power was hard, though no harder than chopping tobacco. It was a big step up for him. And it paid actual cash. Pretty soon he had enough money to meet his bills and even to buy a few items on installment.

As the years wore on, however, something always rankled him. White men—many with no more education than he had—rose up through the ranks to become managers or supervisors, taking spots in comfortable offices with bathrooms down the hall.

Blacks cleaned those toilets—ones they themselves were forbidden to use. For them, the company built a "colored" bathroom outside across the railroad tracks, behind the coal pile.

Why can't black folks get some of the better jobs? Boyd asked his bosses. And they "would tell us we had no chance," he recalled.[52]

The question Boyd raised—"Why can't black folks get some of the better jobs?"—was a question that the litigation team heard many times from plaintiffs and class members they represented. It was the question that the litigation team sought to address in its effort to define a theory of discrimination that would help bring about the change African Americans wanted. In 1966, Boyd began to take action on behalf of his coworkers to find an answer to his question.[53] The president of the Reidsville, North Carolina, NAACP chapter was J. A. (Jay) Griggs, related to but not the lead named plaintiff in *Griggs*, who was named Willie Griggs. Boyd was active in the Reidsville Chapter, and he and Jay Griggs were neighbors. On many occasions, Boyd complained to Jay Griggs about the racially discriminatory practices at Dan River and about the fact that African American employees at the Reidsville facility of the American Tobacco Company were beginning to take steps to seek relief from racial discrimination at that plant. (The litigation team represented the plaintiff in the American Tobacco case.)[54] Jay Griggs had assisted a number of African Americans in preparing charges to file with the EEOC, so he finally told Boyd to fill out a charge to be filed with the EEOC or stop complaining.[55] Jay Griggs knew and had worked with Julius Chambers, a very active LDF cooperating attorney with an office in Charlotte, North Carolina, on other important civil rights cases, and he was to become one of the lead attorneys in *Griggs*. Jay told Boyd about Chambers. So Boyd, with the assistance of Jay Griggs, composed a petition to give to J. D. Knight, the superintendent at the Dan River Station. The petition stated that the signees had given Duke Power satisfactory service for a number of years and, therefore, were justified in requesting the opportunity for promotion to jobs in coal handling, maintenance, and other "inside" departments.[56] All fourteen of the African American employees signed the petition. The petition was dated March 1, 1966, and the plaintiffs left it on Knight's desk the same day.

When Knight arrived at work on the morning of March 3, he scheduled a meeting around 10:00 a.m. with the plaintiffs to find out what the petition was all about. The plaintiffs had selected Lewis Hairston to be their spokesperson at the meeting because "he was the kind of guy who was afraid of nothing, no how," and he had "more nerves" than some of the others had. Hairston boldly told Knight that the plaintiffs "wanted a crack at some of the better jobs" because the most the plaintiffs could earn was $1.65 per hour and the white employees started at $1.81 per hour. Knight's response was that no one without a high school diploma would be promoted to an inside job because Duke Power was moving into the atomic age. He also said the plaintiffs could be considered for promotion to inside jobs under the same policy Duke Power had adopted in September 1965 for white employees in coal handling; that is, if the plaintiffs who did not have a high school diploma successfully passed the test battery, they could be promoted to inside jobs as if they had a high school education. The plaintiffs also complained to Knight about the segregated facilities, such as showers, drinking fountains, and locker rooms.[57]

After the meeting with Knight, the plaintiffs concluded that Duke Power did not consider their petition meritorious. A few days later, the plaintiffs went to Chambers's office in Charlotte and, with his assistance, prepared a charge of racial discrimination to be filed with the EEOC. The plaintiffs met at a funeral home in Reidsville on March 14, 1966, to sign fourteen separate but identical EEOC charges to be filed with the EEOC. For example, Willie Griggs's charge read as follows:

> I, Willie S. Griggs, employee of the Duke Power Steam Station, Draper, North Carolina, wish to enter a complaint of discrimination because of my race, against the company. On the [1st] day of March 1966, I requested to be considered for a high paying job [] classification whenever a vacancy occur[s] in higher classified jobs. I was told on the 3rd day of March by the company officials that it would be necessary to take a test to qualify [] for any job above the level that I am working in. I feel I am being discriminated against because of my race. There

has not been any tests given prior to my request to be upgraded to a higher paying job. Therefore, at this time, I feel before a test goes into effect, the present employees should be given the right, based on seniority, to advance to better job opportunities. In the past, my seniority rights to a higher paying job has been denied because of my race.

The EEOC received the charges on March 15, 1966. A day later, a Duke Power official, A. C. Thies, met with some of the plaintiffs at the Dan River Station. This meeting took place before the EEOC had served a copy of charges on Duke Power in April, so the company did not know that the plaintiffs had, in fact, filed their EEOC charges. The plaintiffs again raised the issue of the unfairness of subjecting them to the test battery as condition for consideration for inside jobs. This raised the possibility that Duke Power would provide tuition refunds for those who opted to obtain a high school diploma or its equivalent instead of passing the test battery. But when pressed about which courses Duke Power would approve for tuition refund, Thies told them that they would have to talk with the superintendent of the Dan River facility and that courses would be reviewed on an individual basis. Prior to this meeting, however, Thies had discussed with the superintendent what courses might be available locally to allow the plaintiffs to obtain a high school diploma.[58] Duke Power made no mention whatsoever of the tuition refund in its September 22, 1965, memo to supervisors notifying them that it had adopted a policy on September 10, 1965, to provide employees in jobs in coal-handling, watchman, and labor positions who did not have a high school education the option of passing the test battery for promotion to inside jobs.[59] Eventually, only one person, Willie Boyd, opted to take advantage of the tuition refund program. Only five employees, *two* blacks and *three* whites who did not have a high school education, took the test battery; none passed.

The EEOC initiated its investigation of the plaintiffs' charge on April 21, 1966, when several of its investigators visited the Dan River Steam Station. In its final report, the EEOC investigators stated that Duke Power officials were reluctant initially to cooperate and gave misleading answers to their questions. The next day, the investigators toured the steam station, during which they saw for themselves the racially segregated locker rooms, drinking fountains, showers, and toilet facilities. The investigators returned to the Dan River facility on April 26, 1966, to do a thorough investigation of the plaintiffs' EEOC charges that they were unable to do on their earlier visit. Two days later, on April 28, 1966, Thies sent a memo to all of the superintendents at Duke

Power's stations advising them to immediately take steps to move all of their employees into one locker room. The reason for this decision, as stated in the memo, was that even though Duke Power had "no specific segregation of our negro employees into one Locker Room since last July 1965, we are now informed that we are in violation of Title 7, of the Civil Rights Act of 1964, by permitting our negro employees to occupy separate facilities."[60] Immediately after these facilities were desegregated, plaintiff Lewis Hairston, whose duties as a laborer included, among others, cleaning the white locker room and toilet facilities, used the shower in the formerly all-white locker room. After this episode, white employees refused to use the shower for a period of time.[61]

On May 4, 1966, just over a week after the last visit by the EEOC investigators, Duke Power wrote a letter to the EEOC denying the allegations that its practices with respect to the plaintiffs were in violation of their rights under Title VII. Duke Power also laid the foundation for a potential defense it might raise in the case based on Section 703(j) of Title VII. This section, the so-called anti–preferential treatment section, provides that Title VII does not require an employer "to grant preferential treatment to any individual or group" because of an imbalance between, for example, African Americans in the employer workforce and the relevant labor market from which it selects its employees.[62] Other phrases that described this defense and that began to surface more and more after the Supreme Court decided *Griggs* are "quota hiring" and "reversed discrimination." In this respect, Duke Power stated that to consider the plaintiffs for promotion on seniority alone would contravene its promotion policy and would "amount to preferential treatment of Negro employees—something that is not required under Section 703(j) of Title VII."[63]

Based on the investigators' final report, the EEOC issued an administrative decision on September 21, 1966, in which it found reasonable cause to believe that the allegations the plaintiffs made in their charges constituted a violation of their rights under Title VII. On the same date, the EEOC notified the plaintiffs of their right to bring a civil action and notified Duke Power that it would undertake an effort to conciliate the plaintiffs' charge. On October 5, 1966, an EEOC conciliator, Jules Gordon, met with officials of Duke Power to discuss the possibilities of resolving the case without the need for the plaintiffs to sue in federal court. Duke Power and Gordon met for several hours but were unable to resolve the plaintiffs' charges because Duke Power disagreed with EEOC's finding of cause. Duke Power's position then, and throughout the litigation, was that its employment practices, including its use of the test battery, complied with its obligations under Title VII.

The litigation team filed the complaint in *Griggs* in the U.S. District Court for the Middle District of North Carolina on behalf of the plaintiffs on October 20, 1966, which was about three months after the EEOC issued its first testing guidelines.

7. *Griggs* in the District Court

Julius Chambers and I were the lead attorneys for the plaintiffs in *Griggs*. Chambers was born in 1936 in Mt. Gilead, North Carolina, which was a small rural community east of Charlotte.[1] The first school he attended, Mt. Gilead Elementary School for Negroes, had outside toilets, wooden floors, and no library. Chambers's father operated an automobile repair shop. One of the events that led Chambers to become a civil rights lawyer was the refusal of a white client of his father's to pay for repair work on a truck. His father, who owned a garage and service station, had tried, without success, to hire a lawyer to represent him in collecting a fee of about $2,000 from the client. This incident outraged Chambers, who was about twelve years old at the time, and he decided right then to pursue a career that would change how African Americans were treated. The loss of income from this episode meant that his father did not have the funds to send Chambers to the same boarding school his brother and sister had attended. Chambers then attended a segregated public school in Troy, North Carolina, which was about twelve miles from his home in Mt. Gilead. The segregated bus on which he rode to school passed a more modern high school for whites. Chambers graduated from high school in May 1954, the same year the Supreme Court decided *Brown v. Board of Education*. He then earned his undergraduate degree in history from North Carolina College for Negroes (now North Carolina Central University) in Durham, where he graduated summa cum laude and was named the most outstanding student. While in college, he was forced off of an interstate bus by a white driver because he refused to move to the back and give up his seat for a white person.[2]

Chambers earned a master's degree in history from the University of Michigan and then entered the University of North Carolina Law School in Chapel Hill in 1959, graduating in 1962. Chambers had wanted to attend the University of Michigan School of Law, but at that time, Michigan had a quota of one African American student for each entering class and had already filled that quota the year Chambers applied. (Amalya Kearse, an African American lawyer who became a judge on the U.S. Court of Appeals for the Second Circuit, was the individual selected when Chambers applied to Michigan Law

School.)[3] The University of North Carolina Law School had admitted its first African American student under court order only eight years earlier.[4] Chambers was the first African American editor-in-chief of the *North Carolina Law Review* and, as such, was the first African American to become editor-in-chief of a law review at any historically white school in the South. His selection as editor-in-chief was widely noted in the press.[5] He graduated first in his class academically.[6] However, his experience with racial discrimination while in law school mirrored his experience in society at large.[7] He was selected as a member of the Order of the Coif (a prestigious legal honor society) and the Order of the Golden Fleece (the highest honor society at the University of North Carolina Law School). Even though he excelled academically in law school, because of his race not a single white law firm in North Carolina was willing to offer him employment as a lawyer.[8] One of his law professors advised him that he should accept the fact that he would not be hired by a white law firm. The law professor was also critical of his interest in working with a civil rights organization because he thought civil rights work "would put him in a certain category that would prevent him from escaping that category."[9] Similarly, I heard many stories from other African Americans that those of us becoming law teachers when I did in the mid-1970s should avoid teaching civil rights courses or engaging in civil rights research because doing so would not be considered favorably in the tenure process.

Chambers earned a master's degree in law from Columbia University Law School in 1964. In 1963, he was the first intern hired by the LDF under a program that later became the Earl Warren Legal Training Program. At the end of his LDF internship, Chambers returned to Charlotte and opened up a one-person law firm in a cold-water walk-up office—the same week that President Johnson signed the Civil Rights Act of 1964. He immediately became active in representing African Americans in all kinds of racial discrimination cases and spent many hours traveling by car across North Carolina doing so. His car was firebombed in New Bern, North Carolina, in January 1965, about six months after he returned to the state, while he was addressing a civil rights rally.[10] Then, on November 22, 1965, his home in Charlotte was firebombed, as were the homes of several civil rights activists, and the office of the racially integrated law firm that he established was set afire in 1971.[11]

Chambers's one-person law firm eventually became one of the first racially integrated firms in the South—Chambers, Stein, Ferguson & Lanning—in 1968.[12] The other founding members of the firm were Adam Stein, James E.

Ferguson II, and Jim Lanning. Stein, born in New York, first became associated with Chambers during an internship through the law student Civil Research Council in the summer of 1965 when he participated in the first phase of the enforcement project. Stein grew up in Washington, D.C., where his home was a frequent meeting place for liberal Democrats. James (Jim) Ferguson, who is African American, was born and raised in Asheville, North Carolina, and had been a civil rights activist while in high school, participating in marches and sit-ins that led to the desegregation of Asheville's restaurants and businesses. He graduated summa cum laude in 1964 from North Carolina Central University, the same school from which Chambers received his undergraduate degree. He then earned his law degree from Columbia University Law School. While attending law school, he worked as a summer intern with Chambers and then joined the firm after he received his law degree. Ferguson had been all set to return to Asheville to practice law but ultimately decided, at Chambers's urging, to join Chambers's firm. Jim Lanning, who is white, graduated from the University of North Carolina Law School in 1968. Prior to joining the firm, he had been an attorney with the legal services of Charlotte. I joined the firm as a partner in 1970.

When I left the firm in 1975, the number of lawyers had grown from four to eleven. All of the attorneys in the firm played a role at one level or another in some of the most important civil rights cases of the last century, including, in addition to *Griggs,* the Supreme Court's busing case of *Swann v. Charlotte-Mecklenburg Board of Education* and the Title VII cases of *Albemarle Paper Co. v. Moody* on monetary relief to victims of unlawful employment discrimination. Many days, various members of the firm would gather in the law library for "rapping" sessions, exchanging "war stories," and refilling our emotional tanks for future civil rights battles in the courts and elsewhere. Many of the attorneys who practiced with and then left the firm have moved on to other positions, including judicial, academic, and political office. Charles Becton served for nine years on the North Carolina Court of Appeals, and Jim Lanning, Fred Hicks, Yvonne Evans, and Rebecca Thorne served as state district court judges. John Nockleby became a professor at Loyola Law School, Los Angeles. In 1992, Melvin Watt and Eva Clayton became the first two African Americans elected to Congress from North Carolina since the nineteenth century. Melvin Watt's district was the subject of the Supreme Court's 1993 voting rights case, *Shaw v. Reno.* Chambers left the firm in 1984 to become the third Director-Counsel of the LDF, and in 1992, he became the chancellor of North

Carolina Central University, his undergraduate alma mater.[13] He returned to private practice with the renamed firm in 2001 after stepping down from his position as chancellor.

Conrad O. Pearson and Sammie Chess, Jr., were two other attorneys who participated in some of the early proceedings in *Griggs*. Pearson was a pioneering civil rights attorney in North Carolina.[14] He was Thurgood Marshall's classmate at Howard University Law School. After graduating from Howard, he participated in the first lawsuit to desegregate graduate schools in the South, serving as cocounsel in a civil rights action filed in state court to gain the admission of an African American to the School of Pharmacy at the University of North Carolina.[15] The NAACP named Pearson as its first general counsel for North Carolina, and in this role he served as a link for North Carolina with the LDF. He participated in the successful lawsuit that attacked the systematic exclusion of African Americans from juries in North Carolina, and he served as counsel in the case to desegregate public schools in Durham.[16] The work of Pearson and his colleagues, including Chambers, in the desegregation case drew praise from presiding Judge Gordon, who found that their level of legal skills was "advocacy in its highest form."

Sammie Chess graduated from the same racially segregated high school in High Point as I did. He received his law degree in 1958 from North Carolina Central Law School, a historically black school. In 1971, Chess became the first African American Superior Court judge in North Carolina upon his appointment by the governor. Both Pearson and Chess participated in a number of other civil rights cases in North Carolina in addition to *Griggs*.

THE CASE

Thirteen of the fourteen African American employees at the Dan River Station joined as plaintiffs in *Griggs*. Jesse Martin, the other African American, decided not to join the case because Duke Power had promoted him to learner in the previously all-white job category in the coal-handling department about two months before the litigation team filed a complaint in federal court. Martin's promotion came only after the EEOC had initiated its investigation of the plaintiffs' charge. Willie Griggs appears as the first named plaintiff of the thirteen plaintiffs in the case. Griggs's name appears first because the plaintiffs had decided among themselves, with the agreement of Griggs, that he was the youngest among them and had the least to lose should Duke Power retaliate against any of them for filing the lawsuit.[17] Griggs, who had completed the tenth grade, was thirty-two years of age, married, and the father of four children when he applied for employment at the Dan River Steam Station in 1963. Prior to his employment with Duke Power, he had work as a laborer at local farms and as a laborer and a truck driver with another employer in the area. He applied for work at Duke Power on the recommendation of his friend and eventual coworker, Jesse Martin. Griggs became the thirteenth African American employee hired as a laborer when he began work at Duke Power Company on March 13, 1963, just over a year prior to the enactment of the Civil Rights Act of 1964.[18]

The major issue in *Griggs* was the legality of the educational and testing requirements. The claim about racially segregated locker rooms, toilets, and showers was mooted when Duke Power integrated those facilities,[19] and the district court ruled against the plaintiffs on the overtime issue, on which no appeal was taken.[20] The litigation team sought only broad injunctive relief and specifically did not seek back pay because each time back pay had been requested in the litigation team's earlier cases, the defendants had asked for a jury trial. So, in keeping with the litigation team's concern about trying racial discrimination cases before a potentially hostile all-white southern jury, a decision was made, temporarily, not to include a claim for back pay until the issue of the right to a jury trial in other similar LDF cases had been resolved. The litigation team did, however, request in the complaint that the court grant "such additional relief as may appear to the [c]ourt to be proper and just." In a later case handled by the litigation team, *Albemarle Paper Co. v. Moody*, the Supreme Court held that the prayer for "such additional relief" included back pay but that defendants in Title VII cases were nonetheless not entitled to a jury trial. It is probably because the litigation team did not specifically ask for back pay in the complaint that Duke Power did not move to have the case tried before a jury.

An overwhelming number of employers hired outside counsel to represent them in employment discrimination cases, but Duke Power decided to have its in-house corporate counsel represent it in *Griggs*. Its lead counsel was George Ferguson. Ferguson was assisted by William Ward and Carl Horn. Ferguson graduated from the University of North Carolina in 1956 and worked with Duke Power from 1962 until he retired in 1988. Horn was Duke Power's general counsel, and Ward was its chief trial counsel. Shortly after receiving the complaint and summons, Horn sent a memo, dated October 26, 1966, to Ward to review the complaint before assigning the case to Ferguson. Horn also suggested that Ward might want to assist the less-experienced Ferguson, since the case had been filed in federal court. Ward then sent Horn's memo to Ferguson and indicated his willingness to assist in the case. Ferguson responded, "I insist! We need more practice before the U.S. Sup[reme] C[our]t."[21] Undoubtedly, Ferguson anticipated that the case might eventually end up in the Supreme Court.

Duke Power's answer to the complaint generally denied the allegation in the lawsuit. Its major affirmative defense was grounded in Section 713(b) of Title VII. Section 713(b) provides a complete defense for defendants who plead and prove that they relied, in good faith, on a written interpretation or opinion of the EEOC. Without specifically citing Section 713(b) in its answer to the complaint, Duke Power claimed that its policies and practices were lawful because they "were [taken] in good faith and in reliance upon written interpretations of the office of the General Counsel" of the EEOC.[22] The written interpretations on which Duke Power relied presumably were the original 1966 EEOC guidelines on testing and an opinion of the general counsel of the EEOC.

About six months after the complaint was filed, Duke engaged Dr. Dannie Moffie to conduct a validation study of its test battery. Dr. Moffie conducted the study in the spring of 1967 and concluded that the correlations between tests and job performance for all job levels were in general small and not statistically significant. In light of the inconclusive results in his validation study, Dr. Moffie recommended in his May 1, 1967, report to Duke that additional studies be conducted but under much more controlled conditions, preferably in one plant where the administration of the tests and the evaluation of employees in the study were highly controlled.[23]

Some efforts were undertaken to settle the case before and shortly after the complaint was filed. As a condition for exploring settlement, Duke Power informed the EEOC conciliator, Jules Gordon, that it would be willing to discuss settlement, but only if the litigation team withdrew the request made in the complaint that the court expedite the case on its docket.[24] The litigation team absolutely refused to agree to that condition. The parties did explore settlement possibilities about a year after the filing of the complaint after the district court judge then handling the case, Judge Edwin Stanley, urged the parties at the initial pretrial conference to explore settlement pursuant to a local court rule that required litigants to have a full and frank settlement discussion. After the parties met to discuss settlement, I drafted a proposed settlement letter, which Chambers sent to Duke Power on October 13, 1967. The proposal included exempting the plaintiffs from the educational and testing requirements for consideration for promotion out of the laborers' jobs; providing on-the-job training for the plaintiffs for positions in the coal-handling department and the "inside" departments; discontinuing the use of the test battery until it had been validated (but the tests could remain in use for the purpose of conducting a validation study); reporting to plaintiffs' counsel for at least two years on the progress it had made in hiring and promoting African American applicants and employees; and paying plaintiffs' counsel reasonable attorneys' fees and costs of the litigation.[25] Duke Power rejected all of the plaintiffs' proposals for settlement. A critical comment made in a memo to Ferguson by a high-ranking official who had authority to accept, reject, or suggest its own settlement proposals captured Duke Power's attitude about the case: "Based on Mr. Chambers' overall approach to this matter, I would suggest that we see him in Court. If we agree to the [proposals] in his letter, we would be, in essence, admitting that we are guilty of discrimination at Dan River, which we are not."[26]

Duke Power, like all of the defendants in the early cases, objected to the case proceeding as a class action. Judge Edwin M. Stanley, who had been appointed to the district court by President Eisenhower, presided over all of the proceedings until Judge Eugene Gordon assumed responsibility shortly before trial. Judge Stanley allowed the case to go forward as a class action. The resolution of the class action issue was not a particularly difficult one for Judge Stanley to decide in favor of the plaintiffs in light of the successes the litigation team had obtained in the seminal case of *Hall v. Werthan Bag* and other Title VII cases litigated in the Middle District.[27] In *Griggs,* Judge Stanley, as other courts had begun to do on a regular basis, accepted the plaintiffs' broad definition of the class to include African Americans currently employed by Duke Power as well as African Americans who might thereafter seek employment, provided the plaintiffs could show that at least one African American had sought and had been denied employment.

Pretrial discovery of evidence under the Federal Rules of Civil Procedure permits each side to obtain evidence from the other before trial. The litigation team's pretrial discovery in *Griggs* did not involve the kind of trench warfare by defendants that the litigation team frequently met in other cases. Duke

Power's pretrial discovery was limited to taking the depositions of all thirteen plaintiffs, and the plaintiffs' pretrial discovery consisted of taking the depositions of knowledgeable officials and supervisors of Duke Power in addition to a series of written interrogatories soliciting information about, for example, the test battery, the jobs, salaries, and the educational background of African American and white employees. The major issue of contention between the parties was whether the litigation team was entitled to evidence of Duke Power's employment practices prior to the key July 2, 1965, date. This evidentiary issue was not resolved until the trial.

Since the major issue in *Griggs* was whether Duke Power's requirement of education and a test battery was lawful under the safe-harbor provision of a "professionally developed ability test" under Section 703(h) of Title VII, it became obvious early in the case that the litigation team would need an expert witness. I initiated the process of selecting a testing expert by contacting Dr. Kenneth Clark. Dr. Clark and his wife, Mamie, were a team of African American psychologists who were the architects of the doll studies on the harmful effects of racism on African American children in segregated schools that the Supreme Court cited in the infamous footnote 11 in *Brown v. Board of Education*.[28] Dr. Clark was unavailable to serve as our testing expert, but he recommended several potential experts, including Dr. Robert L. Thorndike of Columbia University, Dr. Anne Anastasi of Fordham University, and Dr. Raymond A. Katzell of New York University. The litigation team held conferences with all of them either individually or several at a time in May and June 1966 to begin mapping out our litigation strategy on challenging the adverse impact of testing on the employment opportunities of African Americans. Out of this group, Dr. Thorndike agreed to work with us in *Griggs*.

Judge Gordon became the presiding judge in *Griggs* shortly before the trial began in February 1968. He graduated from Elon College in North Carolina in 1941. While attending Elon, he also studied at Duke University Law School, and a week after graduating from Elon, he received his law degree from Duke. President Johnson nominated him for a vacancy on the U.S. District Court for the Middle District of North Carolina on April 30, 1966. He took his seat on the federal bench on June 12, 1964, less than a month before the enactment of Title VII as part of the Civil Rights Act of 1964. In addition to serving as the trial judge in *Griggs,* Judge Gordon was the trial judge in *Robinson v. Lorillard Corp.,* another landmark employment discrimination case, and in a number of LDF school desegregation cases in North Carolina, including

Scott v. Winston-Salem/Forsyth County School Board. In *Scott,* he ordered the desegregation and transfer of 2,000 teachers to different schools in the Winston-Salem public school system in the middle of the 1969–1970 school year. Despite the fact that his decision angered many people, Judge Gordon said that the result in *Scott* was the one decision of which he was most proud.[29]

The trial in *Griggs* began on Tuesday, February 6, 1968. Chambers was unable to attend the first day of trial because of a scheduling conflict. However, Chambers and I had mapped out our final trial strategy several days before the trial began. Since I was not then a member of the North Carolina bar, Chambers asked David Dansby, an African American attorney from Greensboro and a member of the North Carolina bar, to be my "second-chair" at the trial on the first day. My first unpleasant order of business at the beginning of the trial was to inform Judge Gordon that our test expert, Dr. Thorndike, had been unable to arrange his schedule to be available at the trial. The case originally had been set for trial in November 1967, then reset for trial for February 5, 1968, and then reset again for February 6, at the request of the plaintiffs. Dr. Thorndike, who lived and worked in New York, had arranged his schedule to be available when the case was first scheduled for trial in November and also when it was rescheduled for February 5, but he could not be available on February 6. Judge Gordon was quite displeased that our expert was not available when the trial began. He was, nevertheless, sympathetic yet stern in reminding me that the trial had been rescheduled on several occasions at the request of the litigation team. However, he accepted the recommendation of Duke Power's counsel to proceed with the trial but advised me to check with Dr. Thorndike about when he would be available. Both sides waived opening statements, and we proceeded to put on the case for the plaintiff. The judge had a good appreciation of the contentions in the case because the parties had set out their respective positions in the final pretrial order entered by Judge Stanley on October 6, 1967.

The trial strategy Chambers and I had settled upon was not to call any of the plaintiffs to present live testimony at the trial. Rather, we decided to establish the facts on the basis of the evidence we had obtained through pretrial discovery. This strategy meant that, except for the testimony of plaintiffs' expert on testing, the case-in-chief for the plaintiff consisted of introducing into evidence a number of exhibits, including, among others, the depositions of each of the plaintiffs taken by Duke's counsel, the depositions of a number of officials and supervisors taken by the plaintiffs, and exhibits relating to the educational and testing requirements. Duke Power did not object to the introduction of the plaintiffs' depositions but reserved the right to call them for cross-examination. Of course, if the case had to be tried before a jury, it would have been necessary for the plaintiffs to testify at the trial, and we would have called as witnesses some of the officials of Duke Power in the presentation of the plaintiffs' case-in-chief. The litigation strategy was also based on the fact that in nonjury cases, comprehensive and well-crafted proposed findings of fact and conclusions of law play an important role in litigation in federal courts because they are helpful to the judge who, under Rule 52 of the Federal Rules of Civil Procedure, has an obligation to set out the facts relied upon to decide the merits of cases. Because this case would be tried without a jury, I had begun to draft the plaintiffs' proposed findings and conclusions even before the case was set for trial, and in doing so, Chambers and I had a road map for the factual narrative we wanted to establish through the plaintiffs' evidence. All of the plaintiffs were present at the trial, but Ferguson, Duke Power's chief counsel, elected not to call any of them. Duke Power wanted to use their depositions to argue that their testimony proved its case that none of them had been the victim of unlawful employment discrimination. In addition to other documentary evidence, the litigation team introduced into evidence the EEOC's 1966 testing guidelines and the test battery—Wonderlic and Bennett Mechanical—and the manuals for the use of both.

Strong evidence as to the adverse impact of the test battery on the plaintiffs and the class of African Americans they represented simply was not available because only three employees—one white and two blacks—had opted to take the tests, and none had passed. Also, the overwhelming number of new applicants for jobs in the "inside" departments had declined to take the test battery, including those who had completed high school. But since a passing score on the test battery was, in effect, a substitute for a high school education, there were statistical data available for the proposition that African Americans completed high school at a substantially lower rate than whites. The statistical evidence on completion rates for African Americans and whites could properly be considered by the trial court under the doctrine of judicial notice. Judicial notice is a rule in the law of evidence that allows proving a material fact without independent evidence if the truth of that fact is so notorious or well known that it cannot be refuted.

I did not want to close the plaintiffs' case-in-chief because we needed the testimony of our testing expert, so I asked Judge Gordon to permit me to call my secretary in New York for an update on our efforts to reach Dr. Thorndike. Judge Gordon was agreeable but again admonished me that he did not "want [plaintiff's] expert running [his] court" and that he felt that our test expert "had not cooperated too well" with respect to the trial date.[30] I still could not reach Dr. Thorndike, but Ferguson advised the court that, in the interest of moving the trial to a conclusion, he was willing to begin putting on evidence in Duke Power's case-in-chief. Without waiving any claims or arguments on behalf of the plaintiffs, I told the court I had no objections. In fact, I was quite agreeable to proceed in that manner in light of Judge Gordon's tolerant understanding of my situation with respect to our testing expert. However, Ferguson's willingness to move forward with his case was motivated, in part, by the desire for his witnesses, all of them high-level Duke Power officials, to return to their duties as soon as possible.

The only live testimony presented at trial other than the parties' expert witnesses on the testing issue was that of A. C. Thies, Duke Power's Vice President of Production and Operations. Ferguson put Thies on the stand as Duke Power's witness. Thies's testimony on direct examination by Ferguson added very little to the evidence the litigation team had not already introduced into evidence in the plaintiffs' case-in-chief, and that evidence included the pretrial deposition of Thies. On cross-examination, I had Thies repeat for Judge Gordon what we already knew from plaintiffs' evidence: that Duke Power had never undertaken to develop written job descriptions (except to respond to plaintiffs' interrogatories) and that the content of the jobs at Duke Power was determined essentially by the "practice and many years of doing these jobs, and by an understanding between the superintendent and the man in any classification as to what his duties should be."[31] Thies also testified, on cross-examination, that the passing scores for the test battery under the policy of allowing non–high school graduates in coal-handling, watchman, and laborer positions to be considered for "inside" jobs was "a good bit lower requirement than a High School education, and [he] felt like [Duke Power was] bending over backwards to accept [success on the test battery] in lieu of a [H]igh [S]chool education."[32] According to Duke Power's testing expert, Dr. Moffie, the only reason the company had adopted the test battery was to determine whether an individual had the characteristics of a high school graduate; the test simply was not adopted to predict the probable capability of an individual to do any particular job. Duke Power offered no evidence whatsoever that either having a high school diploma or successfully passing the test battery provided any information about the ability of applicants or employees to perform any job or classes of jobs at the Dan River steam plant. On cross-examination, Thies testified,

> I am perfectly willing to admit to you that there are people without a High School Education, who are in the operating jobs in the inside departments, for instance, at Dan River, who have done a satisfactory job. I'm not denying that at all. I can't deny that because we certainly have them there who have done this job, who have been there for over ten years. I don't think there is anything magic about a High School education.[33]

In effect, Thies's testimony was essentially that Duke Power had found that many non–high school graduates performed quite well on inside jobs and that high school graduates sometimes turned out to be incompetent.

At the conclusion of trial on the first day, Judge Gordon reminded me yet again in rather stern words that we needed to have our expert or "some other expert" available to testify when he scheduled the trial to resume on Friday, February 9. The fact that Judge Gordon had not foreclosed the possibility that we would be allowed to use "some other expert" if Dr. Thorndike was still unavailable when trial resumed turned out to be both a challenge and an opportunity. The challenge was that I had approximately two days to find out if Dr. Thorndike could rearrange his schedule to testify or to find another testing expert in the event he could not. I rushed back to New York immediately after the first day of trial to deal with the testing-expert dilemma. The challenge was that I could not contact Dr. Thorndike. So after a few rather frantic phone calls, I was able to contact Dr. Katzell, who had consulted with the litigation team earlier. Dr. Katzell recommended that I contact Dr. Richard Barrett. The opportunity was that I was able to contact Dr. Barrett on Tuesday, February 7, and, fortunately, he agreed to be our expert.

Dr. Barrett, an industrial psychologist, had started his career as an industrial engineer and later earned his Ph.D. in industrial psychology from Western Reserve University in 1956. He was exceptionally familiar with, among others, the Wonderlic and Bennett Mechanical Tests. His involvement with the issue of the impact of standardized testing on the equal employment opportunity of African Americans began in the early 1960s when he did a routine selection study for a large insurance company. Ten percent of the sample was African American, and he analyzed the candidates' performance on the test used by the insurance company. The analysis was inconclusive, but it inspired him to get a grant from the Ford Foundation to do a more extensive study of the differences in performance on tests by different ethnic groups. The results of the larger study were published in an influential book, which he coauthored.[34] The study concluded that tests that might be useful in predicting job success for one ethnic group may not be useful for other ethnic groups and that separate validation standards for the different groups may be necessary. His participation in *Griggs* was, as he later wrote, "the beginning of a lifetime involvement" in employment discrimination law and policies, including consultation with the EEOC on employee selection procedures. After participating in *Griggs*, Dr. Barrett would later testify as a testing expert in over 100 other employment discrimination cases and author books and articles on employment testing,[35] and he also served as the litigation team expert in *Albemarle Paper Co. v. Moody*, which shaped the *Griggs* disparate impact theory in a powerful way.

In light of the short amount of time he had to go over the testing evidence in *Griggs*, Dr. Barrett flew to Greensboro on Wednesday, February 7, to meet with Chambers and me to go over his trial testimony. He read our deposition of Thies and studied other portions of the evidence on the educational and testing practices of Duke Power. He testified as our expert on Friday, February 9, was cross-examined by Ferguson, and left immediately thereafter to return to New York. The evidence was indisputable that Duke Power had adopted its test battery without any attempt to identify the critical skills of the jobs for which the test was used to select applicants, nor had it undertaken a meaningful validation study. In light of these indisputable facts, our approach on direct examination was to have Dr. Barrett testify about the professionally accepted standards for personnel selection when a test was used. The process, briefly, included careful job analysis, analysis and assessment of essential job characteristics, selection of the test or tests, and then a validation study. Dr. Barrett also explained the concept of validation for the court. Responding in layman's terms, Dr. Barrett testified that a "test or other selection procedure is valid to the extent to which people who score high, perform well, and people who score low, perform poorly."[36] He testified that the process used by Duke Power to select the Wonderlic and Bennett Mechanical Tests did not conform to professionally accepted standards for personnel selection because of the absence of clear job descriptions. He also testified that somewhat less than 50 percent of high school graduates would achieve a score of 20 on the Wonderlic and that, according to the manual for the Bennett Mechanical, 65 percent of those who took the test for the job of mechanic helper would score a 39 or above, while 55 percent of unskilled applicants, and only 45 percent of candidates for the lead-men job, would achieve that score. Dr. Barrett added that validation of the selection device was highly recommended, when possible.

On cross-examination, Ferguson asked Dr. Barrett whether his article on differential validation advocated special treatment for African Americans because, as a class, they tend to perform less well on pen-and-paper tests than do whites. He answered in the affirmative and also stated that special treatment could be given in the form of appropriate training. He also affirmed his view that, based on his research, differential validation was appropriate, because the purpose of a test was not to determine whether applicants scored high or low but whether they could adequately perform the jobs in question. The court sustained an objection to Ferguson's question asking Dr. Barrett for his opinion on whether instead of using differential validation "minorities should raise their standards, because industry can't afford to relinquish their standards in the competitive world of today."[37]

Duke Power called Dr. Dannie Moffie as its expert on the testing issue. The only job descriptions Dr. Moffie saw were those that Duke Power had prepared in response to the plaintiffs' interrogatories, and they were not prepared until after the lawsuit was filed. Dr. Moffie had not visited the Dan River Steam Station until about a week before he testified at trial.[38] Even though he was engaged in research along the same lines as Dr. Barrett, unlike Dr. Barrett he had not engaged in research on differential validation, a subject that arose in the examination of Dr. Barrett and involves studies to determine whether lower scores on a test were predictive of successful job performance that was equivalent to that predicted by higher scores of a different group.[39] Duke Power did not challenge Dr. Barrett's testimony that the passing scores on the test battery were more stringent than the high school diploma requirement in that the passing scores would eliminate about half of the high school graduates even if the test battery was a substitute for the high school diploma. Although Drs. Barrett and Moffie agreed with the then-applicable standards adopted by the American Psychological Association for selecting employee screening policies, including pen-and-paper tests, they disagreed on the critical issues in the case of whether those standards had been utilized in the selection of Duke Power's testing battery and whether the test battery was a "professionally developed ability test" within the safe-harbor provision of Title VII and consistent with the EEOC 1966 testing guidelines. A factual matter that was beyond dispute was that, at the time of trial, Duke Power had only recently taken steps to try to validate the test battery and that Dr. Moffie recommended the test battery because other utilities were using them.

After the trial, I spent a considerable amount of time carefully preparing proposed findings of fact, conclusions of law, and the posttrial brief.[40] Dr. Barrett sent me some very helpful proposed findings on the testing issue.[41] The litigation team faced several problems similar to those it had faced in *Quarles*. The first problem was to advance a theory or theories of discrimination. Second, the evidence the plaintiffs introduced at trial had to support those theories. Third, the litigation team had to be prepared to meet and rebut any defense asserted by Duke Power. The problems facing Duke Power were similar. First, Duke Power had to advance a theory of nondiscrimination. Second, it had to argue that the evidence supported its theory. The primary sources on which each party had to rely were the statute, Title VII, and its legislative history. The statutory provisions offered little or no assistance on the set of problems each side faced. Sections 703(a)(1) and 706(g) strongly supported Duke Power's argument that plaintiffs had to prove intentional discrimination because of race in order to win on the liability issue. Section 706(g) provided that a court may grant appropriate relief if the "court finds that the respondent has intentionally engaged in or is intentionally engaging in" an unlawful employment practice. Section 703(a)(2) offered the best option to the litigation team for an argument that the disparate treatment theory was not the only theory available to plaintiffs to prove a violation of Title VII because, unlike Section 703(a)(1), it did not use the term *discriminate*. In addition, Section 703(h) was a provision on which both parties could rely. Section 703(h) provided, in relevant part, that it was not a violation of Title VII for "an employer to give and act upon the results of any professionally developed ability test provided such test, its administration or action upon the results is not designed, intended, or used to discriminate because of race, color, religion, sex or national origin."[42] The litigation team could and did make the argument that even if the tests were "professionally prepared," Duke nevertheless "used" them in a way that adversely affected the employment opportunities of the plaintiffs because of their race. As a defense, Duke Power could and did argue that the Wonderlic and Bennett Mechanical tests were "professionally developed."

In the final analysis, the litigation team advanced two theories of discrimination in the district court. The first was the *Quarles* present effects of past discrimination theory. There were factual similarities between *Quarles* and *Griggs*. Both involved facially neutral employment practices—a seniority system in *Quarles* and an educational requirement and a test battery in *Griggs*. The defendants in both cases had engaged in a long history of racial discrimination against African Americans in their employment practices prior to the enactment of Title VII. One of the differences between *Quarles* and *Griggs* was that the defendants in *Quarles* admitted pre-Act discrimination against African Americans; Duke Power, on the other hand, denied throughout the case that it had ever discriminated against African Americans and was insistent during pretrial discovery and at trial that the evidence should be limited to its employment practices after Title VII's effective date of July 2, 1965. Perhaps one of the reasons Duke refused to admit that it had engaged in racial discrimination in its employment practices before the effective date of Title VII was that it was a federal contractor. As a federal contractor, it was contractually bound not to discriminate because of race. An admission that it had engaged in racial discrimination before July 2, 1965, had the potential of subjecting Duke to sanctions for violating its federal contractual obligation. During pretrial discovery and at the trial, Judge Gordon sustained Duke Power's objections to any of plaintiffs' evidence showing that Duke openly discriminated against African Americans prior to July 2, 1965, but he allowed the litigation team to make a proffer of such evidence for the record. Under the proffer-of-evidence rule, a trial court allows a party to introduce evidence into the record even though the court does not consider that evidence in deciding the case on the merit. The purpose of the proof of evidence rule is that it is a time-saving procedure in the event an appellate court rules that the trial court erred in not considering the evidence in the first instance. However, after the trial, and based upon the briefs filed by the parties, Judge Gordon ruled that evidence of Duke Power's discriminatory employment practices before July 2, 1965, was competent and relevant and would be considered for purposes of this case only. He also ruled that "[a]lthough company officials testified that there had never been a company policy of hiring only Negroes in the labor department and only whites in other departments, the evidence is sufficient to conclude that some time prior to July 2, 1965, Negroes were relegated to the labor department and prevented access to other departments by reasons of their race."[43]

The second argument advanced by the litigation team was that the disparate treatment theory, which requires proof of intentional discrimination, was not the only theory of discrimination embraced in Title VII. Duke Power and other defendants regularly argued that Title VII could be violated only if plaintiffs proved as a factual matter that they were the victims of intentional discrimination. In addition to grounding its argument in the legislative history, Duke Power relied heavily on Section 703(h) and more specifically the provision that a court can order relief where it finds that a defendant "has intentionally engaged in or is intentionally engaging in an unlawful employment practice." In the posttrial brief, the litigation team made a frontal attack on this argument by advocating an alternative effects test, an argument that the EEOC had first made in its amicus brief:

> The Supreme Court has long held that the validity of an act must be "tested by its operation and effect." . . . In *Griffin v. Illinois*, 351 U.S. 12 (1962), the Supreme Court stated: "A law [or as here, a seniority system] non-discriminatory on its face, may be grossly discriminatory in its operation." This principle has been applied by the court with special vigor in determining validity of acts which result in the denial of equal rights to Negroes.
>
>   The administrative and judicial interpretations of the National Labor Relations Act, upon which the provisions of Title VII are in a large measure patterned, follow this principle. Section 8(a)(3) of the N.L.R.A. prohibits an employer from discriminating with regard to hire, tenure, or terms and conditions of employment "to encourage or discourage" union membership. In *Erie Resistor Co. v. N.L.R.B.*, 373 U.S. 221 (1963), at issue was whether an employer discriminated within the meaning of that law by giving super-seniority to replacements for economic strikers. The employer defended granting super-seniority to non-striking employees on the ground that its conduct was not intended to discriminate against the strikers but flowed from the necessity to keep its plant open during the strike. The N.L.R.B. found that the employer's conduct violated Section 8(a)(3) and the Supreme Court agreed, stating (373 U.S. at 229):
>
>   . . . the employer may counter [a finding of discrimination] by claiming that his actions were taken in the pursuit of legitimate business ends and that his dominant purpose was not to discriminate or to invade union rights but to accomplish business objectives acceptable under the Act. *Nevertheless, his conduct does speak for itself—it is discriminatory and it does discourage union membership and whatever the claimed overriding justification may be, it carries with it unavoidable consequences which the employer not only foresaw but which he must have intended.*[44]

This was not the first time in the litigation campaign that the LDF argued that the disparate treatment theory was not the only theory of discrimination that violated Title VII. The litigation team had advanced this argument in some of the other early cases that were beginning to come to trial. For example, in *Lea v. Cone Mills Corp.*,[45] the litigation team made the same argument in the case in which Chambers and I were the lead counsel and filed the complaint on September 19, 1966, before it filed the complaint in *Griggs*. The trial court ruled in favor of the plaintiffs on the merits, but it did not address the litigation team's argument that specific intent was not the only theory of relief under Title VII.

A substantial portion of the litigation team's posttrial brief argued that the tests were not professionally developed. This argument was based substantially on the legislative history of Section 703(h) and the 1966 EEOC testing guidelines. The litigation team advised Judge Gordon that *Griggs* was one of the first cases to call for a judicial interpretation of Section 703(h) in regard to employment tests and that the court had to decide whether, as a "matter of first impression, the clause is to be read as giving employers virtually *carte blanche* to use any personnel test as long as it was professionally prepared," the reading Duke Power wanted the court to adopt, "or whether it was to be read in light of the basic anti-discriminatory purpose of Title VII and construed so as not to undercut that purpose—as the plaintiffs urge the court to construe the statute."[46] The fundamental argument the litigation team made on this issue was that in order for Duke Power's test battery to pass statutory muster under the "professionally developed ability tests" proviso, it must measure the skills that an employee or applicant needs to perform. The litigation team further argued that since it was undisputed that Duke had not validated its test battery, it did not fall in the safe harbor of Section 703(h). In addition to the EEOC guidelines, to which the litigation team asked Judge Gordon to defer, the litigation team also relied upon a line of voting rights cases challenging facially neutral or color-blind criteria that had an adverse effect on opportunities of blacks to register to vote.

Duke Power's argument was essentially threefold. First, it argued that Title VII operates prospectively and, for that reason, provides no remedy for discrimination before July 2, 1965, the effective date of Title VII. Second, and related to the first, Duke Power argued that the plaintiffs must prove that it engaged in intentional discriminatory conduct after July 2, 1965, and that the plaintiffs had failed to introduce any evidence on this point. Without specifically saying so, Duke Power's arguments urged Judge Gordon to reject the *Quarles* present effects of past discrimination theory. Duke Power also claimed foul play on the part of the litigation team in claiming that it had been blindsided because it had no notice prior to the filing of plaintiffs' posttrial brief that the legality of its educational requirement was an issue in the case.[47] This argument was not particularly meritorious in light of the fact that the evidence was undisputed that the test battery was a substitute or deemed to be the equivalent of a high school education and the only live testimony at trial was the parties' expert witnesses on testing. Nevertheless, Duke Power, relying upon an opinion letter of the Office of General Counsel of the EEOC issued on October 2, 1965, argued that educational qualifications do not violate Title VII. Third, Duke Power invoked the business necessity defense in support of its educational and testing requirements and relied on *Whitfield v. United Steelworkers of America* to support this defense. The factual basis for its business necessity defense was the testimony that Duke Power had had a poor experience with some employees in higher-skilled jobs without a high school education who refused to accept promotions when vacancies occurred because they felt they were unable to do the job. Recognizing that Judge Butzner had held in *Quarles* that the *Whitfield* business necessity defense did not preclude a finding of liability under Title VII, Duke Power's argument was essentially that its case with respect to its educational requirement was more akin to the facts in *Whitfield* than to *Quarles*.[48] The EEOC did not file a posttrial amicus brief in *Griggs* as it had done in *Quarles*.

Judge Gordon heard posttrial arguments on June 28, 1968. I presented the posttrial argument on behalf of the plaintiffs. Judge Gordon issued his opinion on September 30, 1968. He held that the plaintiffs had failed to prove that Duke Power had intentionally violated Title VII. Judge Gordon specifically rejected the *Quarles* present effects of past discrimination theory. In addition, he held that the high school education requirement did not discriminate against the plaintiffs on the basis of race, that Duke Power's test battery was professionally developed within the meaning of Section 703(h), and that the legislative history of Title VII indicated that it was to apply prospectively and not retroactively.

Judge Gordon rejected the plaintiffs' reliance on the *Quarles* present effects of past discrimination theory on several grounds. First, although he found as a fact that the plaintiffs "labor under the inequities resulting from past discrimination promotional policies of" Duke Power, Judge Gordon specifically rejected Judge Butzner's interpretation that "present consequences of past discrimination are covered by the Act" because, he said, based on a strict textual statutory interpretive approach, "[t]here is no reference in the Act to 'present consequences'" and "under no definition of the words therein are the terms 'present consequences of past discrimination' and 'unlawful employment practice' to be given synonymous meanings."[49] Second, he held that *Griggs* and

Quarles were distinguishable in that the defendant in *Quarles*, Philip Morris, had failed to prove a business necessity for the challenged seniority system at issue in that case, but Duke Power had a "legitimate *business purpose* for its educational and testing standards and for applying those standards to its departmental structure."[50] In an apparent rebuke to the plaintiffs, Judge Gordon stated that "[i]n light of this Court's holding that the defendant's policy of making a high school education a prerequisite to departmental transfers is nondiscriminatory, it would appear to be in the derogation of the plaintiffs' interest to abolish the use of test scores as a substitute for the high school requirement."[51] In this respect, it appears that Judge Gordon gave some credence to Duke Power's view that it had bent over backwards to open up opportunities for advancement for the plaintiffs out of the laborers' jobs, even though he had granted the plaintiffs' motion to strike the "bent over backwards" testimony of one of Duke Power's officials.

In addressing specifically the litigation team's "professionally developed ability test" argument, Judge Gordon wrote:

> The plaintiffs apparently read Section 703(h) to allow tests only when they are developed to predict a person's ability to perform a *particular* job or group of jobs. That is if the job requires only manual dexterity, then the Act requires an employer to utilize only a test that measures manual dexterity. [The 1966] Guidelines on employment testing procedures set out by the [EEOC] fortify that appraisal of the Act.

Stating that he could not agree with the plaintiffs' interpretation, he continued:

> Nowhere does the Act require that employers may utilize only those tests which accurately measure the ability and skills required of a particular job or group of jobs. Nowhere does the Act require the use of only one type of test to the exclusion of other non-discriminatory tests. A test which measures the level of general intelligence, but is unrelated to the job to be performed is just as reasonable a prerequisite to hiring or promotion as is a high school diploma. In fact, a general intelligence test is probably more accurate and uniform in application than is the high school education requirement.[52]

Judge Gordon made several critical factual findings that proved a strong basis for seeking to overturn his decision on appeal. First, he ruled that

> [t]he two tests used by [Duke Power] were never intended to accurately measure the ability of employees to perform the particular job available. Rather they are

intended to indicate whether the employee has general intelligence and overall mechanical comprehension of the average high school graduate, regardless of race, color, religion, sex, or national origin. The evidence establishes that the tests were professionally developed to perform this function and therefore are in compliance with the Act.

The Act does not deny an employer the right to determine the qualities, skills, and abilities required of his employees.

The defendant's expert testified that the Wonderlic Test was professionally developed to measure general intelligence, i.e., one's ability to understand, to think, to use good judgment. The Bennett Test was developed to measure mechanical understanding of the operation of simple machines. These qualities are general in nature and are not indicative of a person's ability to perform particular tasks. Nevertheless these are qualities which the defendant would logically want to find in his employees.[53]

Under Judge Gordon's interpretation of a "professionally developed ability test," any employer could require applicants for employment for any job to successfully pass the Law School Admissions Test (LSAT), which is a standardized test used to make decisions for admission to most law schools, because it was professionally prepared by testing experts. Or a taxi company could require taxi cab driver applicants to have a Ph.D. because it wanted its drivers to be able to have a high-level intellectual discussion with its customers.[54]

Judge Gordon did not directly address the plaintiffs' argument that specific intent was not always required to prove a violation of Title VII. He did address it indirectly when he held that the plaintiffs had failed to carry the burden of proof that Duke Power had intentionally discriminated against them because of race or color.[55]

Judge Gordon entered an order dismissing the action on the merits on October 9, 1968. The LDF filed a notice of appeal to the U.S. Court of Appeals for the Fourth Circuit on October 19.

8. In the Fourth Circuit: Judge Sobeloff's Blueprint for the Disparate Impact Theory

The decision to appeal Judge Gordon's decision in *Griggs* to the U.S. Court of Appeals for the Fourth Circuit was easy. First, his decision created a clear intradistrict conflict with Judge Butzner's opinion in *Quarles*. Judge Butzner had accepted the LDF's present effects of past discrimination theory; Judge Gordon had specifically rejected it. Second, *Griggs* involved a novel issue of law on the proper interpretation of the meaning of a "professionally developed" test. Although there were other cases pending that raised the issue of the meaning of "professionally developed," Judge Gordon's decision in *Griggs* was the first case to decide the issue squarely. Third, Judge Gordon had rejected, although impliedly, the LDF's argument that specific intent—the disparate treatment theory—was not the only theory of discrimination applicable to prove a violation of Title VII.

Shortly after I received Judge Gordon's decision, I sent copies to both Al Rosenthal and George Cooper, who wrote me separate memos. Al informed me that Cooper had approached him to discuss the case and that both were willing to draft the appellate brief.[1] Three days later, Cooper sent me a memo in which he extended his condolences for the adverse decision from Judge Gordon and expressed his optimism that the Fourth Circuit would at least reverse Judge Gordon's rejection of the *Quarles* present effects theory.[2] By the time Judge Gordon decided *Griggs*, Judge Butzner had become a member of the Fourth Circuit, joining the court in July 1967.

Cooper had a keen interest in working on *Griggs* because he was then working on the final edits of an article on testing and seniority discrimination that was eventually published in the *Harvard Law Review*.[3] The article eventually became most influential in the courts' endorsement of the disparate impact theory. Also, Cooper and Richard Sobol, his coauthor, were serving as cocounsel in several testing and seniority discrimination cases that raised novel issues like those raised in *Quarles* and *Griggs*.[4] They decided to write an article about those issues, which they believed might have some influence on how the courts would decide them. Cooper and Sobol later explained what they were attempting to accomplish in the article:

Along with other civil rights lawyers, we began to examine how [Title VII] might be made more effective than its state predecessors had been. Several ideals suggested themselves. First, the nature of the discrimination was based on class—not that Jack was treated worse than John, but that a certain group of people was treated worse than another group, and therefore a class or group approach to enforcement was essential. Second, subjective appraisals had to give way to objective evaluations. Third, these objective evaluations had to relate to the actual job.

    This article was an attempt to develop an enforcement theory based on these three ideas. It argues for an "effect-oriented" approach to evaluating discrimination, rather than the "intent-oriented" approach followed by earlier laws. Because it was the first attempt to develop and elaborate this approach, the article received a lot of attention.[5]

The article developed the theoretical underpinnings of the disparate impact theory. Cooper and Sobol did not specifically use the term *disparate impact* in their article. Instead, they articulated the new theory in terms of "effect-oriented," "adverse impact," and "adverse effects"—but these are simply alternative labels for the disparate impact theory.[6] The historical and legal underpinnings for the Cooper-Sobol article paralleled and overlapped with, in substantial part, the same historical and legal dynamics driving the LDF's litigation campaign.

    The article had not been published by the time of the posttrial argument in the district court. However, Cooper had shared a draft of the article with members of the litigation team prior to its publication in the June 1969 issue of the *Harvard Law Review*. I do not recall whether I read a draft of the article prior to the posttrial argument in *Griggs* in 1968, but in any event, even if I had read it, I could not cite it because it had not been published at that time. However, Greenberg, Al, Gaby, and I had read the draft by the time the notice of appeal was filed in the Fourth Circuit, and the litigation team welcomed the willingness of Cooper to participate with Al in drafting the appellate brief.[7] The article provided a powerful theoretical foundation that supported an argument that specific intent or proof of "evil motive" was not the only theory of discrimination applicable to employment claims under Title VII. Cooper had a major role in drafting not only the plaintiffs' brief in the court of appeals but also the plaintiffs' petition for certiorari and briefs in the Supreme Court. Barrett, our testing expert, worked with us on the appellate brief.

    Cooper wrote an outstanding draft of the brief for the plaintiffs that the litigation team filed in the Fourth Circuit with only a few minor substantive changes. The brief identified three issues for review, but before addressing those issues, the litigation team succinctly identified for the court the importance of the case because Judge Gordon's decision had generated quite a controversy about employment testing under Title VII:

> This case presents, as a matter of first impression at the Court of Appeals level, a question that is crucial to the efficacy of Title VII. . . . Does the Act cover pattern and practices which effectively discriminate against [African Americans] when those patterns and practices are superficially color-blind? If the Act does not cover such patterns and practices, as Duke Power Company argues, employers will be free to grant gross preferences to whites, and the ability of Title VII to provide true equal job opportunities will be largely nullified.[8]

Judge Sobeloff later picked up this point when he stated that "[t]he decision we make today is likely to be as pervasive in its effect as we have been called upon to make in recent years."[9]

The first issue the litigation team asked the court of appeals to resolve was the intradistrict court split between *Griggs* and *Quarles* on the viability of the present effects of past discrimination theory. Here, the main argument was that a rejection of the *Quarles* theory, as Judge Gordon had done, would "freeze" an entire generation of African Americans into the overtly discriminatory employment practices that existed before Title VII. The "freezing" theory had also been adopted by Judge Butzner in *Quarles.* There was strong support for this argument because an overwhelming number of lower courts had expressly followed *Quarles,* and Judge Gordon's ruling rejecting the theory was simply contrary to the developing law under Title VII. The argument on the present effects theory was essentially an updated and more expansive treatment of the same legal argument that the litigation team had made before Judge Gordon in the district court.

The second issue the litigation team asked the court of appeals to decide was whether Title VII barred an employer from using educational and testing requirements to make employment decisions when the relationship between such employment selection criteria and satisfactory job performance was unknown to the employer and such requirements were known to discriminate against African Americans because of race in light of centuries of educational and cultural discrimination. At bottom, the argument on the second issue asked the court of appeals to hold that facially neutral or color-blind employment selection criteria that have an adverse effect on the employment opportunities of African Americans violated the antidiscrimination mandate of Title VII unless justified by business necessity. Here, for the first time in an appellate Title VII case, the argument was made that Section 703(a)(2) supported the disparate impact theory of discrimination. The substance of the argument based on Section 703(a)(2) was that "[i]n light of the racial characteristics on which they are based, an unnecessary educational or test requirement which screens out [African Americans] at three or more times the rate of whites clearly tends to [in the language of Section 703(a)(2)] deprive or otherwise adversely affect [an African American's] status."[10]

There was no significant statistical evidence of the adverse impact of the testing and educational requirements on African American applicants or employees in the trial record because only three current employees had taken and failed the tests. Also, no evidence had been introduced at trial on the impact of the educational requirement on the employment opportunities of African Americans. However, because Duke Power had adopted the testing requirement as a substitute for a high school diploma, the structure of the argument as to the adverse impact of these criteria on African Americans was based, in part, on 1960 census data:

> The appellants, who were born black, received a different education in segregated schools . . . [because] they [completed whatever educational level they obtained] . . . before the 1954 *Brown* decision began the erosion of pervasive practices of segregation and discrimination. The resulting inferior education and a tendency to earlier dropping out of school . . . led them to conclude that they could not make use of further education. . . . Based on 1960 census data only 12% of North Carolina [African American] males had completed high school, as compared to 34% of North Carolina white males. At the time of the 1950 census, when the school door had closed for many of the [plaintiffs], the disparity was even worse—8% for [African Americans] and 27% for whites. . . . These statistics make one very salient point. If requirements such as a high school diploma or passage of "intelligence" test could freely be imposed by any employer, every employer in North Carolina and throughout the South could create a promotional preference of three or more to one in favor of whites. The free use of such requirements, which the District Court's ruling would permit, would effectively hold [African American] employment opportunities to a bare minimum.[11]

The LDF did not at any stage in the litigation—district court, court of appeals, or Supreme Court—advance the argument that Title VII flatly prohibited the use of all facially neutral objective criteria, such as educational or testing requirements, that have an adverse impact on employment opportunities for African Americans. Rather, the argument was that, assuming proof of the disparate impact of an objective selection criterion on the employment opportunities of African Americans, the critical issue was whether there was a "business need" or business necessity for such criterion. Here, the argument was that the *Quarles* business necessity defense was applicable not only to seniority systems but also to any facially neutral or color-blind selection criterion that had an adverse impact on any class or group protected by Title VII. It was clear that Duke Power could not satisfy the "business need" standard because it had admitted that it had made no effort whatsoever to do so.

Although the litigation team relied upon a few constitutional Equal Protection Clause cases in support of its disparate impact argument in the court of appeals, those cases did not provide the theoretical foundation for the argument. The wisdom of not grounding the disparate impact theory solely in the Fourteenth Amendment Equal Protection Clause became manifest in the Supreme Court's 1976 decision in *Washington v. Davis,* in which the Court drew a sharp distinction between Title VII and the Fourteenth Amendment, rejecting the disparate impact theory for discrimination claims based on the Equal Protection Clause.

In response to Duke Power's argument that its test battery fell within the safe harbor of the "professionally developed" provision of Section 703(h) of Title VII, the LDF relied upon the 1966 EEOC guidelines on testing and the legislative history of the testing provision. The 1966 EEOC guidelines made a distinction between "professionally developed" and "professionally prepared" and took the position that "professionally developed" means a test that fairly measures the knowledge or skills required by the particular job or class of jobs that the applicant seeks or fairly affords the employer a chance to measure the applicant's ability to perform a particular job or class of jobs. To hammer home this distinction between "professionally prepared" and "professionally developed," the LDF reductio ad absurdum argument was that if "professionally developed" were interpreted to mean "any test developed by professionals at its inception," then employers could "use a typing test to select ditch diggers or use the College Board to select janitors." The legislative history argument was straightforward: Section 703(h) was not included in Title VII to exempt tests from Title VII's broad prohibition of discriminatory practice. Rather, it was included only to assure that the "extreme implications of *Motorola* did not creep into the interpretation of Title VII."[12]

As to the third issue, the LDF asked the court to give deference to the EEOC guidelines because that agency's interpretation of Section 703(h) was not so clearly wrong that it should be rejected by the courts. In other words, the argument was that Judge Gordon had failed to give deference to the EEOC guidelines on testing when he ruled that a facially neutral employment test is protected by Section 703(h) as long as the test is professionally prepared, even if it provides no information about the ability of the test-taker to perform the job or jobs for which he or she is being considered.

The Department of Justice and the EEOC filed a joint amicus brief urging reversal of Judge Gordon's decision. There had been some misunderstanding between the Department of Justice and the EEOC as to which agency should take the lead role on appeal. The EEOC, apparently without conferring with the Department of Justice, filed a motion in the court of appeals to file an amicus brief in its own name and to participate in the oral argument in support of the plaintiffs. After some discussion between the two agencies, the Department of Justice informed the court of appeals that it and the EEOC had agreed to file a joint amicus brief on behalf of the United States. Later, the Department of Justice requested and received permission to participate in the oral argument because the case "present[ed] serious issues arising under Title VII."[13]

The government's fundamental argument was that Title VII prohibits not only disparate treatment discrimination but also "practices which appear even handed on their face but which, in actual effect, place [African Americans] at a disadvantage by building upon a pattern of pre-Act discrimination."[14] This argument was in effect that Title VII embraces two separate theories of discrimination—disparate treatment and disparate impact—even though the government did not attempt to ground the two different theories in the two different provisions of the Act, either 703(a)(1) or 703(a)(2). Yet the United States' argument did not abandon completely the view that an element of intent, i.e., pre–Title VII intentional discriminatory conduct, undergirds the disparate impact theory. The government urged the appellate court to endorse the disparate impact theory on the basis that doing so would not break new legal ground because the Supreme Court had already endorsed the theory in constitutional challenges to the denial of voting rights and in equal protection cases. Here, the government was essentially arguing that precedents from constitutional law supported the disparate impact theory in statutory or Title VII claims. Although not specifically stated as a separate ground for reversal, the government also argued that Judge Gordon erred in rejecting the *Quarles* present effects of past discrimination theory because doing so was contrary to the overwhelming weight of judicial precedent, including cases raising similar issues under the National Labor Relations Act. Finally, the government argued that it was unnecessary for the court to address Judge Gordon's ruling that Section 703(h) legitimates any "professionally prepared" test because the tests in *Griggs* were used as a substitute for the educational requirement and, by virtue of that fact, were also clearly "used to discriminate because of race."[15]

Duke Power advanced essentially three arguments in its brief in support of the decision by Judge Gordon. First, Duke Power argued that its adoption of the high school diploma requirement was based on business necessity, namely, that the requirement was necessary to upgrade the quality of its workforce and that great weight and deference should be given to the factual findings in its favor on this point by Judge Gordon because he had to make a credibility assessment of Duke Power's chief witness. Second, Duke Power argued that Title VII prohibits only disparate treatment, that is, intentional discrimination. Here, Duke Power placed heavy emphasis on Section 706(g), which is one of only a few statutory provisions in Title VII that specifically uses the term *intent* or *intentionally*. Duke Power also argued that *Quarles* prohibits disparate treatment. By advocating solely for an intent-based theory of discrimination, Duke Power only indirectly engaged the LDF's and the government's arguments that Title VII embraces other theories of discrimination, such as the *Quarles* present effects of past discrimination and the disparate impact theory.

Duke Power's third argument was that its test battery was "professionally developed" within the meaning of Section 703(h). Fundamentally, Duke Power was attempting to support the "professionally prepared" construction of the statutory phrase "professionally developed" adopted by Judge Gordon. In doing so, Duke Power made a rather ingenious *in terrorum* argument, namely, "the [plaintiffs were], in effect seek[ing] 'a *Motorola* decision' . . . [by] contending that even if the high school and test requirements are imposed equally on all employees, such requirement would be unlawful because they are unjustifiably based on racial characteristics."[16] Alternatively, Duke Power asserted a good-faith defense based on Section 713(b) and on an opinion issued by the general counsel of the EEOC on October 2, 1965, only three months after the effective date of Title VII, which stated that employment decisions based on educational qualifications did not violate Title VII. The United States challenged Duke Power's reliance on that opinion by arguing that the opinion was not a written interpretation within the meaning of 713(b) because it failed to conform to the EEOC interpretation of that Section and that, even if it did, Duke Power had offered no proof at trial that it relied upon the opinion.[17]

Finally, Duke Power invoked a still-controversial argument grounded in the so-called anti–preferential treatment provision of Title VII when it argued that promoting one of the plaintiffs who neither had a high school diploma nor passed the tests over a white applicant who had satisfied both of these criteria would constitute unlawful preferential treatment prohibited under Section 703(j). The litigation team informed the court of appeals in its reply brief that Duke Power had quite nicely joined the issue that was the crux of the case when it boldly asserted that "Congress has made it clear that an employer can set his qualification, educational or otherwise, as high as he likes without violating Section 703 of Title VII . . . so long as they are applied without discrimination."[18] This bold, unqualified assertion by Duke Power was at the heart of *Griggs* in the court of appeals and in the Supreme Court.

The court of appeals judges who decided *Griggs* were Simon Sobeloff, Herbert Boreman, and Albert Bryan.[19] Judge Sobeloff's opinion, in which he concurred in part and dissented in part from the majority opinion written by Judge Boreman, became the blueprint for the disparate impact theory later endorsed by the Supreme Court. Judge Sobeloff was born in Baltimore, Maryland, the son of Russian Jewish immigrants. He earned his law degree from the University of Maryland School of Law in 1915 but was admitted to the bar in 1914 before he received his LL.B. and after receiving one of the highest scores on the Maryland bar admission examination. He held many different legal positions in public office before his appointment to the court of appeals, including serving as the solicitor general of the United States. As solicitor general, he presented the argument on behalf of the United States in *Brown II*, in which the Supreme Court endorsed the "all deliberate speed" remedial order to implement *Brown I*. President Eisenhower nominated Sobeloff to the U.S. Court of Appeals for the Fourth Circuit in 1955, but his appointment was delayed for a year mainly because of opposition by some southern senators who believed he might use the position to advocate on public school desegregation in the wake of the *Brown* decisions and on other controversial matters of the day.[20] Judge Sobeloff served as the chief judge of the Fourth Circuit from 1958 until 1964, during a period in which the LDF and other organizations were heavily engaged in trench warfare litigation to enforce the *Brown* decisions.[21] Judge Sobeloff wrote several important school desegregation decisions from

North Carolina and Virginia, striking down certain school districting plans and ordering a speedier implementation of the *Brown* decisions.

In an article on the deceased judges who sat on the Fourth Circuit from 1941 to 1998, Judge Sobeloff's court of appeals colleagues expressed admiration of him for his "great contributions toward race relations," his advocacy for "removing the basis of racism," and his willingness to advance the argument that from his perspective, racism was "morally and constitutionally untenable," and his view that for courts to allow racism to persist would perpetuate community resistance to desegregation. His colleagues also recognized his legacy of "educated and well-reasoned opinions that formed the basis of many of the Supreme Court decisions and provided a profound and permanent influence on American law."[22] One of those decisions was *Swann v. Charlotte Mecklenburg Board of Education,* in which the Supreme Court approved of busing and numerical goals as remedial schemes in school desegregation cases.[23] Supreme Court Justice William O. Douglas described Judge Sobeloff as an activist "in civil rights affairs, working against school segregation, working for a federal anti-lynching bill, working against censorship of the press, and working for civil rights of all minorities."[24] He also has been called the "champion of the underdog."[25]

Neither Judge Boreman nor Judge Bryan had a reputation for being particularly sympathetic to civil rights claims. Judge Boreman was born in Middlebourne, West Virginia, and received his law degree from West Virginia University College of Law in 1920. He served as a federal district court judge in West Virginia for five years prior to his appointment to the Fourth Circuit in 1959. President Eisenhower appointed him to both positions. Judge Boreman has been described as "a conservative of conservatives" and as "one of the most conservative judges in a conservative circuit." He had a reputation of never antagonizing the more liberal judges on the court of appeals. Despite being an elder statesman on the court of appeals, he regularly assisted the aging Judge Sobeloff to his seat in the courtroom as Judge Sobeloff neared the end of his term.[26]

Judge Bryan was born in Alexandria, Virginia, and received his law degree from the University of Virginia. President Truman appointed him to the U.S. District Court for the Eastern District of Virginia in 1947, and President Kennedy appointed him to the court of appeals in 1961. Judge Bryan has been described as a "conservative in the deepest old Virginia sense" and a "legal conservative and a strict constructionist."[27] His colleagues knew him as a courtly, conservative Virginia gentleman whose personal style was low-key, modest, and polite, with a dry wit.[28] When opposition surfaced to his nomination to the Fourth Circuit on the grounds that he had shown racial bias in the school desegregation cases he had handled in the district court or at least had failed to act in the spirit of the Supreme Court's rulings, Judge Sobeloff wrote a very strong and supportive letter on his behalf to the American Bar Association. In that letter, Judge Sobeloff emphasized, among other matters, that the accusations were unjust and utterly without foundation and that those who were vetting Judge Bryan should be reminded that the district court on which he sat was located in a state—Virginia—the leaders of which unfortunately took the initiative in mounting a massive resistance movement to the implementation of *Brown*. One of the school desegregation cases Judge Bryan sat on as a district court judge was *Griffin v. County School Board of Prince Edward County*. Virginia had initiated a coordinated effort, in light of the holding in *Brown v. Board of Education,* known as massive resistance, to maintain segregation of its public schools. Prince Edward County took the unusual and extreme measure of closing all of its schools after being ordered to integrate its public schools. In short, Judge Sobeloff concluded that there was no just grounds for criticism and that Judge Bryan had behaved in the school desegregation cases "as an honest judge should" even though he had, on occasion, been reversed by the court of appeals.[29]

Greenberg usually reviewed all appellate briefs raising novel and important issues, so he sent me a memo indicating his interest in *Griggs* and also stating his interest in arguing the case in the court of appeals. The case was set for argument on April 10, 1969, and the litigation team worked with Greenberg in preparation for the argument. George Ferguson argued the case for Duke Power, and Gary Greenberg of the Department of Justice and Russell Specter with the General Counsel's office of the EEOC shared the argument on behalf of the United States as amicus curiae. The parties' arguments in the court of appeals paralleled, in substantial part, the positions they had advocated in their appellate briefs.[30]

The practice in many of the federal courts of appeals is that the panel of three judges who are assigned to hear and decide the merits of a case meet in a postargument conference to discuss the judges' views on how the case should be decided and who will draft opinions. At their postargument conference, Judges Sobeloff, Boreman, and Bryan were unable to reach a conclusion as to the proper disposition of *Griggs,*[31] but they clearly recognized that the case presented a novel and difficult question as to the proper interpretation of Title VII.[32] Judge Sobeloff had the initial responsibility of drafting the *Griggs* opinion. Because he already had a rather heavy load for cases for which he was to draft opinions, Judge Sobeloff asked the Chief Judge of the Fourth Circuit, Clement Haynsworth, to assign the opinion drafting responsibility in *Griggs* to another panel member. Chief Judge Clement Haynsworth then assigned the task to Judge Boreman.[33] Judge Boreman accepted the assignment, then sent a memo to Judge Haynsworth and all of the other circuit judges, acknowledging that he and his fellow panelists agreed that the case "pose[d] some rather difficult problems," but he said he would "do [his] best with it."[34]

The general practice in the Fourth Circuit, at least at the time of the *Griggs* argument, was to circulate drafts of opinions not only to the other panelists but to all the other court of appeals judges as well. On October 2, 1969, Judge Boreman circulated a copy of the proposed "trial run" opinion only to Judges Sobeloff and Bryan for their reactions, and he specifically stated that he was not at that time circulating the opinion to other members of the court. He also stated that he was not expecting an immediate response because he recognized that they would probably need time to carefully consider his draft and that he was willing to discuss any questions they might have.[35]

Judge Bryan's response to Judge Boreman's draft came only one day later, informing Judges Sobeloff and Boreman that the draft opinion was acceptable to him, and he returned his copy to Judge Boreman specifically noting his concurrence without any suggested changes.[36] Several weeks later, Judge Sobeloff sent an October 22, 1969, memo to Judge Boreman informing him that he had read the draft "with much appreciation," that *Griggs* was "an important case," and that the issue posed was "a difficult one." However, Judge Sobeloff advised Judge Boreman that he wanted to listen to the tape of the oral argument and review the record before responding to the invitation for comments on the draft opinion.[37] Apparently quite displeased with Judge Sobeloff's response, Judge Boreman sent the tape immediately, pointedly informing Judge Sobeloff that he had spent a lot of time during the summer of 1969 on the case because all the panelists recognized that it presented a difficult question and saying that he hoped Judge Sobeloff would not find his draft "wholly unacceptable."[38]

Later, and apparently still frustrated about not having received comments on his draft opinion from Judge Sobeloff, Judge Boreman sent a November 13, 1969, memo to all the circuit judges—not just to Judges Sobeloff and Bryan— along with his draft opinion. In that memo, Judge Boreman told his colleagues that only a week earlier, Judge Sobeloff had orally informed him that he was preparing a dissent when they talked during the Fourth Circuit annual judicial conference. Judge Boreman also advised his colleagues of the concurrence of Judge Bryan.[39] Thereafter, all communications about the case were sent to all members of the court. In response to Judge Boreman's November 13 memo, Judge Sobeloff pointedly informed his colleagues that Judge Boreman was "quite correct that I am not in agreement with the draft opinion" and that he was working on an "alternative opinion."[40]

The *Harvard Law Review* published the Cooper and Sobol article that first articulated the theoretical support for the disparate impact theory in its June 1969 issue. None of the parties cited the article in their briefs because it had not been published before the briefing deadline had passed or before the oral argument. However, Judge John Butzner, the author of *Quarles* and by then a member of the court of appeals, sent a November 14, 1969, memo to Judge Boreman and the other circuit judges about the law review article. He noted that the article contained a great deal of material pertinent to *Griggs* and specifically noted that Cooper and Sobol were critical of Judge Gordon's decision on the test issue. Judge Butzner also pointed out that the U.S. Court of Appeals for the Fifth Circuit had decided *Local 189*—on July 28, 1969, after the argument in *Griggs*—and appeared to "find [Judge Gordon's] opinion in *Griggs* was unpersuasive in its departure from the [EEOC]'s interpretation of § 703(h)."[41] Earlier, I had sent a copy of *Local 189* to the clerk of the court of appeals on August 4, 1969, shortly after the case was handed down. I asked the clerk to call the case to the attention of the *Griggs* panel in support of the litigation team's argument that Judge Gordon had erred in rejecting the *Quarles* present effects of past discrimination theory.[42]

The Cooper and Sobol article apparently was influential in shaping Judge Sobeloff's thinking about the issue in *Griggs.* He cited the article several times in the first draft of his opinion, which he circulated to his colleagues just about a week after the article had been called to his attention by Judge Butzner, and in his published concurring and dissenting opinion.[43] It appears that none of the members of the court of appeals was troubled by the fact that one of the authors of the article, Cooper, was also "of counsel" for the *Griggs* plaintiffs. That was not the case in *Local 189* in the Fifth Circuit, in which both Cooper and Sobol appeared as counsel for some of the plaintiffs. Judge John Minor Wisdom, one of the liberal judges on the Fifth Circuit and the author of *Local 189*, had cited the Cooper and Sobol article in that landmark decision. Several weeks after *Local 189* had been decided, counsel for the union defendant filed a petition requesting that the entire court rehear the case on the basis that Judge Wisdom had included footnote references to the Cooper and Sobol article, which had been published after oral argument. Although it is commonplace for judges and/or their law clerks to do their own research on issues raised by the parties, the union in *Local 189* argued in its rehearing petition that, by citing the Cooper and Sobol article when both were counsel for some of the plaintiffs in the case, the court had relied upon an ex parte communication in violation of the union's constitutional right to due process of law. There was a rather testy exchange of communication among the judges on the Fifth Circuit about the union's allegation, but in the final analysis, the court denied the petition.[44] The view expressed by the union in *Local 189* on the court's citing articles by plaintiffs' counsel in employment discrimination cases apparently had wide support with the Title VII defense bar. For example, a defense attorney complained that the majority of law review articles, at least in the early years of Title VII litigation, were written by attorneys and consultants to plaintiffs in pending cases such that they could reasonably be regarded as supplemental briefs prepared by plaintiffs' attorneys while their cases were pending appeal. The defense's attorney specifically cited the Cooper and Sobol article as an example of this practice.[45]

On November 21, 1969, Judge Sobeloff circulated a draft of his proposed opinion to all of the circuit judges. As his covering memo informed his colleagues:

> This opinion was drafted with several not necessarily reconcilable objectives in mind. First, I wanted to persuade my colleagues on the panel. Second, if that endeavor were successful, I intended to use the draft as a majority opinion. But third I wished to prepare something I could use as a dissent if I could not prevail upon the brethren. The result is a hybrid which is precisely tailored for neither a majority opinion nor a dissent. Yet you will see what I am driving at and I present it in its present form for your consideration.
>
> If the opinion is to speak for the court, I will revise the introduction and set out the facts. If, on the other hand, it is to be a dissent, I should perhaps square off more explicitly with the opposing opinion.[46]

Immediately after receiving and reviewing the draft, Judge Bryan advised Judge Sobeloff that his proposed opinion was "admirable in thought and thesis, the force of the reasoning would be generally recognized but that he had not left the postargument conference of the panel with any impression of the differences he expressed in his draft."[47] He concluded by saying he would suspend his concurrence until he had given a more thorough review of both opinions. However, two days later, Judge Bryan informed his colleagues that despite Judge Sobeloff's potent and pointed dissent, he nevertheless adhered to his prior concurrence in Judge Boreman's draft opinion. Judge Butzner wrote that he was glad to see that Judge Sobeloff's suggested opinion would align the Fourth Circuit with the Fifth Circuit (presumably with *Local 189*), that the reasoning was compelling, and that he hoped the panel would accept it.[48] Judge Butzner also urged the panel to try to agree upon an opinion that would adopt the requirement that tests must be job related.[49] Later, Judge Butzner wrote Judge Sobeloff to offer his congratulations because his "views, though in the dissent, will command wide respect," and he said he was pleased Judge Sobeloff "spoke out so forcefully, because Title VII is one of the most important statutes of recent years," and that his interpretation of that statute "will strike the mark of race all too often banishing [African Americans] from advancement."[50] Judge J. Braxton Craven then noted that he was in the delightful position of having complimented Judge Boreman on his draft opinion and of being able to bestow the same on Judge Sobeloff. His conclusion was that Judges Sobeloff and Boreman did "not lock horns," but on balance he was persuaded by Judge Sobeloff's opinion, even though both viewpoints were appealing, and that he was glad that presently he did not have to vote.[51] Judge Harrison L. Winter found the draft to be "very persuasive" and expressed his hope that the panel would adopt it because he thought Judge Sobeloff was "unquestionably right."[52] In addition to Judge Bryan, only Chief Judge Haynsworth agreed with Judge Boreman. Judge Haynsworth expressed the opinion that if there was a "real business need" for education or testing requirements, an employer should not be required to prove job-relatedness of a small progression in an employment unit.[53]

About five days after receiving Judge Sobeloff's draft, Judge Boreman circulated a rather stinging and critical nine-page response. His response stated, in part,

> It occurs to me that Judge Sobeloff's overriding fear is that my proposed disposition of this case would lead to widespread use by employers of a sham educational or testing requirement as a subtle, but effective means of discriminating against Negroes. I thought I had said enough throughout the draft submitted by me to dispel any such fear. I proposed to decide the case squarely and completely upon its own facts and circumstances. There was a valid business

purpose back of Duke's educational requirement and obviously there was not a sham which appears to be Judge Sobeloff's burning concern.

I would agree that an employer is not allowed to adopt an educational or testing requirement as an effective means of discriminating against Negroes . . . [and I included] the specific warning . . . [in footnote 8] [which states]

This decision is not to be construed as holding that *any* educational or testing requirement adopted by *any* employer is valid under the Civil Rights Act of 1964. There must be a genuine business purpose in establishing such requirements and they cannot be designed or used to further the practice of racial discrimination. . . .

Here, a company whose business had become and was expected to continue to become more and more complex instituted an educational requirement which was to apply to white as well as Negro employees. . . . It was uncontroverted that Duke had practiced discrimination in hiring Negroes only in the Labor Department and in view of this discrimination it was my conclusion that relief should be provided for those employees who were discriminatorily hired and who were subject to further discrimination by this requirement which would have the effect of "freezing" them in the Labor Department.

Judge Sobeloff seems to think that we should go further and strike down the use of any general educational or testing requirement even in the special case such as this where every fact and circumstance points to the conclusion that there was a genuine business purpose to be served and no purpose to discriminate in the adoption of the initial educational requirement. . . .

I am not persuaded that I should join in a ruling which would invalidate the establishment of a good faith educational or testing requirement designed to further business purposes. . . .

Under different circumstances I might well agree with much of Judge Sobeloff's proposed opinion. However, I am . . . certain that Congress did not intend to give employment opportunities which are more than equal . . . or to give Negroes preferential treatment or privileged treatment over white employees. . . .

Of course, we disagree as to the legislative history of the Act but, according to my analysis, I am not persuaded that blind acceptance of an incorrect [EEOC] administrative interpretation is "settled doctrine."

I have presented my views in the proposed draft which was not prepared in haste but after much study and reflection. I respect Judge Sobeloff's views and his right to state them. I am not going to apologize for disagreeing with him or declining to join in his opinion which he proposes to write as a majority opinion.[54]

The exchange of memos among the members of the court of appeals in response to Judge Sobeloff's effort to try to rally a consensus for his proposed opinion for the panel and the court showed that four of the seven active judges favored an opinion in line with his proposal (Sobeloff, Winter, Butzner, and Craven), and three (Haynsworth, Bryan, and Boreman) supported Judge

Boreman's draft opinion. However, the original panel that heard *Griggs* had the final say as to what the ultimate decision would be. In light of the fact that Judge Boreman decided to stand by his earlier draft and Judge Bryan reaffirmed his concurrence, Judge Boreman's original draft became majority decision of the court of appeals in *Griggs.* Judge Sobeloff revised his draft to concur in part and dissent in part.[55] The majority opinion by Judge Boreman, along with Judge Sobeloff's dissent, was issued on January 9, 1970.

Judge Boreman's decision for the majority did not make any changes in the "trial run" draft he originally circulated to the panel in October 1969. The majority opinion affirmed in part and reversed in part the decision of Judge Gordon. First, the majority specifically endorsed the *Quarles* present effects of past discrimination theory. While agreeing with Judge Gordon that Title VII operates only prospectively, the majority nevertheless held that it provides a remedy for present and continuing effects of past discrimination.[56] Second, Judge Boreman deemed it crucial to divide the group of fourteen African American employees into three clusters in order to determine whether each group had been the victim of unlawful employment discrimination under the *Quarles* theory. The first group of plaintiffs, Group A as designated by Judge Gordon on remand, was the four plaintiffs who had been hired after 1955, did not have a high school education or its equivalent, and, to be promoted out of the category of laborer, had to either obtain a high school diploma or its equivalent or successfully pass the tests. The plaintiffs in this group were the lead plaintiff, Willie Griggs, and Clarence Purcell, Eddie Broadnax, and David Hatchett. The majority deemed that a decision on whether this group was the victim of unlawful employment discrimination raised a novel issue as to whether Duke Power could condition future employment opportunities outside of the Labor Department on the educational and testing requirements because there were "no cases directly in point."[57] The court specifically rejected plaintiffs' argument that the present effects theory supported Group A's claim for relief and in doing so addressed the critical issue in the case. That issue was legality under Title VII of Duke Power's educational and testing requirements.

The majority rejected all of the arguments that the litigation team and the government advanced challenging the legality under Title VII of Duke Power's educational and testing requirements. However, as a threshold matter, the majority endorsed the business necessity defense even though it characterized the defense as either a "business purpose" or a "business motive."[58] First, the majority held that Judge Gordon was correct in holding that Duke Power did not adopt the educational and test battery with the specific intent to discriminate against African Americans. The majority found that Duke Power did so for the business purpose of assessing whether potential employees for the "inside" departments had the ability to perform tasks in higher-skilled jobs because its business was becoming more complex, and its experience was that some of its employees without a high school education did not have an intelligence high enough to enable them to advance upward through its lines of promotion, and that Duke Power had adopted the test battery only after consultation with its expert witness, Dr. Moffie. Second, the majority rejected the argument that the educational and testing requirements must be job related to fall within the safe-harbor provision of Section 703(h), which exempts professionally developed tests from the antidiscrimination mandate of Title VII. With respect to the issue of job-relatedness, the majority specifically declined to give deference to the EEOC testing guidelines because its review of the legislative history of the Tower Amendment led it to conclude that Congress did not intend to mandate that employers had to use only those tests that measure the ability and skills required of a job or a group of jobs. In so holding, the majority agreed with Judge Gordon that tests do not have to be job related to be valid under Section 703(h).

According to the panel majority, the four plaintiffs in Group A were not entitled to any relief. The reasons for not granting relief to these plaintiffs were that, even though Duke Power had engaged in intentional discrimination against all the plaintiffs before the effective date of Title VII, the evidence supported Judge Gordon's finding that Duke Power had adopted the testing requirements without an intent to discriminate, and Duke Power had a genuine business purpose for adopting this employment practice. The panel majority, further agreeing with the decision of Judge Gordon, also rejected the view that an employer must prove that an employment test is job related in order to successfully assert the Section 703(h) statutory safe-harbor defense based on a professionally developed test. The majority also specifically rejected the position of the EEOC that tests must be proven to be job related if they have an adverse effect on a protected class and did so on the ground that the EEOC's position was contrary to the Act's legislative history. Based on its factual and legal conclusions that Duke Power had not intentionally adopted the test battery to discriminate against African Americans and that Title VII did not require tests to be job related, the majority held that the plaintiffs in Group A were not the victims of unlawful employment discrimination:

Having determined that Duke's educational and testing requirements were valid under Title VII, we reach the conclusion that those four [African American] employees without a high school education who were hired after the adoption of the educational requirement are not entitled to relief. These employees were hired subject to the educational requirement: each accepted the position in the Labor Department with his eyes wide open. Under this valid educational requirement these four plaintiffs could have been hired only in the Labor Department and could not have been promoted or advanced into any other department irrespective of race, since they could not meet the requirement. . . . Furthermore, since the testing requirement is being applied to white and [African American] employees alike as an approximate equivalent to a high school education for advancement purposes, neither is it racially discriminatory.[59]

The second group, Group B, was made up of the four plaintiffs who had a high school education or who, by the time of the appeal, had completed a course of study that was equivalent to a high school education. The Group B employees were Jesse Martin (not a plaintiff in the case), Herman Martin, Robert A. Jumper, and Willie Boyd, the spokesperson for the plaintiffs, all of whom had been promoted out of laborers jobs after the complaint was filed in October 1966. Judge Boreman found the claims of Group B to be essentially moot because "it does appear that [Duke Power] is not now discriminating in its promotion and transfer policies against [African American] employees who have a high school education or its equivalent."[60]

The third group, Group C, was composed of the six plaintiffs who were hired prior to 1955, when Duke Power instituted its educational requirement for new applicants for vacancies in the "inside" departments but not for applicants for positions in the coal-handling and labor departments. The plaintiffs in this group were Junior Blackstock, William Purcell, Clarence Jackson, Lewis Hairston, Eddie Galloway, and James Tucker. The majority found that Group C's members were the victims of unlawful discrimination under the *Quarles* present effects of past discrimination theory. Here, the majority overruled Judge Gordon's rejection of the present effects theory because it conflicted with other persuasive authority, including *Quarles*. It then specifically adopted Judge Butzner's theory and reasoning in *Quarles* that even though an employer may not have engaged in post-Act intentional discrimination, the present and continuing effects of pre-Act discrimination constitute a violation of Title VII. The majority thus agreed with the "anti-freezing" and "anti-lock-in" principles of *Quarles*. Although the majority agreed with Judge Gordon's view that Title VII was intended to have prospective application only, it held that remedying the present and continuing effects of past discrimination is consistent with the prospective application construction of Title VII. Applying the present effects of past discrimination theory to the claims of these six employees, the majority held that Duke Power could not, consistent with the mandate of Title VII, require the plaintiffs in Group C to obtain a high school education or successfully pass the test battery as a condition for promotion out of the laborer jobs because similarly situated white employees (who were hired before 1955 and did not have a high school education) with jobs in the "inside" departments were not subject to these requirements.

Judge Sobeloff, concurring in part and dissenting in part, wrote a very powerful opinion. He established the perspective of his decision at the beginning of his opinion:

> The decision we make today is likely to be as pervasive in its effect as any we have been called upon to make in recent years, and puts this circuit in direct conflict with the Fifth Circuit (in *Local 189*). . . .
>
> This case presents the broad question of the use of allegedly objective employment criteria resulting in the denial to [African Americans] of jobs for which they are potentially qualified. . . . Today we are faced with an . . . issue, [analogous to that faced by Judge Butzner in *Quarles*], namely the denial of jobs to [African Americans] who cannot meet the educational requirements or pass standardized tests, but who quite possibly have the ability to perform the jobs in question. On this issue hangs the vitality of the employment provision (Title VII) of the 1964 Civil Rights Act: whether the Act shall remain a potent tool for equalization of employment opportunity or shall be reduced to mellifluous but hollow rhetoric.[61]

He agreed with Judges Boreman and Bryan in finding that the six Group C plaintiffs were entitled to relief, but he reshaped the present effects of past discrimination theory to eliminate the need for the plaintiffs to prove intentional discrimination in cases challenging facially neutral employment policies and practices. Judge Sobeloff's decision to delink completely the past discrimination element of the *Quarles* theory was also a major development in the history of the evolution of the disparate treatment theory. Specifically citing the two substantive provisions of Title VII, Section 703(a)(1) and (a)(2), Judge Sobeloff wrote:

> The statute is unambiguous. Overt racial discrimination in hiring and promotion is banned. So too, the statute interdicts practices that are fair in form but discriminatory in substance. Thus it has become well settled that "objective"

or "neutral" standards that favor whites but do not serve business needs are indubitably unlawful employment practices. The critical inquiry is *business necessity* and if it cannot be shown that an employment practice which excludes blacks stems from legitimate needs the practice must end.[62]

Here, Judge Sobeloff argued that Title VII supports two theories of discrimination: disparate treatment, an intent-based theory that requires proof of intentional discrimination, and disparate impact (even though he did not use that label), which is an "effects-based" theory that does not require proof of discrimination.

He specifically disclaimed any notion of grounding the disparate impact theory on intentional conduct. He spelled out his argument on the disparate impact theory in his treatment of the business necessity defense:

> A man who is turned down for a job does not care whether it was because the employer did not like the color of his skin or because, although the employer professed impartiality, procedures were used which had the effect of discriminating against the applicant's race. Likewise irrelevant to Title VII is the state of mind of the employer whose policy, in practice, effects discrimination. The law will not tolerate unnecessary harsh treatment of Negroes even though an employer does not plan this result. The use of criteria that are not backed by valid and corroborated business needs cannot be allowed, regardless of subjective intent. There can be no legitimate business purpose apart from business need: and where no business need is shown, claims to business purpose evaporate.[63]

Judge Sobeloff acknowledged that Duke Power did not intentionally adopt the educational and testing policies to discriminate against African Americans because, at least as to the educational policy, it could not be foreseen in 1955 that Congress would enact Title VII. But he declared that by "continuing to utilize those selection practices *now* after the enactment of Title VII, courts open the door to wholesale evasion by Duke Power and that other employers would be sure to follow."[64]

Both the majority and Judge Sobeloff relied upon the same legislative history on Section 703(h) in their treatment of the "professionally developed" defense. However, they disagreed on the deference that should be accorded the EEOC guidelines on testing, and they also disagreed on whether Duke Power had shown that its educational and testing requirements were job related. The majority gave more credit to Dr. Moffie, Duke Power's expert witness, in concluding that the tests were job related. Judge Sobeloff gave more credit to Dr. Barrett's testimony that they were not.

Judge Sobeloff also anticipated an issue that the Supreme Court subsequently would address in another landmark LDF case about when an employer can test job applicants at the entry level to determine whether they may eventually fill a higher position in the future rather than jobs to be filled immediately.

In light of the disheartening ruling from the Fourth Circuit majority and the strong dissent from Judge Sobeloff, the litigation team was faced with a difficult question: What step should we take next?

9. *Griggs* in the Supreme Court

The Fourth Circuit decided *Griggs* in January 1970, shortly after I moved to North Carolina to join the Chambers firm. Greenberg selected William L. Robinson (Bill) to replace me as the head of the employment litigation program. Bill, an African American, graduated from Oberlin College in 1963 and from Columbia Law School in 1966. While at Columbia, Bill spent a substantial amount of time in the Deep South doing legal research on voting rights and sit-in demonstration cases. Before joining the LDF, he was the executive director of the Law Students Civil Rights Research Council (LSCRRC). In this role, he worked with civil rights lawyers across the South and assigned law students from northern-based law schools to work under the supervision of civil rights lawyers. Bill joined the LDF in 1967 but mostly handled cases involving public accommodations, school desegregation, and public housing before becoming the head of the employment discrimination litigation campaign. Bill left the LDF in 1973 to become the associate general counsel for the EEOC (the head of its systemic litigation program) and then served as the executive director of the Lawyers Committee for Civil Rights Under Law (LCCRUL) from 1979 to 1988. He became the founding dean in 1989 of the District of Columbia School of Law and the University of the District of Columbia School of Law after the law school merged with the university. Bill won the first Title VII case in the Supreme Court that involved a substantive issue. In that case, *Phillips v. Martin-Marietta Corp.,* the Court held that an employer's policy that excluded mothers of preschool-age children from certain jobs was prima facie evidence of unlawful sex-based employment discrimination.

After the Fourth Circuit's decision in *Griggs,* the issue of whether the litigation team should seek Supreme Court review arose. There was some strong opposition to filing a petition for certiorari. Some thought *Griggs* was an essentially flawed case to take to the Supreme Court. For example, Cooper sent a letter to Greenberg urging the LDF not to seek review in the Supreme Court. Greenberg shared the letter with Bill.[1] Cooper's position was that the LDF should accept the fact that the litigation team had won a significant victory because the Fourth Circuit squarely endorsed the *Quarles* present effects of past discrimination theory. However, Cooper argued that, although the powerful dissent by Judge Sobeloff carried with it a "clear presumption in favor of certiorari," he had "strong feelings that a certiorari petition would be unwise" for several reasons. Cooper's reasons included the failure to introduce comparative or statistical evidence in the trial court showing that African Americans did worse on the Wonderlic and Bennett tests than did similarly situated whites; that Duke Power had not chosen the tests wholly arbitrarily; that the panel's majority decision did not affect four of the named plaintiffs (Group A); that the jobs at the Dan River Steam Station sounded fairly complex and dangerous in light of testimony that Duke Power was transitioning from coal to atomic-generated power; that Duke Power was willing to waive the test battery for any current employee who obtained a high school diploma through its subsidized program; and that the case presented "a most unappealing situation for finding the tests unlawful." Finally, Cooper pointed out that other cases were in the litigation pipeline that offered a more favorable factual context to raise the testing issue. One of the cases Cooper specifically noted was *Moody v. Albemarle Paper Company*,[2] which Chambers and I would be trying in the spring of 1970 and on which Cooper would be consulting to help develop data on the adverse impact of the same tests at issue in *Griggs*.[3]

I had several long and rather spirited conversations with officials at the Department of Justice and the EEOC who, like Cooper, argued that the LDF should not seek Supreme Court review. John Pemberton, then the deputy general counsel for the EEOC, drafted a letter to Greenberg urging the LDF not to seek Supreme Court review. Many of the reasons Pemberton advanced on behalf of the EEOC tracked almost verbatim the reasons advanced by Cooper. In addition, Pemberton argued that the tests at issue in *Griggs* were widely used in industrial and commercial employment and were precisely the kind of tests Congress sought to protect in enacting Section 703(h) of Title VII covering "professionally developed" tests. However, Pemberton never sent the letter to Greenberg.[4]

Bill, Chambers, and I were strongly in favor of filing a petition for certiorari even though we were aware of the powerful arguments advanced by Cooper and others against doing so. One issue affecting the decision of whether to file the petition was that social change litigation of the nature generally undertaken by the LDF often carried substantial risks. As described by two former LDF attorneys, "[l]itigating test cases is playing with dynamite" because even though "much good can result from a successful test case, . . . much damage can result from an unsuccessful one."[5] The risk of having the Supreme Court hear and decide *Griggs* was that the Court could affirm the Fourth Circuit's majority opinion that Title VII prohibits only intentional discrimination. If the Court adopted that interpretation of Title VII, it would result in a major setback in the LDF's efforts to make Title VII a powerful change agent for equality in the workplace. There were a number of issues that had to be considered in deciding whether to take the risk. These included, among others, how much damage would be done if the LDF lost the case in the Supreme Court, the potential for pursuing the disparate impact theory in other cases the LDF or others were litigating, and whether the interests of the plaintiffs in particular cases were consistent with the interests of others who would benefit or lose from whatever the outcome might be in the Supreme Court. Moreover, the reality of chance is an ever-present consideration. Much of what occurs in the courts is not subject to control, such as the defection of the plaintiffs or capitulation of defendants, disagreement among counsel, unanticipated precedents, and the effect of public sentiment and political currents on adjudication.[6]

Bill, Chambers, and I had several long conversations weighing the pros and cons of recommending to Greenberg that the LDF seek Supreme Court review. All of us favored filing a petition for certiorari, and one of the strongest factors in our favor was the powerful opinion by Judge Sobeloff. I flew from Charlotte, North Carolina, to the LDF's headquarters in New York for a meeting with Greenberg, at which Bill and I discussed our recommendation with him. I am sure that Greenberg had already seriously considered the pros and cons of seeking review in the Supreme Court in light of discussions he had had with others, including Al and Cooper. The meeting did not last very long, and, at the end of the meeting, Greenberg agreed to go forward with seeking review in the Supreme Court. Greenberg's reasons were that he thought "*Griggs* was a good case for appealing the testing issue" and that, even though some of our "academic advisors, the Justice Department, and the EEOC disagreed and advised against appealing the testing issue," he "thought the discriminatory impact of testing would be better understood in a case where an IQ test was being used to evaluate someone who wanted to be a coal handler than in some other kind of case." Greenberg then balanced the risk of losing in the Supreme Court against the potential payoff of winning: "If we won, the payoff could be enormous; if we lost we would be no worse off—a better case was unlikely to arise. I decided to go ahead."[7]

After Greenberg made the decision to take the case to the Supreme Court, Cooper then played a major role in drafting the plaintiffs' petition for certiorari and the plaintiffs' briefs on the merits after the Supreme Court granted certiorari. The focus of the petition for certiorari was directed toward the educational and testing policies. The question the Court was asked to review was framed in terms of whether Title VII embraced the disparate impact theory of discrimination: "[w]hether the intentional use of psychological tests and related formal educational requirements as employment criteria violate Title VII, Civil Rights Act of 1964, where: (1) the particular test and standards used exclude [African Americans] at a high rate while having a relatively minor effect in excluding whites, *and* (2) these tests and standards are not related to the employer's jobs." The plaintiffs borrowed the eloquent prose of Judge Soberoff to help frame the reasons certiorari should be granted: "'The decision we make today is likely to be as pervasive in its effect as any we have been called upon to make in recent years' . . . [because] the broad question [is] the legality of the use of allegedly objective employment tests resulting in the denial of [African Americans] for jobs for which they are potentially qualified."

The plaintiffs argued that the Court should grant review for two reasons. The first concerned the panel majority's endorsement of objective criteria that have an adverse impact on the employment opportunities of African Americans without a concomitant obligation that such criteria be job related. If that were allowed to stand, such a rule would be an open invitation for employers to engage in racial discrimination despite the qualifications of many African Americans to successfully perform the jobs at issue. The second reason was that the court of appeals' decision was in direct conflict with other circuit courts of appeals holding that facially neutral objective criteria that have an adverse effect on the employment opportunities of African Americans constitute a violation of Title VII. This second reason focused on a line of circuit court cases involving seniority discrimination and facially neutral policies challenged on constitutional grounds, such as the use of grandfather clauses for voter registration that limited the opportunities of African Americans to vote. A split in the circuits on an important legal issue is a basis on which the Court often decides whether to review a case.

The LDF filed its petition for certiorari on April 9, 1970. In its response, Duke Power did not specifically challenge the issue of whether the disparate impact theory was a viable theory of discrimination under Title VII. Rather, the company framed the issues raised by the plaintiffs as attacking the factual findings of the lower courts, which had held that the tests were "professionally developed" and that the company had a "legitimate business reason" to use the educational and test requirements to determine which individuals were qualified to perform skilled jobs. Although probably not intending to do so, Duke Power underscored the novelty and importance of the issues in the case by arguing that "[i]nsofar as [it] can determine there has been no judicial determination that the use of educational requirements constitutes an unlawful employment practice under Title VII." Duke Power also attempted to support its opposition against review by invoking the *Whitfield* case, which provided the doctrinal foundations for the *Quarles* business necessity defense. Finally, Duke Power argued that the constitutional cases on which the plaintiffs relied in support of the disparate impact theory were inapplicable in a statutory civil rights claim involving a private employer.[8]

The United Steelworkers of America, AFL-CIO, with the consent of the LDF,[9] filed an amicus brief urging the Court to grant the petition for certiorari. Duke Power refused to consent to the filing of the Steelworkers' brief, so the union had to file a motion for leave to file its brief. The Steelworkers had an interest in the case because of its long-standing efforts to eliminate the use of non-job-related tests and standards as employment criteria for advancement. The union deemed such devices as irrelevant to an employer's need for determining the competency of individuals to perform certain jobs. The Steelworkers also believed such tests unfairly weighed against those who had received inadequate or inferior education and that they were culturally biased. Characterizing the lower court decision as "dangerously wrong," the Steelworkers urged the Court to grant certiorari because "the case pose[d] an issue which, perhaps more than any other, will determine whether Title VII can succeed in according minorities employment opportunities."[10] Further, the Steelworkers argued that even though it is difficult to document instances in which employers openly condition job opportunities on factors such as race, "the same result can be achieved—whether or not so intended—by the utilization of factors neutral on their face but which are unfairly slanted against minority groups."[11] The Steelworkers, in effect, endorsed the disparate impact theory of discrimination.

The LDF's petition for certiorari was on the list of cases that Chief Justice Burger circulated to the Justices for the Court's May 22, 1970, conference. At these conferences, which are attended only by the Justices, the Court decides what action it will take on pending cases, including whether to grant or deny petitions for certiorari; votes on the merits of cases that have been argued; and makes opinion-writing assignments to particular Justices for cases that have been argued. At one point in the history of the conferences, the Chief Justice circulated a "dead list," which is a list of cases that receive no attention during the conferences. If a case is on the dead list, the Court will not grant certiorari.[12] Any Justice could remove a case from the dead list for discussion, but unless such action was taken, the petition would be denied. However, the practice had been changed to the "discuss list" by the time the litigation team filed the petition for certiorari in *Griggs*.[13] Pursuant to the discuss list procedure, any Justice could add cases to the list that he or she deemed worthy of discussion. Unlike the dead list procedure, in which every case was discussed unless it was on the list, the revised process allowed no case to be discussed unless it was placed on the special discuss list.[14]

In their best-selling and highly acclaimed and often harshly criticized book on the inner workings of the Supreme Court, *The Brethren*, Bob Woodward and Scott Armstrong stated that Chief Justice Warren Burger placed the *Griggs* petition for certiorari on the "dead list" because he thought the Fourth Circuit's compromise decision was sensible. The authors also stated that although Justice Brennan had recused himself from participating in the case because he had once represented Duke Power, he convinced Justice Stewart to take *Griggs* off the "dead list."[15] Justice Potter Stewart sent a note to Chief Justice Burger requesting that *Griggs* be placed on the discuss list.[16] Chief Justice Burger then included *Griggs* on the "special list" of cases for discussion for the conference scheduled for May 22, 1970.[17]

The Court decided at the May 22 conference to invite the Solicitor General of the United States to file a brief expressing the views of the United States on whether to grant the petition for certiorari.[18] There is no definitive public information on how many affirmative votes are needed to seek the views of the Solicitor on whether to grant or deny a petition for certiorari,[19] but when sought by the Court, the Solicitor General's decision on whether the Court should grant or deny a petition for certiorari can carry a great deal of weight in private actions in which the federal government has an interest. The Solicitor at the time was Erwin Griswold, who served in that role from 1967 to 1973 under Presidents Johnson and Nixon. While dean of the Harvard Law School, Griswold had testified as an expert witness in the LDF graduate school desegregation case of *Sipuel v. Oklahoma Board of Regents*, which challenged the denial of an African American female's application to Oklahoma's all-white law school.[20]

Griswold urged the Court to grant the petition for certiorari in *Griggs* on the ground that the issue presented for review was one of high importance "because the use of employment criteria of the kind utilized by [Duke Power] . . . is widespread in many parts of the country today . . . yet these criteria bear no relationship to employees' ability to perform the jobs for which they are used."[21] Besides noting that the court of appeals' decision had specifically rejected the EEOC guidelines on testing, the Solicitor General did not place heavy emphasis on the need for the Court to decide the degree of deference the courts should give to the EEOC's substantive interpretations of Title VII. Griswold also urged the Court to adopt the *Local 189* present effects of past discrimination theory with the accompanying business necessity defense as the correct framework of analysis under Title VII for facially neutral selection criteria that have an adverse effect on the employment opportunities of minorities.[22]

The Court granted the plaintiffs' petition for certiorari on June 29, 1970, just over a month after the Solicitor General filed his brief in support of certiorari. Justice Douglas's law clerk had framed the issue neatly in a cert memorandum: "As Judge Sobeloff argues, [the testing issue] is a question of pervasive importance if Title VII is to mean anything practical. As seems always to be the case, tests of good faith and subjective motives don't carry very far in remedying racial discrimination, while the objective approach may do some good and certainly is easier to administer."[23] Seven justices voted in favor of granting certiorari and only Chief Justice Burger, President Nixon's first Supreme Court appointee, voted against.[24]

Cooper drafted the plaintiffs' brief on the merits. The litigation team made only a few suggested changes or additions to Cooper's draft. The fundamental argument the LDF made was that facially neutral objective criteria that have an adverse effect on the employment opportunities of African Americans must be shown to be related to job performance to survive a challenge under Title VII. This argument, in a nutshell, was the argument advocating the disparate impact theory. With respect to evidence of the adverse impact of the testing requirements, the plaintiffs relied upon EEOC decisions. With respect to the adverse impact of the educational requirement, the LDF relied upon the same 1960 data from the U.S. Bureau of Census that it had relied upon in the court of appeals.[25]

The LDF urged the Court to adopt a job-relatedness standard to justify the adverse impact of facially neutral objective criteria on the employment opportunities of African Americans because

[t]he rationale of the job relatedness doctrine is clear. If a test, or education (or other objective requirement) is job related, employees are hired or promoted on the basis of their ability, which is fair. But where a test or educational requirement is not job related, hiring and promotion is done on the basis of educational and cultural background, which given the fact of schooling, housing and other factors affected by race is only thinly veiled racial discrimination.[26]

The LDF's brief was the first time the argument was made before the Supreme Court that Title VII embraces two theories of discrimination. The disparate treatment theory is supported by Section 703(a)(1) of the statute. The structure of the LDF's argument required the litigation team to harmonize several statutory provisions that make specific reference to "intent," more specifically Sections 703(h) and 706(g). To deal with this statutory construction problem, the litigation team first argued that the disparate impact theory is fully supported by 703(a)(2): "The emphasis on result rather than motive is clear in Section 703 (a)(2) [employers] and 703 (c)(2) [unions] of Title VII which define unlawful practices as those which 'tend to deprive' or 'adversely affect' because of race without reference to the employer's reasons for the practices."[27] Second, the litigation team argued that Section 706(g) authorizes courts to award injunctive relief "[i]f the court finds that the respondent has intentionally engaged in or is intentionally engaging in an unlawful practice charged in the complaint." As to how the reference to "intent" in Section 706(g) should be construed, the litigation team's argument was that "[t]he only reference to intent is in the remedial provision, Section 706(g), and its purpose is designed only to assure that employers are not subjected to injunctions for accidental events."[28]

Section 703(h), covering professionally developed ability tests, was another statutory provision that had to be dealt with in structuring the argument for the disparate impact theory. Section 703(h) provides a safe harbor for ability tests as long as they are "*not designed, intended or used*" to discriminate because of race. Here, the LDF made several arguments. The first was a straightforward textual argument, namely, that Section 703(h) on its face applies only to tests and therefore has no applicability to the educational requirements. The second, and perhaps the strongest, argument was that Duke Power's tests were not professionally developed because they failed to satisfy the EEOC's 1966 guidelines on employment testing. The guidelines adopted an interpretation of "professionally developed" to mean "a test which fairly measures the knowledge or skills required by the particular job or class of jobs which the applicant seeks, or which fairly affords the employer a chance to measure the applicant's ability to perform a particular job or class of jobs."[29] This argument was bolstered by the fact that Duke Power had admitted that it had not undertaken any study or investigation to determine whether its tests were job related.

Third, as a fallback argument in the event the Court rejected the disparate impact theory, the litigation team argued that to the extent proof of intent is the only theory of liability under Title VII, the totality of the circumstances under which Duke Power adopted the tests provided a strong inference of discriminatory intent. The evidence showed that Duke Power had adopted the test requirement only shortly after it had abandoned its practice of overtly discriminating against African Americans; that this happened very shortly after Title VII became effective; and that the testing policy, which was an alternative for advancement for those employees without a high school education, was adopted only in response to pressure from white employees who did not have a high school education even though the plaintiffs had also made a similar request. Further, the litigation team argued that whatever intent Duke Power had in adopting the tests, they were in fact used to discriminate against the plaintiffs because whites in the inside departments without a high school education were permitted to advance to higher-paying jobs without taking the tests or obtaining a high school education.

Finally, the LDF's brief also had to address the legislative history on the professionally developed statutory provision in Section 703(h)—the Tower Amendment—which was included as a result of the rather contentious congressional debate in light of the *Motorola* hearing officer's decision from Illinois striking down the use of a test on the grounds that it was culturally biased against African Americans. Congressional sponsors of Title VII objected to Senator Tower's original proposal to address the *Motorola* issue on the grounds that it was so loosely worded that it would permit employers to use any professionally designed test, even if it had a discriminatory effect. Senator Tower withdrew his original amendment and subsequently introduced a much abbreviated, watered-down version, which became Section 703(h) because the sponsors of Title VII found it to be in accordance with the intent and purpose of the act. Based on this legislative history, the LDF argued that the provision was designed to do nothing more than to clarify the basic mandate of Title VII.[30]

The EEOC withdrew its original 1966 guidelines on testing after *Griggs* had been argued in the court of appeals and issued new revised testing guidelines effective August 1, 1970.[31] The 1970 guidelines broadly defined a covered "test" to include not only pen-and-paper tests, but "any performance measure used as a basis for any employment decision" designed to measure eligibility for hire, transfer, promotion, training, or retention. The revised definition of a "test" included, for example, measures of general intelligence, mental ability and learning ability, formally scored, quantified or standardized, scored interviews, and scored application forms. In the section defining discrimination, the 1970 guidelines adopted the position that any test that adversely affects hiring, promotion, transfer, or any other employment or membership opportunity is a violation of Title VII unless it has been validated and that employers giving or acting upon the result of a test prove that alternative employee selection procedures are unavailable. The LDF also relied upon these revised testing guidelines in support of its argument that employment practices having an adverse impact on African Americans must be job related.[32]

The Solicitor General informed the Court that the federal government agreed with the LDF's basic argument that the "rights created by Congress when it enacted Title VII of the Civil Rights Act of 1964 may no more be frustrated by apparently neutral employment practices, not justified by business necessity, which have racially exclusionary effects than by overtly discriminatory practices."[33] The Solicitor General also grounded its argument in support of the disparate impact theory solely on Sections 703(a)(2) and 703(h) but made no argument distinguishing between the theory of discrimination under Sections 703(a)(1) and 703(a)(2) and made a much stronger argument than did the LDF in urging the Court to give great deference to the EEOC guidelines on testing. Relying on a fairly detailed examination of the legislative history of Section 703(h) and the Tower Amendment, the Solicitor General argued that Section 703(h) does not provide a safe harbor for tests unless those tests are shown to be job related.[34]

Two additional amicus briefs were filed in support of the LDF, one by the United Steelworkers of America and one by the State of New York. The LDF consented to the filing of the amicus briefs, but, as with the Steelworkers' amicus brief on certiorari, Duke Power withheld its consent. Agreeing with what it deemed to be solid grounds for reversal set out in the LDF's brief, the Steelworkers deemed it important to bring to the Court's attention what thirty-four years of representation in the metal industries had taught the

Steelworkers, namely, that "unless [the] Court strikes down non-job-related tests and standards, the unhappy plight of minority employees in American industry cannot end."[35] The amicus brief filed on behalf of the State of New York by Louis J. Lefkowitz, its Attorney General, urged the Court to reverse the court of appeals decision because it posed a challenge to the potency and effectiveness of New York's fair employment laws, which were quite similar to Title VII, and that New York had sought to eliminate hiring, promotion, and union admission standards that had a disparate impact on minorities when those standards were not job related.[36]

Duke Power made a number of arguments in its response to the LDF's main brief. The first was that the educational requirement was adopted in good faith to serve a legitimate business purpose and that the testing requirements constituted a reasonably satisfactory substitute for the high school education requirement. The second argument was that the tests were professionally developed within the meaning of Section 703(h) and fell within the safe-harbor protection of that section because they were not administered, scored, designed, intended, or used to discriminate because of race. The third argument was that the Supreme Court should defer to the findings of the lower courts because the plaintiffs had failed to introduce any evidence that Duke Power had intentionally discriminated against its African American employees in the adoption of educational and testing requirements. A major argument Duke Power made throughout its brief was that the factual findings of Judge Gordon were not clearly erroneous and that substantial deference should be accorded to those findings in this case, particularly since the case involved an element of intent. Another argument Duke Power made throughout its brief was that the legislative history of Title VII made clear that an employer has an unqualified right to determine job qualifications and to make employment decisions based on those qualifications.[37]

Duke Power's response to the LDF's argument that Section 703(a)(2) supports the disparate impact theory of discrimination was that it

> does not agree that the employer's intent under Sections 703(a)(2) and 703(c)(2) is immaterial, but even if it is assumed *arguendo* that is correct with respect to those sections, it is obviously erroneous with respect to section 703(h).... The fact that Sections 703(c)(2) and 703(a)(2) *may* be susceptible of an interpretation that Congress intended to emphasize *result rather than motive* is not determinative as to 703(h) because the plain language of 703(h) removes it from concomitant consideration with any other section of the title and makes it an island unto

itself. . . . The crucial inquiry is whether the employer "designed, intended, or used" such test to discriminate on the basis of race, color, etc. To hold an employer liable for giving and acting upon the results of such tests, the claimant must at the very least adduce some evidence which shows, either directly or inferentially, that the employer "designed, intended, or used" the tests to discriminate on the basis of race, color, etc. This record contains no such evidence.[38]

Like the LDF and the Solicitor General, Duke Power placed heavy emphasis on the legislative history of Section 703(h), the Tower Amendment, in support of its argument that educational and testing requirements that have an adverse impact on African Americans can survive a Title VII challenge without the need for an employer to prove that these devices are job related. Duke Power construed the legislative history of 703(h) as permissive for employers to insist on job-related tests but said that nowhere in that history did there appear a requirement that employers use only those tests that are job related. If, Duke Power argued, the Supreme Court were to accept the arguments of the LDF and the Solicitor General that Title VII bars employers from using tests that have an adverse impact on African Americans if the tests are not job related, then doing so would unleash "unbridled authority in a Federal Commission to meddle in and eventually control the relationship of private employers and their employees."[39] The bottom line in Duke Power's argument was that Congress intended to adopt only the disparate treatment theory of discrimination and that an employer could use any employment criteria, even if not job related, unless a plaintiff proved that the criteria had been selected, used, or intended to limit the employment opportunities of African Americans because of their race.

The U.S. Chamber of Commerce, with the consent of the LDF and Duke Power, filed an amicus brief urging the Supreme Court to affirm the court of appeals. The concern of the Chamber of Commerce was that endorsement of the disparate impact theory by the Court would have "substantial and far-reaching consequences on American industry" in that "tests and educational requirements constitute the only objective means available to employers to perform the necessary task of selecting among applicants or employees on the basis of individual merit when previous experience is not relevant or available in quantified form."[40] To substantiate its concern, the Chamber of Commerce informed the Court that 55 percent of all companies in the United States employing more than 1,600 employees used the Wonderlic Test and that over 20 percent used the Bennett Mechanical Comprehension Test. It also urged the

Court not to give any deference to the EEOC guidelines on testing because the agency had completely disregarded discriminatory intent as a crucial finding in the enforcement of Title VII. The Chamber also advanced an argument that eventually bore fruit in later Supreme Court disparate impact cases when it claimed that "[w]hile test validation is a desirable objective, it is often an elusive one because of the prohibitive expense and difficulty involved, particularly in view of the infant state of the art of industrial psychology in securing an adequate and representative sample."[41] Rather, the Chamber urged the Court to defer to the judgment of testing specialists on whether a test is professionally developed. In its argument, the Chamber asserted that the EEOC construed Title VII "as broadly as possible in order to maximize the effect of the statute on employment discrimination without going back to Congress for more substantive legislation," departed from previous notions of discrimination in doing so, and went beyond other agencies' readings of the law, disregarding intent "as crucial to the finding of an unlawful employment practice."[42]

The Court denied the motion of the Solicitor General to participate in the oral argument[43] but granted Duke Power's motion to allow the Chamber of Commerce to participate in the oral argument. The Court heard argument in *Griggs* on December 14, 1970. Greenberg argued on behalf of the plaintiffs. Greenberg emphasized several important points at the beginning of his opening argument. First, he made clear that the plaintiffs were asking the Court to recognize the disparate impact theory and that theory was supported by the mandate in Section 703(a)(2) of Title VII, which makes it unlawful for an employer "to limit, segregate, or classify his employees . . . in any way which deprives or tends to deprive any individual of any employment opportunity, or otherwise affects his status as an employee because of" race or other forbidden reasons. Second, before making his affirmative argument, Greenberg advised the Court that he wanted to make crystal clear that the LDF's position was that the business necessity or job-related defense of the disparate impact theory would not require employers to hire or promote unqualified African Americans: "No employer, we submit, under the statute is required to employ anyone who is unable to do the job and any employer may use test and educational requirements which predict whether an employee . . . can do the job." But Greenberg emphatically argued that

> if the test is used or the educational requirement that is used screens out members
> of a race or of a group protected by the statute and does not predict who can do

the job, otherwise does not have predictive validity as the industrial psychologist used the term, and as this record uses the term, then it cannot be justified merely on good faith because good faith or intent . . . is an illusive concept which is regularly and frequently advanced in civil rights cases.[44]

Much of the colloquy between the Supreme Court and Greenberg during his opening argument focused on clarification of factual matters in the record; it was only near the end of his argument that the conversation turned to the heart of the case.

> Chief Justice Burger: Would it be a violation of the Act if an employer had a general policy that he would not hire anyone in any capacity if they did not meet certain potential promotability qualifications?
>
> Greenberg: That would not be a violation of the Act if he could demonstrate that kind of capacity to be promotable is necessary to do the job and necessary for the operation of his plant. Then it might not be a violation either if it did not disproportionally screen out members of a protected race or national group.
>
> Chief Justice Burger: That's the key to your case.
>
> Greenberg: That's the key.
>
> Chief Justice Burger: The impact of any test screens out one particular category whether it happens to be women or Negroes or Orientals or whatever. Then it is at least suspect.
>
> Greenberg: Then it must be justified in terms of some sort of validation of its [ability to predict ability to do the jobs].
>
> Chief Justice Burger: Let's say a power plant in the State of Maine on the assumption that there would be an almost all-white population there. The power plant in the State of Maine had a high school or other aptitude test that was directed to promotability and did not have any adverse impact on any particular racial group or national origin group.
>
> Greenberg: Then . . . I would suggest that they might be depriving themselves of people who could otherwise do the job very well, but that would not be the problem.
>
> Chief Justice Burger: No violation problem.

During Ferguson's argument for Duke Power, the Court focused on the safe-harbor defense in Section 703(h) and the Tower Amendment. The Chief Justice stated, "There is a claim that the test is inherently an unfair test, so far as Negroes are concerned," and then asked whether he understood the claim correctly. Ferguson responded, "They claim the tests as to Negroes are unfair because they are culturally deprived and therefore placed at a competitive disadvantage."

Chief Justice Burger: And what they are asking is that you tailor a new test that will be directed at the particular job ahead.

Ferguson: Yes sir, I would respectfully submit to you that the legislative history of the Act clearly shows that general intelligence and aptitude tests that Congress intended they should be used. And I point specifically to Senator Tower's amendment. . . . Senator Tower's original amendment stated: "It is an effort to protect the system whereby employers give general ability and intelligence tests to determine the trainability of employees."

I would point out even more particularly to you . . . the [Senator] Clark-[Senator] Case interpretive memorandum prepared by the Justice Department which states this. There is no requirement in Title VII that employers abandon bona fide qualification tests where because of differences and background and education, members of some groups are able to perform better on these tests than members of other groups. An employer may set his qualifications as high as he likes.

Justice Stewart: Well nothing that I heard you read would say that the tests could be non-job related. Said they can be as high as he likes.

Ferguson: Yes sir.

Justice Stewart: Question: But it doesn't say they can be wholly irrelevant to the job that he is hiring employees to fill.

Ferguson: Well may I answer that this way? The Bennett and the Wonderlic are, of course, professionally developed tests. That alone we realize is not enough. The courts below found that we had a genuine business purpose in adopting a high school education requirement or they found that the tests were a reasonably satisfactory substitute for the high school education requirement. Now if we assume that the tests are professionally developed ability tests and that Congress intended to allow the use of general aptitude and ability tests then and in that event the crucial inquiry becomes this. Are the tests designed, used or intended to discriminate? [T]he two tests in question here were designed by professional psychologists. . . . What about the intent? Well once the employer establishes a legitimate business purpose for employment practice, testing or otherwise, then that practice is nondiscriminatory even if it operates to prefer whites over blacks.

Justice Stewart: That statutory word used is kind of a slippery and ambiguous word in this context. It could be read couldn't it, and as I gather how your brothers and the other side read it and if their use results in discrimination then they are used to discriminate and on the other hand it could be read as if they . . . are not subjectively used for purposes of discrimination then they are all right. I simply suggest that that's not the clearest words in the world in this context.

Lawrence M. Cohen, with the law firm of Lederer, Fox & Grove of Chicago, Illinois, presented the argument on behalf of the U.S. Chamber of Commerce. Chief Justice Burger engaged Cohen in the following colloquy that focused on the most important issues in the case:

Chief Justice Burger: Mr. Cohen let me put this question to you if I can. Assume an area of the country where, I suppose in the Southwest, there are people whose primary language is Spanish and have a rather limited comprehension of English. Suppose an employer provided for farm workers that they must pass the test something like a literacy test in English. On the face of that it would be a rational request generally from employers. I am sure it's impact in the Southwest in that particular area for the farm workers might have no relationship at all to the job, might or might not. Wouldn't that bring it under the act if the impact was there?

Cohen: I think that this is really the heart of this case. Most educational tests today unfortunately or aptitude tests have a discriminatory impact on one or more racial groups. This is the problem of the social economic status of these groups is historically involved. . . . When Congress enacted Title VII it knew that educational requirements and tests had a potential discrimination of the type you have just referred to. It didn't outlaw the use of tests, it didn't prohibit the use of educational requirements. It tried to reach a compromise where employers could use such tests and use such educational requirements as long as they were not a pretext or a subterfuge use for discrimination.

Chief Justice Burger: Does it go that far that it must be subterfuge, or is it on the impact?

Cohen: It is whether on the basis of the evidence of the case did the employer use or intend that the test be discriminatory. That is the words, for example, in 703(h). Our fear here really is that if a business necessity test is adopted of the type that petitioners have urged in this Court the result will be that employers won't be able to use any objective tests.[45]

Cohen later made one of the most telling concessions made in the argument: "The trouble is that educational requirements or tests never can be shown to be essential so . . . the employer must fall back and use something other than objective criteria, because under the EEOC's definition of a test, any objective means of selecting employees is considered a test."

Chief Justice Burger then revisited the hypothetical case of the employers in the Southwest requiring a command of the English language for fruit pickers and farmworkers:

Chief Justice Burger: Let me be sure I understand your response to my hypothetical question. If the fruit pickers and farm workers down in the Southwest have this English language test you would regard that as not very job related?

Cohen: No, my feeling is that you could never prove that that was a business necessity for that task, nor was it job related in a sense that the employees had to have that skill in order to perform the job. It probably would not, if it had not as

> I understand the petitioners' position, if it had not been validated which includes job relatedness under the EEOC's guidelines the employer could not use it.

The concession by Cohen in answer to Chief Justice Burger's hypothetical bodes well for the possibility of a favorable decision for the plaintiff.

The exchange between Chief Justice Burger and Cohen provided the opportunity for Greenberg, in rebuttal, to focus the Court's attention on the fact that the evidence was undisputed that Duke Power had made no effort whatsoever to validate its testing and educational requirements, that is, that it had put on no evidence that the requirements were job related. To underscore his response, Greenberg called the attention of the Court to the testimony of Dr. Moffie for Duke Power and summarized it:

> A high school education would merely tell you that you have the necessary abilities as defined by a high school education and if the company *feels* that this is required in those jobs that is all it tells you. That's what the company and [its] amici are saying, if the company *feels* that you ought to have these qualifications then the company ought to have the right to do it.

Greenberg then tied this argument back into the theory of discrimination—disparate impact—that the LDF was asking the Court to embrace as a correct interpretation of Section 703(a)(2).

The Court held a conference on December 18, 1970, four days after oral argument, at which it discussed a possible decision in the case. The handwritten conference notes of Justice Douglas offer one insider's account of how each Justice voted at the conference and the influence of Judge Sobeloff's decision on the outcome in the case:

> Burger: This case involves the use of intelligence tests for transfers from one department to another. The impact is severe on Negroes. This case is difficult and close. I hesitate to affirm, but it is a small plant with little turnover. Tests and standards must be related to the job. If there was no history of past discrimination, I would have no problems. The arbitrary requirement of a high school diploma has a severe impact. I can affirm if Sobeloff's standards were accepted.
>
> Black: It is a new act. There are difficulties in complying with it. This company was doing its best to comply with it. I am inclined to affirm. [Sobeloff's] standards do not suit me, as that is a legislative function.
>
> Douglas: I would reverse and remand. The employer has the burden of showing that these tests were job related.
>
> Harlan: [I] agree with [Bill Douglas]. [These] tests must be job related. Administrative practice points that up. [It] is very difficult to affirm. Reversal is

not on the Constitution, but on the act. Sobeloff's view of the act is right. I would reverse and remand the tests must be job related.

Stewart: [I] agree with [Bill Douglas] and [John Harlan]. [I] would reverse. [I] cannot affirm.

White: [I] reverse. Does job relatedness refer to a particular job or a future job? [The] tests were not job related in either sense. Promotion was from inside the company [they] can screen out people who never would get beyond one job.

Marshall: Not everyone employed need be qualified for higher jobs. I stay with the U.S. position, not with Sobeloff—[I would] reverse.

Blackmun: [I am] inclined to reverse. [The] legislative history favors Duke. [I] agree with Byron [White] on the difficulties of the case. [An] employer has the right to hire only those promotable employees people like to work up through the ranks. [I] would not restrict the employer to only a present job.

Burger: An employer has a right to test for more than a particular job. [I am] flexible, and can do the job by reversal or affirmance.[46]

There were clearly six votes to reverse the court of appeals—Justices Douglas, Harlan, Stewart, White, Marshall, and Blackmun. These six favored a definitive reversal, finding a basis in Title VII for the holding that all employment testing must be narrowly job related. Given that the employers could easily use testing schemes in a discriminatory fashion, the six Justices who favored reversal saw this outcome as the only result that would square with the overarching and antidiscriminatory mandate of Title VII. It seems apparent from Justice Douglas's notes that the Court, except possibly Justice Black, had no difficulty in agreeing with the LDF's argument that the disparate impact theory is a theory of discrimination under Title VII. It also is clear from Justice Douglas's notes that the Court accepted the fact that there was sufficient evidence in the record to demonstrate the "severe impact" of both the test and the high school education requirements on the African American plaintiffs. The major focus of the conference discussion was Judge Sobeloff's construction of Section 706(h): the testing and the high school diploma requirements had to be job related. Justice White raised an issue that was neither briefed by the parties nor specifically addressed in *Griggs* itself, namely, whether an employer may test applicants or employees at the entry-level position to determine their possibility for promotion to higher levels of jobs. The Court did not address this issue in *Griggs*, but it did address this question in the next major disparate impact case, *Albemarle Paper Co. v. Moody.*

The papers of Justice Harry Blackmun provide additional insights on the outcome of *Griggs* in the Supreme Court. Pursuant to his long-standing practice as a federal judge, including his term on the Supreme Court, Justice Blackmun, shortly before the oral argument, would review the briefs submitted by the parties and any memos prepared by his law clerks. He would then dictate a memo to himself summarizing the arguments and setting out his responses.[47] His preargument memo in *Griggs* began by noting that "[h]ere again is one of those sensitive cases where procedures which seem innocuous and neutral on their face, and which have been employed in the past without challenge, are now subjected to litigation and are claimed to be illegal."[48] He stated that initially he was persuaded that the Fourth Circuit's analysis of the history of the legislative debate about the Tower Amendment was "correct," namely, that congressional intent was to permit employers to use professionally developed tests even if they were not job related. However, Justice Blackmun expressed some uncertainty about his first impression about the court of appeals being correct in its interpretation of the legislative history in light of the fact that the "EEOC itself construes the legislative history as do the petitioners here . . . that ability tests must have some relation to the job in order to come within the blessing of the statute." Recognizing that the legislative history is not "without meaning or assistance," he expressed doubt about whether it was "conclusive" as to the proper interpretation of whether a test must be job related to fall within the meaning of professionally developed.

Justice Blackmun wrote that the issue of the proper interpretation of the meaning of "professionally developed" was not an "easy issue" for him. On the one hand, he noted that the phrase could be construed literally to uphold any test that is prepared by a professional or, on the other hand, "less literally, to wit, [it could include] the added requirement that the test, although 'professionally developed' must be job-related." In resolving this major interpretive issue, Justice Blackman in the final analysis "lean[ed] at [that] moment toward reversal" because he "would not be intellectually offended in any way if the statute was construed to mean job related." However, he was concerned about preserving the right of any employer to upgrade his employee staff as much as he can but recognized that Title VII "puts the brakes on this ambition up to a point." An example he used to illustrate the "brakes" Title VII puts on an employer was the situation in which an employer requires an applicant for a janitor's job to be a college graduate.

Justice Blackmun's conference notes affirm much of what is in Justice Douglas's notes but add a couple of additional insights. His notes indicate that a majority of the Justices were in favor of reversing the court of appeals.[49] The views of the Justices, according to Justice Blackmun's notes, were as follows: Chief Justice Burger indicated that he would be "uneasy on affirming" but "could go for a job related test but to call [for] allowing room too" and "could affirm if standards were stated along Sobeloff's route"; he seemed to deem the case "not too important."[50] Justice Black was "inclined to affirm" because Title VII was a "new act," and "the company was doing its best to comply" so a "competency test [was] needed," but he also indicated he might be willing to "reverse and remand" and that the Court should "decide only what [the Court] had to decide." Justice Douglas voted to reverse because he thought "Judge Sobeloff had the right approach," that the employer has the burden of proof,[51] and he would "remand for appropriate finding." Justice Harlan "agreed with [Justice] Douglas" to reverse and further stated that he "place[d] much emphasis on an administrative interpretation [of the EEOC] which is [in favor of] job relationship" and that he believed the "legislative history [is] not too clear." Justice Stewart also voted to reverse because he agreed "with Justices Douglas and Harlan." Justice White voted for reversal, but he said it was a "difficult question as to what 'job related' means' or 'promotable jobs' means," but he was unwilling to go "so far as to require tests only for specific job for [illegible] hirees." It is unclear from Justice Blackmun's conference notes how Justice Marshall voted. His notes indicate an "X" for affirmance with no name so it is difficult to tell whether the "X" represents himself or Justice Marshall. But at the end of the conference there were clearly six votes to reverse the court of appeals decision. It was also clear that Judge Sobeloff's dissenting opinion played a substantial role in the votes to reverse. Chief Justice Burger had made specific reference to Judge Sobeloff as agreeing with the LDF's argument in his first draft of his opinion for the Court, but specific identification of Judge Sobeloff was omitted in the published opinion.[52]

Only Justice Black was inclined to affirm the Fourth Circuit. Justice Douglas's notes indicate that only Justice Black was inclined at the conference to affirm the court of appeals, and the docket sheet for the conference, maintained by Justice Brennan, also shows that only Justice Black voted to affirm.[53] Chief Justice Burger appeared undecided. The Chief Justice always votes first at the conferences and is then followed by the other Justices based on seniority on the Court. After the apparent 6–2 split for reversal had been revealed, Chief Justice Burger spoke again, this time defending the use of general employment tests but again equivocating as to whether he stood with the six or the minority position. The Supreme Court's traditional practice is to allow the most senior Justice in the majority to assign the writing of the opinion, and Burger by the final remark positioned himself as prospectively aligned with the majority and thus was able to reserve to himself the writing of the opinion in *Griggs,* a posture far more conducive to his shaping of the final result than the alternative of writing for himself and Justice Black in dissent.

Any uncertainty about the final outcome in *Griggs* was resolved when all of the Justices agreed to join Chief Justice Burger's first draft of the opinion to reverse the court of appeals with only a few changes suggested by some of the Justices. He circulated a first draft of the opinion on January 26, 1971, just over a month after oral argument and the conference vote.[54] A Justice indicates agreement with a proposed draft opinion by sending an unqualified letter to the author to "please join me," which really means, "I join you." The "please join me" letter means the Justice agrees to the draft as written. Justices White and Marshall sent "please join me" letters to Chief Justice Burger with no suggestions or comments.[55] Justice Stewart expressed his general agreement with Chief Justice Burger's first draft but expressed concern about a section that would permit employers to administer a test at the hiring stage to determine the eligibility of new hires for promotions to higher-level jobs in the future.[56] The issue of whether an employer may, consistent with Title VII, test for the capability of applicants to be able to perform jobs at a high level had come up as a question from the Court in oral argument in Greenberg's rebuttal argument. Greenberg's response was that Title VII would probably permit an employer to do so if there was proof of rapid and frequent promotions, but not in a situation like Duke Power's where the employer's workforce was fairly stable.[57]

The specific paragraphs of Chief Justice Burger's draft that caused concern for Justice Stewart were these:

> To comply with Title VII employment tests or practices must be job-related in terms of measuring capability to perform the particular job, not broadly aimed at providing work for men with high educational credentials.
>
> This does not preclude, of course, testing requirements that take into account capability for the next succeeding position or immediately related future promotions, so long as such long range requirements fulfill a genuine business need to fill the higher position.
>
> In the present case the Company made no such showing. Nor has it been shown that the high school completion or test requirement is a valid measure of a person's ability to perform in the higher positions.[58]

Justice Stewart's concern was that the last two paragraphs were based on the reality that not everyone can be promoted but that "[i]f an employer is allowed to refuse to hire a job applicant because the applicant cannot pass a test for a better or higher job, the employer [would] be able, if he wishes, to discriminate against applicants who are fully qualified for the jobs for which they apply." He asked Chief Justice Burger to consider eliminating the last two quoted paragraphs because he thought they were not necessary in deciding the case. Chief Justice Burger accepted Justice Stewart's suggestion and revised those two paragraphs in the final opinion by noting that it was not necessary for the Court to reach that issue in *Griggs* but that, in any event, Duke Power had not put on any evidence that its tests were used to determine future promotability.[59] (The Court did, however, address this precise question in *Albemarle Paper Co. v. Moody.*)

Justice Harlan indicated his willingness to join the opinion but made two suggestions, which Chief Justice Burger accepted. The first was to change the disposition of the case in order to distinguish clearly between the plaintiffs who had received relief in the appellate court—those hired before 1955—and those who had been hired after 1955. Justice Harlan wanted the disposition to make clear that the decision would apply to only those four plaintiffs hired after 1955 because it was only the claims of these four plaintiffs that were before the Court. Justice Harlan's second suggestion was that Chief Justice Burger had insufficiently treated the legislative history of the Tower Amendment on which the court of appeals had relied: "I would think that this legislative history should be faced up to, although I think it is adequately answered by reliance on the EEOC guidelines to which you have already referred in your opinion. In other words, what I am suggesting is that the discussion of the legislative history might be specifically correlated with what you have already said about the EEOC guidelines."[60]

There was some concern in Justice Blackmun's chambers that certain language in Chief Justice Burger's draft would limit an otherwise broader interpretation of Title VII. This concern was called to the attention of Justice Blackman by one of his law clerks in a January 26, 1971, memorandum.[61] The clerk pointed out that although "the CJ holds that Title VII requires demonstration of job-relatedness of tests and diploma requirements where the requirements unequally exclude blacks from employment opportunities," the way Chief Justice Burger framed the question would permit "a narrower reading, limiting the holding to cases of prior intentional discriminatory practices." The Chief Justice had framed the question to be decided as whether Title VII prohibits the use of diploma and test requirements as a condition of employment in or transfer to jobs (a) when neither standard is shown to be significantly related to successful job performance, (b) both requirements operate to disqualify Negroes at a substantially higher rate than white applicants, and (c) the jobs in question formerly had been filled only by white employees as part of a long-standing practice of giving preference to whites. The law clerk's memorandum pointed out that including subsection (c) in the question gave the incorrect impression that the Court's holding did not apply in the absence of that condition or comparable past purposeful discrimination. The clerk's memorandum further pointed out that subsection (c) was magnified by language in the draft, which stated:

> The objective of Congress in the enactment of Title VII . . . was to achieve equality of opportunities and remove barriers that have operated in the past to favor an identifiable group of white employees over other employees. . . . Under the Act, practices, procedures or tests neutral on the face, and even neutral in terms of intent, cannot be maintained if they operate to "freeze" the status quo of prior discriminatory employment practices.[62]

This language, the clerk pointed out, seemed to suggest that in the absence of prior intentional discriminatory employment practices, a selection criterion that is neutral on its face and neutral in terms of intent is legal. He suggested that the draft of the opinion should be clarified so that it was clear that subsection (c) and the above-quoted language did not leave open the possibility of the narrower reading. It appears that Justice Blackmun did not ask Chief Justice Burger to clarify the concerns raised by his law clerk, and the published opinion retained the issue with subsection (c) and the above-quoted language.

Chief Justice Burger circulated a revised draft of his opinion on February 5, 1971, and advised the other Justices that the new draft took into account some of the problems some of the other Justices had raised with respect to the first draft. In addition to noting that the legality of entry-level testing for future promotability was an open question, the second draft added two footnotes in response to Justice Harlan's concern of the need to shore up the argument that the legislative history of Section 703(h) supports the Court's decision that tests must be job related.[63] Chief Justice Burger had used the term "denigrating" in his drafts but deleted it in the final opinion at the suggestion of Justice

Blackmun, who said that the origins of that word "just might be offensive in some quarters."[64]

The Court handed down a unanimous 8–0 decision in *Griggs* on March 8, 1971, reversing the decision of the court of appeals. The decision in *Griggs*, like that in *Brown v. Board of Education*, was very short, covering only thirteen pages in the official Supreme Court reports; *Brown I* covered fourteen pages and only a very few case citations. *Griggs* generated a vast amount of news coverage, but not at the same level as had *Brown*. The Court agreed with the LDF's argument that Title VII endorses the disparate impact theory when it held that "[t]he Act proscribes not only overt discrimination but also practices that are fair in form, but discriminatory in operation. The touchstone is business necessity. If an employment practice which operates to exclude [African Americans] cannot be shown to be related to job performance, the practice is prohibited."[65] The Court accepted the factual finding of the district court that the plaintiffs introduced no evidence at trial to show that Duke Power had intentionally adopted the educational and testing employment criteria to discriminate against African Americans. However, the Court held that such proof was unnecessary under Section 703(a)(2) because "Congress directed the thrust of the Act to the *consequences* of employment practices not simply the motivation."[66] The Court held that the touchstone was business necessity, adopting the precise characterization that the LDF outlined in its brief.[67] The Court also relied upon the "freezing principle"[68] that underlay the present effects of past discrimination theory that Judge Butzner had first adopted in the LDF seniority case of *Quarles v. Philip Morris*, even though the Court did not cite *Quarles*. The Court did not categorically state that the disparate impact theory was based on an interpretation of Section 703(a)(2) until eleven years after *Griggs*, when it decided *Connecticut v. Teal*.

There was no direct evidence of statistical data in *Griggs* on the adverse impact of the testing and educational requirements on African Americans. However, the LDF argued in its brief, and the Court agreed, that the adverse effects of these employment standards could be determined by relying, in part, on studies of the same tests conducted in other places. Since the tests used by Duke Power were the same as those used in previously reported EEOC decisions the LDF relied upon in its brief,[69] the Court was willing to accept statistical findings in those other decisions. At the LDF's urging, the Court also considered data from the State of North Carolina in assessing the high school education requirement. The 1960 census showed whites were approximately three times as likely as African Americans to have a high school education. While there was no specific evidence that these statewide data or the data from other EEOC decisions reflected the relevant labor market population at Duke Power, the data were nonetheless indicative of adverse racial impact to be relied upon. The Court agreed with this argument by the LDF. Finally, the Court supported its finding of adverse impact, as the LDF had urged,[70] by relying on nonstatistical information, observing that the inferior segregated education of African Americans inevitably had an adverse impact on their ability to perform well in testing procedures.

Once the Supreme Court had established the doctrinal foundations for the disparate impact theory, it then construed Section 703(h) as imposing upon the defendants the burden to prove the job related/business necessity defense. There was no dispute about the fact that both the test and the educational requirements had been adopted without meaningful study of their relationship to job performance ability, and the evidence showed that white employees who had not completed high school or taken the tests were allowed to progress to higher-paying jobs for which the educational and testing requirements were imposed.[71]

The Court later endorsed its findings on educational differences in *Griggs* in its seminal disparate treatment case, *McDonnell Douglas v. Green,* in which the LDF had a substantial role in writing the Supreme Court brief on behalf of the respondent, Percy Green. In that case, the Court observed that "*Griggs* was rightly concerned that the childhood deficiencies in the education and background of minority citizens, resulting from forces beyond their control, not be allowed to work a cumulative and invidious burden on such citizens for the remainder of their lives."[72] Even before Congress codified the disparate impact theory in the Civil Rights Act of 1991, legislative history indicated that *Griggs* had an influence on the thinking of some in Congress about the broader question of what is unlawful discrimination. For example, a 1971 Senate report concluded that

> employment discrimination as viewed today is a far more complex and pervasive phenomenon. Experts familiar with the subject now generally describe the problem in terms of "systems" and "effects" rather than simply intentional wrongs, and the literature on the subject is replete with discussions of, for example, the mechanics of seniority and lines of progression, perpetuation of the present effect of pre-act discriminatory practices through various institutional devices, and testing and validation requirements.[73]

A question that has intrigued many is what motivated Chief Justice Burger, who was widely viewed as a conservative, to author such a landmark civil rights decision.[74] One explanation is that Burger saw himself as a judicial moderate, but the press had labeled him as a judicial conservative and compared him unfavorably with his predecessor, Chief Justice Earl Warren, who was the author of the unanimous opinion in *Brown v. Board of Education.* Some argue that Chief Justice Burger decided that one way to counter this unfavorable comparison was to vote with the liberal wing of the Court on civil rights cases and to author some liberal opinions. Doing so, he thought, would confuse his liberal detractors in the press. *Griggs* is deemed to be one of his liberal opinions.[75] Another suggestion is that Chief Justice Burger's attempt to lead the Court often forced him to moderate his conservative views.[76] Steve Ralston, a career LDF staff attorney since 1964, has expressed an opinion on this question that is shared by some others: "We always suspected Chief Justice Burger really had no idea at all what he was doing when he wrote *Griggs.*" Similarly, Professor Charles Craver of George Washington University National Law Center stated: "I don't think Chief Justice Burger fully appreciated what he was holding in *Griggs* . . . a totally separate proof structure, the far-reaching ramifications of disparate impact. . . . And I don't think Congress in 1964 was sure it was creating that approach. *Griggs* changed everything."[77] Judge Sobeloff later noted in a letter to an attorney in North Carolina that "the unanimous opinion of the Supreme Court [in *Griggs*] was very gratifying."[78]

10. The Maturation of the *Griggs* Theory

Much work remained to be done after the Supreme Court's decision in *Griggs* to establish the legal edifice that made the disparate impact theory a revolutionary theory of equality. The LDF's post-*Griggs* strategies focused more closely on two interrelated and overlapping priorities. The first strategy was to flesh out questions either left unanswered by or not raised specifically in *Griggs,* namely, whether the disparate impact theory applies to subjective criteria, the allocation of the evidentiary burdens on the parties, the use of statistical evidence to prove unlawful discrimination, and the substance of the business necessity test. The second strategy focused on the relief courts should award to remedy unlawful employment discrimination. It was impossible to pursue these two strategies in a sequential order, similar to what was done in the *Brown* litigation to control the sequence in which the law develops, because, by the time the Supreme Court decided *Griggs,* there was a substantial increase in the litigation of employment discrimination by others who had their own agendas and priorities. Thus, the order of discussion of the coverage of the issues in this chapter and in chapter 11 is an attempt to provide some coherence to the developments of the legal edifice built on *Griggs.* The subject of this chapter is the first strategy, and the subject of chapter 11 is the second strategy.

Before focusing more specifically on these two litigation strategies, it should be noted that *Griggs* had an immediate impact on the employment testing business. One of the immediate effects of *Griggs* was to "throw job testing into a state of confusion."[1] Psychological Services, Inc., one of the earliest pioneers in the publication of employment tests, "lost half of its business when *Griggs* came out."[2] Within a year after *Griggs,* the American Management Association, a global not-for-profit membership-based organization that provides management development and educational services to employers, published a book providing a nontheoretical approach to selecting and using employment tests.[3] Since *Griggs,* the literature on employment tests and test validation strategies has expanded substantially.

A limited study of the impact of *Griggs*—the Petersen study, which was published a few years after the Supreme Court's ruling—investigated three issues: (1) whether employers would discontinue the use of tests rather than validate them; (2) the degree of effort employers might make in validating tests, who would do the validations, what techniques would be employed to validate, and the potential scope of employee testing validation studies; and (3) what future impact *Griggs* might have on selection procedures.[4] The study concluded that, as a direct result of *Griggs*, 15.1 percent of the employers using tests before *Griggs* dropped them because the costs and time involved did not seem to warrant testing as an aid in the selection process or because of a possible violation of Title VII if tests were not validated.

The real repercussions of *Griggs* showed up in the validating practices. There was a 25 percent increase in validation efforts after *Griggs*, particularly in the use of managerial and professional tests. Before *Griggs*, employers relied primarily upon in-house psychologists and statisticians to do validations studies, but after *Griggs*, there was a trend toward using more outside psychologist-consultants to validate tests, especially in medium-sized companies. Smaller firms were the most likely to drop testing altogether, while companies with midsize workforces appeared to be the hardest hit by *Griggs* in terms of test validation. In terms of the future impact of *Griggs*, the study concluded that it seemed likely that employers would continue to use tests as an integral part of the employee-selection process, but with more attention to validation, particularly for upper-level jobs. Anecdotal evidence also indicates that *Griggs* had an immediate impact on personnel testing behavior.[5] The challenge *Griggs* posed for employers, industrial psychologists, human relations personnel, and test vendors was to develop valid job-related employment criteria, and thus one of the effects of *Griggs* was to create sustained full employment for them. As one commentator put it, *Griggs* assured that "industrial psychologists [would] . . . not [be] idle."[6]

The decade following *Griggs* was the most intensive period of the litigation campaign. Because the courts had decided most of the procedural and jurisdictional issues that employers and unions had raised during the early years of the campaign in favor of the plaintiffs, a large number of the LDF cases, practically all of which had been allowed to go forward as class actions, began to move rapidly toward trials on the merits. The litigation team had a docket of more than 100 active cases at the time the Supreme Court decided *Griggs*,[7] many of which were disparate impact cases. The time required to prepare this large number of cases for trial simply mushroomed after *Griggs* because of the need, for example, to examine and analyze voluminous records of employers and unions, respond to broad-based objections by defendants to the plaintiffs' pretrial discovery demands, prepare numerous plaintiffs for depositions and for trial, take depositions of fact and expert witnesses for plaintiffs and defendants, develop statistical evidence, prepare trial exhibits, and respond to summary judgment motions filed by defendants. The preparation of the cases for trial and the trials themselves were essentially David and Goliath confrontations[8] because the employers in many of the cases were large, well established, nationally known, and willing to incur substantial expenses, including attorney's fees, to aggressively defend employment discrimination cases. Also, the defendants in many of the cases were international and local labor organizations that sided with employers to protect the seniority rights of white employees, even though well before Title VII, unions were legally obligated under the duty of fair representation to equally represent the employment interests of white *and* African American employees in unionized bargaining units.[9]

Two attorneys who became full-time members of the LDF litigation team after *Griggs* were Barry Goldstein and Morris (Mike) J. Baller. Barry and Mike, among the liberal Jewish attorneys who came to work for the LDF, both eventually worked almost full-time on employment discrimination cases. They had the major responsibility for the litigation campaign from about 1973, when Bill Robinson left to become associate counsel of the EEOC, until about 1975. Later, Peter Sherwood, an African American attorney who joined the LDF in early 1974, had responsibility for the day-to-day operations of the litigation campaign. Barry and Mike, with some assistance from other LDF[10] and cooperating attorneys, had major roles in some of the most important post-*Griggs* cases. Barry did his undergraduate work at Harvard and graduated from Columbia Law School in 1970. On his second day in law school, Barry met Bill and offered to work with the LDF, for free; this was an offer Bill could not refuse. Bill also arranged for Barry to spend a summer internship, under the auspices of the Law School Civil Rights Research Committee, with John Walker, an African American cooperating attorney in Little Rock, Arkansas.[11] After Barry completed a fellowship at Cambridge University, Greenberg, on Bill's recommendation, hired Barry for a six-month term to assist on the cases against United States Steel Corporation and the United Steelworkers, pending in Birmingham, Alabama.[12] The trial in the steel cases, which began in June 1972 and continued on an intermittent basis for the next six months, was among the most contentious, yet noteworthy, cases handled by the litigation team.[13] Barry's six-month term eventually turned into an eighteen-year stint with the LDF, including several years as the director of its Washington, D.C., office. After leaving the LDF, Barry entered private practice, where he continued to engage in class action civil rights litigation and served as counsel in a number of landmark settlement agreements with one of the premier private public interest law firms in California.[14]

Mike received his undergraduate degree from Harvard and graduated from Harvard Law in 1970. He began his association with the LDF prior to becoming a member of the litigation team, when he received a Reginald Heber Smith Community Lawyer Fellowship, a "Reggie,"[15] to work with the LDF's National Office of the Rights of Indigents (NORI) program in New York. Greenberg established NORI as a subsidiary of the LDF, and it was the first private national poverty law program. Its purpose was to provide legal assistance for the poor in much the same way as the LDF did for African Americans.[16] Mike was with the LDF from 1970 until 1975. He then joined the Mexican American Legal Defense Fund as a staff attorney, later becoming its coordinator of litigation and senior vice president for legal programs. After a stint as a partner in another law firm, he eventually became a law partner of Barry's in California.

The cooperating attorneys, particularly those in southern states, continued to play a major role in the litigation campaign. I had become a partner in Chambers's firm in Charlotte, North Carolina. Chambers and I had the major responsibility for the firm's employment discrimination docket, but other attorneys with the firm, particularly Jonathan Wallace, handled a substantial number of the firm's employment discrimination cases. Gaby, who also had left the LDF for private practice in Texas, had a substantial docket of employment discrimination cases and did a substantial portion of the work on the cases litigated in Texas. Some of the other cooperating attorneys who were heavily involved in the spate of cases that came to trial before and after *Griggs* included Oscar Adams and U. W. Clemon with the firm of Adams, Baker & Clemon in Birmingham, Alabama; Henry Marsh and Sam Tucker with the firm of Hill, Tucker & Marsh in Richmond, Virginia; John Walker and Philip Kaplan in Little Rock, Arkansas, where the firm of Walker, Kaplan, Lavey & Mays was Arkansas' first racially integrated law firm; Howard Moore and Peter Rindskopf of Moore, Alexander & Rindskopf in Atlanta, Georgia; and Bobby Hill and Fletcher Farrington of Hill, Jones & Farrington in Savannah, Georgia.[17]

Of these, Oscar Adams, who participated in establishing the first racially integrated law firm in Alabama, Adams and Burg, was the first African American to serve on any appellate court in Alabama when Governor Fob James appointed him to the Alabama Supreme Court in 1980. U. W. Clemon, in 1974 the first African American elected to the Alabama State Senate since Reconstruction, became the first African American federal judge in the state upon his appointment by President Carter in 1980. Henry Marsh was elected the first African American mayor of Richmond, Virginia, in 1977.

SUBJECTIVE CRITERIA AND *GRIGGS*

In addition to facially neutral objective selection criteria that test cognitive abilities and the seniority rules involved in cases such as *Quarles* and *Local 189,* employers often used noncognitive or subjective criteria jointly or solely in making employment decisions. It is difficult to draw a bright-line rule between objective and subjective employment criteria. As a general rule of thumb, objective decision making is thought of as an employment decision that is uninfluenced by personal prejudice, bias, or stereotypical assumptions and includes such things as pen-and-paper tests, educational requirements, arrest and conviction records, height and weight requirements, or licensing requirements. Subjective-based employment decisions are based on the judgment of the decision makers and include such factors as "leadership ability or potential," "ability to motivate others," "personality," "ability to fit in," and "ability to handle interpersonal relationships." Perhaps the overwhelming majority of employment and personnel decisions employers make are subjective in nature in the sense that they are based on the personal judgments and assessments of supervisors and upper-management personnel. Also, employment decisions that rely heavily on subjective factors most frequently occur in promotions to higher-level positions.[18] Subjective factors are difficult to quantify. Early in the litigation campaign, the issue arose whether subjective criteria that had an adverse impact on the employment of African Americans could also be brought under the disparate impact theory.

The first case challenging subjective criteria under the disparate impact theory, not specifically addressed by the Supreme Court until the *Wards Cove* decision in 1989, was *Rowe v. General Motors Corp.* In *Rowe,* there were two methods by which an hourly paid employee could obtain a transfer or promotion to a salaried supervisor's job. Under the first method, an employee made a request to a supervisor. Under the second method, a supervisor could recommend an hourly paid employee for a salaried position. The selection committee, all of whom were white, made the ultimate decision on whether the employee would be promoted. The process never began unless and until the employee received the endorsement of his foreman. General Motors acknowledged that since all of the personnel who made recommendations for salaried positions were white, the method for promotion enabled the white foremen, if so inclined, to exercise racial discrimination in selecting candidates. Under the social structure at that time, African Americans may very well have been hindered in obtaining recommendations from their white foremen since there were often no familial or social associations between the two groups. The litigation team presented strong statistical evidence to support their claim of the adverse impact of the subjective selection process on African Americans.

A major issue in the case was whether the plaintiffs could rely upon the *Griggs* disparate impact theory. The district court rejected the use of the disparate impact theory, relying in substantial part on the district court's decision in *Griggs*. By the time the Fifth Circuit decided *Rowe*, however, the Supreme Court had ruled in *Griggs*. Based on the evidence and legal argument the litigation team presented in *Rowe*, the Fifth Circuit concluded that five aspects of the promotion and transfer practices, when taken together, had a disparate impact on employment opportunities for African Americans. These five aspects were as follows: (1) the foreman's recommendation was the single most important factor in the promotion process; (2) the foremen were given no written instructions pertaining to the qualifications necessary for promotion; (3) standards were vague and subjective; (4) employees received no notice of promotional opportunities or the qualifications necessary for the job; and (5) there were no safeguards in the procedure designed to avert discriminatory practices. Acknowledging a long history of racial discrimination against African Americans by General Motors, Judge Brown, who authored the Fifth Circuit's decision in *Rowe*, stated that "[w]e and other [courts] have expressed skepticism that [African Americans] dependent on decisive recommendations from Whites can expect non-discriminatory action." Relying on the Supreme Court's freezing principle endorsed in *Griggs*, Judge Brown wrote that "[a]ll we do today is recognize that the promotion/transfer procedures which depend almost entirely upon the subjective evaluations and favorable recommendations of the immediate foreman are a ready mechanism for discrimination against African Americans much of which can be covertly concealed and, for that matter, not really known to management."[19] For almost a decade after

Rowe, the LDF and others relied upon *Rowe* to successfully challenge subjective criteria under the *Griggs* disparate impact theory.[20]

After *Rowe,* a split developed in the courts of appeals in the early 1980s on whether the *Griggs* theory may be used to challenge employment decisions based on a disparate impact of facially neutral subjective promotion practices or procedures. After declining to grant certiorari in some earlier cases, including a petition for certiorari filed by the Department of Justice,[21] the Supreme Court finally addressed the issue in *Watson v. Fort Worth Bank & Trust. Watson* was a race discrimination case brought on behalf of an African American woman who had been rejected in favor of white applicants for four promotions to a supervisory position with the Fort Worth Bank & Trust. The bank had not developed precise and formal selection criteria for the positions but instead relied upon the subjective judgment of supervisors who were familiar with the applicants and with the nature of the jobs to be filled. All of the supervisors were white. The criteria these white supervisors used to evaluate applicants included accuracy of work, alertness, personal appearance, supervisor-to-worker relations, quantity of work, physical fitness, attendance, dependability, stability, ambition, friendliness, courtesy, job knowledge, and experience. Watson presented statistical evidence that these subjective criteria had a significant adverse impact on promotional opportunities of African Americans. The Fifth Circuit, following its earlier precedents, held that subjective criteria, even when they have an adverse impact on African Americans, are to be analyzed under the disparate treatment theory and cannot be analyzed under the disparate impact theory.[22]

The Supreme Court solicited the view of the Department of Justice on whether review should be granted.[23] Although the Department of Justice had joined the LDF in urging the Supreme Court to adopt the impact theory in *Griggs,* it supported the employer in *Watson,* asking that the Court hold that the *Griggs* disparate impact theory was not applicable to subjective criteria.[24] The reason the Department of Justice supported the employer is that by 1987, the controversy over the legality of affirmative action was in full swing, the Reagan and Bush administrations had launched a full-scale attack on the disparate impact theory, and the conservative majority of the Supreme Court was beginning to issue decisions that undercut the theory. A number of organizations filed briefs asking the Justices to hold that subjective criteria could not be analyzed using the disparate impact theory.[25] One of the main arguments advanced by these parties was that applying disparate impact analysis to subjective criteria would present employers, big and small, with a Hobson's choice. Employers would either have to spend staggering sums of money to hire statisticians, industrial psychologists, and consultants to conduct validation studies on any and all selection criteria that might not withstand a disparate impact challenge in light of the *Griggs* business necessity defense or adopt quotas to ensure that plaintiffs would not be able to statistically prove disparate impact in the first instance.[26] One group supporting the bank made the *in terrorem* argument that the application of the disparate impact theory to subjective criteria would impose an insurmountable rebuttal burden under the business necessity defense and thus of necessity would eliminate the legitimate use of subjectivity in employment decisions.[27]

The LDF joined with the Mexican American Legal Defense and Educational Fund, the Employment Law Center, and the Center for Law in the Public Interest to file a friend of the court brief in support of *Watson.*[28] One of the main purposes of the brief, joined by the LDF, was to respond to the arguments made by the Department of Justice and to point out that the Court in broadly construing Title VII had repeatedly rejected the Department of Justice's argument in LDF cases such as *Griggs, Moody,* and *Franks,* and in other cases such as *Connecticut v. Teal.* Another argument was that, irrespective of an employer's good intentions, the use of subjective selection criteria may unfairly restrict employment opportunities of minorities and women because such criteria leave substantial room for deeply ingrained unconscious discriminatory biases. The unconscious discriminatory bias argument is, in effect, what might be called the clone theory of equality. Under the clone theory of equality, the decision maker, usually a white male, tends to select only those candidates who possess or aspire to possess the same ideals, cultural background, socioeconomic status, or political philosophy as the decision maker. The clone theory is based in substantial part on unconscious racism or sexism.[29]

In a unanimous decision written by Justice O'Connor, the Court held that subjective selection practices can be analyzed under the disparate impact theory. The first justification for doing so was that if disparate impact analysis was confined to objective criteria, employers would be able to substitute subjective criteria having substantially the same adverse impact as objective criteria, and *Griggs* would become a "dead letter" and "largely nullified" and "might be effectively abolished."[30] The Court was cognizant of the possibility that all an employer had to do to avoid the unfavorable evidentiary requirements of the disparate impact theory would be to introduce a single subjective component into its decision-making process because "[h]owever one might distinguish 'subjective' from 'objective' it is apparent that selection systems that combine both types would generally be considered subjective." The second justification was that the disparate treatment theory alone would not be adequate to ferret out subconscious stereotypes and unlawful prejudices. An example of such stereotyping that Justice O'Connor provided from the factual record was a statement made to Watson when she applied for a teller's position that the teller's job was a big responsibility with "a lot of money . . . for blacks to have to count."[31]

THE PROOF STRUCTURE IN DISPARATE IMPACT CASES

The next major Supreme Court disparate impact case after *Griggs* was *Albemarle Paper Co. v. Moody,* an LDF case decided in 1975 in which the Court addressed several important issues, one of which was the order and allocation of the burdens of proof in disparate impact cases. The Supreme Court had not explicitly addressed this issue in *Griggs* because it had simply stated that "Congress placed on the employer the burden of showing that any given requirement [that had a disparate impact on a protected class] must have a manifest relationship to the employment in question."[32] The order and allocation of the burdens of proof on the parties in a civil action is a very technical legal subject, but it governs the fact-finding process and factual disputes that lie at the heart of virtually every discrimination case. The allocation of the burdens of proof during trial often has a significant effect on the outcome of a case and frequently may be dispositive of which party wins or loses.[33]

The Supreme Court's first encounter with the proof structure in employment discrimination cases was its 1973 decision in *McDonnell Douglas Corp. v. Green,* a leading case on the disparate treatment theory. *McDonnell Douglas* did not begin as an LDF case, but the LDF assumed a major role after the Supreme Court agreed to hear the case. Al Rosenthal, a member of the litigation team, with assistance from Bill Robinson, wrote the Supreme Court brief on behalf of the black plaintiff, Percy Green, when Green's attorney, Louis Gilden of St. Louis, Missouri, sought the assistance of the LDF.[34] With respect to the proof structure, the Supreme Court held that a plaintiff must first introduce evidence that supports a finding of a prima facie case of unlawful discrimination.[35] The prima facie case doctrine requires a plaintiff to introduce evidence that, standing alone, is sufficient to entitle the plaintiff to a judgment on the merits in his or her favor. Second, assuming the plaintiff establishes a prima facie case of unlawful discrimination, the burden shifts to the defendant to rebut the prima facie case, which the defendant can do by introducing evidence that a legitimate nondiscriminatory reason explains the adverse employment action. Third, the plaintiff can still win the case by convincing the fact finder—judge or jury—that the employer's claimed reliance on a legitimate nondiscriminatory reason is pretextual because it is not the real reason or is unworthy of credence. The tripartite *McDonnell Douglas* proof scheme of the prima facie case, legitimate nondiscriminatory reason, and pretext has become a deeply entrenched mantra and has made that case the most cited in civil rights law.[36]

In *Moody,* the Court tailored the *McDonnell Douglas* burden allocation proof scheme for disparate impact claims. First, a plaintiff must establish a prima facie case of disparate impact discrimination. The principal evidentiary route for establishing a prima facie case of disparate impact is with statistical evidence. Second, if a plaintiff establishes a prima facie case, the defendant must prove that the challenged facially neutral employment practice is justified by business necessity. Third, even if the employer's evidence satisfies the business necessity test, a plaintiff can still establish a violation of Title VII by showing that the asserted business justification is pretext for unlawful discrimination. One way a plaintiff can prove pretext is with evidence of an alternative to the challenged facially neutral practice with a less discriminatory effect that at the same time equally well serves the employer's legitimate interest in efficient and trustworthy workmanship.[37] The significance of the *Moody* proof allocation to the maturation of the disparate impact theory is that, until overturned by the Supreme Court in its 1989 decision in *Wards Cove Packing Co. v. Atonio,* the burden imposed upon employers under the business necessity defense was a substantial one—the burden of persuasion—that was difficult to meet in a large number of the disparate impact cases.

STATISTICAL EVIDENCE AND THE
TEAMSTERS TRILOGY

It was obvious from the beginning of the litigation campaign that statistical evidence would be crucial in proving claims of employment discrimination in both disparate impact and disparate treatment cases. Because the *Griggs* disparate impact theory focuses on the effects—or as the Supreme Court said in *Griggs,* the *consequences*[38]—of a facially neutral employment policy or practice, statistical evidence is indispensable to establishing a prima facie case under this theory. One of the first legal questions raised in Title VII cases was whether the plaintiff could rely on pre-Act discriminatory conduct to prove unlawful discrimination. Section 703(j) of Title VII, often referred to as the anti–preferential treatment or the anti–"reverse discrimination" provision, stood as a potential limitation on the use of pre-Act (July 2, 1964) statistical evidence to prove unlawful employment discrimination. Section 703(j) provides that

> [n]othing contained in [Title VII] shall be interpreted to require any employer
> . . . to grant preferential treatment to any individual or to any group because of the
> race, color, religion, sex, or national origin of such individual or group on account
> of an imbalance which may exist with respect to the total number or percentage
> of persons of any race, color, religion, sex, or national origin employed by the
> employer . . . in the available work force.[39]

The sponsors and supporters of Title VII agreed to the inclusion of Section 703(j) to allay the concerns of opponents that reliance on statistics to prove unlawful discrimination would result in federally mandated quotas to achieve "racial balance" in the workplace, thus forcing employers to make race-based hiring decisions.[40]

Shortly after the effective date of Title VII, the EEOC explored the use of statistical evidence to prove unlawful employment discrimination. EEOC staff attorney Sonia Pressman, at the request of Charles Duncan, the first general counsel of the EEOC, wrote a memorandum, dated May 31, 1966, on the use of statistical evidence to prove unlawful discrimination. Pressman, a Jewish refugee of Hitler's Germany, graduated first in her class from the University of Miami School of Law and was the first woman to be employed in the EEOC's Office of General Counsel. Pressman pointed out that Section 703(j) was a potential limitation on the use of statistical evidence to the extent that the data reflected pre-Act discrimination (except in those cases where the defendant had some obligation prior to July 2, 1965, not to engage in unlawful employment discrimination). To avoid this possible limitation, Pressman recommended that the EEOC limit its statistical data on hiring, transfers, and promotions to the post–Title VII period (after July 2, 1965) because information on the employer's *current* work complement might include employees who were hired before Title VII became effective. Hugh Davis Graham, a noted historian and the author of a highly acclaimed book on civil rights, rather harshly criticizes the Pressman memorandum because he construed it as purporting to provide a legal foundation for the EEOC's endorsement of the disparate impact theory. Graham's criticism is that, although Pressman recognized Section 703(j) endorsed a substantial legislative limitation on the use of statistical evidence, she nevertheless urged the EEOC "to pursue in the courts an affirmative theory of nondiscrimination," one that the employer cannot satisfy "merely by silently and passively ceasing his past discrimination and posting EEOC notices," and to pursue an enforcement policy that would ensure that "Negroes are recruited, hired, transferred, and promoted in line with their ability and *numbers*."[41]

Beginning with the very first case it filed under Title VII, the litigation team regularly relied on statistical evidence that included both pre– and post– Title VII data, and did not, as the Pressman memorandum suggested, limit its demands for statistical evidence to the post–Title VII period. The defendants in the early Title VII cases rarely, if ever, raised Section 703(j) as a ban on the use of statistical evidence. For example, in a case that I tried in 1970, the defendant simply argued, without relying on Section 703(j), that "[a] mere head count of Negro versus white employment in various job categories is not proof" of unlawful discrimination.[42] The courts allowed the plaintiffs to rely upon pre-Act evidence, statistical and nonstatistical, because such evidence was highly relevant in evaluating whether facially neutral practices perpetuated into the post-Act period the discriminatory effects of pre-Act discrimination and because the LDF had included a claim under Section 1981 in addition to Title VII.[43] In addition, the litigation team had a strong argument based on a line of cases in which the courts had endorsed the liberal use of statistics to prove discrimination in activities such as juries, schools, and voting,[44] based on the evidentiary maxim that "[i]n the problem of racial discrimination, statistics often tell much and Courts listen."[45] These earlier cases relied upon the so-called prima facie rule or rule of exclusion based on statistical evidence, which originated in the 1889 Supreme Court case of *Neal v. Delaware,* and which courts regularly applied in employment discrimination cases. The lower courts were virtually unanimous in liberally endorsing the use of statistical evidence and often accorded critical, if not decisive, weight to statistical evidence in finding for the plaintiffs in the LDF cases.[46]

The Supreme Court first sanctioned the use of statistical evidence to prove unlawful discrimination under Title VII in *McDonnell Douglas,* a disparate treatment case. Although McDonnell Douglas relied upon Section 703(j) to support its argument that the prima facie case theory adopted by the court of appeals granted preferential treatment to African Americans, it did not specifically argue in the Supreme Court that the section bars or otherwise precludes the use of statistical evidence in Title VII cases.[47] The brief the litigation team wrote on behalf of the employee, Green, argued that the trial court had unduly limited Green's access to statistical evidence and supported the argument with a long line of lower court cases approving of the use of statistics by plaintiffs.[48] The Supreme Court agreed with the LDF's argument when it held that "statistics as to [the employer's] employment policy and practice may be helpful to a determination of whether [the employer's] refusal to rehire [the plaintiff] in this case conformed to a general pattern of discrimination against blacks."[49]

The Supreme Court eventually endorsed the use of statistical evidence in its 1976 Term in a trilogy of Title VII cases brought by the Department of Justice—*Teamsters v. United States, Hazelwood School District v. United States,* and *Dothard v. Rawlinson. Teamsters* was the lead case in the trilogy. The principal legal argument the employer made in *Teamsters* was that because of Section 703(j), "statistics can never in and of themselves prove the existence of a pattern or practice of discrimination, or even establish a prima facie case shifting to the employer the burden of rebutting the inference raised by these figures."[50] The structure of the company's argument was essentially that allowing the plaintiffs to rely on statistical evidence to prove unlawful discrimination would, contrary to the specific language of Section 703(j), impose an obligation on employers to make race-based employment decisions to reduce the disparity in order to avoid a violation of Title VII. This, the employer argued, would lead to quota hiring that Congress meant to prohibit under Section 703(j).[51]

The Supreme Court rejected the employer's argument and, in doing so, rejected a construction of Section 703(j) that would impose an absolute bar on the use of statistical evidence in Title VII cases. The Court held that its precedents, including *McDonnell Douglas,* "make it unmistakably clear that '[s]tatistical analyses have served and will continue to serve an important role' in cases in which the existence of discrimination is a disputed issue," and for that reason, "[s]tatistics are equally competent in proving employment discrimination."[52] In addressing the employer's argument based on Section 703(j), the Court held that when statistical evidence is used to establish a prima facie case or to shift the burden of proof to the defendant, such evidence is not proffered to support an erroneous theory that Title VII requires an employer's workforce be racially balanced. Rather, the Court said that "[s]tatistics showing racial or ethnic imbalance are probative in a case ... only because such imbalance is often a telltale sign of purposeful discrimination; and that absent explanation, it is ordinarily to be expected that nondiscriminatory hiring practices will in time result in a work force more or less representative of the racial and ethnic composition of the population from which employees are hired." The Court approvingly cited the trend in the lower courts, including groundbreaking cases handled by the LDF that broadly endorsed the use of statistical evidence to prove unlawful discrimination,[53] but it issued a cautionary admonition on the use of statistical evidence: "We caution only that statistics are not irrefutable; they come in infinite variety and, like any other kind of evidence, they may be rebutted. In short, their usefulness depends on all of the surrounding circumstances."[54] The concurring opinion by Justice Brennan in *Hazelwood* made clear the significance of the *Teamsters* trilogy: "It should be plain ... that the liberal substantive standards for establishing a Title VII violation, including the usefulness of statistical proof, are reconfirmed."[55]

Cases such as *Griggs* and *Teamsters* were a kind of wake-up call to employers and unions,[56] so their counsel began to defend employment discrimination cases more seriously and vigorously by relying on computer-generated discovery on statistics and hiring experts on statistics, testing, and labor market economics.[57] In response to this development, it became necessary for the litigation team to also engage in more sophisticated statistical methodologies and to use statistical and other experts.[58] Just as with the issue of testing, the use of statistical evidence by the parties in employment discrimination cases often involves a battle of experts, and the trial judges are called upon to choose which expert's testimony to credit.

In 1978, the year following the *Teamsters* trilogy, the EEOC, the Civil Service Commission, the Civil Rights Commission, and the Department of Justice adopted the Uniform Guidelines on Employee Selection. The Uniform Guidelines adopted a broad definition of "selection procedures" that may be subject to disparate impact claims. That definition includes "[a]ny measure, combination of measures, or procedures used as a basis for any employment decision and [s]election procedures including the full range of assessment techniques from traditional paper and pencil tests, performance tests, training programs, or probationary periods and physical, educational, and work experience requirements through informal or casual interviews and unscored application forms." The Uniform Guidelines broadly define an "employment decision" to include "hiring, promotion, demotion, membership (for example, in a labor organization), referral, retention . . . licensing and certification, to the extent that certification is covered by Federal equal employment law, and other selection decisions, such as selection for training or transfer . . . if they lead to any of the decisions listed above."[59]

The *Griggs* disparate impact theory, coupled with the EEOC's broad definition of selection procedures, the courts' sanctioning of the liberal use of statistical evidence to prove unlawful discrimination, and the endorsement of broad-based class actions were clear indications that, although Title VII speaks in terms of discrimination against individuals, the major problem of unlawful discrimination is not isolated cases of bigotry toward particular persons but rather institutionalized or structural practices and policies such as testing, subjective standards, and seniority rules that systematically limit the employment opportunities of blacks, women, Asians, Latinos/as, and Native Americans.[60]

MOODY AND *ROBINSON*: A RIGOROUS TEST OF BUSINESS NECESSITY

The LDF was involved in two of the most important cases that led to a rigorous test of business necessity: *Moody v. Albemarle Paper Co.* and *Robinson v. Lorillard. Moody,* like *Griggs,* was one of the earliest class action cases filed in the litigation campaign.[61] As we did in *Griggs,* Chambers and I served as lead counsel in *Moody.* The defendants were Albemarle Paper Company, located in Roanoke Rapids, North Carolina, and a union, Halifax Local No. 425, United Papermaker and Paperworkers, AFL-CIO. Francis V. Lowden and Paul Thompson, with Hunton, Williams, and Gay of Richmond, Virginia, were lead counsel for Albemarle; and Warren Woods, with Wilson, Woods & Villalon of Washington, D.C., was lead counsel for the union. Although the litigation team filed the complaint in *Moody* before it filed the complaint in *Griggs, Moody* did not come to trial until July 1971, about four months after the Supreme Court's decision in *Griggs.* A major reason for the substantial delay is that *Moody* was one of the most litigious cases in the litigation campaign. The defendants filed round after round of every motion they could conceive of to try to get the case dismissed to avoid a decision on merits. One motion even asked the court to require the plaintiffs to post a security bond in the amount of $100,000 to be used to pay taxable costs and attorney's fees should the plaintiffs lose on the merits; the court denied the motion.

The facts of *Moody* were to a large extent a combination of a classical *Quarles v. Philip Morris*–type seniority discrimination claim and a classical *Griggs*-type testing and educational selection criteria claim. The lead plaintiff, Joe P. Moody, was a remarkable individual who lived in Roanoke Rapids. He was the son of a sharecropper and the second oldest of eight children. His family lived in a rural part of North Carolina. As one of the older children, he never learned to read or write because he was required to work to help support his family and thus had very little time to go to school. He started working at Albemarle Paper in 1952. Although Moody never learned the alphabet, he had the uncanny ability to memorize complex mechanical designs and operations and did so by making illustrations and markings in notebooks. He often employed an individual to be his secretary when he found it appropriate to communicate with others in writing. Even though he could not read or write, Moody was a very articulate individual and eventually became a lifelong civil rights activist and leader and continued in that tradition after Albemarle hired him. Moody suffered personal racial attacks because he was a rather vocal civil rights activist. During pretrial discovery, the litigation team learned that there were a number of whites who could neither read nor write but who had been hired or promoted to jobs involving work on sophisticated machinery or other jobs in which only whites were employed. The facts in *Moody* typified the lack of success that African American plaintiffs had in enlisting the assistance of their unions to escape the racially discriminatory terms and conditions under which they were employed.[62]

Although the company hired African Americans only as laborers, Albemarle, like Duke Power and many other employers, simply refused to admit that it had intentionally engaged in racial discrimination prior to the effective date of Title VII.[63] However, the evidence the litigation team introduced at trial was more than sufficient for the trial judge to find that prior to January 1, 1964, Albemarle's lines of progression were strictly segregated on the basis of race, and that the lines of progression to which African American employees were traditionally assigned were lower paying than the whites' lines of progression.

Albemarle's adoption of educational and testing practices paralleled, in substantial part, those challenged in *Griggs*. Albemarle first adopted a high school education requirement in the early 1950s. Like Duke Power in *Griggs*, Albemarle claimed that justification for the educational requirement was the need to select qualified applicants who had the skills to perform technological innovations associated with the modernizing of its Roanoke Rapids mill. It then added a testing requirement in the mid-1950s for employment in the skilled lines of progression that were limited to whites. The tests were the Revised Beta Examination and the Bennett Mechanical Comprehension Test. The Beta test is a written nonverbal test designed to measure the intelligence of non-English-speaking individuals or illiterates. In 1963, about two years before the effective date of Title VII, Albemarle stopped using the Bennett test because it had not been validated and replaced it with the Wonderlic. The official who made the decision to discontinue the Bennett and adopt the Wonderlic admitted he was not an expert in industrial testing but relied on his graduate work in psychology from Vanderbilt University in making the decision to use testing as a screening criterion. Albemarle made no attempt to validate its test battery until after the Supreme Court decided *Griggs*.[64] Again, like Duke Power in *Griggs*, Albemarle adopted a policy for waiving the high school education requirement for certain African American employees for promotion to white jobs in certain skilled lines of progress provided they successfully passed the test battery. A few African Americans who scored successfully on the test battery were then permitted to transfer to formerly all-white jobs.

The litigation team engaged Dr. Raymond Katzell, a psychologist at New York University, as its expert witness on the education and testing issues. Dr. Katzell, along with Dr. Richard Barrett and others, coauthored an important book on employment testing that recognized differential validation; the EEOC testing guidelines endorsed the differential validation testing guideline that was in force at the time *Moody* came to trial.[65] Albemarle took a pretrial deposition of Dr. Katzell in April 1969, more than two years before the trial began in July 1971. Dr. Katzell's testimony was that although Albemarle's tests had been prepared by professionals in industrial psychology, they had not been validated for the purpose for which Albemarle used them because no effort had been made to determine their validity according to professionally accepted validation standards. Dr. Katzell also testified that the high school education requirement should be validated.[66]

Two significant legal developments occurred shortly before the trial in

Moody. First, the Supreme Court decided *Griggs* in March 1971. Second, on July 1, 1971, the U.S. Court of Appeals for the Fourth Circuit handed down a landmark decision on the business necessity defense and back pay in the LDF's case of *Robinson v. Lorillard Corp. Robinson* was one of the first appellate court cases to flesh out the scope of the business necessity test the Supreme Court had adopted in *Griggs.* The named plaintiffs in *Robinson* were eight African American male and female employees of the Lorillard cigarette manufacturing plant located in Greensboro, North Carolina. Lorillard had transferred the facility from New Jersey to Greensboro in 1956. While operating in New Jersey, Lorillard had engaged in racially discriminatory employment practices that were the subject of investigation under New Jersey civil rights laws;[67] the company had set up the new plant in Greensboro on a strictly racially segregated basis, employing African Americans only in the all-black departments. The North Carolina Employment Service assisted Lorillard in its discriminatory employment practices by referring African Americans, at Lorillard's request, to jobs at Lorillard that were reserved for African Americans. The LDF filed a complaint in *Robinson* on August 1, 1966. The history of racial discrimination in *Robinson* followed essentially the same pattern in the tobacco manufacturing industry, as was the case in *Quarles,* and, like *Quarles, Robinson* was a seniority discrimination case.

The lead plaintiff in the case was Dorothy Robinson, an African American female. Like many other African American plaintiffs in the LDF's employment discrimination cases, Robinson had lived under and endured the disadvantages of living in a racially stratified society all of her life. As a young child, she noticed that African Americans were expected to call white persons "Mr.," "Mrs.," or "Miss," but white persons called African Americans, including adults, by their first names. Her father wanted her to get a good education, but he did not make enough money to realize this dream. She had operated a restaurant with her husband before her employment with Lorillard and regretted that she was prohibited from serving white customers under then-current state racial segregation laws. Motivated by the racial disparities that she saw around her, Robinson joined the local NAACP chapter in the early 1950s. In 1957, Lorillard hired Robinson and assigned her to a job sweeping floors. She was gravely concerned about the fact that no white employees swept floors and decided that she was not going to sweep floors for the rest of her life. Lorillard told her that it could not employ her to work in jobs white women performed because of racially restrictive state laws. Although she was technically in the racially segregated service department, she worked on the filter-making floor where most of the employees were white. She and several other African Americans transferred from the service department to the filter-making department as soon as they were permitted to do so in 1962. However, when there was a cutback in the number of employees in the filter-making department in 1965, Robinson had to return to the service department, even though she had worked for Lorillard longer than many of the white employees in the filter department. She and other African American employees made substantially less money than white employees who were no better qualified and who had less seniority at the plant.

LDF attorney William (Bill) Turner and Adam Stein, a partner in the Chambers firm, tried *Robinson* in May 1969 before Judge Gordon, who was also the trial judge in *Griggs*. By the time the case was tried, the legal developments, including *Quarles, Local 189*, and a long line of other cases, strongly supported the plaintiffs' claims, and the Cooper and Sobol *Harvard Law Review* article on seniority and testing had been published. Judge Gordon delayed issuing his opinion on the merits for almost a year and later acknowledged that he had done so in the hope that the delay would pressure the parties to settle the case.[68] During the delay, the U.S. Court of Appeals for the Fourth Circuit decided *Griggs* on January 9, 1970, endorsing the *Quarles* and *Local 189* present effects of past discrimination theory, thus overruling Judge Gordon's earlier rejection of that theory in *Griggs*. Stein sent a lengthy letter to Judge Gordon shortly after the Fourth Circuit's decision in *Griggs,* setting out the reasons *Griggs* compelled a decision in favor of the plaintiffs.[69]

Several months after the court of appeals reversed him in *Griggs,* Judge Gordon finally decided *Robinson.* In the face of controlling authority from the Fourth Circuit in *Griggs,* Judge Gordon had very little choice but to rule in favor of the plaintiffs on the merits based on the present effects of past discrimination theory. In light of his earlier rejection of the *Quarles* theory in *Griggs,* it seems ironic that he so aptly describes the theory as follows:

> The present effects of this seniority system might be illustrated as follows: if two race cars are placed evenly, one beside the other, and started at the same instant, one being allowed to accelerate to 50 m.p.h. in 7 seconds and the other in 10 seconds, with both vehicles to remain at 50 m.p.h. indefinitely, there will be an evident distance gap between the two. Even though the constant speed limit of 50 m.p.h. affects each car equally, it also serves to preserve and perpetuate the gap created when, at an earlier time, one car was denied an advantage allowed the

other. Persuasive and controlling authority has termed such practice unlawful when applied to an individual's employment status because of race, color, religion, sex, or national origin.[70]

George Cooper was astounded by Judge Gordon's decision, particularly the race car analogy, because it seemed to him that the judge was not the same person who had decided *Griggs* several years earlier.[71] After rejecting all of the reasons the defendants advanced to justify the challenged departmental seniority provision, Judge Gordon ruled in favor of the plaintiffs and entered a remedial order directing Lorillard and the union to implement a company-wide seniority system. He also ordered class-wide back pay but declined to award attorney's fees to the victorious plaintiffs.

Lorillard and the unions appealed to the U.S. Court of Appeals for the Fourth Circuit. At the time, it was becoming clear to defendants that the *Griggs* decision would require substantial changes in eliminating racial discrimination in the workplace. For example, in *Robinson*, the union's brief on appeal, incredibly, did not even mention *Griggs*. Lorillard at least acknowledged *Griggs* but never attempted to distinguish it and impliedly conceded that *Griggs* controlled the case.[72]

The Fourth Circuit panel consisted of Judge Simon Sobeloff, whose separate opinion in *Griggs* became the legal blueprint for the Supreme Court's adoption of the disparate impact theory in *Griggs*; Judge Albert Bryan, who wrote the majority opinion of the Fourth Circuit in *Griggs* that rejected the disparate impact theory; and Judge John Butzner, who, sitting as a district court judge, decided the seminal case of *Quarles*, establishing the doctrinal foundations for the present effects of past discrimination theory. The litigation team was indeed very pleased when it was notified of the appellate judges who would be deciding *Robinson*. The fact that Judge Bryan was a member of the appellate court panel was not a major cause for concern because, although *Robinson* was argued in the court of appeals on February 11, 1971, the Supreme Court had overturned his rejection of the disparate impact theory in *Griggs* on March 8, 1971. Bill Turner argued the case in the court of appeals on behalf of the plaintiffs.

The Fourth Circuit affirmed the finding of liability in an opinion authored by Judge Sobeloff, who by then had become a senior judge. Judge Sobeloff circulated a draft of his opinion to the other two members of the panel (and the other judges on the court) on June 21, 1971. The next day Judge Butzner readily agreed to concur in the decision because he felt "confident that [Judge Sobeloff had] correctly decided the many complex issues [the case presented]."[73] Judge Bryan's only difficulty with the draft was that Judge Sobeloff had not fixed a beginning date for the back pay awards to class members. However, Judge Sobeloff persuaded him to concur in the opinion on the grounds that fixing the beginning date was an issue left open for decision by the lower court.[74] The apparent animosity between Judges Sobeloff and Bryan about how *Griggs* should be decided did not manifest itself in *Robinson*.

The significance of Judge Sobeloff's opinion in *Robinson* to the maturation of the disparate impact theory is twofold. The first was the test of business necessity that he endorsed. The second was the remedy of class-wide back pay. After noting that "[t]he business necessity test has evolved as the appropriate reagent for detecting which employment practices are acceptable and which are invalid because based on factors that are the functional equivalent of race," Judge Sobeloff held that *Griggs, Local 189,* and other cases, taken together,

> conclusively establish that the applicable test is not merely whether there exists a business purpose for adhering to a challenged practice. The test is whether there exists an overriding legitimate business purpose such that the practice is necessary to the safe and efficient operation of the business. Thus, the business purpose must be sufficiently compelling to override any racial impact; the challenged practice must effectively carry out the business purpose it is alleged to serve; and there must be available no acceptable alternative policies or practices which could better accomplish the business purpose advanced, or accomplish it equally well with a lesser differential racial impact.[75]

Judge Sobeloff adopted a stringent three-part test of business necessity. He then held that none of the reasons advanced by Lorillard satisfied the test. Those three reasons were that its seniority system was consistent with industry practice, that the company had agreed to the challenged seniority system only under union pressure, and that employees would perform more efficiently if they had prior experience in a particular department. Judge Sobeloff rejected all three reasons on the grounds that the maintenance of the status quo of industry practice cannot validate unlawful discrimination, that rights under Title VII cannot be bargained away either by an employer or by a union, and that Lorillard produced no evidence that employees would perform better in jobs simply because they might have worked within the same department.[76] Also, he categorically rejected the argument that a facially neutral seniority system satisfied the business necessity test because, he said, seniority is necessarily an inefficient means of assuring effective job performance.[77]

On June 21, 1971, the same day that Judge Sobeloff circulated his draft opinion to his colleagues, Judge Wilfred Feinberg, who had been appointed to the U.S. Court of Appeals for the Second Circuit in 1966 to a seat vacated by then Judge Thurgood Marshall, filed his opinion in *United States v. Bethlehem Steel Corp. Bethlehem Steel,* like *Robinson,* was a seniority discrimination case; it had been filed by the Department of Justice. Like Judge Sobeloff, Judge Feinberg also adopted a rigorous business necessity test. While accepting the *Local 189* definition of business necessity that requires proof of "an overriding legitimate, non-racial business purpose," Judge Feinberg expanded upon that definition by holding that "[n]ecessity connotes an irresistible demand. To be preserved, the seniority and transfer system must not only directly foster safety and efficiency of a plant, but also be essential to those goals. . . . If the legitimate ends of safety and efficiency can be served by a reasonably available alternative system with a less discriminatory effect, then the present policies may not be continued."[78]

Judge Feinberg sent a copy of his opinion in *Bethlehem Steel* to Judge Sobeloff, who, in turn, sent Judge Feinberg a letter of "congratulations and admiration" and a draft of his opinion in *Robinson.* Judge Sobeloff further observed that "[t]here is a very unusual coincidence" in the two opinions because Judge Feinberg had "referred to Judge Butzner's opinion in *Quarles* as a seminal opinion and [he] did the same thing [in *Robinson*]." On a rather lighter note, Judge Sobeloff concluded that "[a] mean-minded critic might suggest some copying here, but that is impossible" because "[i]t is just a case of two minds with a single thought."[79] Judge Feinberg responded, stating that "[r]egarding Judge Butzner's opinion in *Quarles,* I guess everyone agrees that it had a tremendous impact and what better adjective is there than 'seminal.'"[80] Judge Sobeloff inserted a footnote in *Robinson* noting that his opinion was in full accord with Judge Feinberg's decision[81] but decided not to revise his draft opinion because a "major rewriting would be necessary to do the case [*Bethlehem Steel*] justice."[82]

The Supreme Court decision in *Griggs* and Judge Sobeloff's decision in *Robinson* were the legal precedents that governed the trial in *Moody.* Judge John Larkins had been the trial judge in *Moody* for almost five years until it was assigned to Judge Franklin Dupree. Judge Dupree, a native of North Carolina and a graduate of the University of North Carolina School of Law, had been very active in Republican politics before President Nixon appointed him to the federal bench. He has been characterized as "the epitome of the old-school Southern lawyer" who had "a reputation as an excellent defense lawyer" but was an "ardent conservative" and could be "at turn coldhearted and grandfatherly."[83]

Judge Dupree put *Moody* on a "rocket docket" schedule, a trial schedule some courts adopt that puts a case on a highly accelerated timetable. Lawyers whose cases are put on a rocket docket must adhere to strict and often short deadlines. One of the reasons Judge Dupree put *Moody* on a rocket docket schedule might have been that the case was one of the oldest on the docket of the federal court for the Eastern District of North Carolina. Another reason might have been, as Chambers later opined, that "the judge didn't like us."[84] In just over a two-month period between a May 17, 1971, pretrial conference and the start of the trial on July 26, 1971, Judge Dupree issued a series of orders on discovery, redefined the class, and entered a gag order barring all parties and their counsel from communicating directly or indirectly with potential or actual class members who were not formal parties to the action without his prior approval.[85] As a result of Judge Dupree's rocket docket schedule, to comply with each round of orders and the right time lines, I worked almost full-time on *Moody* from May 1971 through the end of a nine-day trial that took place between July 26 and August 5, 1971.

By the time the case came to trial, it was rather obvious to counsel for Albemarle and the unions, as well as to Judge Dupree, that the seniority system was unlawful under *Griggs* and *Robinson*. For this reason, counsel for Albemarle informed the judge at the beginning of the trial that "without admitting any guilt," the defendants had agreed to the entry of an injunction requiring the defendants to use a company-wide or plant seniority system for job advancement rather than the challenged departmental seniority system. Judge Dupree nevertheless entered findings of fact and conclusion of law finding that the department seniority system violated Title VII because the plaintiffs' evidence essentially compelled that finding.[86] The defendants had also drafted a proposed consent decree on the seniority discrimination issue and had given a copy to Judge Dupree before the trial began.[87] It was obvious to Chambers and me that one of the strategies of the defendants in conceding that the plaintiffs were entitled to both a judgment on liability and appropriate relief on the seniority discrimination issue was to deny Moody and other black employees their day in court to put on the public record their stories of the racially discriminatory treatment to which they had been subjected for years at the hands of the defendants. Chambers and I decided, nevertheless, to call some of the plaintiffs as witnesses to put their stories on the public record because this was the first time in their lives they had the opportunity to memorialize how they had suffered from racial discrimination in employment.

The major issue in *Moody* after the defendants conceded liability on the seniority discrimination issue was the legality of the educational and testing requirements under the disparate impact theory. Albemarle's earlier deposition of Dr. Katzell, and the fact that Albemarle had validated neither the educational nor the test requirements, demonstrated an exceptionally high probability that Albemarle would lose on these issues unless it satisfied the *Robinson* rigorous business necessity defense. So what did Albemarle do? After *Griggs* came down from the Supreme Court in March 1971, Albemarle retained Dr. Joseph Tiffin, an industrial psychologist at Purdue University, as its testing expert to perform a validation of its test battery. Dr. Tiffin was one of the pioneering scholars in industrial psychology. He began his work on the study in April or May 1971 and finished it just prior to trial in July 1971. The Tiffin report concluded that both the Beta and the Wonderlic tests could properly be used as Albemarle was using them. His conclusion was that at least one of Albemarle's three tests was significantly related to job performance on nine of ten job groups studied. Dr. Tiffin used the concurrent criterion-related validation method. He selected and grouped jobs from the middle to upper range of ten lines of progression in five different departments. All employees in those jobs, except a few who refused, took the tests for correlation purposes. The supervisors of these employees were then asked to rate their job performances but were given no guidelines to make this assessment. No separate study was made of the correlation between test scores and job performances of African American employees. In three instances, Dr. Tiffin obtained perfect correlations between test scores and supervisory ratings. Such dreamlike perfection is highly unlikely to occur even with the best of tests unless there is some outside influence brought to bear.

Chambers and I received the Tiffin report on July 19, 1971, just ten days before the trial began. Dr. Katzell was unable to arrange his schedule to testify at trial. Fortunately, however, Dr. Richard Barrett, the LDF's testing expert in *Griggs*,[88] agreed again, on short notice, to be our testing expert in *Moody*. We did not get the report to Dr. Barrett until July 29, 1971, less than a day before he would have to testify, as Judge Dupree wanted to have the experts testify back-to-back. Judge Dupree denied the litigation team's request for at least a day to prepare Dr. Barrett for trial because we had received the Tiffin report only shortly before the trial began. His decision was consistent with his "rocket docket" philosophy to quickly dispose of the case. However, we were able, through Dr. Barrett's testimony, to expose serious defects in the hurriedly put together Tiffin report by pointing out that the study failed to conform to a number of professionally acceptable standards on test validation approved by the American Psychological Association. After consulting with Dr. Barrett, it seemed clear to Chambers and me that Albemarle had probably engaged Dr. Tiffin not to do an objective validation study but rather to do a report that would provide it with a defense under the *Griggs* business necessity test as fleshed out in *Robinson.*

Like Judge Butzner in *Quarles,* Judge Dupree, accompanied by counsel for the parties, conducted a personal tour of the Roanoke Rapids mill before he issued his decision. He concluded, based on the tour, that the efficient operation of the highly sophisticated and technically complex machinery required employees with a high level of native intelligence, prolonged training, and experience.[89] On November 9, 1971, Judge Dupree ruled in favor of Albemarle on the testing issue on the grounds that the Tiffin validation study supported a finding that the tests were job-related under the *Robinson* business necessity test. However, he found that the high school education requirement, when used in conjunction with the test battery, was unlawful because the test battery alone was adequate to measure aptitude for skills required for jobs for which they were used. He thus enjoined continued use of the high school education requirement.[90] He denied the plaintiffs and their class back pay but awarded the plaintiffs their attorney's fees. Judge Dupree's denial of back pay led to a landmark decision on back pay in *Moody* in the Supreme Court.

On appeal to the Fourth Circuit, George Cooper, who had drafted the LDF's brief in the Supreme Court in *Griggs,* again drafted the plaintiffs' brief on the testing issue. In addition to Chambers and me, other LDF attorneys who participated in the preparation of the appellate brief were Mike Baller, Bill Robinson, and Eric Schnapper. While the case was pending on appeal, the publisher of the Wonderlic test released a study in which 251,258 job applicants, including 38,452 African Americans, took the test. The study concluded that "the vast amount of data studied in this report confirms that a very stable differential in raw scores achieved by Negro Applicant Population exists and that where Education, Sex, Age, Region of Country and/or Position applied for are held constant, Negro-Caucasian Wonderlic Personnel Test Score differentials are consistently observed."[91] I sent a copy of this report to the court of appeals prior to argument.[92] The court of appeals[93] and other courts[94] relied upon the study to strike down the Wonderlic test because of its adverse impact on African American workers.

The three appellate judges assigned to *Moody* were Judge Braxton Craven, Jr., and the two judges who joined the majority opinion in *Griggs,* Judges Herbert S. Boreman and Albert Bryan. Both Judges Boreman and Bryan had become senior judges by the time they participated in *Moody.* Cooper and I split the oral argument; he argued the testing issue, and I argued the back pay issue. The panel issued a split decision authored by Judge Craven on February 20, 1973.[95] Judge Boreman joined Judge Craven in reversing Judge Dupree on the testing issue; Judge Bryan would have affirmed on the testing issue. Judge Craven, joined by Judge Bryan, voted to reverse Judge Dupree's denial of class-wide back pay; Judge Boreman voted to uphold the denial of back pay. *Griggs* and *Robinson* were the key cases on which the court of appeals relied in holding that Albemarle's test battery was unlawful under the disparate impact theory. The court agreed with the litigation team's argument that a major flaw in the Tiffin study was the total absence of an acceptable job analysis and the reliance on subjective ratings of supervisors who were given only vague standards by which to judge job performance: "We agree that some form of job analysis resulting in specific and objective criteria for supervisory ratings is crucial to a proper concurrent validation study. . . . To require less is to leave the job relatedness requirement largely to the good faith of the employer and his supervisors."[96] Here, the court found that the widely respected Cooper and Sobol *Harvard Law Review* article on testing and seniority supported its rejection of the vague supervisory evaluation as satisfying the obligation for objective job criteria.[97] Another major flaw in the Tiffin study was that it sanctioned the use of the complete test battery when the study had clearly indicated that only one test was valid. Albemarle's principal argument in support of its business necessity defense was that there was nothing wrong with adopting a test battery to assure that all employees in the labor pool were qualified, even though the tests could not predict whether a particular employee would move out of the labor pool to a skilled or unskilled line of progression. The court rejected this argument because Albemarle offered no proof to support the argument.

Albemarle and the union filed petitions for certiorari in the Supreme Court. Although the litigation team opposed the petitions for certiorari, the Supreme Court agreed to hear the case. Chief Justice Burger and Justices White, Blackmun, and Rehnquist voted in favor of granting certiorari, and

Justices Douglas, Brennan, Stewart, and Marshall voted against doing so. Justice Powell did not participate in any of the proceedings in *Moody,* probably because he had been a partner in the Hunton and Williams firm, which represented Albemarle.[98]

Albemarle's principal argument in the Supreme Court on the testing issue was essentially twofold. First, it argued that the court of appeals had committed a "grievously and astonishingly" major error of fact and law in its ruling on the testing issue because the litigation team had introduced absolutely no evidence, statistical or otherwise, to prove that its tests had an adverse impact on African Americans and that this evidentiary defect was not cured by the EEOC's attempt to do so in its brief in the court of appeals based on one of the exhibits introduced at trial.[99] Second, it argued that, even if the litigation team had proven the adverse impact of its tests, Judge Dupree had correctly credited the Tiffin study in finding that the tests had been sufficiently validated to satisfy the job related/business necessity mandate of *Griggs.* With respect to its second argument, Albemarle launched a major and broadside attack on the deference that the courts, including the court of appeals in this case, were giving to the EEOC testing guidelines. The issue of differential validation, which the Supreme Court addressed in its decision on the merits, was injected into the case by Albemarle[100] and its amici, the American Society of Personnel Administration,[101] even though it was not an issue before the court of appeals and was not identified as an issue in Albemarle's petition for certiorari.

The LDF's argument in its merits brief not only pointed out that the evidence of record supported a finding of the disparate impact of the Wonderlic test on the employment opportunities of African American employees but also cited numerous lower court post-*Griggs* decisions that had found that the Wonderlic screens out African Americans. The point of citing this list of cases was, in effect, an argument that the Supreme Court would be justified in taking judicial notice of the adverse impact of the Wonderlic on African Americans.[102] Many of these cases were litigated by the LDF litigation campaign. As was done in the court of appeals, the brief also pointed out the numerous inadequacies in Dr. Tiffin's study that failed to comply with the EEOC testing guidelines. The Department of Justice filed a brief in support of the LDF's position and in defense of the EEOC testing guidelines.

The Supreme Court heard arguments on the case on April 14, 1975. Chambers argued the case for the plaintiffs. The defendants had agreed that Frank Lowden would argue the testing and educational issues for Albemarle and

Warren Woods would argue the back pay issue for Albemarle and the union. Lowden recognized, as he candidly stated to the Court, that his argument was unfocused and disjunctive and for that reason he had not been able to reach the heart of Albemarle's argument on the testing and educational requirements.[103] When the red light on the attorney's podium in the Supreme Court came on, Lowden ended his argument by saying, "I really have not got down to the argument, but I best let Mr. Woods take up the other subject." It was fairly clear to all of those in the courtroom that Lowden's assessment of his argument was right on point. James Turner of the Civil Rights Division presented the argument on behalf of the Department of Justice and the EEOC. There were very few questions from the Justices during the argument, but most of them focused primarily on the back pay issue. There were four solid votes at the conference to affirm the court of appeals on the testing issue—Justices Marshall, White, Stewart, and Brennan. Justices Rehnquist and Blackmun were inclined to reverse. Justice Douglas did not participate in the vote at the conference, and, as noted earlier, Justice Powell did not participate in any aspect of the case.[104] Chief Justice Burger passed, so this meant that Justice Brennan, as the senior Justice in the majority, had the responsibility to assign the writing of the opinion, and he assigned it to Justice Stewart. After Justice Stewart circulated a draft of his opinion to the conference, Justices Douglas, Brennan, White, and Marshall joined the opinion. Justice Marshall, while joining the opinion, filed a separate concurring opinion limited to the back pay issue. Justice Rehnquist, who was initially inclined to reverse, also joined the opinion, and he too limited his separate concurring opinion to the back pay issue. Although Chief Justice Burger styled his opinion as concurring in part and dissenting in part, a close reading of his opinion indicates that he thought the court of appeals' decision should be reversed on both the testing and back pay issues.

The Court summarily rejected Albemarle's argument that the plaintiffs had failed to establish a prima face case of disparate impact of the tests and focused on the issue whether Albemarle had shown its test to be job related. The Court also rejected Albemarle's all-out attack on the EEOC guidelines when it reiterated that they were entitled to great deference even though they did not constitute administrative interpretations of Title VII. The Court then held that "[t]he message of these Guidelines is the same as that of the *Griggs* case—that discriminatory tests are impermissible unless shown, by professionally acceptable methods, to be 'predictive of or significantly correlated with important elements of work behavior which comprise or are relevant to the job or jobs for which candidates are being evaluated.'"[105] The Court found that the Tiffin validation study was significantly flawed in four respects and, for these reasons, could not survive the *Moody* test of business necessity. First, the Court found that the results of the Tiffin study were not statistically significant in demonstrating that success on the tests had any relationship to the ability of the test-takers to be more successful job performers. Second, the Tiffin study was flawed because it compared the test results with subjective supervisory ranking without a proper job analysis and description: "There was no way of knowing precisely what criteria of job performance the supervisors were considering, whether each of the supervisors was considering the same criteria or whether, indeed, any of the supervisors actually applied a focused and stable body of criteria of any kind."[106] It did not escape the Court's attention that the numerous deficiencies in the Tiffin study were, in all probability, the result of Albemarle's hasty effort to do a validation study in the heat of litigation because it was undertaken only a few months before trial when it had used a nonvalidated test battery for a number of years before then: "It cannot escape notice that Albemarle's study was conducted by plant officials, without neutral, on-the-scene oversight, at a time when this litigation was about to come to trial. Studies so closely controlled by an interested party in litigation must be examined with great care."[107] The third reason was that the Tiffin study was flawed because it was conducted on an unrepresentative group of employees. The fourth reason was that Albemarle had made no showing that differential validation was not feasible for testing in the lower-level jobs.

The Court also reached an issue in *Moody* that had been raised by Justice Stewart in response to a draft of Chief Justice Burger's opinion in *Griggs,* but which the Court found unnecessary to resolve there. That issue was whether an employer may test employees for employment in entry-level jobs to assess their potential for qualifying for upper-level jobs as they become vacant. Again, relying on the EEOC testing guidelines, the Court held that an employer may test new employees for future promotions if the new employee is likely, within a reasonable period of time, to progress to jobs at a higher level. While agreeing with the court of appeals that Judge Dupree had committed reversal error in finding that Albemarle had satisfied the business necessity test, the Court decided that the plaintiffs should not be entitled to an immediate injunction against the test program because two prongs of the disparate impact analysis—the business necessity defense and that a properly validated test may nevertheless be a violation of Title VII with "pretext" evidence—had only been clarified in *Moody*. Thus, taking what it deemed to be the more prudent course, the Court left it to the district court to fashion appropriate relief and to call for additional evidence, if appropriate, in light of its approval of the EEOC's guidelines.

11. Make Whole Remedies:
Moody and *Franks*

The effectiveness of a law is determined as much by the remedies or relief it provides as by the substantive theories for determining its violations. The terms "remedies" and "relief" have a chameleonic character.[1] As used in this chapter, they mean the nature and scope of redress a court awards to plaintiffs who have proven they have been victims of or harmed by unlawful employment discrimination. The development of effective remedies, like new theories of discrimination, was an important goal in the LDF's campaign. The strategy of the litigation team to establish a substantial body of law on remedies eventually led to two landmark Supreme Court civil rights cases on remedies. These cases are *Albemarle Paper Co. v. Moody* and *Franks v. Bowman Transportation Co., Inc.,* in which the Court endorsed a set of substantive and procedural rules on remedies advocated by the litigation team that were critical in making the disparate impact theory a revolutionary theory of equality. Of the two cases, *Moody* is the first and most important in placing significant limits on a court's discretion to deny complete relief because the Court affirmed a substantial body of law on remedies the litigation team had established in the lower courts.

The major issue in *Moody* and *Franks* was the limits on the discretion courts have under Section 706(g) of Title VII to deny successful plaintiffs full relief that would restore them to the jobs and economic status they would have had but for unlawful discrimination. Section 706(g) provides that upon a finding of unlawful employment discrimination, a court *may* enjoin the defendants from engaging in such unlawful practice and order such affirmative action as may be appropriate, which may include, but is not limited to, reinstatement or hiring of employees, with or without back pay or any other equitable relief as the court deems appropriate. Section 706(g) specifically mentions only three remedies—injunctive relief, back pay, and affirmative action, which may include reinstatement or hiring—but it does not limit courts to these forms of relief because it also authorizes courts to award *any other equitable relief as the court deems appropriate.* A court's authority to award relief under Section 706(g) is limited by several other provisions in Title VII. The first is that a court shall not award any relief to an individual who has been denied an employment opportunity for any reason not prohibited by Title VII. The second, found in Section 703(j), is that Title VII does not require an employer to grant preferential treatment to any individual or group to eliminate any statistical imbalance between the number of protected individuals or groups in the employer's workforce and the relevant cohort in the relevant labor market. Section 703(j) was a very controversial provision with respect to whether plaintiffs could rely upon statistical evidence to prove unlawful employment discrimination; it was and remains a critical provision on the reach and limits of discretion courts have to award relief to address economic injuries caused by unlawful discrimination.

As a general proposition, the purpose of the relief courts award is to enforce a right or to redress the harm or injury a plaintiff has suffered because of the violation of a right. A threshold problem this general proposition raises, as it applies to employment discrimination cases, is identifying the nature of the harm caused by the unlawful discrimination. No one really disputes the fact that unlawful discrimination causes both economic and noneconomic injuries. The economic injuries include diminished earning opportunities that a plaintiff and a class would have had but for discrimination and loss of or diminution of employee benefits. Noneconomic or personal injuries include pain and suffering, emotional distress, inconvenience, mental anguish, and loss of enjoyment of life. In *Moody,* the Supreme Court affirmed the decisions of lower courts that Title VII, as originally enacted, provides relief only for economic injuries: "Title VII deals with legal injuries of an economic character occasioned by racial or other antiminority discrimination."[2] In a later case, the Court explained that economic injury consists specifically of the unlawful deprivation of full wages earned or due for services performed, or the unlawful deprivation of the opportunity to earn wages through wrongful denial of employment opportunities.[3]

Between 1965 and the enactment of the Civil Rights Act of 1991, Congress provided remedies only for economic injuries for violations of Title VII. Congress amended Title VII in the Civil Rights Act of 1991 to include remedies for noneconomic injuries, but only in disparate treatment cases.[4] Successful plaintiffs in employment discrimination cases brought under Section 1981 are, as a general rule, entitled to relief for both economic and noneconomic injuries caused by unlawful discrimination. There are a couple of potential reasons Congress added noneconomic remedies for violations of Title VII in the 1991 Act. The first and perhaps most important is that because Section

1981 provides relief for both economic and noneconomic injuries in race discrimination cases, it was unfair to deny similar kinds of remedies in unlawful sex discrimination cases.[5] Second, there is congressional recognition that Congress probably had a very myopic view of the nature of discrimination in employment when it enacted Title VII in 1964.[6]

In *Moody,* the Supreme Court held that although Section 706(g) gives courts wide discretion in providing relief to redress economic injuries caused by unlawful employment discrimination, those courts must exercise that discretion to accomplish the congressional goal in enacting Title VII. The Court then identified two purposes. Specifically citing *Griggs,* the Court held that the first and primary purpose of Title VII is prophylactic: to achieve equality of employment opportunities and remove barriers that have operated in the past to favor white employees over other employees. The second purpose of Title VII is to make persons whole for economic injuries they suffered because of unlawful employment discrimination. The second purpose endorses the "make whole" theory of relief. The make whole theory requires courts not only to restore, as far as possible, successful plaintiffs to the positions they would have had but for discrimination but also to deter similar conduct in the future. The contested remedy in *Moody* was an award of back pay to the class on whose behalf the suit was brought. *Franks* extended the make whole remedy to all forms of relief, including retroactive awards of seniority standing.

THE PRE-*MOODY* PRECEDENTS

The Supreme Court in *Moody* affirmed a long line of cases decided by the lower courts that fleshed out the make whole remedy. The foundations for those remedies were the successes the litigation team achieved in the lower courts, stretching back to the early days of the litigation campaign. One of these early successes was convincing the courts to allow plaintiffs to bring broadly defined class actions. Because practically all the LDF cases were filed as class actions, it was not unusual for the litigation team to find itself representing large classes of 100 or 200 or more African American employees and applicants.[7] Representing these large and broadly defined classes, however, presented the litigation team with manageability and litigation costs problems. To alleviate these problems, the litigation team asked the courts to bifurcate the trial proceedings under Rule 42(b) of the Federal Rules of Civil Procedure. Most of the courts were generally quite willing to do so because bifurcation enhanced both economy and efficiency in the management of their dockets.[8] Bifurcated proceedings soon became designated as Stage I and Stage II proceedings. In Stage I, or the liability-determining phase, the parties and the courts focused on the issue of whether the plaintiffs had satisfied their obligation to prove the defendants had engaged in unlawful employment practices. If the plaintiffs were not successful in the liability stage and the plaintiffs did not appeal an adverse decision on liability, the case was over. If the plaintiffs were successful on the liability issue, the trial then proceeded to Stage II, or the remedy-formulating phase.[9] With respect to dealing with the manageability problem, in Stage II the courts could assign a magistrate or appoint a special master to conduct a hearing and make recommendations to the trial judge on back pay claims or monitor compliance with the judgment on relief.

One of the major benefits of bifurcation for the litigation team was that it did not have to put every member of these large class actions on the stand in the liability phase to testify about his or her own story of discrimination. They could tell their personal stories of discrimination in Stage II. There was also the possibility that a finding of liability in favor of the plaintiffs in Stage I might encourage employers and unions to seriously consider settlement.[10] The terms "Stage I" and "Stage II" soon became an integral part of the lexicon in employment discrimination law, and the designations have appeared periodically in Supreme Court employment discrimination cases.[11] The Supreme Court eventually acknowledged that class action employment discrimination cases are essentially a two-stage trial proceeding.[12]

A second early success was convincing the courts that Title VII cases should be tried before judges and not juries. If the courts had rejected this argument, it is highly unlikely that the make whole remedy would have developed as it did because jurors—particularly jurors in the southern states in which most of the litigation team's cases were filed—probably would not have been sympathetic to black plaintiffs because of their own racial biases.

As the Supreme Court later did in *Moody,* the courts in the early cases handled by the litigation team defined the nature of the injury inflicted by unlawful racial discrimination in employment as economic.[13] As a general proposition, an injunction permanently enjoining defendants from engaging in employment practices found to be unlawful was sufficient to prevent defendants from engaging in those practices in the future. The remedy of a permanent injunction rarely, if ever, raised any significant remedial problem because the courts held that absent clear and convincing proof of no reasonable probabilities of future unlawful employment discrimination, a grant of injunctive relief was mandatory.[14] For this reason, cases challenging testing and educational employee selection criteria did not pose any substantial remediation problems. The LDF achieved a high degree of success in most of the cases in which these practices were used.[15] Some courts, aware of the fact that the standards for test validation involved a new and complicated area of the law after *Griggs,* were willing to allow some employers a reasonable amount of time to conduct a proper validation study rather than enjoin the use of a challenged test outright.[16]

THE RIGHTFUL PLACE THEORY

The seniority discrimination cases presented more difficult remedial issues under the make whole theory, but it is this category of cases in which some of the most important remedies for employment discrimination were established. Although back pay, discussed later, is the remedy for economic injury suffered in the past, something more was necessary in the seniority discrimination cases. One court defined the crux of the problem in the seniority discrimination cases to be how far defendants must go to undo the effects of past discrimination.[17] The litigation team urged the courts to construe their remedial authority in this class of cases broadly. The Supreme Court's 1965 voting rights case, *Louisiana v. United States,* strongly supported the litigation team's argument because, in that case, the Court held that a court has not merely the power but the duty to render a decree that will, so far as possible, eliminate the effects of past discrimination as well as bar like discrimination in the future. The courts, including the Supreme Court, frequently cited the *Louisiana* case in endorsing the make whole theory of relief.[18]

The goal of the litigation team from the beginning of the campaign was to establish a body of law on remedies that would make the plaintiffs whole for the economic injury they suffered because of discrimination and to prevent the perpetuation of that kind of injury. The courts, particularly the liberal trial and appellate judges in the Fourth and Fifth Circuits, were receptive to construing broadly the remedial authority they had under Section 706(g). The first remedial theory the litigation team advocated and the courts endorsed was the rightful place theory of relief. Although the courts, parties, and federal agencies, such as the EEOC and the Department of Justice, repeatedly used the term *rightful place*, it is in effect simply another name for the make whole relief endorsed by the Supreme Court in *Moody.*

The rightful place theory was first advocated in a law student Note in the *Harvard Law Review* in 1967,[19] and it substantially influenced the judicial acceptance of the rightful place theory.[20] Both the litigation team and the EEOC, as a friend of the court, relied upon the student Note in *Quarles v. Philip Morris, Inc.*, which was the first case in which a court had accepted the litigation team's new theory of discrimination, namely, the present effects of past discrimination. Judge Butzner, the trial judge in *Quarles,* found the Note to be a "perceptive analysis of both the issue of seniority discrimination and 'its [remedial] solution'" and decided to "freely" draw upon it in deciding whether "present consequences of past discrimination are covered by [Title VII]" and, if so, the remedy he should grant the plaintiffs.[21] Judge Butzner applied the theory in *Quarles* when he ordered Philip Morris and the Tobacco Workers Union to institute a plant seniority system to replace the "lock-in" effect of the challenged departmental seniority system.[22]

On the issue of appropriate relief, Judge Butzner declined the invitation of the LDF and the EEOC to, in his view, abolish the departmental structure and merge the seniority rosters of the respective departments according to seniority. This essentially would have been the Sadie Hawkins remedy. He also declined the proposal by Philip Morris and the union that would continue to subordinate the employment opportunities of black employees to white employees regardless of seniority. Although recognizing that he had the power to issue a far-reaching decree to invalidate the separate lines of progression and affirmatively require the company and union to grant the same seniority rights, training privileges, assignments, and opportunities to black employees as white persons of the same continuous service date, Judge Butzner opted for a more modest decree. He thus decided that the remedy should permit African American employees in plaintiffs' class, i.e., those employed before January 1, 1966, to train and advance on the same basis as white employees with comparable ability and employment seniority. This approach was designed to disturb as little as possible the efficiencies of Philip Morris's department structure. Taking a lead from the defendants' own agreement modifying and loosening interdepartmental transfers, Judge Butzner issued a fairly intricate and detailed decree to unlock African Americans from the formerly racially discriminatory and less desirable department.[23]

Judge Wisdom gave more careful attention than Judge Butzner to the issue of the appropriate remedy. He stated the crux of the remedy issue as posing the problem of how far the employer must go to undo the present effects of past discrimination.[24] On this issue he found the *Harvard Law Review* student Note on seniority quite helpful because it articulated three potential remedial schemes. The first was the "freedom now," or the Sadie Hawkins, approach that would be a complete purge of the "but-for" effect of pre-Act discrimination by allowing African American employees to immediately displace incumbent white employees who had less employment seniority. The second, the "status quo" theory, advocated by the defendants, would continue the effects of past racial discrimination so long as the defendants had adopted policies and practices that ended explicit racial discrimination. The third theory, "rightful place"—which stands between "freedom now" and "status quo," would provide African American workers the right to bid for future vacancies based on plant or employment seniority rather than a seniority arrangement that "locks in" past discrimination. Judge Wisdom endorsed the "rightful place" theory because he believed that it would be in accordance with the history and purpose of Title VII. His reasoning for adopting the rightful place theory was based on his view that Title VII should be construed to prohibit the future awarding of vacancies on the basis of a seniority system that "locks in" prior racial discrimination, that white employees should not be bumped out of their present positions by the African American discriminatees, and that plant or company seniority should govern new job openings.[25]

The courts regularly applied the rightful place theory in the seniority discrimination cases. Under the rightful place theory, members of the plaintiff class are awarded the first opportunity to move into the jobs historically closed to them because of race and to "carry over" their seniority with them in the new jobs.[26] The courts began, at the request of the litigation team, to flesh out in a rather expansive fashion the scope of affirmative remedial action under the rightful place theory. The litigation team's 1974 success in *Pettway v. American Cast Iron Pipe Co.* (ACIPCO) became a landmark template for the kinds of remedies courts regularly awarded under the rightful place theory. Judge Tuttle was the author of the Fifth Circuit's opinion in *Pettway,* and he relied upon the many decisions of the Fifth Circuit and other courts of appeals that had endorsed and applied the theory. *Pettway,* in the words of the Fifth Circuit, was the "most sweeping of all our employment discrimination decisions" at the time it was decided.[27] ACIPCO had a departmental seniority system (though no union was involved) and a rather haphazard and ill-defined no-transfer policy between departments. Because of ACIPCO's wage progression structure and transfer practices, African American employees were deterred from transferring to white jobs or departments. The transfer and promotion practices, together with the mechanism by which they operated, including testing, educational standards, departmental seniority, the absence of the posting of job vacancies or a job-bidding system, and the lack of red-circling or rate retention upon transfer, were shown to have a severe adverse impact on the ability of African American employees to move into better and higher-paying jobs historically reserved for whites.

The litigation team tried the case before Judge Seybourne H. Lynne. Judge Lynne has been described as a "Southern patrician,"[28] but it was rather obvious that, from the beginning of the case, he was disinclined to rule in favor of the plaintiffs on any issue raised in the case. In fact, Judge Lynne had dismissed *Pettway* and four other cases early in the litigation campaign on the grounds that the failure of the EEOC to attempt to conciliate the claims was a jurisdictional prerequisite to suit in federal court, but the court of appeals overruled him on this issue.[29] Judge Lynne eventually ruled against the plaintiffs on the merits after a very long trial in October 1971.

When the Fifth Circuit decided the case, Judge Elbert Tuttle directed that Judge Lynne grant the plaintiffs and members of their class practically all of the rightful place relief the litigation team requested. He wrote that on remand,

> the district court should issue an injunction requiring: (1) the posting of vacancies plant-wide; (2) the selection of "qualified" personnel for the vacancies on the basis of plant-wide seniority; (3) transferring members of the class shall retain their plant-wide seniority for all purposes including promotion, lay-off, reduction-in-force, and recall; (4) advanced entry into jobs for which an employee in the class is "qualified" or for which no specific training is necessary; (5) red-circling of members in the class; (6) establishment of specific residency periods in lines of progression where the company has established prerequisite training as a "business necessity."[30]

Advanced entry, or job skipping, allows members of the class to bypass, or "skip over," jobs lower in a progression scheme if it is decided that experience or training in such jobs is not necessary to the safe and efficient performance of higher-level jobs. Red-circling is a remedy requiring that black victims of unlawful discrimination be paid at the same higher rate they received in segregated jobs and departments when considerations of business necessity require them to enter entry-level lower-paying jobs in white lines of progression, and they must be paid at this higher rate until they reach a job that pays more than the higher rates earned in segregated jobs or until they voluntarily freeze themselves in the new job.

Other kinds of relief included the requirement that defendants keep records of their employment decisions made after a decree had been entered and to file periodic or annual reports with the courts in order for the courts to monitor the defendants' compliance with the injunctive orders and to allow counsel for the plaintiffs to inspect records of compliance for the same purpose.[31] Changes in apprenticeship and on-the-job training programs were ordered and residency requirements were established to assure that class members were properly trained and at the same time not unduly delayed in reaching their rightful place.[32] In appropriate cases, defendants were ordered to provide copies of the decrees to each employee or to post notice of the decree in conspicuous places in the workplace in order to curb the possible chilling effect on the rights of class members to exercise their rights under the decree.[33] Frequently, the courts retained jurisdiction so the courts could review the progress of compliance and, if necessary, to modify the decree to effectuate the rightful place remedy.[34] Employers were also sometimes ordered to engage in affirmative action recruitment programs to increase the number of African Americans in an employer's workforce.[35]

The rightful place theory of relief opened up thousands of jobs for African Americans that had previously been denied to them because of race in industries such as steel, tobacco, paper and pulp, transportation, railroad, trucking, and textiles. One of the ironies of this development is that employment opportunities in many of these industries were on the decline just as the law began to be a potent tool in eliminating discrimination in employment. However, the remedial principles the litigation team advanced and the courts endorsed remained good law, even as the nation moved from a smokestack to a service workplace society.

MOODY, BACK PAY, AND OTHER MONETARY COMPENSATION

Although back pay is one of the specific remedies identified in Section 706(g), that section is silent on whether the make whole remedy includes class-wide back pay. The issue of class-wide back pay was one of the most hotly con-tested remedial issues in the litigation campaign. Beginning with the October 29, 1969, Seventh Circuit decision in *Bowe v. Colgate-Palmolive Co.,* the courts began to regularly allow class back pay as the remedy for the economic injury for past discrimination. *Bowe* was a sex discrimination case in which the em-ployer argued on appeal that only members of a class action who have actually filed charges of unlawful employment discrimination with the EEOC were entitled to back pay, even if they were entitled to benefit from nonmonetary injunctive relief, such as rightful place relief. The court rejected this argument by holding that it was illogical to allow class-wide nonmonetary relief but not other forms of relief, including back pay. The court found that the rulings in *Quarles* and *Jenkins,* major LDF class action cases, supported its decision.

Building on *Bowe,* the litigation team litigated a number of pioneering cases on class-wide back pay cases that ultimately led to the Supreme Court's decision in *Moody. Robinson v. Lorillard Corp.* was one of the earliest of the LDF's class back pay decisions. The claim for class-wide back pay evolved over the course of the proceedings in the trial court. The complaint did not spe-cifically ask for class back pay but did request the court to grant "such other additional relief as may appear to the court to be proper and just." The request for additional relief was included in every complaint the litigation team filed. However, at an early hearing on whether the case could be brought as a class action, a member of the litigation team unequivocally advised the court that only injunctive relief for the class was sought, that back pay was sought only for the eight named plaintiffs, and no back pay was sought for other class members.

Robinson was tried in early May 1969, but the litigation team had not spe-cifically asked for class back pay until after the trial and the posttrial argu-ment. Two significant developments occurred after trial and before Judge Gordon issued his decision in March 1970. First, the Seventh Circuit decided *Bowe* and the EEOC sent a copy of the ruling to Judge Gordon, urging him to grant class-wide back pay. Second, on December 15, 1969, the Supreme Court decided *NLRB v. J. H. Rutter-Rex Mfg.Co.,* in which it rejected a challenge to an NLRB back pay award by the employer, who argued that the NLRB had inordinately delayed its back pay decision. The Court held that it was unfair to impose the adverse economic consequences on the victims of the employ-er's unfair labor practice because of the inordinate delay the NLRB had taken to resolve the back pay remedy. In January 1970, Judge Gordon still had not decided the case, so Turner and Stein filed a formal motion asking Judge Gordon to issue a decision on the merits, "one way or the other," and for the first time in the case specifically requested class back pay. Candidly admitting that the awarding of class back pay may not have been warranted had Judge Gordon decided the merits of the case earlier, the litigation team argued, based on *Rutter-Rex,* that Judge Gordon's long delay in reaching the merits of the case now entitled the plaintiffs to class-wide back pay.[36]

Judge Gordon finally decided *Robinson* in March 1970. However, without explication or discussion, but specifically noting that the plaintiffs had requested class back pay only after trial, he simply ordered the plaintiffs to submit suggested methods to determine back pay for each member of the class and any instructions he should give to a special master should he decide to appoint one to make recommendations on back pay for the class.[37] The Court of Appeals for the Fourth Circuit affirmed the award of class back pay.[38] The appellate panel consisted of Judges Sobeloff, who wrote the opinion, Bryan, and Butzner, each of whom had been involved in other key cases. Judge Sobeloff ruled that back pay is not punitive in nature but is rather a form of affirmative relief that is intended to restore class members to their rightful economic status absent the effects of unlawful discrimination. He also expressed his full agreement with *Bowe* that there was no justification for treating a case as a class action for injunctive relief but not for other forms of relief. Judge Sobeloff agreed with the litigation team's argument that Lorillard's waiver argument was without merit because Rule 54(c) of the Federal Rules of Civil Procedures imposes an obligation on the court to grant necessary relief, even if the winning party has not demanded such relief in the pleadings. After the Fourth Circuit refused Lorillard's motion to stay proceedings while it sought review in the Supreme Court, the company asked Senator Edward Brooke to arrange a meeting of the parties to discuss settlement. Counsel for the parties met with Senator Brooke in Washington, D.C., on October 6, 1971, and agreed to a settlement of $725,000 for the class back pay award and attorney's fees. The settlement in *Robinson* pales in comparison to the amount of back pay in the millions of dollars obtained in later LDF class action cases either in litigation or from settlement.

The Supreme Court eventually decided the issue of whether back pay could be awarded to class members in class actions in *Moody,* in which the relevant facts on the class back pay issue paralleled in many respects the unfolding of the back pay claim in *Robinson.* The complaint the litigation team filed in the case in 1966 did not specifically ask for back pay but, consistent with the litigation team's pleading practice at that time, did request "such other additional relief as may appear to the court to be equitable and just." In addition, in *Moody*, a member of the litigation team advised the trial judge at the hearing on whether the case could proceed as a class action that no back pay was sought for persons other than those named in the complaint. The reason a request for class back pay was not made in the complaint was that the state of the law as to the availability of class back pay and the right to a jury trial had not been decided in 1966. Shortly after the Fourth Circuit decided *Robinson*, Chambers and I informed Judge Dupree, the trial judge, and counsel for Albemarle and the union that the litigation team would be seeking class-wide back pay.

Chambers and I clearly had the impression that Judge Dupree was not favorably disposed to rule in favor of the plaintiffs on the class back pay or that he wanted to limit the size of the class if he had to award class back pay. This impression is based, first, on his entering a series of rather onerous and time-consuming orders relating to the class status that he handed down during the two months before trial—May 28 through July 26, 1971. Among other things, Judge Dupree required that, within two weeks of an order, the litigation team had to specify from records the team had obtained from Albemarle how each class member claiming back pay had been denied employment opportunities because of race, the exact amount of back pay each member claimed he was due, and a suggested form of notice to be sent to each class member. Second, Judge Dupree, like other judges in some of the litigation team's cases, also entered a very broad gag order prohibiting all counsel, including members of the litigation team, from communicating with actual or potential class members who were not formal parties to the action without his express approval to contact members and his approval of the proposed communications to be discussed with each member to be contacted.[39] Courts have the authority to regulate the conduct of the parties and their attorneys in class action cases, including communications between counsel and class members, but that authority is not boundless. The litigation team challenged the constitutionality of the gag order on First Amendment grounds in a motion for leave to communicate with class members, but Judge Dupree never decided the motion.[40] Our impression of Judge Dupree's inclination is reinforced by his writing, on his copy of the slip opinion in *Robinson*, "MIGAWD" by a sentence in the opinion, which stated that "[w]here some employees now have lower expectations than their coworkers because of the influence of one [of the] factors [in Title VII], they are entitled to have their expectations raised even if the expectations of others must be lowered in order to achieve the statutorily mandated equality of opportunity."[41] It is reasonable to assume that the notation stands for "My God!"[42]

After the Fourth Circuit approved class-wide back pay in *Robinson*, Judge Dupree entered an order acknowledging, as he had to, that class back pay could be awarded if plaintiffs were successful on the merits of the claim. But he was not through with his orders regulating the class action aspect of the case. In the same order, he required that notice of the case be sent by first-class mail to each member of the class and that such notice be published, at the expense of the plaintiffs, in the *Daily Herald,* a newspaper published in Roanoke Rapids, North Carolina.[43] The notice required all class members seeking back pay to file a written proof of claim, under oath, with the clerk of the court, setting out in detail the nature of the claim of discrimination and the amount of back pay sought.[44]

The possibility of an award of attorney's fees also did not escape Judge Dupree's scrutiny because he also ordered the filing of detailed information about the fee arrangement between plaintiffs and their counsel *and* the details of any fee arrangement that the plaintiffs had with anyone acting on their behalf and the source of any fees provided on their behalf. It seemed rather obvious that Judge Dupree knew that the litigation team included LDF attorneys, although the LDF name was rarely, if ever, listed on any pleadings in cases in which LDF attorneys were involved, and its name was certainly not listed on any of the pleadings in *Moody*. Perhaps by ordering the disclosure of the fee arrangement, Judge Dupree may have thought it would dissuade the litigation team from pursuing class back pay, but if that was his purpose, he did not achieve that result. Working with a dedicated team of individuals like Joe Moody, Bob Valder, and some of the secretaries in the Chambers law firm, the litigation team was able to respond to the avalanche of onerous and time-consuming orders that Judge Dupree imposed, and Chambers and I were prepared to begin trial as scheduled on July 26, 1971.

The case was tried on the merits before Judge Dupree over a two-week period from July 26 to August 5, 1971. On August 6, the day after the trial concluded, Judge Dupree called Judge Gordon, the district court judge in *Robinson*. The handwritten notes by Judge Dupree of this telephone conversation indicate that he wanted to explore Judge Gordon's rationale for awarding class-wide back pay in *Robinson*.[45] Judge Dupree's notes indicate that Judge Gordon "seemed to have no particular reason for having awarded back pay" and that he did so because he "figured [the plaintiffs] would get it on appeal"; that he was "sorry" he had awarded class back pay; and that he advised Judge Dupree that unless there were "compelling reasons to award back pay," then Judge Dupree would be "warranted in not doing so." His notes concluded with the impression that Judge Gordon "obviously . . . got a mess to work out with the back pay problem [in *Robinson*]."

Judge Dupree denied back pay for two reasons. The first was that neither Albemarle nor the union had engaged in bad-faith noncompliance with Title VII because they had begun as early as 1964 to eliminate their overt discriminatory practices against African Americans, and Albemarle had consistently paid higher wages at all levels of employment than other industries in the area. With respect to the last point, the clear implication was that even though Albemarle was found to have engaged in overt intentional racial discrimination, African Americans who worked for Albemarle were nevertheless economically better off than they would be working with some other racially biased employers in the area. The second reason was that Albemarle and the union had suffered prejudicial harm because the claim for class back pay was not affirmatively requested until nearly five years after the complaint had been filed.[46]

The Fourth Circuit reversed Judge Dupree's denial of back pay in a 2–1 decision written by Judge Craven and joined by Judge Bryan. Judge Craven relied heavily on *Robinson* in overturning Judge Dupree's denial of class-wide back pay. The most important issue in the case was the standard that should be applied to guide courts' discretion to award or deny class-wide back pay. The litigation team urged the Fourth Circuit to adopt, for awards of class back pay, the special circumstances rule the Supreme Court had adopted in *Newman v. Piggie Park Enterprises, Inc.* for awards of attorney's fees and which other courts had adopted for attorney's fees awards under Title VII.[47] The court of appeals agreed with the argument,[48] and, until the Supreme Court's ruling in *Moody*, other courts generally followed the Fourth Circuit in adopting the special circumstances rule on class back pay.[49] The instances in which the courts found special circumstances to deny class back pay were exceedingly rare.[50] However, some courts of appeals rejected the special circumstances rule.[51]

In light of *Robinson* and other court of appeals cases the litigation team had won on class back pay,[52] Albemarle and the union were essentially swimming upstream when they sought review in the Supreme Court on the class back pay issue. The Supreme Court agreed to hear the case over the objection of the litigation team. The litigation team argued very strongly in its Supreme Court brief on the merits in favor of the special circumstances rule on class back pay. After the argument, with Justice Powell recused, there were four votes to affirm the court of appeals on the back pay issue even though the Court eventually rejected the special circumstances rule: Justices Brennan, White, Stewart, and Marshall. There were two votes to reverse: Justices Blackmun and Rehnquist. Justice Douglas did not attend the conference on *Moody* but later joined fully in the majority opinion. Chief Justice Burger passed at the conference, so it fell to Justice Brennan, as the senior justice in the majority, to assign the writing of the opinion, and he chose Justice Stewart for this responsibility.[53]

In *Moody,* the Court endorsed class back pay but rejected the special circumstances rule. Finding that back pay had an obvious connection to the primary purpose as defined in *Griggs,* the Court concluded that if, upon the finding of a violation in Stage I, employers faced only the prospect of an injunctive, nonmonetary order, they would have little incentive to shun practices of dubious legality. The Court observed that it is the reasonably certain prospect of a back pay award that "provide[s] the spur or catalyst which causes employers and unions to self-examine and to self-evaluate their employment practices and to endeavor to eliminate so far as possible, the last vestiges of an unfortunate and ignominious page in this country's history."[54] The litigation team had made this "spur or catalyst" argument in its brief.[55] The Court then fashioned a rigorous rule that substantially limited the discretion a court has to deny back pay to a class or otherwise: "It follows that, given a finding of unlawful discrimination, back pay should be denied only for reasons which, if generally applied, would not frustrate the central statutory purposes of eradicating discrimination throughout the economy."[56] In crafting its rule on the scope of a district court's discretion, the Court was apparently impressed with the argument that the litigation team had made that class-wide back pay would encourage voluntary compliance.

> The experience in Title VII litigation since 1973, when the [c]ourts of [a]ppeals established clear standards on the exercise of discretion, indicates that the voluntary resolution of employment discrimination suits have been advanced. Governmental agencies and private litigants have concluded many consent decrees in Title VII actions which have provided wide-ranging relief, including back pay.
>   Rather than obstructing the elimination of employment discrimination, a

clear judicial standard governing the award of back pay will serve the national purpose of ending employment discrimination by causing employers and unions to carefully evaluate, and to change, where discriminatory, their employment practices without first being subjected to administrative or judicial proceedings.[57]

The Court applied its new rule on back pay to reject the reasons on which Judge Dupree had relied to deny back pay. The first was really an unfettered good-faith defense. The litigation team had urged the Court to reject the good-faith defense on the authority of *Griggs*. The Court agreed that a good-faith defense to back pay is totally inconsistent with the rationale for the *Griggs* disparate impact theory because Congress directed the thrust of the Civil Rights Act to the consequences of employment practices, not simply an employer's motivation for the practices.[58] *Moody* essentially sounded the death knell for the good-faith defense to the back pay remedy except to the extent it may be applicable to some of the sex discrimination cases. As to the second reason Judge Dupree had denied back pay, namely, prejudice to the defendants because of the five years' delay in asking for class back pay, the Court had a twofold approach. First, the Court agreed with the Fourth Circuit that the mere fact that the litigation team's request for class back pay came only shortly before trial did not preclude an award of back pay because, under Rule 54(c) of the Federal Rules of Civil Procedure, trial courts have an obligation to grant necessary relief even if not specifically requested in the complaint, if appropriate. Second, the Court found that further proceedings in the district court would be necessary to determine whether, in fact, Albemarle and the union were actually prejudiced by the "tardy delay" in asking for back pay and, if so, whether the delay was excusable. Finally, the Court summarily rejected Albemarle's and the union's argument that back pay could be awarded only to those class members who had actually filed charges with the EEOC.

Justice Marshall wrote a separate concurring opinion in which he expressed doubts about whether Albemarle or the union would be able to prove they had actually been prejudiced by the plaintiff's delay in specifically seeking class back pay. Based on his long career as a preeminent civil rights advocate, he brought a real-life perspective to the issue when he correctly observed that any tardiness in asserting a claim for class back pay was excusable in light of the uncertain state of law during the early years of litigation under Title VII. Justice Rehnquist changed his vote on back pay after he reviewed Justice Stewart's draft opinion. He joined Justice Stewart's opinion but, in a separate concurrence, he addressed an issue not raised by either party: whether there was a Seventh Amendment right to a jury when back pay was sought. He expressed his view that there may be a right to a jury trial if back pay had to be awarded as a matter of course rather than left to the discretion of the trial court, but he saw no reason to resolve that issue in *Moody*. Justice Blackmun joined in the judgment but disagreed with the majority's holding that good faith is never a sufficient reason to deny back pay. He illustrated his concern about the absolute bar of good faith as a defense with reference to sex discrimination cases where employers might find themselves on the horns of a dilemma of an obligation to comply with state "female protective" laws and the more stringent ban on sex discrimination mandated by Title VII. Chief Justice Burger concurred with the majority's holding that the availability of back pay was committed to the sound discretion of the trial court, but he also agreed with the arguments of Albemarle and the union that good faith was a defense because otherwise employers and unions would have little incentive to eliminate marginal unlawful employment practices unless ordered to do so by a court. It was fairly obvious that in *Moody*, Chief Justice Burger was beginning to retreat from his landmark decision in *Griggs*.

The litigation team had scored another exceptional victory on class back pay in its landmark case of *Pettway v. American Cast Iron Pipe Co.*, decided before the Supreme Court issued its opinion in *Moody*. The district court judge in *Pettway* denied all relief except attorney's fees. On appeal, Fifth Circuit Judge Tuttle wrote a rather long opinion reversing Judge Lynne. In its ruling, the Fifth Circuit went much further than any other court of appeals at that time by providing some guidelines on a multitude of issues that had to be addressed in implementing an order on class back pay relief. It is clear from the sources Judge Tuttle cited in his opinion that he had carried out a fairly exhaustive examination of the substantial body of case law on the subject in setting out guidelines for the computation of class back pay in Stage II proceedings. His guidelines covered suggestions on the use of special masters; negotiations between the parties; the EEOC's assistance in determining amounts to be awarded as back pay; the beginning and ending of the period for computation of back pay for each class member; methods for computing back pay; and the components of the back pay award including but not limited to interest, overtime, shift differentials, and fringe benefits, such as vacation, sick time, and pension plan adjustments.[59] He placed a heavier burden of proof on defendants disputing back pay claims than on the individual class members claiming that pay. Judge Tuttle espoused two basic principles that became the overarching framework for determining back pay awards: that unrealistic exactitude is not required and that any uncertainty in determining what a victim of unlawful employment should have earned but for discrimination is to be resolved against the defendants.[60] *Pettway* thus became a primer on back pay awards (and other forms of relief) in employment discrimination law.[61]

FRANKS AND THE INNOCENT VICTIM DOCTRINE

The Supreme Court decided *Franks* during the term following *Moody. Franks* is the only case in which a member of the litigation team, Mike Baller, served as lead trial counsel, prepared the brief then argued the case in the court of appeals, wrote the petition for certiorari and the briefs on the merits, and argued the case in the Supreme Court. *Franks* was a class action case against an interstate trucking company, Bowman Transportation, and a union. Prior to 1968, the departments within the company were almost totally segregated by race, including jobs as long-haul or over-the-road drivers, which were essentially limited to whites. After 1965, the lead plaintiff in the case, Harold Franks, had attempted, without success, to transfer out of the tire shop in which only African Americans were employed. He had been denied the opportunity to do so because of Bowman's racially discriminatory policy of hiring only African Americans in the tire shop. The facially neutral seniority provisions in the collective bargaining agreement between Bowman and the union had the effect of locking African Americans into the all-black jobs and departments. The posture of the case in regard to Franks's claims was the classical seniority discrimination dispute the litigation team had litigated in a number of other cases, such as *Quarles, Robinson, Pettway,* and *Moody.* The lower courts found in favor of Franks on the seniority discrimination claim and ordered that he and his class be allowed full seniority carryover upon transfer to departments and jobs historically reserved for whites.

Had Franks been the only plaintiff in the case, his claim would have been essentially a disparate treatment case. However, the more important remedial issue in the case involved the claim of another plaintiff, Johnnie Lee, who had applied for an over-the-road driving job after the effective date of Title VII and had been turned down because of his race. In response to the substantial number of applications from African Americans for over-the-road jobs, Bowman finally relented and began to hire African Americans for these jobs. Lee was eventually hired as an over-the-road driver, and the litigation team sought as part of the relief for the subclass he represented—rejected black applicants for the over-the-road driving jobs who were later hired—retroactive rightful place or constructive seniority based on the dates they originally applied, rather than a seniority standing based on the dates they were actually hired. The district court refused to award constructive seniority under the rightful place theory on the grounds that the seniority system was not discriminatory on its face or as applied to the plaintiffs in Lee's subclass. The court of appeals affirmed the denial of constructive seniority to Lee's subclass.

The principal issue before the Supreme Court was whether courts are prohibited, as a matter of law, from granting, as part of the remedy to African American jobs applicants unlawfully refused employment, the full or constructive seniority they would have obtained but for the racially discriminatory refusal to hire them at an earlier date.[62] The issue raised in *Franks* was essentially the same as the back pay issue before the Court in *Moody*, even though it arose in a different remedial context. As a general proposition, back pay claims involve only the interests of plaintiffs and defendants and can be awarded without consideration of the impact of such an award on the employment expectancies or seniority interests of so-called innocent third parties.[63] There have been repeated references to "innocent third parties" in some Supreme Court civil rights cases, but rarely, if ever, is the identity of those deemed to be "innocent third parties" made explicit. Contextually, however, this group is essentially those the Supreme Court described in *Griggs* as "an identifiable group of white employees."[64]

An important issue the LDF raised in *Franks* required the Supreme Court to address the impact of remedies under the rightful place theory on the seniority expectancies of white employees or "innocent third parties." Mike had to get special permission to argue the case before the Supreme Court because one of the rules for admission is that an applicant must have been a member of a state bar for at least five years before seeking admission, and Mike had not met this requirement. One of the most memorable events for Mike about the Supreme Court argument was the presence of Justice Douglas at the oral argument. Justice Douglas had suffered a stroke in December 1974 and did not regularly participate in Supreme Court proceedings, including oral arguments, because he spent months convalescing. Justice Douglas was not on the bench for the case that was argued before *Franks*. Nor was he on the bench when Chief Justice Rehnquist called *Franks* for argument. However, shortly after Mike stood up to begin his argument, Justice Douglas entered the courtroom in his wheelchair and took his usual place at the bench. As Mike described that event, it could not have been a bigger thrill for him, and even though Justice Douglas did not ask any questions during the entire argument, "his eyes were sparkling and he had obviously made the effort to come in" for the *Franks* argument.[65] Throughout the argument, there were a series of questions on the potential impact of retroactive seniority relief for the members of the subclass on innocent white employees and whether allowing retroactive seniority relief constituted preferential treatment for African Americans.[66]

The Court met in conference on November 5, 1975, two days after the oral argument in *Franks*. All of the Justices at the conference, except Chief Justice Burger, tentatively voted to reverse the court of appeals on the denial of retroactive seniority relief to members of Lee's subclass, even though it appears from Justice Blackmun's notes on the conference that there were serious differences as to what the appropriate relief should be in light of the *Moody* make whole theory of relief.[67] Chief Justice Burger was the only Justice who voted to affirm the court of appeals. Justice Douglas voted at the conference to reverse, but he resigned from the Court on November 12, 1975, so his participation in the case came to an end on that date. Because of the resignation of Justice Douglas and the fact that Chief Justice Burger was the only one to vote to affirm, it fell to Justice Brennan as the senior Justice in the majority to assign the opinion writer. He opted to write the opinion himself. Chief Justice Burger and Justice Powell, joined by Justice Rehnquist, each wrote opinions concurring in part and dissenting in part.

In his opinion for the Court, Justice Brennan first decided the threshold issue of whether Section 703(h) of Title VII, which protects "bona fide" seniority systems, limits a court's remedial authority under Section 706(g). After a rather lengthy discussion of the legislative history on the compromise that led to the inclusion of Section 703(h), he concluded that "[t]here is no indication in the legislative materials that § 703(h) was intended to modify or restrict relief otherwise appropriate once an illegal practice occurring after the effective date of the Act is proved—as in the instant case, a discriminatory refusal to hire."[68] The Court then held that Section 703(h) was irrelevant because the relief the plaintiff sought would not result in a modification or the elimination of the extant system. He also found that Section 703(h) was only a definitional provision and did not expressly qualify or proscribe relief otherwise available under Section 706(g). The Court then focused on the remedy that should be awarded in light of the make whole theory of relief it had endorsed in *Moody*. The Court emphatically rejected the argument that the *Moody* rightful place and make whole theory of relief was limited to relief in the form of back pay.[69] The majority and the dissenters agreed that the *Moody* make whole theory of relief governs the exercise of discretion under Section 706(g) in deciding how to remedy a diminished seniority standing suffered by victims of unlawful hiring discrimination. However, they disagreed on whether that discretion should be exercised in favor of constructive seniority or monetary relief. The disagreement on constructive seniority versus monetary relief centered in substantial part on the weight, if any, that should be given to the interest of so-called innocent white males who obtained a superior competitive seniority standing as a result of racial discrimination because they were hired ahead of identifiable African American males found to be actual victims of hiring discrimination. The majority, agreeing with the LDF, found that its decision in *Moody* should control in favor of the identifiable unnamed victims of the plaintiff's class.

Relying on the *Moody* make whole purpose of Title VII, the Supreme Court held that adequate relief for victims of unlawful discrimination ordinarily requires the slotting of the victims in the position in the seniority system that they would have held had they been hired at the time of application. Under the majority's holding, a claim for retroactive or constructive seniority should be treated like back pay under the *Moody* standard and should be denied only for reasons that, applied generally, would not frustrate the purposes for which Congress enacted Title VII. *Franks* and *Moody* established a strong yet rebuttable presumptive entitlement rule in favor of all forms of relief deemed necessary to satisfy the rightful place and make whole purposes of Title VII.

The innocent victim doctrine first surfaced in the Supreme Court in *Franks* in a dispute between the majority and dissenters over whether the *Moody* presumptive entitlement rule on back pay applied equally to nonmonetary forms of rightful place relief, such as retroactive seniority. Unlike monetary relief, which impacts only the economic interests of employers and unions, an award of rightful place seniority relief often diminishes the employment and income expectancies of incumbent white employees. The majority rejected the argument that the employment expectancies of innocent white incumbent employees were presumptively entitled to greater protection than the right to rightful place relief of actual victims of unlawful employment discrimination:

"[A] sharing of the burdens of past discrimination [by innocent white incumbent employees] is presumptively necessary [because it] is entirely consistent with any fair characterization of equity jurisprudence."[70] Chief Justice Burger characterized the majority's view as "robbing Peter to pay Paul," a view that he had expressed at the oral argument. The dissenters argued for the adoption of a rule that would grant actual victims of discrimination monetary compensation, or front pay, which it deemed to be an appropriate exercise of equitable discretions in balancing the interests of actual victims and innocent white employees. The debate between the majority and dissenters was a prelude to disagreement among the Justices on the affirmative action remedy pursuant to which race would be one factor in implementing this country's commitment to equality.

The lower courts' response to the innocent victim problem was the adoption of the no-bumping doctrine in the seniority discrimination cases.[71] In *Patterson v. American Tobacco Co.*, an LDF case, the Fourth Circuit led the way in the adoption of the no-bumping rule. The court of appeals, grounding its endorsement of the no-bumping rule in the exercise of equitable discretion, reasoned that bumping would adversely affect the innocent employees who had done no wrong and who themselves may have been the victims of discrimination and that the domino effect of bumping would mean that employers and employees would likely have their working lives rearranged by courts from time to time in the future as various other unlawful employment practices were identified. The court decided that the more equitable resolution of the problem under the *Moody* guidelines was to protect the innocent victims as to their current jobs but to award victims a monetary award, front pay, to compensate them for the economic loss between the date of the entry of seniority relief until a slot opening occurred in the future in which they could be slotted in their rightful place. The court in *Patterson* framed the monetary relief as back pay, but it is deemed to be the seminal and leading case on the front pay remedy as an ameliorative remedial theory to accommodate the *Moody* presumptive entitlement rule to right place relief and the innocent victim and antibumping rules. Front pay is to compensate a victim of unlawful employment discrimination for future economic loss between the date of the court's judgment and award of back pay and the date the victim is placed in his rightful place. Red-circling or wage-circling can be seen as another form of front pay that courts awarded in the seniority discrimination cases.

STAGE II PROCEDURAL RULES

Before the Supreme Court addressed the issues in 1977 in *Teamsters v. United States,* the litigation team was involved in a series of cases primarily in the Fourth and Fifth Circuits about the procedural rules for determining the relief for individual class members, including back pay awards, because the process of deciding what jobs each member would have had but for unlawful discrimination "create[d] a quagmire of hypothetical judgments."[72] Before *Teamsters,* the litigation team had addressed this problem, and the lower courts had endorsed many of the approaches advocated by the litigation team. In *Johnson v. Goodyear Tire & Rubber Co.,* which, argued by Gaby, was one of the earliest LDF cases to address the procedure for determining individual awards of back pay, the Fifth Circuit endorsed a separate hearing procedure to determine on an individual basis which class members would be entitled to back pay because individual circumstances vary. In a later LDF case, *Pettway v. American Cast Iron Pipe Co.,* which was argued on appeal by Barry Goldstein and decided about a month after *Johnson,* Judge Tuttle wrote a very influential opinion for the Fifth Circuit on procedures for awarding back pay in class actions. In a rather exhaustive section on back pay, Tuttle reviewed a number of other back pay cases. His review led him to make a distinction between class actions in which the class is small or the time period for calculating back pay awards is short and those in which the class size, the ambiguity of promotion or hiring, or the multiple effects of discrimination that has extended over a period of time calls forth a quagmire of hypothetical judgments. He advocated the individual-by-individual approach endorsed by *Johnson* in cases in which the class is comparatively small. But with respect to large classes, he suggested alternative approaches such as a class-wide award, a formula approach, a representative employee earnings formula, or approximations based on a group of employees not injured by discrimination that is comparable in size and length of employment.[73]

In both *Johnson* and *Pettway,* the Fifth Circuit held that, with respect to the burden of proof, each class member was the beneficiary of a presumption of entitlement to back pay based on the liability finding made in Stage I. In order to benefit from the presumption, each individual member had to prove that he was a member of the class and put on evidence of how the violation found in Stage I adversely affected him economically in terms of reduced pay or income.[74] The Fourth Circuit approved an approach to the procedures for determining back pay for members of a class in *United Transportation Union Local No. 974 (Rock) v. Norfolk & Western Ry.*, which Mike Baller and I tried in the district court and which Baller argued on appeal. In addition, the Fourth Circuit held that any judgment on back pay should run against the employer and union jointly and severally or against the employer solely with the right to partial indemnity from the union as to assure that class members who have suffered economic injury are made whole by the responsible party.[75] And in *Russell v. American Tobacco Co.*, which Peter Sherwood and I argued on behalf of the plaintiffs, the Fourth Circuit rejected a union's argument that it should not be liable for back pay because it was a nonprofit organization with meager assets.

In *Teamsters*, the Court weighed in on the process for determining which class members in a class action case are entitled to individual relief:

> When the Government seeks individual relief for victims of the discriminatory practice, a district court must usually conduct additional proceedings after the liability phase of the trial to determine the scope of individual relief. The petitioners' contention in this case is that if the Government has not, in the course of proving a pattern or practice, already brought forth specific evidence that each individual was discriminatorily denied an employment opportunity, it must carry that burden at the second, "remedial" stage of the trial. [But] . . . as is typical of Title VII pattern-or-practice suits, the question of individual relief does not arise until it has been proven that the employer has followed an employment policy of unlawful discrimination. The force of that proof does not dissipate at the remedial stage.
>
> The proof of a pattern or practice supports an inference that any particular employment decision, during the period in which the discriminatory policy was in force, was made in pursuit of that policy.[76]

As to the allocation of the burdens of proof, the Court held that in the remedial stage, the plaintiffs need only show that an alleged individual discriminatee unsuccessfully applied for a job and therefore was a potential victim of the discrimination found in the liability phase. Upon that very liberal quantum of evidence, the burden of proof then shifts to the employer to demonstrate that the individual applicant was denied an employment opportunity for lawful reasons.

The procedure endorsed in *Teamsters* contemplated the possibility of a series of mini-trials, sometimes referred to as the *Teamsters* hearings, in which class members presented evidence on their entitlement to individual relief, including back pay. The Court did not mandate that a *Teamsters* hearing be conducted in each class action to determine individual relief; it was, however, an option open to the district court. *Teamsters* followed the lower courts in imposing a much lighter burden on the individual class member to prove a prima facie entitlement to relief, including back pay, because each class member was the beneficiary of a strong inference that he was a victim of unlawful discrimination at the hands of the defendants, while the defendants had a much greater burden to prove during a *Teamsters* hearing that the individual claimants were entitled to no individual relief or much less relief than requested. *Teamsters* hearings also presented the defendants the prospect of additional costs in terms of discovery and fees for their own attorneys, as well as for the plaintiffs. The possibility that a court had discretion to order *Teamsters* hearings in class action cases on individual relief, possibly resulting in hundreds of hearings, and the costs associated with *Teamsters* hearings were a tremendous inducement to defendants to settle.

ATTORNEY'S FEES

Title VII gives the courts discretionary authority to award the prevailing party, other than the United States, a reasonable attorney's fee, including expert fees as part of the costs of the litigation.[77] Congress included the attorney's fee provision to encourage the private bar to represent civil rights claimants who had meritorious employment discrimination claims because it was persuaded that effective enforcement of the statute would have to rely in substantial part upon private litigation in addition to enforcement by federal agencies. However, the private bar faced a dilemma. On the one hand, as pointed out earlier, the plaintiffs in employment discrimination cases generally do not have the financial resources to pay the up-front litigation costs and attorney's fees. On the other hand, the issue of entitlement to a statutory fee award is not decided until after the plaintiff has obtained prevailing party status, which often does not occur until years after the filing of a complaint because of long delays occasioned by, for example, discovery disputes, numerous motions filed by defendants, and the almost inevitable appeals. I have often observed that the life span of an employment discrimination case from the date of the filing of a complaint in court to the final resolution on the merits is anywhere from three to five years, or more.[78] Without some expectation that a court would award reasonable fees to successful plaintiffs at the end of this long process, the overwhelming majority of the private bar could not afford, and was thus unwilling, to represent impecunious plaintiffs, particularly in a developing area of the civil rights law such as Title VII.

The employment discrimination litigation team had a major role in the development of standards for awards of reasonable attorney's fees because doing so was critical to the effective enforcement of Title VII and standards were needed to guide the lower courts in the exercise of their discretionary authority to award attorney's fees. The Supreme Court first addressed this issue in 1968 in *Newman v. Piggie Park Enterprises, Inc.*, which arose under Title II of the Civil Rights Act of 1964. The LDF urged the Court to endorse a rule directing lower courts to presume that prevailing plaintiffs in fee-shifting civil rights cases are entitled to counsel fees unless "very special circumstances render such a disposition unjust."[79] The Court adopted the LDF's proposed standard. *Piggie Park* established a very strong presumption in favor of reasonable fees to prevailing plaintiffs. The fact that salaried LDF attorneys served as counsel for the plaintiffs did not constitute a special circumstance because the right to an award of fees belongs to the plaintiffs and not their attorneys.[80]

The litigation team's lawyers urged the lower courts to adopt the *Piggie Park* rule on counsel fees for Title VII cases, and eventually those courts did so. Some courts in the early Title VII cases found reasons under the special circumstances rule either to deny counsel fees outright or otherwise to award unreasonably low fees for successful plaintiffs. For example, in *Lea v. Cone Mills Co.*, an LDF case, the district court denied the plaintiffs' attorney's fees based on its conclusion that the plaintiffs, African American females, were testers, rather than applicants, who were not seriously interested in employment with Cone Mills. The court of appeals reversed, specifically endorsing the applicability of the *Piggie Park* special circumstances standard. On remand, the trial court, without making any findings of fact, awarded $10,000 for approximately 515 hours of work, which amounted to less than twenty dollars per hour. This rather paltry hourly rate paled in comparison to the market rate for successful and experienced attorneys handling cases in federal courts. The court of appeals affirmed the award, relying primarily on the grounds that the district court had not abused its discretion in setting the amount.[81] In another LDF case that became a landmark on the business necessity defense and class back pay, *Robinson v. Lorillard Corp.*, Judge Gordon denied fees on the sole ground that "while more meritorious defenses have in some cases been presented, the defenses here cannot be fairly characterized as extreme." The

Fourth Circuit reversed, holding that the *Piggie Park* special circumstances standard was equally applicable to Title VII.[82]

Defendants in employment discrimination cases can also obtain the status of prevailing party under Title VII because the fees provision speaks in terms of prevailing party—not prevailing plaintiffs. In light of the courts' adoption of a strong presumption in favor of reasonable attorney's fees for prevailing plaintiffs, absent special circumstances, the issue inevitably arose whether the same rule applies to prevailing defendants who successfully obtain a judgment in their favor on the liability issue. The Supreme Court addressed this issue in 1974 in *Christiansburg Garment Co. v. EEOC*. The LDF had an exceptionally strong interest in how the Court should decide the issue of the standard for fee awards for prevailing defendants for several reasons. First, the EEOC does not face the same economic problems as private plaintiffs in funding its litigation; funding for its operation is paid by the taxpayers. Second, a rule that would entitle prevailing defendants to an award of statutory fees, absent special circumstances, as urged by Christiansburg, would have a chilling effect on the continuation of the LDF's employment litigation campaign, which had been so instrumental in the development of employment discrimination jurisprudence. The LDF thus filed an amicus brief to advise the Court that, based on its experience in having been involved as counsel for plaintiffs in hundreds of cases against large and small companies and unions, the rule sought by Christiansburg would be a major disincentive to the enforcement of Title VII by private attorneys general that the Court itself had endorsed in *Piggie Park*. The LDF asserted that bringing and maintaining claims under Title VII, often involving complex and difficult issues, and particularly those brought as across-the-board class actions challenging systemic practices, involved substantial resources both in personnel and in funds:

> Lawyers' fees and expenses, expert witnesses and expenses, salaries of research analysts and computer personnel, and other funds expended as ordinary costs of litigation must be found. Such resources are beyond the reach of ordinary Title VII plaintiffs, who are most likely blue collar workers at the lowest rung of the salary scale. Indeed, it is because of their position economically that such workers have sought out the aid of the courts to achieve equality of opportunity for themselves and others similarly situated. Even in class actions, groups of workers rarely have the funds necessary to carry out their side of the litigation without the assistance of organizations such as the Legal Defense Fund. . . . [I]t is obvious that given the fact that Title VII plaintiffs usually cannot afford to bear the costs of their own side of litigation, it would be impossible for them to bear the costs of the defendant's side as well.[83]

The Supreme Court rejected the applicability of the special circumstances rule to claims by prevailing defendants in Title VII cases. Instead, the Court concluded that equitable considerations embodied in Title VII justified a different standard for prevailing defendants. The Court then held that prevailing defendants in a Title VII case may be awarded a statutory award of fees from a losing plaintiff only when a court, in the exercise of its discretion, has found that a plaintiff's action was frivolous, unreasonable, vexatious, or without foundation, even though the case was not brought in subjective bad faith.[84] The standard the Court adopted was essentially the same urged by the EEOC and the LDF. However, the Court hastened to add that, in applying these criteria, district courts must resist the understandable temptation to engage in post hoc reasoning that, because the plaintiff did not ultimately prevail on the merits, the plaintiff's case should be deemed unreasonable or without foundation. This hindsight logic, reasoned the Court, could discourage all but the most airtight claims, for seldom can a prospective plaintiff be sure of the ultimate success.[85] The LDF had addressed the hindsight problem in its amicus brief when it argued that the development of Title VII law had been gradual and had taken dramatic shifts from time to time and that even district courts, like the one in *Griggs*, often err in deciding cases and must, at times, be reversed by appellate courts.[86] One court has said that fees to prevailing defendants under the *Christiansburg* standard "are to be sparingly awarded."[87]

For many years prior to *Christiansburg*, one of the leading cases on statutory awards of attorney's fees was the Fifth Circuit's decision in *Johnson v. Georgia Highway Express, Inc.*, a Title VII case handled by the litigation team. The plaintiffs had won on the merits. The LDF and the cooperating attorney on behalf of the plaintiffs sought $30,145.50 in fees for the 659.5 hours they had devoted to the case. The district court awarded them only $13,300. The court of appeals reversed and identified twelve factors as guidelines (the *Johnson* factors) district courts should consider in determining a reasonable fee: (1) time and labor involved; (2) novelty and difficulty of the issues; (3) skill required; (4) loss of other employment in taking the case; (5) customary fee; (6) whether the fee is fixed or contingent; (7) time limitations imposed by the client or circumstances; (8) amount involved and results obtained; (9) counsel's experience, reputation, and ability; (10) undesirability of the case; (11) nature and length of the relationship with the client; and (12) awards in similar cases. The court based its guidelines on an analysis of fee-award cases previously decided by the Fifth Circuit and by other appellate and district courts, the then extant recommendations by the American Bar Association, and an earlier district court case on fees that was handled by the litigation team.[88] The Supreme Court later replaced the *Johnson* twelve-factor test with the lodestar method as the now-predominant method for calculating a reasonable fee.[89] The lodestar method decides a reasonable fee based on the number of hours reasonably expended on the litigation multiplied by a reasonable rate. Adjustments upward or downward can then be made if appropriate, using, for example, some of the *Johnson* factors.

The developments on the availability of reasonable attorney's fees under the specific statutory provisions in Titles II and VII played a significant role in the enactment of the Civil Rights Attorney's Fees Award Act of 1976.[90] In the wake of *Piggie Park*, some courts began to award fees regularly to prevailing plaintiffs in civil rights cases even if they were brought under laws, such as Section 1981, that did not specifically provide for a statutory award of fees.[91] The litigation team and other lawyers bringing racial discrimination cases regularly added a claim under Section 1981 in addition to a claim under Title VII. The Supreme Court ended the practice of awarding fees in such instances in 1975 when it held that courts should award fees only when Congress had specifically declared by legislation that doing so was appropriate.[92] Congress responded immediately with the enactment of the Civil Rights Attorney's Fees Award Act of 1976. The Fees Award Act provides for statutory awards of fees, among others, in employment discrimination cases brought under Section 1981.

Another development on fees undertaken by the litigation team was to convince the courts to award interim fees, particularly in cases in which the plaintiffs had been successful on the liability issue and the defendant had appealed. The argument in support of interim fees was that in cases where the liability has been decided in favor of the plaintiff, the litigation has been protracted, and there is a strong likelihood that it will continue for some time in the future, the continuing financial drain on the resources constitutes a cash-flow problem for the plaintiffs. The cash-flow problem under these circumstances might induce defendants to engage in an economic war of attrition in an attempt to deprive plaintiffs of their victory. In addition, the legislative history of the Civil Rights Attorney's Fees Award Act of 1976 supported interim awards of fees. The courts were receptive to the LDF's argument that interim fees could be awarded sometimes in appropriate cases.[93]

It is my opinion that during the first several decades of the litigation campaign and particularly for cases in the campaign's earliest years, the LDF and its cooperating attorneys lost millions of dollars in fees because they did not maintain contemporaneous records of the time devoted to the litigation.[94] During the course of the first decade of developments of the litigation campaign, the courts' broad construction of Title VII, and Section 1981, coupled with the positive developments on awards of attorney's fees to prevailing plaintiffs, led to an increase in the number of members of the private bar willing to represent employment discrimination claimants. In later years, as the Supreme Court began to take a more conservative approach to employment discrimination issues and to establish more onerous rules on awards of attorney's fees to prevailing plaintiffs, the number of such members of the private bar declined substantially.

12. *Griggs* and Affirmative Action: *Weber* and *Johnson*

Affirmative action as a remedy for discrimination has generated a great deal of controversy in the long history of the efforts to implement this nation's commitment to equality. However, a major problem in the debate about the legality of affirmative action is the lack of a commonly accepted or widely shared meaning of the concept. In a 1981 article, I addressed this problem by locating it in its historical context:

> This nation unquestionably has a long way to go to achieve a society in which the status of being black is as irrelevant as the color of one's eyes. The affirmative action concept embodies a policy decision that some forms of race-conscious remedies are necessary to improve the social and economic status of blacks in our society. That policy decision, however, cannot be isolated from the history that gave rise to the affirmative action concept. When viewed in light of that history—decades of blatant public and private discrimination against blacks *as a group*—the underlying premise of affirmative action is manifest: If the chasm between "equality" as an abstract proposition and "equality" as a reality is to be bridged, something more is needed than mere positive prohibitions of positive acts of discrimination and the substitution of passive neutrality. That something more, the affirmative action concept dictates, must include race- [or sex-] conscious remedies.[1]

The more provocative conceptions of affirmative action are "preferential treatment," "quotas," and "reverse discrimination." The notions of affirmative action and reverse discrimination are so closely intertwined so as to make clear delineations between them extremely problematic. Both concepts have doctrinal foundations in the same statutory and constitutional provisions. There appears to be a consensus, however, that a claim of reverse discrimination arises only when the form of affirmative action is articulated in terms of specific race- or sex-conscious decisions in favor of African Americans or women.[2] Even though it is difficult to distinguish affirmative action from reverse discrimination, the cases and literature strongly suggest that reverse discrimination is often used as a code word for discrimination against white males.[3] Affirmative action in the context of discrimination has usually been thought of as a remedy for past, present, or continuing discrimination or a way to foster the values of inclusiveness and diversity.

There is no clear consensus on the origins of the affirmative action remedy. Some trace it back to post–Civil War civil rights legislation, enacted when, after passage of the Fourteenth Amendment, Congress adopted a series of programs with benefits expressly limited to African Americans.[4] Others have expressed the view that the origins of the affirmative action remedy first surfaced during the New Deal.[5] Yet others have taken the position that the concept is grounded in presidential Executive Orders.[6] However, there appears to be a consensus that, between 1963 and 1969, the affirmative action remedy moved from historical obscurity to become perhaps the single most important remedy for discrimination.[7] The philosophy underlying the concept of affirmative action—that is, the idea that something more is needed than a rule of law mandating "passive neutrality"—was one of the motivating concerns that led the LDF litigation team to advocate the disparate impact theory of discrimination. This is not to say that affirmative action in the fullness of the debate that emerged in later years entered into the development of the LDF's litigation strategy when that program was initiated in the mid-1960s. Rather, the point is that controversy over affirmative action evolved only over time with the maturation of the *Griggs* disparate impact theory and the make whole theory of relief, which the Supreme Court eventually endorsed in *Moody* and *Franks*.

The issue of affirmative action did not escape the attention of Congress during the legislative debates on Title VII in 1964. One commentator stated that "[p]erhaps no charge was made more frequently by opponents of Title VII, both in and out of Congress, than that Title VII would require or authorize the imposition of racial quotas upon employers and labor organizations."[8] Although the congressional proponents of Title VII rebutted the racial quota charge on numerous occasions, the Senate leadership added Section 703(j) to quell the persistent concerns that the Act would require employers to maintain racially balanced workforces. Section 703(j) provides that nothing in Title VII *requires* defendants to "grant preferential treatment to any individual or any group because of race, color, religion, sex or national origin" to remedy an imbalance between the number of minorities in an employer's workforce and the number in the labor market from which the employer draws its employees.[9]

CONTROVERSY OVER AFFIRMATIVE
ACTION EMERGES

The broad-based enthusiasm for federal civil rights legislation that was so manifest in the efforts that led to the Civil Rights Act of 1964 began to wane in the 1970s, when the worldwide economic recession started to have an impact on the American economy. By the mid-1970s, the continued expansion of the middle class was no longer assured and, because of the progress made in developments under Title VII, white males, in particular, found themselves competing in the workplace not only with other white males but also with African Americans, other minorities, and women. As affirmative action began to emerge as an effective remedy for the continuing effects of decades of racial discrimination, white males began to seek judicial redress for their own claims of unlawful discrimination. Affirmative action thus became one of the more controversial issues in civil rights enforcement because it was claimed that affirmative action that took race or sex into account constituted reverse discrimination against white males and was, for that reason, legally and morally indefensible. One commentator viewed the controversy over affirmative action this way:

> To its critics, affirmative action is both a euphemism for discrimination against white men and a system that bureaucratizes the entire society at the cost of meritocratic decision making; it is a symbol for all that has gone wrong with American society since the sixties. To its supporters, it is a first step towards remedying the crime of slavery and eliminating the discriminatory preferences that have guaranteed white men the easiest path to wealth and power; it is a symbol of justice, and promise of a future of hope.[10]

The controversy about the legality of affirmative action led to the splintering of the civil rights coalition that played a significant role in the passage of the Civil Rights Act of 1964. The segment of the coalition that opposed affirmative action argued that equality requires adherence to a strict color-blind notion of equality as both a strategy and a goal and that the only way to accomplish this goal is to assure that each individual has access to all spheres of public activity—social, economic, and religious—regardless of race, sex, or ethnic origin. The advocates of this view believed the original vision of the civil rights movement was concerned with *equality of opportunity.* But by the mid-1970s, much of the civil rights leadership began to splinter, with one segment becoming preoccupied with *equality of results,* which meant all groups should be represented in institutions and occupations of society roughly in proportion to their representation in the population. The term *equality of results* is a different label for affirmative action or, the more emotionally charged term, *quotas.* Adherents of the *equality of results* view were labeled social engineers.[11] The segment of the civil rights coalition that endorsed affirmative action argued that it was appropriate as a tool of civil rights public policy because, on balance, it is useful, if not necessary, in overcoming entrenched racial hierarchy or societal discrimination.[12] Another commentator who has written extensively about unions and the struggle by African Americans for equality in the workplace offered this explanation of the splintering of the civil rights coalition:

> Because Title VII as initially interpreted and enforced by the courts reached beyond individual relief to attack long-established patterns of discrimination and hence was becoming a major instrument of social change, the law came under powerful and repeated attacks. As the AFL-CIO became an adversary of the law and many labor unions resisted compliance with the Civil Rights Act, the coalition that was decisive in securing the adoption of Title VII disintegrated.[13]

Another potential explanation about the splintering of the civil rights coalition is the absence of any meaningful discussion about whether the different constituencies may not have subscribed to the same conception of *equality* while instead each proceeded on the assumption that all other constituencies of the coalition did. However, when affirmative action began to emerge as a strategic remedy for discrimination, it became obvious that there was an absence of unanimity about the meaning of equality. Also, one of my colleagues explained that the history that led to the split of the LDF's immense success in developing pro-plaintiff employment discrimination legal theories and remedies may have led to the rise of reverse discrimination claims.

THE SUPREME COURT ENDORSES AFFIRMATIVE ACTION

The courts have addressed the issue of the legality of affirmative action in three broad categories of cases: those involving laws and policies specifically requiring affirmative action,[14] those involving judicially imposed affirmative action as remedy after a judicial finding of unlawful employment discrimination,[15] and those involving affirmative action plans voluntarily adopted in the absence of a judicial finding of liability.[16] Also, the Supreme Court has adopted different legal rules for determining whether affirmative action is permissible depending upon whether the challenge is based on the Equal Protection Clause of the Constitution or a civil rights statute, such as Title VII. The focus of this chapter is on the legality of voluntarily adopted affirmative action under Title VII and the influence of *Griggs* on the legal rule the Supreme Court adopted for this category.

Prior to the enactment of the Civil Rights Act of 1991, *Steelworkers v. Weber* and *Johnson v. Transportation Agency, Santa Clara County,* were the leading Supreme Court Title VII cases on the legality under Title VII of voluntarily adopted affirmative action plans. The contexts in which the two cases arose are attributable, in substantial part, to the *Griggs* disparate impact theory and the legal edifice built on that theory. Although the Supreme Court had not been consistent in its guidelines on the evidentiary showing required to satisfy the business necessity defense,[17] the courts, including the Supreme Court in *Moody,* had clearly decided that a validation study provides the most probative evidence of business necessity. It is generally recognized, as a plurality of the Supreme Court eventually acknowledged in *Watson,* that validation studies are costly and time-consuming.[18] It has been estimated, for example, that an employer seeking to validate a single employee selection criteria, such as an arithmetic test for mechanics, could expect to incur costs ranging from $20,000 to $100,000.[19] Yet, as late as 1976, more than a decade after the enactment of Title VII and a year after the Supreme Court had decided *Moody,* one management lawyer pointed out that many employers were still oriented to the threat of strikes or organizing campaigns or to the daily struggle over labor contract negotiations and had not come to realize the full implication of the landmark employment discrimination cases.[20]

The twin developments of an emergence of a coherent body of substantive law on the disparate impact theory and a substantial body of remedial measures based upon the rightful place and make whole theories sent a clear message to defendants in employment discrimination cases: either affirmatively prove that the facially neutral practices that result in disparate impact are mandated by business necessity or face a substantial risk of liability, including the imposition of costly remedies by the courts, and bad publicity.[21] The either-or message in the post-*Griggs* developments was bolstered by other developments that were taking place simultaneously with the LDF's litigation campaign. Although presidential Executive Orders have been on the books since 1941, effective enforcement of these orders did not begin to occur until after the election of President Kennedy, when his Executive Orders imposed an obligation on private employers to take affirmative action to assure that employees were treated fairly during their employment without regard to race, color, religion, sex, or national origin. In the early years after the presidential orders began to require affirmative action, employers had little to fear if they did not honor the obligation because of ineffective enforcement by federal authorities. That state of affairs began to change in the late 1960s, after the enactment of Title VII and the Supreme Court's decision in *Griggs,* when the federal government began taking steps to effectively enforce employers' affirmative action obligations under Executive Orders.

In 1969, the Office of Federal Contract Compliance (OFCC) issued an order known as the Philadelphia Plan that required all bidders for federal contracts to submit acceptable affirmative action plans. The bids had to include an obligation to make good-faith efforts to achieve specific goals and timetables on minority manpower utilization. The emphasis on goals and timetables soon began to attract the attention of employers. Just over a month after the Supreme Court decided *Griggs,* the Third Circuit, on April 21, 1971, upheld the Philadelphia Plan in *Contractors Association of Eastern Pennsylvania v. Secretary of Labor.* The Association, which consisted of more than eighty contractors in a five-county area near Philadelphia who were subject to the federal Executive Order, challenged the legality of the affirmative action obligations of the Philadelphia Plan on a number of grounds. They asserted that the Plan was social legislation enacted by the executive branch that was authorized by neither constitutional nor statutory authority and violated the anti–preferential treatment provision of Section 703(j) of Title VII; Title VII, because it interfered with the protection afforded bona fide seniority systems under Section 703(h); the basic mandate of Section 703(a) of Title VII, because it required reverse discrimination by forcing members of the Association to refuse to hire white tradesmen and to classify employees because of their race; Title VI of the Civil Rights Act of 1964, which prohibits racial and other forms of discrimination in any program receiving federal financial assistance; and the equal protection mandate of the Fifth Amendment by imposing contradictory duties on recipients of federal assistance to grant preferential treatment on the basis of race and, at the same time, prohibit discrimination because of race. It was obvious that the Association's and the union defendants' primary objective was to protect the seniority expectancies of its largely white membership they had obtained only because of a history of discrimination against African Americans.[22]

The Third Circuit upheld the legality of the Philadelphia Plan on the grounds that it fell within the implied authority of the President and his designees to implement the affirmative action provision of Executive Order 11246 and that the Plan was prohibited by neither Title VII nor Title VI. In so doing, the court found support in *Griggs* and relied on the "freezing" principles of *Griggs* and *Quarles* in rejecting the Association's argument that Title VII bars affirmative action:

> To read § 703(a) [of Title VII] in the manner suggested by the [Association] we would have to attribute to Congress the intention to freeze the status quo and to foreclose remedial action under other authority designed to overcome existing evils. We discern no such intention either from the language of the statute or from the legislative history. Clearly the Philadelphia Plan is color-conscious. Indeed, the only meaning which can be attributed to the "affirmative action" language which since March 1961 [date of President Kennedy's Executive Order] has been included in successive Executive Orders is that Government contractors must be color-conscious.[23]

Another important post-*Griggs* development was that the EEOC was beginning to flex its administrative muscle with the filing of cases in its own name with the new judicial enforcement authority it received from Congress in 1972. Even after obtaining judicial enforcement authority, the EEOC continued its long-standing practice of filing amicus briefs that, more often than not, supported the arguments of the LDF litigation team and plaintiffs in other cases, whether brought individually or with the support of some other public interest organization. And the federal agencies with primary responsibility for enforcing the laws and Executive Orders on employment discrimination—the EEOC, Department of Justice, Department of Labor, and the Civil Service Commission (now the Office of Personnel Management)—adopted Uniform Guidelines on Employee Section Procedures in 1978, which broadly defined selection practices subject to challenges under the disparate impact theory.

One way employers and unions could possibly reduce their exposure to very costly and time-consuming litigation was voluntarily to adopt affirmative plans pursuant to which they would take race and sex into account in making hiring and promotion decisions. By doing so, they could reduce the statistical disparities between minorities in their workforces and the relevant labor markets and could substantially reduce the probability that a plaintiff would be able to establish a prima facie case under the disparate impact theory and thus avoid the obligation to prove that facially neutral employment practices are mandated by business necessity. But employers faced another dilemma if they voluntarily adopted the affirmative action option: the prospect of *reverse discrimination* claims, so-called, by white males.[24]

Many employers chose the option of voluntarily adopting affirmative action plans. And, as expected, employers began to be hit with "reverse discrimination" claims by white males.[25] These developments set into motion the events that led to *Steelworkers v. Weber,* the first Supreme Court decision to address the legality of voluntarily adopted affirmative action plans when challenged solely under Title VII. Fundamentally, *Weber* raised the issue of whether, in the absence of judicial findings of unlawful racial discrimination, employers and unions can voluntarily adopt affirmative action plans that take race or sex into account in making employment decisions.

In 1974, Kaiser Aluminum & Chemical Corporation and the Steelworkers, the defendants in *Weber,* entered into a master agreement covering fifteen of Kaiser's plants in the United States. The agreement contained an affirmative action provision designed to eliminate conspicuous racial imbalances in what were then almost exclusively white craft jobs. The agreement provided that for each of Kaiser's fifteen plants, a goal was set that no fewer than one minority applicant be admitted to the craft training program for every nonminority admitted until the percentage of African Americans craftsmen equaled the percentage of African Americans in the relevant labor force. Eligibility for the craft training program would still be based on plant seniority, but to implement the affirmative action goal, two separate seniority lists based on race were established. For each two vacancies, one African American and one white would be selected on the basis of seniority from the respective racial seniority lists.

Prior to the agreement, Kaiser selected only individuals who had at least five (later changed to three) years of experience in the particular craft jobs; it offered no on-the-job training for craft jobs. Neither the Steelworkers nor Kaiser was willing to admit that they had excluded African Americans from craft jobs because of their race, and the district court found that the evidence at trial did not establish that Kaiser had engaged in racial discrimination in staffing the positions. But as the LDF argued in its amicus brief, the lack of diversity among the parties to the lawsuit explained the absence in the record of evidence on which a finding of past discrimination by Kaiser or the

Steelworkers could be made, even though there was ample evidence to support a finding of potential liability under disparate impact theory with respect to the prior experience requirement for craft jobs.[26] Also, Kaiser conceded in the Supreme Court that its past hiring practices might be open to question insofar as race was concerned.[27] In any event, the Supreme Court held that judicial findings that African Americans had been excluded from craft jobs because of race were so numerous as to make such exclusion a proper subject for judicial notice.

The 1974 agreement between Kaiser and the Steelworkers clearly showed that any potential future liability under Title VII was the major motivating factor in adopting the affirmative action plan.[28] Kaiser also acknowledged that its motivation for entering into the agreement was pressure from the Labor Department, which enforced the Executive Order, to take steps to eliminate the underutilization of minorities in craft jobs, and the fact that the company was a defendant in other race discrimination lawsuits brought by private parties under Title VII.[29] The LDF was involved in one of the cases against a Kaiser plant in Baton Rouge, Louisiana, which eventually settled for $255,000.[30] The other private Title VII case against Kaiser had been in litigation for eleven years.[31] The district court also concluded that the evidence supporting the view that Kaiser's primary motivation for agreeing to the affirmative action plan was a desire to satisfy its affirmative action obligations under the rules adopted by the OFCC and to avoid "vexatious litigation by minority employees."[32] The Steelworkers' motivation for entering into the agreement was substantially that it had been a defendant in a large number of cases, many of which had been brought by the litigation team[33] and the Department of Justice.[34] As one scholar has observed, "[p]robably no industrial union has faced more Title VII trouble than the United Steelworkers of America" because "[t]housands of complaints have been filed against the unions and employers with whom they bargain in basic steel, charging racial discrimination in both the North and South."[35]

In *Weber,* a white employee in the Kaiser facility in Gramercy, Louisiana, brought a Title VII class action against Kaiser and the Steelworkers alleging that the affirmative action provision of the agreement discriminated against him and his class because of their race. Kaiser and the Steelworkers defended the claim on the grounds that the affirmative action plan was a valid exercise of presidential executive power, and it did not violate Title VII because its goal was to remedy societal discrimination against African Americans, even in the absence of past discrimination. The district court ruled in favor of Weber and his class because it concluded that Kaiser had not discriminated against African Americans in the past and that racial quotas were not a legitimate response to societal discrimination. The district court further held that none of the African Americans preferred over more senior white employees was ever a victim of discrimination at the Gramercy facility.[36] A divided panel of the Fifth Circuit affirmed, holding that "[i]n in the absence of prior discrimination, a racial quota loses its character as an equitable remedy and must be banned as an unlawful racial preference prohibited by Title VII."[37] Judge Wisdom, in dissenting, warned that the majority's standard would substantially undercut voluntary compliance with Title VII, which had been encouraged by cases such as *Moody* and *Franks*, by forcing employers and unions to walk a "high tightrope without a net beneath them." On one side of the rope was the possibility of liability to African Americans in private actions, suits by the federal government, and sanctions under Executive Order 11246. On the other side was the threat of private suits by white employees in reverse discrimination cases and possible suits by the federal government. He advocated an "arguable violation" test to determine the legality of voluntarily adopted affirmative actions plan. Under his test, affirmative action plans would be lawful if they were voluntarily adopted by employers and unions in response to an arguable violation of Title VII.[38]

The court of appeals' decision in *Weber* created the "high tightrope" dilemma for employers and unions characterized by Judge Wisdom. This dilemma was compounded by the Supreme Court, which earlier had expressly refused to decide whether Title VII allowed or prohibited private employers and unions from voluntarily adopting affirmative action plans.[39] Both Kaiser and the Steelworkers filed petitions for certiorari in the Supreme Court. The Justices granted review and in their opinions were to say that the case raised only the "narrow statutory issue of whether Title VII *forbids* private employers and unions from voluntarily agreeing upon bona fide affirmative action plans that accord racial preferences in a manner and for the purpose provided in the Kaiser-[Steelworkers] plan."[40] *Weber* was the first case the Supreme Court agreed to hear involving the legality under Title VII of affirmative action plans voluntarily adopted by private employers and unions. The Court was well aware that *Weber* raised a hotly contested civil rights issue that would have far-reaching consequences whether it ruled in favor of Weber or in favor of Kaiser and the Steelworkers.[41]

Only seven of the nine Justices participated in decision in *Weber*. Justice Stevens disqualified himself at the time the Court granted certiorari but did not give a reason for doing so, although it was widely assumed that he did so because of a possible legal or financial conflict of interest arising from his former law practice or his personal investments.[42] Justice Powell attended the conference at which certiorari was granted but did not participate in either the oral argument or the decision because he was recovering from surgery to remove a nonmalignant tumor in his colon.[43] At the conference following the argument, there was some discussion of Justice Powell possibly participating in the case, which led to concern of a potential four-four vote, namely, four Justices who wanted to decide the case in favor of Weber and four Justices who wanted to decide in favor of Kaiser and the Steelworkers.[44]

Chief Justice Burger passed at the conference because he wanted to first ascertain the views of Justice Powell because, in his judgment, "[d]eference to a colleague unavoidably absent from participation in a case so inherently institutionally important commanded no less."[45] The Chief Justice called Justice Powell to inform him of the Justices' tentative vote on the merits and to get some assessment of when Justice Powell might be able to resume his normal duties. Apparently, there was also some discussion at the conference about the possibility of reargument to provide Justice Powell the opportunity to participate if there was a very narrow vote in favor or against reversal of the Fifth Circuit. After reporting the results of his telephone conversation with Justice Powell to the other members of the Court, the Chief Justice decided to vote to affirm the Fifth Circuit. In a memorandum to the conference on his vote, the Chief Justice said that he would "much prefer to have employers free to initiate their own private programs to give minorities preferential treatment," but he could "find no principled basis to avoid the explicit language of the relevant statutory provision [of Title VII] which forecloses such programs based on race."[46] The Chief Justice requested that Justice Brennan designate the Justice to write the opinion for the Court because he was the most senior Justice in the majority to uphold the affirmative action plan. Justice Brennan assigned himself to do so.

Justice Brennan initially circulated a draft of his opinion upholding the affirmative action plan to only the four Justices who had decided to join in a judgment to uphold the plan—Justices Stewart, White, Marshall, and Blackmun—but not to the other Justices who eventually wrote dissents, Chief Justice Burger and Justice Rehnquist, because apparently he wanted to first find out whether he had a majority of the Court with him.[47] Justice Stewart said he would join in the proposed opinion if there were three others also willing to do so. Justice Marshall immediately joined the opinion. Justice White responded that although he recognized there was more than one approach to the case, he might eventually join in the opinion because he preferred to have a majority opinion. Justices White and Blackmun withheld their decisions to join Justice Brennan's draft opinion until they had reviewed the dissenting opinions.[48]

In a 5–2 opinion written by Justice Brennan, the Court held that the plan did not violate Title VII. Perhaps one of the strongest arguments made on behalf of Weber's class was that because the Court had held in *McDonald v. Santa Fe Trail Transp. Co.* that Title VII prohibits discrimination against whites as well as African Americans and because the Kaiser-USWA affirmative action plan, on its face, was not race neutral, it logically followed that the plan violated Title VII. This argument was based on the disparate treatment theory of discrimination and, on the facts of the case, was a classical case of direct evidence of discriminatory intent because no one disputed that race was a factor specifically relied upon in administering the affirmative action plan. Based on a literal or strict construction of the operative language in Title VII, the Court specifically acknowledged that the "argument [was] not without force." However, the Court rejected the literalist or strict construction of Title VII. Rather, the Court turned to a canon of statutory construction that held that "a thing may be within the letter of the statute and yet not within the intention of its makers." Justice Brennan, citing the legislative history, focused on the fact that Congress's primary concern in enacting Title VII was "the plight of the Negro in our economy" and that the goal of Title VII was to "open opportunities for Negroes in occupations which have been traditionally closed to them." Then, relying on the spirit rationale, Justice Brennan held that "[i]t would be ironic indeed if a law triggered by the Nation's concern over centuries of racial injustice and intended to improve the lot of those who had 'been excluded from the American dream for so long' . . . constituted the first legislative prohibition against all voluntary, private, race-conscious efforts to abolish traditional patterns of racial segregation and hierarchy."[49] Justice Brennan invoked the doctrine of judicial notice to support the factual conclusion that because blacks had long been excluded from craft unions, few were able to obtain experience in craftsmen positions. In a memo to Justice Blackmun, one of his clerks stated that Justice Brennan had apparently "cribbed from" Judge Wisdom's dissenting opinion in *Weber* and the LDF's amicus brief in invoking the doctrine of judicial notice on the exclusion of African Americans from craft jobs.[50] The LDF had asked the Court to take judicial notice of the long history of discrimination against African Americans in craft jobs. It deemed it critical for the Court to do so in a case of such importance, as neither party had an interest in fully presenting the factual context in which the case arose and substantial rights of persons not party to the case were at stake. In addition, the LDF marshaled the facts in support of a finding that African Americans historically had had limited opportunities, because of race, to participate in craft jobs.[51]

The appropriate interpretation of Section 703(j) of Title VII, the so-called antipreferential provision, was a major issue in *Weber,* just as it had been with respect to the issue of whether statistical evidence may be introduced to prove or disprove a claim of unlawful employment discrimination. Section 703(j) provides that nothing in Title VII "shall be interpreted to require" any employer or union to grant preferential treatment to any individual or group to correct any racial imbalance in a workforce. The majority and dissenters disagreed on whether this provision is an absolute bar to voluntarily adopted affirmative action plans. And both the majority and the dissenters relied heavily upon the legislative history in support of their views on how this Section should be construed. Based on his review of the pertinent legislative history, Justice Brennan concluded that since Congress, after much debate, chose the term *require* rather than *require or permit,* the "natural inference was that Congress chose not to forbid all voluntary race-conscious affirmative action."[52] Justice Brennan had also proposed to justify the majority's construction of Section 703(j) with the argument that it was too late in the day to argue that Title VII requires race-neutral employment practices in all circumstances, that the Court had not read it that way in cases such as *Griggs* and *Moody,* and that Congress, in enacting the 1972 amendments to Title VII, had expressly considered and rejected proposals to alter the prevailing judicial interpretations of Title VII permitting race-conscious affirmative action.[53] This line of argument was excluded from the official opinion. The Supreme Court held also that its disposition of the case made it unnecessary to consider Kaiser's and the Steelworkers' argument that the plan was justified because it feared that black employees would bring a disparate impact case if they did not adopt an affirmative action plan.[54]

The Court upheld the affirmative action plan at issue in *Weber* but declined to provide bright-line rules on permissible and impermissible plans.

However, the Court did provide guidelines or, as some would say, a three-part test, to determine the legality of a voluntarily adopted affirmative action plan when challenged in a "reverse discrimination" case under Title VII. Those guidelines are whether the plan is designed to break down old patterns of racial segregation by eliminating conspicuous racial imbalances in traditionally segregated job categories and old patterns of racial segregation and hierarchy; unduly trammels the interests of white employees, such as by requiring the discharge of white employees and their replacement with new black hires; or creates an absolute bar to the advancement of white employees because it is a temporary measure that is not intended to maintain racial balance or quotas but is rather adopted to eliminate a manifest racial imbalance.[55]

A key holding in *Weber* was the rejection of Judge Wisdom's "arguable violation" theory, endorsed by Justice Blackmun. He wrote a separate concurring opinion and advocated a theory he deemed appropriate to navigate the practical problems defendants in employment discrimination cases face, namely, potential liability or reverse discrimination claims by whites if an affirmative action plan is adopted. He found Judge Wisdom's "arguable violation" theory to be the most appropriate approach to this dilemma. Justice Blackmun also observed, and probably quite correctly, that Justice Brennan would consider a job to be traditionally segregated when there had been a societal history of purposeful exclusion of African Americans.[56]

Both the majority and dissenting Justice Rehnquist relied heavily on Title VII's legislative history. Justice Rehnquist, joined by Chief Justice Burger, wrote a scathing dissent in which he asserted that Justice Brennan's majority opinion was "a tour de force reminiscent not of jurists such as Hale, Holmes, and Hughes, but of escape artists such as Houdini" because, in his opinion, the Court failed to recognize that "[t]he operative Sections of Title VII prohibit ... discrimination in employment *simpliciter.* ... [I]t prohibits a covered employer from considering race when making an employment decision, whether the race be black or white." With respect to *Griggs,* he wrote: "We have never wavered in our understanding that Title VII 'prohibits all racial discrimination in employment, without exception for any group or particular employees.' In *Griggs v. Duke Power Co.,* our first occasion to interpret Title VII, a unanimous Court observed that '[d]iscriminatory preference, for any group, minority or majority, is precisely and only what Congress has prescribed.'"[57] It apparently was not an oversight that Justice Rehnquist did not discuss the fact that the Court had endorsed the disparate impact theory in *Griggs,* which

Justice Brennan did not cite in his opinion. Justice Rehnquist's interpretation of *Griggs* had ominous implications signaling the death of the disparate impact theory that came to fruition in 1989. Justice Blackmun criticized Justice Rehnquist on the ground that he read the legislative history of Title VII more expansively than the Court had done in *Griggs*.[58] In addition to joining Justice Rehnquist's dissenting opinion, Chief Justice Burger wrote a separate dissent that Rehnquist did not join. With respect to *Griggs,* Chief Justice Burger, specifically citing his unanimous opinion for the Court in *Griggs,* wrote that "[u]ntil today, I had thought the Court was of the unanimous view that '[d]iscriminatory preference for any group, minority or majority, is precisely and only what Congress has proscribed' in Title VII."[59]

Johnson v. Transportation Agency, Santa Clara County, decided by the Supreme Court in 1987, was another closely watched Title VII case on the legality of voluntarily adopted affirmative action plans. The major differences between *Weber* and *Johnson* were that *Weber* was a race discrimination case against a private employer and a union and *Johnson* was a sex discrimination case against a public employer, and the plan in *Weber* was the result of collective bargaining, while the plan in *Johnson* was not. The plan in *Johnson* provided, among other things, that in making promotion decisions within traditionally segregated job classifications in which women have been significantly underrepresented, the employer is authorized to consider as one factor the sex of qualified applicants. Unlike the plan in *Weber,* the plan in *Johnson* set aside no specific number of positions for women or minorities. Rather, the plan contained a long-range employment goal to attain a workforce composed of women, minorities, and disabled persons in approximately the proportion to the composition of the relevant labor market. Santa Clara County had selected a woman, Diane Joyce, for a skilled craft position that Paul Johnson, a white male, also had sought. Both applicants were qualified, but the employer relied upon the affirmative action plan as the tiebreaker in awarding the vacancy to Joyce. Johnson then filed a lawsuit solely under Title VII alleging that he had been denied the job because of his sex. Johnson made no claim of sex discrimination under the Equal Protection Clause of the Constitution. Equal protection challenges to affirmative action plans are analyzed under a strict scrutiny test, which is a more rigorous test than the *Weber* Title VII test.

The main issue in the case was whether a public employer may, consistent with Title VII, voluntarily adopt an affirmative plan that considers gender a factor in making employment decisions. The trial court held that the plan was invalid under the *Weber* test; the court of appeals held that the plan was lawful under *Weber*.[60] The Ninth Circuit also addressed a threshold issue that the Court had not specifically addressed in *Weber,* namely, which party, the employer or the plaintiff, has the greater burden to prove that a voluntarily adopted affirmative action plan either meets or fails the *Weber* test. The Ninth Circuit majority held that the plaintiff has the greater burden of proving that the plan is unlawful under the *Weber* test. The dissenting court of appeals judge held that the employer has the greater burden.

Until the Supreme Court granted the employer's petition for certiorari in *Johnson,* that case did not gain the same widespread publicity that *Weber* had generated because it had escaped the civil rights bar's monitoring radar. Most of the reverse discrimination cases challenging affirmative action plans were closely watched and monitored by civil rights advocates as well as by groups and individuals who opposed such plans. *Johnson,* according to Mike Baller, who had a major role in drafting the Supreme Court brief for the employer, was not one of those cases, as it had not received the same kind of notoriety as had other affirmative action cases.[61] Baller, then living in California, recalls that he received calls from civil rights "friends on the East Coast who were three time zones ahead of me" trying to find out about the case. Baller, who at that time had left the Mexican American Legal Defense and Educational Fund (MALDEF) and was then in private practice, also had not heard about the case. He agreed to make some inquiries and convey the information to those who had called him. He did so by contacting Steven Woodside, who represented Santa Clara County, and then conveyed the information to his East Coast colleagues. Baller, who had extensive experience in employment discrimination and civil rights litigation with both LDF and MALDEF, offered to work with Woodside and his colleagues on the proceedings in the Supreme Court. Woodside accepted the offer and hired Baller to serve as cocounsel in the case, and they coauthored the briefs for Santa Clara County filed in the Supreme Court.[62] The LDF joined a number of other civil rights legal organizations in filing an amicus brief urging the Court to affirm the Ninth Circuit's majority decision.

Upholding the plan, the Court addressed an important preliminary matter about the theory and allocation of the burdens of proof in the affirmative action reverse discrimination Title VII cases in holding that a plaintiff in a reverse discrimination case brought under Title VII has the ultimate burden of proving that the challenged affirmative action plan does not satisfy the *Weber* test. The Court also rejected Justice Scalia's claim, in dissent, "that the obligations of a public employer under Title VII must be identical to its obligation under the Constitution."[63]

On the merits, the Court, in a 5–4 decision written by Justice Brennan, held that the legality of an affirmative action plan adopted by a public employer, when challenged solely in a Title VII action, is to be determined by the *Weber* test. The Court found that Santa Clara County's plan was valid under *Weber*. It also affirmed its earlier ruling in *Weber* that an employer is not required to admit nor point to its own prior discriminatory practices nor even produce evidence of an arguable violation on its part to justify the adoption of an affirmative action plan. Rather, an employer can adopt an affirmative action plan to remedy conspicuous racial or sexual imbalances in traditionally segregated jobs. Translated, the term "traditionally segregated job categories" means societal discrimination. In an earlier case, the Court, in an opinion written by Justice O'Connor, had held that, under the Equal Protection Clause, public employers cannot justify an affirmative action plan on the grounds that it is a remedy for societal discrimination.[64] Justice Brennan rejected Justice O'Connor's view that an employer is legally justified in adopting affirmative action only if the manifest imbalance sought to be remedied would support a prima facie case of unlawful discrimination because such a rule would create a significant disincentive for employers to voluntarily adopt affirmative action plans.[65] Even though Justice Brennan did not cite *Griggs* in either *Weber* or *Johnson,* the rationale upon which he relied was undoubtedly powerfully informed by the legal edifice built on the *Griggs* disparate impact theory. *Weber,* he said, is grounded in the recognition that voluntary employment action can play a crucial role in furthering Title VII's purposes of eliminating the *effects* of discrimination in the workplace and that Title VII should not be read to thwart such effort as a catalyst for employers and unions to eliminate the vestiges of societal discrimination.[66]

Justice White had joined Justice Brennan's opinion in *Weber* but refused to join his opinion in *Johnson*. He took the position that he understood that the notion in *Weber* of "traditionally segregated jobs" meant intentional and systematic exclusion of blacks by employers and unions from certain jobs. Because he said the majority in *Johnson* construed this notion as nothing more than a statistical imbalance between one identifiable group and another in an employer's workforce, he would overrule *Weber* and reverse the decision below.[67]

GRIGGS AND THE BOTTOM-LINE THEORY

Between *Weber* and *Johnson,* the Court decided another case, *Connecticut v. Teal,* involving the legality of a theory that would have made it more difficult, if not impossible, for plaintiffs to successfully challenge facially neutral employment practices that had an adverse impact on African Americans. In 1979, the federal agencies with the major responsibility for enforcing laws prohibiting discrimination in employment in the public and private sectors adopted the Uniform Guidelines on Employee Selection Procedures. After resolving some policy differences on how to address the "either-or" situation employers and unions faced in light of the *Griggs* disparate impact theory and the surge in reverse discrimination claims, these federal agencies endorsed the "bottom-line" theory, on which they earlier had differing views, particularly as to its role in employment discrimination law.[68] The bottom-line theory, as the federal agencies adopted it, holds that if an employer uses multifaceted selection criteria and one of the criteria, though facially neutral, has a disparate impact on African Americans or women, the agencies generally would not take enforcement action if the total selection process resulted in no adverse impact. These agencies specifically recognized the rights of any individual to pursue a claim in court if denied employment because one component of the selection process has a disparate impact on the group of which the individual is a member.[69] The best and least costly way to achieve the bottom line would be to add an affirmative action component to the selection process; by taking this expedient step, employers could avoid the costly and time-consuming requirement under the *Griggs* business necessity defense to validate the criterion in the selection process that produced the adverse impact.

Connecticut v. Teal is a classic case on the operation of the bottom-line defense, which the Supreme Court rejected. The employer, the State of Connecticut, used a multicriteria selection process to fill supervisory vacancies in one of its departments. The selection process first required applicants to pass a written examination. Candidates who failed the exam were eliminated from the list of those who would be subject to further screening procedures, which included a review of past work performance, supervisors' recommendations, and, to a lesser extent, seniority. Connecticut then applied what the court of appeals characterized as an affirmative action component with the end result, i.e., the bottom line, that more African Americans were promoted to supervisor vacancies than had passed the test and satisfied the other selection criteria.

Four of the African Americans who failed the test sued Connecticut under Title VII. They alleged that the selection process was racially tainted because the exam had an adverse impact on African Americans and Connecticut had no defense to the claim because it had not validated the exam. Instead, the state relied upon the bottom-line defense. The trial court analyzed the case as one of disparate impact and held that, because there was no adverse effect on the bottom line, Connecticut did not have to prove that the exam was job related. The plaintiffs lost. The court of appeals reversed.

The lower courts were in agreement that this category of cases should be analyzed under the *Griggs* disparate impact theory. However, they disagreed on whether the bottom-line evidence precluded plaintiffs from establishing a prima facie case or whether it was a defense to a disparate impact case and whether, if treated as a defense, it relieved the employer from having to validate the criterion that caused the adverse impact. The Supreme Court granted certiorari to resolve this conflict. The argument Connecticut made in the Supreme Court was that bottom-line evidence precludes a plaintiff from establishing a prima facie case under the disparate impact theory and, in the alternative, is a defense to a disparate impact case without the need to prove business necessity. In a 5–4 decision with the opinion written by Justice Brennan, the Court categorically rejected the state's argument, holding that the bottom line does not preclude plaintiffs from establishing a prima facie case and does not provide employers with a defense to such a case. In so holding, the Court relied on *Griggs* when it said that a non-job-related test that has a disparate impact and that is used to limit or classify employees is used to discriminate, whether or not it was designed or intended to have this effect and despite an employer's effort to compensate for its discriminatory effect. In order to demonstrate his view and the views of his colleagues who joined in his opinion that the disparate impact theory was now a well-established theory in civil rights jurisprudence, Justice Brennan declared that Congress endorsed the *Griggs* disparate impact theory when it amended Title VII in 1972 to extend coverage to state and municipal employers:

> The legislative history of the 1972 amendments to Title VII . . . demonstrates that Congress recognized and endorsed the disparate-impact analysis employed by this Court in *Griggs*. Both the House and Senate Reports cited *Griggs* with approval, the Senate Report noting: "Employment discrimination today is a . . . complex and pervasive phenomenon. Experts familiar with the subject now generally describe the problem in terms of 'systems' and 'effects' rather than simply intentional

wrongs." In addition, the section-by-section analyses of the 1972 amendments submitted to both Houses explicitly stated that in any area not addressed by the amendments, present case law—which as Congress had already recognized—was intended to continue to govern.[70]

The Court specifically rejected the Department of Justice's invitation to construe Section 703(h) contrary to how it had construed it in *Griggs*. The Court also declined to recognize an exception in this class of cases, either by imposing an additional burden on plaintiffs seeking to establish a prima facie case or in the nature of an affirmative defense when an employer has compensated for a criterion that has an adverse effect by adding an affirmative action component. The EEOC did not join the Department of Justice brief, and the Court specifically noted that fact in its opinion.

The dissenters, in an opinion written by Justice Powell, objected to the majority's decision on the ground that, inter alia, it might force employers to either eliminate tests or rely on expensive, job-related testing procedures, the validity of which may or may not be sustained if challenged. Because of the costs attendant to the validation process, the dissenters concluded that one of the practical effects of the majority's view might well be the adoption of simple quota hiring. A more fundamental issue that divided the majority and dissenters was whether Title VII, as interpreted in *Griggs*, protects individuals or groups. Justice Brennan, although recognizing that the Court had said in *Griggs* that Title VII prohibits procedures that operate as built-in headwinds for groups, decided *Teal* on the ground that it protects individuals rather than groups: "Congress never intended to give an employer license to discriminate against some employees on the basis of race or sex merely because he favorably treats other members of the employees' group." The dissenters, on the other hand, criticized the majority for blurring the line between the *Griggs* disparate impact theory and the *McDonnell Douglas* disparate treatment theory. The dissenters accused the majority of confusing the aim of Title VII, which they agreed was to protect individuals, with the two distinct methods of proof, depending on the theory under which plaintiffs sought relief.[71]

13. The Death Knell for *Griggs*:
The Court's 1989 "Civil Rights Massacre"

Many in the business community strongly opposed affirmative action when, in 1965, the federal government first required employers with government contracts to take affirmative action to increase the number of African Americans, women, and other minorities in their workforces. A major reason for the opposition was that affirmative action constituted reverse discrimination primarily against white males. By the 1980s, the early opposition by employers began to shift more toward an enthusiastic acceptance of affirmative action. Some of the reasons were that employers and unions faced difficulties in defending disparate impact and pattern or practices claims based on the business necessity defense; the EEOC began to enforce Title VII aggressively after Congress gave it enforcement authority in 1972; and employers recognized the benefits of having a diverse workforce at all levels of the business hierarchy, which included economic benefits and better consumer relations.

President Ronald Reagan took office in 1981 during a time when claims of reverse discrimination were on the rise and affirmative action was constantly under attack in the political and legal arenas. During the eight years President Reagan was in office (1981–1989), his administration conducted a sustained political and legal campaign to get rid of the disparate impact theory because of the belief that the disparate treatment theory of discrimination, which requires proof of discriminatory intent, is the only theory of discrimination that is embraced in our national commitment to equality. This meant, of course, that *Griggs* had to be overruled because it established the critical concept of discrimination, the disparate treatment theory, which legitimates affirmative action.[1] President Reagan's election and his appointment of conservative Justices to the Supreme Court were among the most important developments that set into motion events that eventually led to the death of the *Griggs* disparate impact theory during the Supreme Court's "civil rights massacre" of 1989, but as early as 1976 the Supreme Court began to dismantle the disparate impact theory and the legal edifice established on it.

THE FIRST WARNING OF THE DEATH OF *GRIGGS*

The composition of the Supreme Court began to change less than a year after *Griggs,* when President Richard Nixon appointed Justice William Rehnquist to replace Justice John Marshall Harlan and Lewis Powell to replace Justice Hugo Black. Both took their seats on the Court on January 7, 1972. Shortly after the Supreme Court decided *Griggs,* the issue arose about whether the Title VII disparate impact analysis is equally applicable to discrimination cases brought under the Equal Protection Clause of the Constitution. The Court first addressed the issue in *Washington v. Davis* in 1976.

Employment discrimination claims could be brought under the Equal Protection Clause of the Constitution against public employers before and after 1972, but these employers could not be sued under Title VII until Congress amended it in 1972 to include them. The LDF was in the forefront of the endeavor to move the law toward embracing the principles of *Griggs* in equal protection cases before 1972 and, in fact, successfully litigated one of the first cases in which a court was persuaded to do so.[2] By the time the Court decided *Washington v. Davis,* the question of whether the *Griggs* disparate impact analysis was equally applicable to public employers sued only under the Equal Protection Clause was one of the most controversial civil rights issues. The courts of appeals, however, were divided on the issue.[3]

The facts in *Davis* were analogous to those in *Griggs.* The plaintiffs were African American applicants to be police officers in the District of Columbia's police department. They alleged that the department's selection practices, including a written test that African American applicants failed at a rate roughly four times that of whites, discriminated against them because of their race. They did not claim that the police department intentionally selected the test to discriminate against African Americans. Instead, they alleged only that the test's disproportionate impact violated their rights to equal protection.[4] The African American plaintiffs, the police department, the district court, and the court of appeals relied on disparate impact analysis with respect to the testing claim. The black applicants lost in the district court, but the court of appeals ruled in their favor. The court of appeals categorically held that a public employer's intent or lack of intent was irrelevant because the disproportionate impact of the test, standing alone, was sufficient to establish a prima facie case of discrimination under the Equal Protection Clause, thus shifting the burden to the government employer to prove business necessity. The court of appeals then held that the black applicants had proven a prima facie case of differential impact discrimination with respect to the test and the police department had not satisfied the business necessity test because it had validated the test only for success in the police academy but not for actual job performance as a police officer.

The police department sought review in the Supreme Court. The Court, with the issue framed as whether the court of appeals had correctly applied the *Griggs* disparate impact analysis, agreed to hear the case. The LDF filed an amicus brief in support of the African American plaintiffs urging the Court to affirm the court of appeals. During the argument, several of the Justices pointedly questioned whether the *Griggs* disparate impact theory applies to cases brought solely under the Equal Protection Clause. All of the parties responded affirmatively, either directly or indirectly.[5] In deciding the case, the Court, on its own accord, reached out to address a question neither raised in the certiorari petition nor addressed by the parties in their briefs, finding the case appropriate for invoking a rule providing that the Court "may notice plain error not presented." The Court then said the issue was not whether the lower court had correctly applied *Griggs* but rather whether proof of disparate impact of a racially neutral practice or policy, standing alone, establishes a prima facie case of a constitutional violation under the Equal Protection Clause. All of the Justices, in an opinion written by Justice White, rejected the argument that the *Griggs* disparate impact theory applies to Equal Protection Clause cases. To prove a violation under the Equal Protection Clause, the Court held that a plaintiff must prove intentional or purposeful discrimination. As the Court explained in a later case, a plaintiff must prove that a public employer selected the racially neutral criterion causing the disparate impact at least in part "because of," and not merely "in spite of," its adverse effect on an identifiable group.[6] In *Washington v. Davis,* the Court said that while disproportionate impact is not irrelevant, it does not, standing alone, trigger strictest scrutiny in racial discrimination cases based on the Equal Protection Clause.

The Court drew a sharp distinction between the *Griggs* disparate impact theory and the constitutional purposeful discrimination theory. Saying it was "not disposed to adopt [the] more rigorous standard" of *Griggs* for cases based on a constitutional provision, the Court said that the process of adjudicating a Title VII claim, with the need for job validation of qualifying tests, "involves a more probing judicial review of, and less deference to, the seemingly reasonable acts of administrators and executives than is appropriate under the Constitution where special racial impact, without discriminatory purpose, is claimed."[7] A major concern expressed by the Court in rejecting the disparate impact theory in equal protection cases was the likelihood that it could be used to invalidate a range of tax, welfare, public service, regulatory, and licensing statutes that may be more burdensome to the poor and the average black than to the more affluent whites and could be used to challenge tests and qualifications for voting, draft deferment, public employment, jury service, and other government-conferred benefits and opportunities.

SENIORITY SYSTEMS INSULATED FROM THE *GRIGGS* THEORY

In the term following *Washington v. Davis,* the Court continued to restrict the disparate impact theory by insulating race- and sex-neutral seniority systems from the reach of the disparate impact theory. The first and most important of these cases is *Teamsters v. United States,*[8] in which civil rights advocates suffered their first major substantive defeat in a Title VII case in the Supreme Court. It is the same case in which the Court endorsed the liberal use of statistical evidence in employment discrimination cases, established a strong rebuttable presumption in favor of make whole relief for individuals and class members on whose behalf the case was brought, and imposed a heavy burden on defendants to prove that individuals and class members were not entitled to make whole relief after a judicial finding of unlawful discrimination.

Teamsters was the consolidation of two separate Title VII cases in which the Department of Justice charged a company and a union with engaging in a pattern and practice of racial discrimination. Pattern and practice cases require proof of discriminatory intent. A major issue in *Teamsters* was whether a racially neutral seniority system that affords no constructive seniority to victims discriminated against prior to the effective date of Title VII (July 2, 1965) is immunized from the disparate impact theory under Section 703(h), which provides a safe harbor for bona fide seniority systems that otherwise would be prohibited under Title VII. Unions had insisted upon such protection for seniority systems in exchange for supporting Title VII.[9] Following in the wake of cases such as *Quarles v. Philip Morris, Local 189, Papermakers and Paperworkers v. United States,* and *Griggs,* the lower courts regularly found that race- and sex-neutral seniority systems perpetuated into the post–Title VII era the effects of past intentional discrimination that constituted unlawful employment discrimination. In doing so, the lower courts repeatedly rejected the argument that Section 703(h) insulates either unions or employers from liability under the disparate impact theory.[10] Unions were deeply disappointed with this development. As one commentator observed, "[w]ith increasing judicial enforcement of Title VII, organized labor was transformed from a supporter of the law into an opponent of the law."[11] The unions' persistence in adhering to their view that Section 703(h) insulates them from liability under Title VII for bona fide seniority systems finally bore fruit in *Teamsters.*

The fundamental argument the union made in the Supreme Court was that the central purpose of Section 703(h) is to make certain that the mere perpetuation of pre-Act discrimination by facially neutral seniority systems does not violate Title VII. The Supreme Court agreed. In a 7–2 opinion written by Justice White, the Court readily acknowledged that "[w]ere it not for § 703(h), the seniority system in this case would seem to fall under the *Griggs* rationale."[12] The Court also candidly acknowledged a long line of decisions in the courts of appeals that had adopted and expanded upon the seminal seniority discrimination case of *Quarles.* However, the Court, relying on the legislative history of Section 703(h), concluded:

> The unmistakable purpose of § 703(h) was to make clear that the routine application of a bona fide seniority system would not be unlawful under Title VII. As the legislative history shows, this was the intended result even where the employer's pre-Act discrimination resulted in whites having greater existing seniority rights than Negroes. Although a seniority system inevitably tends to perpetuate the effects of pre-Act discrimination in such cases, the congressional judgment was that Title VII should not outlaw the use of existing seniority lists and thereby water down vested seniority right of [white] employees simply because their employer had engaged in discrimination prior to the Act.[13]

Justice White attempted to harmonize the Court's ruling in *Teamsters* with *Quarles* by trying to recast the rationale for *Quarles* as resting on an intent theory rather than the disparate impact theory: "Insofar as the results in *Quarles* and in the cases that followed it depended upon findings that the seniority systems were themselves 'racially discriminatory' or had their 'genesis in racial discrimination,' . . . the decision can be viewed as resting upon the proposition that a seniority system that perpetuates the effects of pre-Act discrimination cannot be bona fide if an intent to discriminate entered into its adoption."[14]

Justice Marshall, concurring in part and dissenting in part, correctly pointed out that the majority overruled almost a decade of legal precedents on seniority discrimination that had developed in the wake of *Quarles* without a single dissent in the six courts of appeals that had endorsed that case. Many of the thirty cases cited by Justice Marshall were cases brought by the LDF litigation team, with some groundbreaking decisions that helped to establish the legal edifice that made *Griggs* a revolutionary theory of equality. In *Teamsters*, however, the Supreme Court did reaffirm the litigation team's success in *Franks v. Bowman Transportation Co.*, which held that Section 703(h) does not bar an award of make whole retroactive seniority relief for post-Act victims of unlawful discrimination. The Court distinguished the two cases on the ground that the plaintiffs in *Teamsters* were seeking relief for the disparate impact of pre-Act discrimination, which required a direct attack on the seniority system, but the plaintiffs in *Franks* were seeking constructive seniority that did not require a change in the seniority system.

In later cases in which it repeatedly emphasized the *Teamsters* rule, the Court left no doubt that its clear intent was to insulate seniority systems where proof is lacking that they were adopted or maintained with the specific purpose or intent to discriminate. In a case decided in the same term as *Teamsters, Trans World Airlines, Inc. v. Hardison,* a religious discrimination case, the Court emphatically stated that, under *Teamsters,* a plaintiff must prove "actual intent to discriminate on [statutorily proscribed] grounds on the part of those who negotiated or maintained the system."[15] Perhaps more important, the Court established the proposition that the seniority rights of employees under a bona fide seniority system trump the rights of employees under Title VII. In a third case, *United Air Lines, Inc. v. Evans,* which was decided on the same day as *Teamsters,* the Court established another hurdle to challenging facially neutral seniority systems. United Airlines had hired Carolyn Evans, a female, as a flight attendant in 1966, at a time when United had a no-marriage rule for female flight attendants. When Evans married in 1968, she was forced to resign under the no-marriage rule. A court of appeals later struck down United's no-marriage rule in a case brought by another female flight attendant in 1968,[16] but that case was decided after plaintiff Evans had been forced to resign. United and the union then agreed to a new collective bargaining agreement that ended the no-marriage rule. United rehired Evans as a new employee in 1972, but United and the union refused to give her the seniority standing that she would have had from 1966 but for the unlawful no-marriage rule. The issue in the case before the Supreme Court was whether Evans had timely filed a charge with the EEOC because, if she had not, then her claim was time barred.

Relying in part on *Franks,* the plaintiff, who was supported by the LDF, argued that Section 703(h) does not bar an award of retroactive seniority relief for post-Act effect of facially neutral seniority systems that perpetuated the present effects of an unlawful rule. In a 7–2 decision written by Justice Stevens, the Court rejected Evans's argument when it held that, although the facially neutral seniority system has a continuing effect on her pay and fringe benefits, she could not pursue the claim because she had not filed a timely charge with the EEOC after she had been forced to resign in 1966. As they had in *Teamsters,* Justices Marshall and Brennan vigorously dissented in *Teamsters, Evans,* and *Hardison.*

In 1979, the Supreme Court continued to erect formidable barriers to challenges to facially neutral seniority systems with its ruling in *California Brewers Association v. Bryant.* The issue there was whether a provision in a collective bargaining agreement is part of a seniority system when it provided greater benefits to permanent employees than it did to temporary employees; the provision required that employees had to work at least forty-five weeks in a single calendar year before they could become permanent employees. The African American plaintiffs in the case alleged that the employer and the union manipulated the system by intermittently hiring African Americans in such a way so as to limit their opportunity to work the necessary number of weeks. The court of appeals held that the facially neutral forty-five-week rule was not part of the seniority system and thus was not subject to the rule announced in *Teamsters*; rather, it was subject to a *Griggs* disparate impact analysis. The Supreme Court reversed, in a 4–3 opinion written by Justice Stewart, with Justices Powell and Stevens not participating. The Court broadly defined a seniority system that is protected under Section 703(h). The Court took the position that the term "seniority system" should be broadly, not narrowly, construed, in view of this nation's long-standing policy of recognizing diverse forms of seniority systems and the necessity of affording significant freedom in their creation. Although the Court did not provide a bright-line definition of a seniority system, it did say that a "seniority system" is a scheme that, standing alone, or in tandem with non-"seniority" criteria, allots to employees ever-improving employment rights and benefits as their relative lengths of pertinent employment increase. The Court further stated that, unlike other methods of allocating employment benefits and opportunities, such as subjective evaluations or educational requirements, the principal feature of any and every "seniority system" is that preferential treatment is dispensed on the basis of some measure of time served in employment.

The LDF litigation team joined with MALDEF in filing an amicus brief in *California Brewers* urging the Supreme Court not to define a seniority system so broadly as to include facially neutral nonseniority-related practices that might otherwise be subject to challenges under the disparate impact theory. The Court responded to this concern positively when it admonished that its ruling in *California Brewers*

> does not mean that § 703(h) is to be given a scope that risks swallowing up Title VII's otherwise broad prohibitions of "practices, procedures, or tests" that disproportionately affect members of those groups the Act protects. [Although employers and unions must be afforded significant freedom to create differing seniority systems] . . . that freedom must not be allowed to sweep within the ambit of § 703(h) employment rules that depart fundamentally from commonly accepted notions concerning the acceptable contours of a seniority system, simply because those rules are dubbed "seniority" provisions or have some nexus to an arrangement that concededly operates on the basis of seniority.[17]

But for this admonition, *Teamsters* and its progeny would have provided employers and unions the opportunity to broadly define seniority systems to include tests and educational requirements that would then be insulated from disparate impact challenges unless proven to have been adopted with the intent to discriminate.[18]

Then, in a 1982 LDF case, *American Tobacco Co. v. Patterson*, the Court held that seniority systems protected under Section 703(h) are not limited to those adopted before the effective date of Title VII but applied also to seniority systems adopted after Title VII. Cooperating attorney Henry Marsh, who had been lead counsel in *Quarles*, argued in the Supreme Court on behalf of the plaintiffs in *Patterson*. In another LDF case also decided in 1982, *Pullman-Standard v. Swint*, the Supreme Court granted certiorari on whether courts of appeals are bound by the facts as found by the trial courts to determine whether the plaintiffs have proven unlawful discrimination. The issue arose particularly because the U.S. Court of Appeals for the Fifth Circuit had held that the ultimate finding of discrimination is a legal, rather than a factual, question. (Courts of appeals may not reverse factual findings on which a decision on the merits is based unless that decision is clearly erroneous; however, they have broader authority to reverse legal error.) In *Swint*, which arose in the context of a determination of the bona fides of a seniority system, the Court held that a court of appeals may reverse a trial court's factual findings of discriminatory intent only if it concludes that the finding of intentional discrimination is clearly erroneous. The effect of *Swint* is to put substantial authority in the hands of federal district court judges to enforce civil rights laws. As the composition of the federal courts changed under the Republican presidency of President Reagan as he appointed many federal judges, the possibility increased that these conservative judges would be less inclined to construe civil rights legislation liberally. However, it should be noted that the LDF was successful in convincing courts to apply the *Swint* rule when plaintiffs convinced trial judges to find, as a factual matter, that defendants had engaged in intentional discrimination.[19]

THE AFTEREFFECTS OF *TEAMSTERS* AND ITS PROGENY

Teamsters and its progeny made it extremely difficult to win seniority discrimination cases because proving intentional discrimination is not an easy undertaking. The Supreme Court in *Teamsters* did not set forth what factors should be examined in determining whether a system is bona fide. However, it did say that some of the determining factors include whether the seniority system operates to discourage all employees equally from transferring between seniority units; whether the seniority units are in the same or separate bargaining units, and if the latter, whether the structure is rational and in conformity with industry practices; whether the seniority system has its genesis in racial discrimination; and whether the system was negotiated and has remained free from any illegal purpose. The litigation team took on the challenge of attempting to formulate a test for evaluating the evidence when a claim is made that an employer and union intentionally adopted or maintained a seniority system that violates Title VII. Based on *Teamsters*, Barry Goldstein and cooperating attorney Demetrius Newton litigated a case in which a court of appeals embraced the test advocated by the litigation team. In *James v. Stockham Valves & Fitting Co.*, at Barry's urging, Judge Wisdom adopted a four-part totality of the circumstances test to evaluate the evidence to determine whether a seniority system was bona fide within the meaning of Section 703(h). Other courts of appeals then adopted the *James* four-part analysis.[20]

   Teamsters gave employers and unions the incentive to seek modification of pre-*Teamsters* judicial decisions in which individuals and class members obtained make whole relief in seniority discrimination cases. Both the employers and unions and the litigation team had some successes in the resulting cases.[21] By 1977, many employers and unions in many industries had made changes in their seniority practices, either voluntarily or by court decrees, that permitted African Americans and others groups protected by Title VII to transfer with full carryover seniority to jobs and departments historically denied to them because of their race and sex.

Teamsters and its progeny constituted an incursion into the effectiveness of Title VII because much of the legal edifice of the Griggs disparate impact theory was established in the seniority discrimination cases. However, even though the Supreme Court insulated facially neutral seniority systems not adopted or maintained with the intent to discriminate, the disparate impact theory retained its revolutionary impact for other facially neutral employment practices and the make whole remedies generally.

THE REAGAN ADMINISTRATION'S ASSAULT ON GRIGGS

Historically, the Justice Department, and particularly its Civil Rights Division, has had a major role in enforcing civil rights laws, including Title VII. After a slow start in enforcing Title VII, the Civil Rights Division became a major force in enforcing employment discrimination laws over which it had jurisdiction.[22] The Department of Justice fully supported and relied upon the disparate impact theory from 1971, when the Supreme Court decided Griggs, until 1981. However, federal support of the theory not only abruptly ended with the election of President Ronald Reagan, who took office in 1981, but the Civil Rights Division during his eight years in office (1981–1989) engaged in an all-out assault on the disparate impact theory and affirmative action.[23] Ronald Reagan became President at a time when affirmative action and civil rights were the subjects of much broad-based political and legal controversy. The Republican platform on which he ran in 1980 declared that "equal opportunity should not be jeopardized by bureaucratic regulations and decisions which rely on quotas, ratios, and numerical requirements to exclude some individuals in favor of others, thereby rendering such regulations and decisions inherently discriminatory."[24] Reagan deemed his election to be a mandate to roll back the gains that had been made in civil rights enforcement since the Civil Rights Act of 1964.[25] Efforts to capture broad-based public support for its attack on affirmative action were consistently cast in the emotionally charged terms of "quotas" or "reverse discrimination," and these terms were used with reckless abandon during the Reagan administration.

A major objective of the Reagan administration's civil rights agenda was getting rid of the *Griggs* disparate impact theory and enshrining forever in our civil rights laws and jurisprudence the proposition that our commitment to equality prohibits only disparate treatment or intentional discrimination. This objective is most clearly stated in a report prepared by the Office of Legal Policy of the Department of Justice. The report, *Redefining Discrimination: Disparate Impact and the Institutionalization of Affirmative Action,* addresses what the Reagan administration deemed to be the "premier" issue in contemporary civil rights jurisprudence, namely, "whether 'discrimination' for purposes of the nation's civil rights laws shall be defined as it has been traditionally understood, and as almost all of those laws facially contemplate, in terms of intentional conduct, or rather as is becoming increasingly prevalent in the courts, in terms of statistically disproportionate results or effects for preferred groups."[26] The purpose of the report, which is more than 150 pages long, was to examine how the "redefinition of discrimination" or the *Griggs* disparate impact "came about and how to assess where it is taking us as a nation."[27] *Griggs* is repeatedly denounced throughout the report. Quoting from one of my articles, the report also candidly acknowledges that *Griggs* established the critically important concept of discrimination on which affirmative action is based.[28]

Redefining Discrimination was not published until November 1987, near the end of President Reagan's tenure in office. However, his administration's endeavor to get rid of the disparate impact theory began much earlier in his administration with the appointment of Clarence Thomas, an African American opposed to affirmative action, as the chair of the EEOC in 1982 and the appointment of William Bradford Reynolds as Assistant Attorney General to head the Civil Rights Division of the Department of Justice in 1981. Reynolds held that position during the eight years of the Reagan administration and was a key spokesperson and strategist for President Reagan's civil rights agenda. Under the leadership of Reynolds, the Civil Rights Division launched an aggressive campaign to reverse more than three decades of civil rights law and frequently advanced arguments in cases that were contrary to arguments that the Civil Rights Division had advanced prior to 1981. The Reynolds Civil Rights Division flatly opposed busing as a remedy in school desegregation cases, even though the Supreme Court had endorsed busing as a remedy in appropriate cases;[29] supported, without success, in the Supreme Court a reversal of an Internal Revenue Service policy dating back to 1970 of denying tax-exempt status to private schools that engaged in racial discrimination in their admission policies;[30] and changed its position in pending civil rights litigation initiated by his predecessors. In a 1982 housing discrimination case, for example, the trial courts specifically noted that the Civil Rights Division, under Reynolds, had shifted its theory from disparate impact, which the Carter Justice Department had relied upon in filing the case, to the disparate treatment theory, which requires proof of discriminatory intent.[31] In other instances, the Civil Rights Division advocated positions in the courts that were unacceptable to the EEOC, and the Supreme Court specifically noted this split in several employment discrimination cases.[32] The Division entered private employment discrimination cases on the side of the employers or white plaintiffs to argue against the disparate impact theory or affirmative action. For example, it supported the position of the employer on the bottom-line theory in the Supreme Court in *Connecticut v. Teal*. If this position had been accepted by the Supreme Court, it would have been a strong incentive to employers to adopt bottom-line employment decisions to avoid challenges posed by the disparate impact theory of a single criterion in a multicriteria selection process.

In testimony before Congress, Reynolds stated that the Reagan administration would "no longer insist upon or in any respect support the use of quotas or any other numerical or statistical formulae designed to provide nonvictims of discrimination preferential treatment based on race, sex, national origin, or religion."[33] He repeatedly advocated the position that only intentional discrimination is prohibited in the national commitment to equality and that laws prohibiting employment discrimination provided a remedy only for identifiable victims of unlawful discrimination. The attack on affirmative action was particularly hard-hitting. The campaign to revise the affirmative action provisions in presidential Executive Orders led by Reynolds during 1984 and 1985 was not successful and was strongly opposed by other members of the Reagan administration.[34] Although affirmative action was controversial, it had gained acceptance in all courts of appeals, frequently at the urging of the Civil Rights Division prior to the Reagan administration.[35] In *Williams v. City of New Orleans*, a private case in which the remedy of affirmative action was an issue and in which the LDF litigation team was involved, the Civil Rights Division filed a motion to intervene in the case and argued that affirmative action is never an appropriate remedy under Title VII, except to remedy past discrimination, in which case it could be ordered only to provide a remedy for identifiable victims of unlawful discrimination. The fact that the Civil Rights Division had not consulted the EEOC prior to seeking intervention generated a sharp rebuke from the EEOC.[36] Had the court of appeals accepted the Civil Rights Division's argument, not only would the EEOC guidelines on affirmative action have been unenforceable, but many of the affirmative action plans voluntarily adopted by employers and unions and consent decrees containing affirmative action components and judicially ordered affirmative action decrees would have become unlawful.

One of the major assaults by the Reynolds Civil Rights Division on affirmative action followed in the wake of the Supreme Court's 1984 decision in *Firefighters Local Union No. 1784 v. Stotts.* The City of Memphis had entered into consent decrees with the African American plaintiffs in 1974 and 1980 to settle an employment discrimination case. However, the decrees did not specifically address how the affirmative action provision would be applied during layoffs. Subsequently, an unforeseen economic crisis made it necessary for Memphis to lay off some of the firefighters. The plaintiffs filed a motion to prevent the city from implementing the layoffs in a way that would reduce the number of African American firefighters who had benefited from the affirmative action provision, and the lower courts modified the decrees to accomplish that result. The Supreme Court held that the lower courts had erred in approving a modification in the affirmative action plan that conflicted with a bona fide seniority plan under the rule it announced in *Teamsters.* Although the Supreme Court expressly stated that it was not deciding whether a public employer, on its own, could have voluntarily and unilaterally adopted the course of action approved by the lower court, the Civil Rights Division nevertheless took the position that *Stotts* sounded the death knell for affirmative action.[37] After *Stotts,* the Civil Rights Division sent letters to over fifty public employers advising them that they had to revise consent decrees to eliminate provisions on affirmative action goals and timetables.[38] President Reagan supported Reynolds on affirmative action when he stated that "Mr. Reynolds' civil rights views reflect my own . . . [the] policies he pursued are policies of this administration, and they remain our policies as long as I am president."[39]

The Civil Rights Division's record on civil rights under Reynolds was repeatedly criticized by civil rights advocates and others as being the most anti–civil rights in the history of the Division.[40] Jack Greenberg, former

Director-Counsel of the LDF, stated that President Reagan attempted to change civil rights law "by administrative and political fiat."[41] Some former career attorneys in the Civil Rights Division of the Department of Justice published articles criticizing Reynolds's civil rights litigation strategies on civil rights.[42] Drew S. Days III, Assistant Attorney General for Civil Rights during the Carter administration, concluded that the Reagan administration "inadequately enforced or otherwise undermined, if not violated outright, settled law in the field of civil rights."[43] Theodore Shaw, a former career attorney in the Civil Rights Division who left the Division because of Reynolds's anti–civil rights campaign and who eventually became the Director-Counsel of the LDF, noted that Reynolds developed a cadre of assistant attorneys general and others who worked tirelessly to turn civil rights enforcement on its head and went on to establish right-wing policy institutes and legal defense funds that sustained the attack on affirmative action.[44]

THE COURT'S "CIVIL RIGHTS MASSACRE" OF 1989

A major legacy of the Reagan administration was the emergence of the solid five-member "conservative bloc" of Supreme Court Justices composed of Chief Justice Rehnquist and Justices White, O'Connor, Scalia and Kennedy. During his first term, Reagan appointed Justice O'Connor in 1981 as the first female Supreme Court Justice to fill the position created by the retirement of Justice Potter Stewart. In 1986, during his second term, Reagan elevated Justice William H. Rehnquist to be Chief Justice to replace Chief Justice Burger and appointed Justice Antonin Scalia to the seat vacated by Justice Rehnquist. In 1988, he appointed Justice Anthony M. Kennedy to the seat vacated by Justice Lewis Powell, who was considered a "swing vote" on the Court during a substantial part of his fifteen-and-one-half-year tenure. With that appointment, President Reagan was able to tilt the Court to a more conservative stance, and, for the first time since World War II, a majority of the Court shared the same political and legal philosophy of a sitting president. Along with the three new Supreme Court Justices, President Reagan appointed 83 judges to the federal courts of appeals and 290 judges to the district courts, so that he had appointed a majority of federal lower court judges, completing a conservative shift in the federal judiciary;[45] his total of 376 appointments was the most by a sitting president.[46]

In a burst of civil rights decisions in 1989 that is perhaps unmatched in the history of civil rights jurisprudence, the Supreme Court's conservative majority decided a number of cases that can be appropriately characterized as a "civil rights massacre." The Supreme Court launched its first judicial salvo in this massacre on January 23, 1989, in the affirmative action case of *City of Richmond v. J. A. Croson Co. Croson* was an Equal Protection Clause challenge to a City of Richmond, Virginia, ordinance that required prime contractors with the city to subcontract at least 30 percent of the dollar amount of the contract to minority business enterprises. The plaintiff in the case, J. A. Croson, a mechanical plumbing and heating contractor, had submitted the only bid for a city project. The city rejected the bid, and Croson filed suit alleging that the ordinance was unconstitutional on its face and as applied to his company. A majority of five Justices, in an opinion written by Justice O'Connor, held that all racial classifications imposed by federal, state, and local governments must meet a strict standard of scrutiny. Although the Court held that a governmental unit may have a compelling state interest to remedy its own past racial discrimination, it also found that there was insufficient evidence in the record to support a finding that the City of Richmond had discriminated against minority contractors in the past. *Croson* was a major disappointment for civil rights advocates.

The continued vitality of the *Griggs* disparate impact theory was not an issue in *Croson* because, in its earlier 1976 decision in *Washington v. Davis,* the Supreme Court held that the disparate impact theory does not apply to constitutional equal protection cases. Nor was the legality of affirmative action plans voluntarily adopted by government employers and challenged under Title VII an issue. This was because in its 1987 decision in *Johnson v. Transportation Agency, Santa Clara County,* the Court had held that *Steelworkers v. Weber* applies when such a plan is challenged solely under Title VII. However, the clear message from *Croson* was that white persons were likely to be more successful in challenging voluntarily affirmative action plans adopted by government employers under the strict scrutiny test in equal protection cases than under Title VII, even though government employers can be sued under both.

A more direct assault on the disparate impact theory came in three of eight employment discrimination cases the Court decided over a short period of about eight weeks during 1989—May 1 to June 22—that sounded the death knell for the *Griggs* disparate impact theory. These cases were *Wards Cove Packing Co. v. Atonio,* which overturned almost eighteen years of judicial developments under the disparate impact theory; *Lorance v. AT&T Technologies, Inc.,* which limited the circumstances under which allegedly discriminatory seniority systems could be challenged; and *Martin v. Wilks,* which liberalized the rules pursuant to which whites and males could challenge affirmative action decrees.

The Court did not sound the death knell for the disparate impact theory until it decided *Wards Cove,* but it had fallen just one vote short of doing so just a year earlier in *Watson v. Fort Worth Bank and Trust Co.* The Court was unanimous in *Watson* in holding that the disparate impact theory applies to subjective criteria. Only eight of the nine Justices participated, as Justice Kennedy had been nominated but did not actually join the Court until three weeks after the argument in *Watson.* A four-Justice plurality of Chief Justice Rehnquist and Justices White, O'Connor, and Scalia, in an opinion authored by Justice O'Connor, went further than the issue on which certiorari was granted to address specifically the evidentiary standards to be applied in light of extending the disparate impact theory to subjective criteria and, by implication, to objective criteria. The plurality's reason for doing so was to respond to arguments advanced by the bank and the Reynolds Civil Rights Division, which had entered the case on the side of the employer to argue against extending the disparate impact theory to subjective criteria.

> Respondent contends that a plaintiff may establish a prima facie case of disparate impact through the use of bare statistics, and that the defendant can rebut this statistical showing only by justifying the challenged practice in terms of "business necessity." Standardized tests and criteria, like those at issue in our previous disparate impact cases, can often be justified through formal "validation studies." . . . [But respondent] warns . . . that validating subjective selection criteria this way is impracticable. . . . Because of these difficulties, we are told, employers will find it impossible to eliminate subjective selection criteria and impossibly expensive to defend such practices in litigation. Respondent insists, and the United States agrees, that employers' only alternative will be to adopt surreptitious quota systems in order to ensure that no plaintiff can establish a statistical prima facie case.[47]

The plurality agreed with the argument when it asserted that "the inevitable focus on statistics in disparate impact cases could put undue pressure on employers to adopt inappropriate prophylactic measures" because "[i]t is completely unrealistic to assume that unlawful discrimination is the sole cause of people failing to gravitate to jobs and employers in accord with the laws of chance" and "equally unrealistic to suppose that employers can eliminate or discover and explain, the myriad of innocent causes that may lead to statistical imbalances in the composition of their work forces." Then, relying on Section 703(j) of Title VII, which it construed as a congressional prohibition against "prophylactic measures" or quotas, the plurality concluded:

> Respondent and the United States are thus correct when they argue that extending disparate impact analysis to subjective employment practices has the potential to create a Hobson's choice for employers and thus to lead in practice to perverse results. If quotas and preferential treatment become the only cost-effective means of avoiding expensive litigation and potentially catastrophic liability, such measures will be widely adopted. The prudent employer will be careful to ensure that its programs are discussed in euphemistic terms, but will be equally careful to ensure that the quotas are met. Allowing the evolution of disparate impact analysis to lead to this result would be contrary to Congress' clearly expressed intent, and it should not be the effect of our decision today.[48]

To eliminate this "Hobson's choice," the plurality deemed it necessary to take "a fresh and somewhat closer examination of the constraints that operate to keep [the disparate impact] theory within its proper bounds."[49] The plurality then identified two sets of restraints. The first set focused on the use of statistical evidence to establish a prima facie case of disparate impact. Here, the plurality said that the plaintiffs would have to do more than simply introduce evidence of statistical disparities to establish a prima facie case of disparate impact discrimination. Rather, the plaintiffs must identify the specific employment practice that caused any observed disparity, and the statistical evidence must be sufficient to raise an inference of causation between the facially neutral employment criteria and the adverse impact. The specificity and causation requirements were imposed in response to the argument of the employer and the Reynolds Civil Rights Division that the plaintiffs should not be able to rely on bare statistics to establish a prima facie case of disparate impact. Without specifically saying so, it appears that the plurality was influenced by the Supreme Court's earlier rejection of the bottom-line defense in *Connecticut v. Teal.* The plurality took the position, also without specifically saying so, that if defendants are precluded from relying on bottom-line bare statistics to rebut plaintiffs' prima facie case, then it is only fair that plaintiffs likewise should not be permitted to rely on bare statistics to establish a prima facie case. Again without specifically saying so, the plurality reversed the liberal use of statistics that the Court had endorsed in the *Teamsters* trilogy in 1977, in which the Court had also relied upon Section 703(j). To underscore its new approach to the use of statistical evidence, the plurality cautioned lower courts against assuming that the plaintiffs' statistical evidence is reliable, and, to guard against this possibility, it provided an evidentiary laundry list on which employers could rely to challenge whether plaintiff statistics were probative. This laundry list includes challenges that the sample size is too small; that the statistics were based on incomplete data, for example, the data exclude applicant flow data; and that the statistical techniques used were inadequate.

The second set of constraints focused on the business necessity defense. The plurality in *Watson* said that the defense is only the lighter burden of going forward with evidence, rather than the much heavier burden of persuasion. As Justice Blackmun correctly observed in his dissenting opinion for himself and Justices Brennan and Marshall, "the plurality's suggested allocation of the burden bears a closer resemblance to the allocation of the burden [the Court] established for the disparate-treatment claims . . . than it does to those the Court has established for disparate-impact claims."[50] To underscore the lighter burden imposed on employers, the plurality stated that employers are not required, "even when defending standardized or objective tests, to introduce formal 'validation studies' showing that particular criteria predict actual on-the-job performance."[51] If a defendant has met its lighter burden of production of evidence on business necessity, then the plaintiff can prove a violation under the disparate impact theory only by convincing the fact finder that there are other facially neutral selection devices without a similarly undesirable racial effect that would equally well serve the employer's legitimate interest in efficient and trustworthy workmanship. But the plurality then stated that even if a plaintiff were to put on evidence on an alternative selection, the costs to the employer in adopting such a practice are relevant in deciding whether there has been a violation in a disparate impact claim. The recognition of a potential cost defense in *Watson* was in direct contradiction to an earlier sex discrimination case, in which the Court had squarely rejected the cost justification defense on the ground that Congress had not included it in Title VII, and for that reason, the Court would not do so either.

In *Watson,* the plurality in effect adopted the view that the disparate impact theory is simply the disparate treatment theory masquerading in drag:

> The distinguishing features of the factual issues that typically dominate in disparate impact cases do not imply that the ultimate legal issue is different than in cases where disparate treatment analysis is used. . . . Nor do we think it is appropriate to hold a defendant liable for unintentional discrimination on the

basis of less evidence than is required to prove intentional discrimination. Rather, the necessary premise of the disparate impact approach is that some employment practices, adopted without a deliberately discriminatory motive, may in operation be functionally equivalent to intentional discrimination.[52]

Wards Cove was one of the most momentous and controversial cases in the 1989 "civil rights massacre." The case had been in litigation for fourteen years prior to the Supreme Court's decision. The plaintiffs, a group of Samoans, Chinese, Filipinos, Japanese, and Alaskan Natives, brought a class action on behalf of nonwhite workers against two companies in the salmon canning industry that operated canneries in a remote part of Alaska. The claims involved the employment practices of the canneries that hired seasonal workers for unskilled cannery jobs and skilled workers for noncannery jobs. The noncannery higher-paying jobs were staffed predominantly by white workers, and the unskilled jobs were staffed by nonwhite members of the plaintiffs' class. In his dissent, Justice Stevens captured the essence of the factual setting in which the case arose when he wrote that the case "bear[s] an unsettling resemblance to aspects of a plantation economy[,]" because of the segregated housing and dining facilities, and the racial and ethnic stratification of jobs.[53] Justice Blackmun was more blunt when he stated, in dissent, that "the salmon industry as described by this record takes us back to a kind of overt and institutionalized discrimination we have not dealt with for years: a total residential and work environment organized on principles of racial stratification and segregation, which as Justice Stevens points out, resembles a plantation economy."[54] The factual description of the case by Justices Stevens and Blackmun drew a sharp disclaimer from Justice White, who wrote the majority's opinion, when he felt compelled to acknowledge that "[o]f course, it is unfortunately true that race discrimination still exists in our country."[55]

The Supreme Court granted the employer's petition for certiorari because some of the issues raised were matters on which the Court had been evenly divided in *Watson*. The difference between the cases was that Justice Kennedy supplied the fifth vote in *Wards Cove*. The Court did an about-face in *Wards Cove* on the liberal use of statistics to prove unlawful employment discrimination that it had endorsed in its 1977 decisions in *Teamsters, Hazelwood,* and *Dothard* when it held that, absent usual circumstances, the only proper statistical comparison is between the number of protected class members in the employer's workforce and the pool of qualified applicants in the labor force. The Court specifically rejected a comparison based solely on current employees. This about-face was intended to create a high evidentiary hurdle that plaintiffs had to overcome to establish a prima facie case under the disparate impact theory. The five-Justice conservative majority in *Wards Cove* then did what the Court had been unable to do in *Watson,* namely, officially sound the death knell for the *Griggs* disparate impact theory by adopting the *Watson* plurality's opinion.[56]

The Court also abolished the business necessity defense in all but name because, each time it made reference to the *Griggs* business necessity defense, it became clear that the defense was nothing more than the legitimate nondiscriminatory reason defense a defendant may advance to rebut a prima facie case of intentional discrimination. The Court described the defense as "any business justification [an employer] offer[s]" that "serves in a significant way, the legitimate employment goals of the employer." The "touchstone of this inquiry" was to be "a reasoned review of the employer's justification for his use of the challenged practice," and, finally, it must be a "legitimate business justification defense." The closest the Court came to candidly recognizing that it overruled eighteen years of developments under *Griggs* was in connection with its reallocation of the burdens of proof: "We acknowledge that some of our earlier decisions can be read as suggesting otherwise. But to the extent those cases speak of an employer's 'burden of proof' with respect to the legitimate business justification defense, they should have been understood to mean an employer's production—but not persuasion—burden."[57] The Court then turned to the final stage of disparate impact analysis. Here, the Court held that, even if the employer proves the now watered-down legitimate business justification defense, plaintiffs could win a disparate impact case only with proof of an alternative to the challenged practice or policy that has a lesser disproportionate impact and at the same time serves the legitimate business goals of the employer. However, the Supreme Court warned that lower courts should proceed with caution in giving too great a weight to any proposed alternative proffered by the plaintiffs because it deemed those courts less competent than employers to restructure their business practices,[58] a concern the Court had also expressed in one of its earlier employment discrimination cases brought by white males.[59]

Although the Court did not expressly overrule the *Griggs* disparate impact theory in *Wards Cove,* it established doctrinal rules regarding statistical evidence, the business necessity defense, causation, and burden-shifting allocations that left little doubt it intended to completely dismantle the *Griggs* disparate impact theory as support for affirmative action under Title VII.[60] As it did in *Croson,* the Court established an almost impenetrable legal barrier against voluntary affirmative action as a remedy to fulfill this nation's commitment to equality. Without the intervention by Congress that eventually led to the rebirth of the *Griggs* disparate impact theory and the legislative overruling or modifications of a host of other civil rights decisions by the Supreme Court, the historic struggle to fulfill the nation's commitment to equality would have, once again, fallen on hard times.

Newspapers and other media repeatedly proclaimed that *Wards Cove* brought about the death of *Griggs,*[61] and this generated more publicity and press coverage than its birth. One of the unanswered questions *Wards Cove* raises is why, if the majority of the conservative Justices subscribed to the view that the disparate treatment theory is the only theory of discrimination that is embraced in this nation's commitment to equality, the Court did not completely overturn *Griggs,* especially when it unanimously adopted that view in *Washington v. Davis* with respect to claims based on the Equal Protection Clause. One answer might very well be that the Court would have had to overturn *Washington v. Davis* because, in *Davis,* the Court drew a clear line of distinction between equal protection claims, in which the disparate impact theory is not applicable, and Title VII claims, in which the Court recognizes the legitimacy of disparate impact claims. Another potential reason is that the Court might have been sensitive to the fact that Congress, in its 1972 amendments to Title VII, expressed its support of the disparate impact theory. In *Connecticut v. Teal,* the Court had cited the legislative history from both the Senate and House deliberations for the proposition that Congress had recognized and endorsed the disparate impact theory in light of the evidence it had before it in 1972 but not in 1964 when it enacted Title VII.[62] Perhaps Justice Blackmun may have articulated quite accurately that the decision in *Wards Cove* reflected the majority's view that by 1989 racial discrimination against nonwhites is no longer a problem in our society.[63] A different way to articulate what Justice Blackmun said is that the conservative majority decided to retain the label but eliminate the substance of the disparate impact theory.

The Court continued the process it initiated in *Teamsters* of insulating facially neutral seniority systems from challenges under the disparate impact in the *Lorance* case. The plaintiffs—females, who were represented by the LDF in the Supreme Court—claimed that the intent and effect of a contested seniority provision was the product of a conspiracy between the employer and a union to protect the seniority standing of junior males over more senior females when females were allowed to work in jobs historically limited to males. The rule had been adopted in 1979 and was first applied to the plaintiffs in 1982 to demote Patricia Lorance and the other two female plaintiffs. The issue before the Supreme Court was when the limitation period begins to run for filing a charge with the EEOC to challenge a facially neutral, but intentionally discriminatory, seniority system. The choice was between the date an employee knows or has reason to know that the intentionally discriminatory seniority system was first adopted or when such a system was actually applied to the plaintiffs. For the litigation team, Barry Goldstein argued to the Supreme Court that the period should begin to run when the system was actually applied to the plaintiff. In a 6–3 opinion written by Justice Scalia, the Court held that the limitation period begins to run as soon as the system is adopted—not from the date the system is applied to the plaintiff or complaining party. Justice Marshall, dissenting, captured the devastating effect of *Lorance* when he wrote that the majority's opinion was the latest example of the Court flouting the intent of Congress by gradually diminishing the application of Title VII to seniority systems. Although *Lorance* arose in the context of a seniority discrimination case, the logic of the decision would seem to apply to any employment system or employment policy alleged to have been intentionally adopted to discriminate.

Martin v. Wilks, decided on the same day as *Lorance,* not only further weakened the *Griggs* disparate impact theory support of affirmative action but also encouraged whites to challenge literally hundreds of consent decrees with affirmative action provisions. The case began in January 1974 as an employment discrimination case filed on behalf of the African American employees and applicants for employment with the city of Birmingham and Jefferson County, Alabama. The long history of egregious discrimination by the city of Birmingham and its across-the-board racially discriminatory practices had been the subject of prior decisions of the Supreme Court and had received national news coverage as part of the civil rights demonstrations of the early 1960s that led to the enactment of the Civil Rights Act of 1964. About a year after the complaint in *Wilks* had been filed, the Department of Justice, in May 1975, also brought a Title VII pattern and practice action, *United States v. Jefferson County,* against the city and others, charging pervasive race and sex discrimination in virtually all aspects of employment. *Wilks, Jefferson,* and several other cases were consolidated for trial. The proceedings in the case were the subject of prominent and continuous press coverage that made the case notorious in the community.[64] After two trials, two appeals, and a finding of discrimination based on massive evidence of discrimination in promotions in the city's fire and other departments, the plaintiffs and the Department of Justice entered into consent decrees with the city of Birmingham and the Jefferson County Personnel Board in 1981, which included affirmative action goals and timetables for the hiring and promotion of African Americans and women in municipal jobs in reasonable proportions to the percentage of these groups in the relevant civilian workforce.

The trial court provisionally approved the consent decrees, scheduled a fairness hearing to provide an opportunity for all interested parties to appear and express their objections to the entry of the decree, and directed that notice be given to all interested parties. Notices of the scheduled hearing were published in two local newspapers. Among others, the white Birmingham Firefighters Association (BFA) and two of its members appeared as amici curiae at the fairness hearing to object to the approval of the consent decrees on the ground that the race- and sex-specific affirmative action provisions constituted "reverse discrimination" against whites. They based their claims on Title VII and the Equal Protection Clause.

The district court eventually approved entry of the consent decree, and the white employees took an appeal. The court of appeals affirmed the denial of the motion to intervene and for a preliminary injunction, and, in doing so, specifically noted that the motion was untimely because the white employees knew at an early stage in the proceedings that their rights could be adversely affected.[65] The court of appeals also addressed the issue on which the Supreme Court granted certiorari in *Wilks,* whether the white firefighters were barred from filing a separate Title VII "reverse discrimination" claim in a case that, of necessity, would constitute a collateral attack on a judicially approved consent decree with its affirmative action provisions.

During the pendency of the appeal, a new group of white firefighters, the *Wilks* group, brought a total of five separate "reverse discrimination" claims against the city of Birmingham and the board, alleging that they were victims of intentional "reverse discrimination" as a result of decisions made by the city pursuant to the consent decree. The city and the board admitted making race-conscious employment decisions pursuant to the consent decree. The petitioners in *Wilks* intervened in the "reverse discrimination" cases because, they alleged, if the relief sought by the "reverse discrimination" claimants was granted, it would foreclose future promotions under the consent decrees and could perhaps result in demotions of African Americans who had benefited from the consent decrees. The United States, represented by the Reynolds Civil Rights Division—though a party to the original consent decrees, and indeed the Civil Rights Division had drafted them—intervened in *Wilks* and realigned itself with the white firefighters and challenged as discriminatory many of the promotions of African Americans the City had made pursuant to the consent decrees.[66] The Civil Rights Division thus switched its position between the time it filed its case in *Jefferson* and the time it reached the Supreme Court, siding with the plaintiffs in the lower courts but with the white employees in the Supreme Court. The district court, after a full trial, dismissed the white firefighters' complaint on the grounds, among others, that it was an impermissible collateral attack on the consent in the *Martin* decrees. The court of appeals reversed and held that the white plaintiffs could proceed with their case because they were not parties to the consent decree.

The *Martin* intervenors, the city, and the Board filed petitions for review in the Supreme Court, which agreed to hear the case. In a 5–4 decision authored by Chief Justice Rehnquist, the Court held that the white firefighters who brought the "reverse discrimination" claims were not collaterally estopped from challenging the consent decrees on the ground that they could not be deprived of their rights in the cases brought on behalf of the African Americans because they had neither intervened nor joined as parties in that action. Prior to *Wilks,* a majority of the courts of appeals had rejected attempts at collateral attacks on consent decrees with affirmative action provisions on the ground that allowing such attacks would discourage voluntary settlements of discrimination claims. *Wilks* not only jeopardized many existing Title VII consent decrees that included affirmative action provisions but also created a different kind of "Hobson's choice" for employers, similar to the one the Court resolved in *Weber* and *Johnson.* If an employer faced a large class action disparate impact claim in which its probability of losing on the merits was strong but it did not settle and eventually lost on the merits after trial, that employer would be subject to substantial injunctive rightful place relief; monetary awards such as class-wide back pay; and attorney's fees. On the other hand, if the employer settled a case that included an affirmative action provision, then the employer would be subject to another round of litigation by white employees who could challenge the affirmative action provision under the rule of *Wilks.*[67]

There were also other cases included in the Supreme Court's set of 1989 civil rights rulings. Included was *Patterson v. McLean Credit Union,* in which the Court severely limited the kinds of racial discrimination claims that can be brought under Section 1981, and *Jett v. Dallas Independent School District,* which made it more difficult to sue municipalities under Section 1981.

Patterson was not a Title VII case, nor did it involve the disparate impact theory because the Court had earlier held that, like *Washington v. Davis,* liability may be found under Section 1981 only upon proof of intentional discrimination.[68] However, the case was an integral part of the 1989 massacre because in it the Court reversed a long line of lower court decisions that, in race discrimination cases brought under Section 1981, provided broad relief including compensatory and punitive damages, which were not then available under Title VII, and because prior to *Patterson,* the coverage of racial discrimination under Section 1981 was as broad as under Title VII.[69] The plaintiff, Brenda Patterson, an African American female, had been hired by the bank as a teller and file coordinator in 1972. She sued the bank for race discrimination after she was laid off in 1982. Relying solely on Section 1981, she alleged that she had been harassed, passed over for promotions, not offered training for higher-level jobs, denied wage increases, and discharged because of her race. Her claim could have been pursued under Title VII, but she elected to proceed only under Section 1981. The harassment claim was based on an allegation that her supervisor frequently stared at her for several minutes at a time; gave her too many tasks, including tasks of sweeping and dusting, jobs not given to white employees; told her on one occasion that blacks are known to be slower than whites, or, as he put it, "some animals are faster than others";[70] and criticized her in meetings while not similarly criticizing white employees. After she lost in both the district court and the court of appeals, the LDF entered the case to represent her in the Supreme Court along with local counsel.

The LDF raised two questions on which the Supreme Court granted certiorari. The first was whether Section 1981 encompasses claims of racial harassment. Every court of appeals deciding the issue—except the Fourth Circuit, out of which *Patterson* arose—had held that racial harassment claims are actionable under Section 1981.[71] The second was whether the district court had erred in instructing the jury that, in order for her to prevail on her claim of discrimination, she had to prove that she was more qualified than the white person who received the promotion. Penda Hair, an LDF attorney, argued the case in the Supreme Court for the plaintiff. However, after the argument, and instead of deciding the issues on the merits, the Supreme Court, on its own initiative, set the case for reargument and specifically directed the parties to address the question of whether its interpretation adopted in *Runyon v. McCrary* in 1976, which extended Section 1981 to private persons, should be reconsidered.[72]

The Supreme Court was bitterly divided on the issue of whether to reconsider *Runyon*, as evidenced by the rather scathing dissents to the order by Justices Brennan, Marshall, Stevens, and Blackmun. The order for reargument, although issued as a per curium decision, was agreed to by only the five conservative Justices. The reargument order sent shock waves throughout the civil rights community and generated a substantial number of amicus briefs urging the Supreme Court not to overturn *Runyon*.[73] Included among the amicus briefs were those filed on behalf of sixty-six members (about two-thirds) of the United States Senate, forty-seven state attorneys general, the American Bar Association, prominent historians, and more than 100 civil rights groups.[74] No fewer than three law reviews published symposia on the case.[75]

One of the main arguments the LDF advocated in its brief on reargument was that Section 1981 should be broadly construed because a major concern of Congress when the statute was enacted was the discriminatory terms and conditions of employment contracts that were being used by former slaveholders. The argument was not that former slaves could not get jobs but rather that, once they did obtain jobs, they were subjected to onerous and discriminatory conditions of employment.[76] One of the main arguments made by the senators and congressmen in their amicus brief was that they had ratified *Runyon* by declining to take action to reverse it legislatively, and that if the Court did reverse the case, Congress would feel compelled to legislatively take action, even though doing so would result in a divisive debate.[77] Chambers, who had been one of the plaintiffs' attorneys in *Griggs*, and who had become the Director-Counsel of the LDF, argued on behalf of *Patterson* in the reargument before the Supreme Court.

In a majority opinion written by Justice Kennedy, the Court first declined to overrule *Runyon* and devoted the first part of the opinion to explaining why five Justices had voted for reargument in the first place. On the merits, the five conservative Justices held that Section 1981 is not to be construed as a general prohibition against racial discrimination in all aspects of the employment relationship because, by its very terms, it prohibits discrimination only in two narrowly defined situations. The first is the initial decision to hire, and if the hiring decision is made on a nondiscriminatory basis but the employer then engages in other forms of discrimination, those posthiring discriminatory acts are not prohibited unless it involves the opportunity to enter into a new and distinct contractual relationship with the employer. Under this limited construction of Section 1981, the Court had no difficulty in ruling that racial harassment is not prohibited under Section 1981, even if it is reprehensible, severe, and pervasive, because it is post–contract formation conduct by the employer. As explained by Justice Brennan, the view of the five conservative Justices would allow an employer to tell an African American applicant that he would offer him the same written contraction of employment as a white person but that the conditions under which he would work would be much worse than a similarly situated white employee, including the fact that he would be subjected to a lot of racial harassment. The second situation would be a limitation on the right to access to the legal process—that is, the right to go into court to enforce a violation of the first right, namely, the right to enter into a contract of hire on a nonracial basis. Justice Brennan correctly described what the Court had done when he wrote that "[w]hat the Court declines to snatch away with one hand it takes with the other" because it reaffirmed the applicability of Section 1981 to private conduct but at the same time gave the statute a needlessly cramped interpretation.

After *Patterson,* the civil rights community expressed concern not only over the loss of a favored civil rights remedy but also over plaintiffs' lost opportunity for any remedy under federal law. Although Title VII covers such claims as harassment, promotion, transfer, and retaliation, employers with fewer than fifteen employees are exempt from coverage under Section 1981. This exemption leaves 14.4 percent of the workforce without coverage when the court held that Section 1981 was no longer available as a remedy.[78]

The Court further limited the reach of Section 1981 in *Jett v. Dallas Independent School District,* decided about a week after *Patterson.* This case involved a racial discrimination claim brought against a public employer by a white male, who sought relief under Sections 1981 and 1983, both of which were enacted during the post–Civil War Reconstruction era. Section 1983, enacted five years after Section 1981, provides a cause of action for damages and other equitable relief against states and municipalities (but not the federal government) for deprivation of rights secured by the Constitution and the laws of the United States. Unlike Title VII, Section 1983, the statute under which the LDF litigated *Brown v. Board of Education,* does not itself provide any rights; it simply provides a remedy for violations of rights found in the Constitution and certain other federal laws. Also, a different set of rules apply in actions brought under

Section 1983, depending on whether the suit is against a state, municipality, or a state official or employee sued in his or her individual capacity.

The questions on which the Supreme Court granted certiorari in *Jett* were whether Section 1981 provides an independent federal cause of action for damages against municipalities, and, if so, whether the cause of action is broader than the damages remedy available under Section 1983. Again, the five-Justice conservative majority, in an opinion by Justice O'Connor, held that, although it was willing to imply a damages remedy for private citizens suing a private employer under Section 1981, the remedial scheme Congress provided in Section 1983 is the exclusive remedy for damages for violations of Section 1981 when the claim is brought against a state actor. The net effect of *Jett* is to require plaintiffs suing state and local governments and their officials under Section 1981 to navigate an exceptionally complex set of rules that the Court had adopted under Section 1983.

Other civil rights cases the Court decided in 1989 included *Price Water-house v. Hopkins,* decided a week after *Lorance,* in which the Court established the legal principles to be applied in mixed-motive cases, those in which there is evidence that an employer relied upon both an unlawful reason and a lawful reason in making an adverse employment decision. The Court also decided *Texas State Teachers Ass'n v. Garland Independent School District,* this time ruling for the plaintiffs, overruling a lower court's rather stringent standard for awarding attorney's fees to prevailing plaintiffs.

One of the effects of this "civil rights massacre" by the Court was to further discourage members of the private bar from representing clients in employment discrimination cases. Many lawyers abandoned the practice of taking Title VII cases because of the increasing hostility of the federal courts to civil rights cases, the willingness the courts exhibited to impose harsh sanctions against civil rights attorneys, and their regularly dismissing employment discrimination and other civil rights cases on summary judgment in favor of defendants.[79] The corpus of cooperating attorneys that was so instrumental in the development of employment discrimination law and often was an integral part of the litigation team began to wane over the years. However, more recently a group of attorneys joined together as the National Employment Lawyers Association (NELA), this nation's largest professional organization exclusively composed of attorneys who represent individual applicants and employees in cases involving employment discrimination and a host of other laws that regulate the employment relationship.

14. The Resurrection of *Griggs*:
The Civil Rights Act of 1991

The irony of the timing of the Supreme Court's 1989 rulings was that 1989 was the twenty-fifth anniversary of the Civil Rights Act of 1964. Julius Chambers, then the Director-Counsel of the LDF, said that the Court's 1988 Term "was one of the worst this nation had experienced in our lifetime and that it had had and would continue to have a devastating effect of the hopes of victims of discrimination."[1] Another LDF attorney, Charles Stephen Ralston, stated that the 1988 Term was the worst in the history of the LDF, which goes back fifty years.[2] Barry Goldstein, the LDF attorney who argued *Lorance* in the Supreme Court, characterized the 1989 civil rights decisions as "ten days that shook fair employment law."[3] Benjamin Hooks, executive director of the NAACP, compared the 1989 civil rights decisions to Birmingham, Alabama, police commissioner Bull Connor's use of attack dogs to break up civil rights demonstrations and to burnings by the Ku Klux Klan.[4] Hooks also characterized the Supreme Court's actions as a "legal lynching of black American hopes . . . to become full partners in the American dream."[5] Another longtime Supreme Court watcher stated that the 1989 civil rights decisions were "almost [a] total defeat for minority employees, and almost a total victory for employers [public and private]."[6] Ralph Neas, executive director of the Leadership Conference on Civil Rights (LCCR), stated that the Supreme Court "did more damage to civil rights law in four weeks in June [1989] than had occurred in the previous four decades."[7] Several senatorial legislative aides who participated in the legislative process that led to the rebirth of *Griggs* in 1991 described the decisions as a "body blow to civil rights organizations."[8] The NAACP closed its 1989 national convention, which was held in Detroit, Michigan, with a call by Benjamin Hooks for a national march on Washington, D.C.[9] Pursuant to this call, hundreds of civil rights activists and sympathizers from more than 200 civic, religious, and labor organizations participated in a silent march around the Supreme Court on August 26, 1989, to dramatize their outrage at the Court.

THE END OF THE SECOND RECONSTRUCTION

The shock waves that rippled throughout the civil rights community from the Court's actions are understandable only in light of the historical context of the ongoing effort to eliminate racism in our society; those rulings brought an end to the Second Reconstruction.[10] The term *Reconstruction* in the civil rights context is a shorthand description of the legal, political, and social efforts to eliminate slavery and its racist legacy that the Supreme Court had endorsed as a matter of law in, for example, its 1857 decision in *Dred Scott v. Sandford.* In a profound statement that undergirds much of the history of racism in this country, the Court, in *Dred Scott,* said that slaves have been "regarded as of an inferior order, and are altogether unfit to associate with the white race . . . and that they have no rights the white man was bound to respect."[11]

Throughout its history, the United States has adopted different legal and policy positions on the legal status of African Americans in the public and private sectors. At first, grounded in the institution of slavery, African Americans were, by law, relegated to the status of property. The First Reconstruction, which some have dated as occurring between the end of the Civil War in 1865 and 1877, focused on eliminating the institution of slavery and according full citizenship to African Americans.[12] During the First Reconstruction, Congress enacted three amendments to the Constitution: the Thirteenth Amendment abolishes slavery and involuntary servitude; the Fourteenth Amendment prohibits states and local governments from denying any citizen the equal protection of the law; and the Fifteenth Amendment guarantees the right to vote. Based on the enactment of these constitutional provisions, Congress also enacted a host of civil rights legislation, including Section 1981, which the Supreme Court emasculated in 1989 in the LDF case of *Patterson v. McLean Credit Union.* The three constitutional amendments and the civil rights statutory regime were adopted to foster political, social, and economic equality for African Americans. One of the distinctive features of the civil rights laws passed by Congress between 1866 and 1875 was the designation of the federal courts as the principal guardian of newly created civil rights.[13] The history of the dismantling of the First Reconstruction has been extensively documented, but it consisted of, among other features, political compromises and Supreme Court decisions that undercut the early post–Civil War civil rights legislation.[14] Even before Congress had completed its legislative civil rights agenda of the First Reconstruction, the Supreme Court began to judicially dismantle it.

The enunciation of the "separate but equal" doctrine by the Supreme Court in *Plessy v. Ferguson* in 1896 and the enactment of the black codes in the southern states were among the major historical events that legitimated the racist treatment of African Americans in education, housing, voting, employment, the administration of justice, and political and civil rights, and it brought the First Reconstruction to an end.[15]

Even though the beginning of the Second Reconstruction has been dated at different historical points,[16] the Supreme Court's decision in *Brown v. Board of Education* is deemed to be one of the seminal developments that ushered it in. During the Second Reconstruction, Congress enacted a host of civil rights statutes as it had done during the First Reconstruction. The congressional legislation included the Civil Rights Act of 1964, of which Title VII is a part. In contrast to its role in the First Reconstruction, the Supreme Court, during much of the Second Reconstruction period, took the lead in liberally construing provisions of civil rights laws, including the Civil Rights Act of 1964, and resuscitating the moribund Reconstruction-era statutes, which included Section 1981.[17] Until it became a victim of the 1989 "civil rights massacre," the *Griggs* disparate impact theory was a major cornerstone of the Second Reconstruction. But, just as the Supreme Court played a pivotal role in bringing about the demise of the First Reconstruction, it also played a pivotal role in bringing about the end of the Second Reconstruction as its membership became more conservative, eventually leading to its 1989 rulings.[18] A prominent civil rights scholar who is deemed to be the father of critical race theory,[19] Derrick A. Bell, advanced a cyclical theory that he deems the best explanation of the uneven history over time in the effort to end racial discrimination in the United States. According to Bell, "[w]hat appears to be progress toward racial justice is, in fact, a cyclical process. Barriers are lowered in one era only to reveal a new set of often more sophisticated but no less effective policies that maintain blacks in a subordinate status."[20] Similarly, a leading authority on the history of the First Reconstruction has said that the dismantling of the [civil rights] legislation of that era, "demonstrated . . . that rights, once won, can be taken away."[21]

The implicit message of the Court's 1989 "civil rights massacre" parallels the explicit message the Court delivered in 1883 in the *Civil Rights Cases,* a key element in the Supreme Court's dismantling of the civil rights legislation that Congress had enacted during the First Reconstruction.[22] The statute at issue in the *Civil Rights Cases* was Section 1 of the 1875 Civil Rights Act, which granted all persons the same accommodations and privileges to the full enjoyment of inns, public conveyances, and theaters and was deemed to be the "capstone of the congressional civil rights program" of the First Reconstruction.[23] At issue in the *Civil Rights Cases* was the scope of the Act. The Supreme Court narrowly construed the statute when it held that it did not apply to the conduct of private white citizens who discriminate against African Americans because of race. A critical part of that decision rested on the Court's view that

[w]hen a man has emerged from slavery, and by the aid and beneficent legislation has shaken off the inseparable concomitants of that state, there must be some stage in the progress of his elevation when he takes on the rank of a mere citizen, and ceases to be the special favorite of the laws, and when his rights as a citizen, or a man, are to be protected by the ordinary modes by which other men's rights are protected.[24]

The *Wards Cove* conservative majority apparently agreed with this view because it construed the *Griggs* impact theory and its legitimization of affirmative action as condoning "preferential treatment" and "quotas," and for that reason believed the impact theory was an undesirable rule of law that treats minorities and women as "special favorite[s]" of the law. The Justices apparently deemed that, by 1989, minorities and women had reached the point in our history when the disparate impact theory was no longer needed and thus proceeded to dismantle *Griggs*. This analysis of *Wards Cove* is underscored by Justice Blackmun's dissent in which he described the understated hypothesis of the majority's opinion: "One wonders whether the majority still believes that race discrimination—or more accurately, race discrimination against nonwhites—is a problem in our society, or even remembers that it ever was."[25] In effect, the Court declared in *Wards Cove* that only the disparate treatment theory, rather than the *Griggs* disparate impact theory, is the "ordinary mode" or the only legal theory that is embraced in our national commitment to equality.[26]

The role the Supreme Court played in bringing about the end of the Second Reconstruction did send shock waves throughout the civil rights community, but it also galvanized a sustained two-year movement by congressional supporters of strong enforcement of civil rights laws and the civil rights community to overturn or modify the Court's June 1989 rulings legislatively. This movement was eventually successful with the enactment of the Civil Rights Act of 1991 in which Congress codified the disparate impact theory, but the success came only after President George H. W. Bush had vetoed an earlier and stronger version of the bill, the Civil Rights Act of 1990. Although a major reason Congress enacted the Civil Rights Acts of 1991 was to codify the disparate impact theory and "confirm statutory authority and provide statutory guidelines for the adjudication of disparate impact" as it stood before *Wards Cove,* the 1991 Act addressed other Supreme Court decisions that Congress deemed to have weakened protection against discrimination in employment. However, consistent with the subject of this book, the principal focus of this chapter is on congressional codification of the *Griggs* disparate impact theory.

The legislative and political maneuvering that led to the 1991 Act has been described by several legislative insiders as a bitter and bruising two-year battle fraught with "partisan bickering and ideological splits" because both *Griggs* and *Wards Cove* raised the "politically explosive issue of quotas."[27] Another legislative aide, who had an insider's role in the legislative process, described its history as a "battle among a philosophically evolving Supreme Court, a Democratically-controlled Congress, and a Republican Executive Branch."[28] The process also involved a confrontation between the civil rights community and the pro–civil rights members of Congress on the one hand and the administration of President George H. W. Bush, conservatives, and the business community on the other. Although the Bush administration was amenable to legislation to minimize the impact of *Wards Cove* and *Patterson v. McLean Credit Union,* it was, as it repeatedly proclaimed throughout the two-year process, opposed to any civil rights bill that supported quotas and affirmative action.[29]

THE CIVIL RIGHTS ACT OF 1990: A FAILED FIRST ATTEMPT

Perhaps the reaction of Congress in moving quickly to redress the Court's "civil rights massacre" legislatively should not have been surprising because it had responded with some frequency in recent years in overturning a number of the Court's civil rights decisions that it deemed to have been wrongly decided.[30] Congress's first attempt to codify *Griggs* began almost immediately after the Court decided *Wards Cove.* On June 23, 1989, just two weeks after *Wards*

Cove, Senator Howard Metzenbaum of Ohio introduced a bill to overturn the case. However, the Metzenbaum Bill—the drafting of which included the participation by some members of the civil rights coalition—was put on hold while some engaged in the drafting of a more comprehensive bill to modify or reverse other Supreme Court civil rights cases deemed to have undermined effective enforcement of civil rights laws.[31] In August 1989, the LDF hosted a two-day session in New York City to begin to map out strategies to legislatively overturn the Court's "civil rights massacre." Approximately eighty of the nation's leading civil rights attorneys and advocates who represented a broad spectrum of civil rights organizations, legal scholars from leading law schools, and private attorneys participated in the sessions.[32]

The congressional legislative efforts were led by longtime civil rights advocates: Representative Augustus F. Hawkins, Chairman of the House Education and Labor Committee, and Senator Edward Kennedy, Chairman of the Senate Labor and Human Resources Committee. The initial goal of the civil rights community and its legislative supporters was to overturn or modify the 1989 "civil rights massacre," but during the course of drafting legislation, the goal was expanded to include earlier Supreme Court cases, as well. Civil rights organizations and activists working with and through the LCCR played a major role in the legislative process. The LCCR, which lobbied on civil rights issues, was composed of religious, labor, and auxiliary organizations as well as civil rights groups, including the NAACP, ACLU, Women's Legal Defense Fund, LDF, National Women's Law Center (NWLC), National Urban League, Lawyers Committee for Civil Rights under Law (Lawyers Committee), Mexican American Legal Defense and Educational Fund (MALDEF), and People for the American Way. Their interaction has been described by an observer in this way:

> Primary responsibility for addressing each of the June 1989 decisions as well
> as other issues possibly to be included in the legislation was assigned to an
> organization according to its particular expertise and interest. The Lawyers
> Committee and LDF took the lead in developing language to overturn the decision
> in *Wilks* because they often litigate class action employment discrimination cases
> that result in consent decrees embodying affirmative action relief. The ACLU
> assisted in that effort because of the constitutional due process issues implicit
> in foreclosing a potential litigant access to the courts. All of the represented
> organizations shared responsibility for developing an appropriate response to
> *Wards Cove* because *Griggs*-based disparate impact litigation dramatically opened

up employment opportunities for women, racial, and ethnic minorities. The WLDF, NWLC, and LDF took the lead on *Price Waterhouse* [*v. Hopkins*] mixed motive cases. The WLDF and LDF, ultimately joined by the AFL-CIO, spearheaded the effort to draft language overturning *Lorance*.[33]

In addition to assisting in drafting proposed legislation, civil rights organizations prepared studies and memoranda that documented the deleterious effects of the Court's 1989 civil rights decisions. Many of these studies were introduced into legislative history through the testimony of civil rights representatives. For example, the Action Fund for the People for the American Way—a nonprofit citizen organization established in 1981 to promote and protect civil and constitutional rights—commissioned Arnold and Porter, a preeminent international law firm well known for its pro bono work and support of liberal causes, to prepare a legal analysis of the combined effects of four of the Court's June 1989 decisions: *Wards Cove, Lorance, Wilks,* and *Price Waterhouse v. Hopkins.* The study, which covered cases in the lower courts over a period of about seven months from June 1989 through January 1990, concluded that these four decisions had had a substantial cumulative effect of undermining the overall effectiveness of Title VII.[34]

The LDF conducted a study of the impact of *Patterson* on Section 1981, covering Section 1981 cases decided by the lower court between June 15, 1989—the date the Court decided *Patterson*—and November 20, 1989. The study was later updated to include cases decided between November 1989 and February 9, 1990. As of February 1990, just over seven months after *Patterson,* the lower courts had dismissed over 158 Section 1981 claims alleging racial discrimination based on harassment, discharge, demotion, promotion, transfer, retaliation, miscellaneous treatment, and contract formation without any opportunity for the plaintiffs to have a hearing on the merits of their claims.[35] The Lawyers Committee, which filed the original case out of which *Martin v. Wilks* arose, conducted a study of the aftermath of *Wilks* in the lower courts. The study concluded that, because of *Wilks,* cases with affirmative action provisions or settled by the parties many years before June 1989 were being subjected to endless and perpetual litigation even by persons who had the opportunity to participate in the original lawsuits. The study also found that *Wilks* discouraged employers from entering into settlements of class action cases because of potential exposure to multiple liability from African Americans, women, and other minorities on the one hand and "reverse discrimination" suits by whites on the other; that the courts were being overburdened with lawsuits seeking to relitigate claims that had already been heard; and that the concept of finality in this class of employment discrimination cases had been destroyed.[36]

On February 7, 1990, identical bills from Representative Augustus Hawkins and Senator Edward Kennedy that eventually led to the Civil Rights Act of 1990 were introduced in the House and in the Senate.[37] The Republicans in Congress generally saw no reason to amend Title VII or Section 1981. They generally hailed the Supreme Court's rulings as a necessary corrective action to end the trend toward legitimating quotas because of the *Griggs* disparate impact theory, and the Bush administration and the business community also strongly believed that no congressional action was necessary to respond to the Court's decisions.[38] The Bush administration did introduce legislation on February 22, 1990, to redress some of the June 1989 civil rights cases, signaling its willingness to work with Congress to overturn or limit *Patterson* and *Wilks*, but its bill was substantially less friendly than the bill proposed by the civil rights community and its legislative supporters. And throughout the two years of legislative proceedings, President Bush and other officials in his administration repeatedly admonished that any amendments to Title VII would be vetoed by the President if they decided it legitimated quotas as a remedy.[39]

After eight months of rancorous congressional and administrative debate, on October 17, 1990, Congress passed the Civil Rights Act of 1990, codifying the *Griggs* disparate impact theory.[40] If enacted as introduced, the Civil Rights Act of 1990 would have overruled in whole or in part the seven decisions that the Supreme Court handed down in 1989 as well as other decisions from 1986 and 1987.[41] By another count, the 1990 Act would have "overturn[ed] 25 Supreme Court decisions to some degree."[42] However, on October 22, 1990, two weeks before the congressional elections of 1990, President George H. W. Bush vetoed the Civil Rights Act of 1990 and the Senate failed by only one vote to override the veto.[43]

President Bush's veto made him only the third president to veto a civil rights bill; the only other two were Andrew Johnson and Ronald Reagan. Prior to his veto, President Bush met with William T. Coleman, an African American Republican who had been the Secretary of Transportation during the Ford administration and who had become chairman of the LDF's Board of Directors; Coleman had requested a face-to-face meeting with the President to discuss the President's threat to veto the bill. During this meeting, Coleman made an "impassionate pitch" to the President not to veto the bill,[44] but President Bush vetoed the 1990 Act nevertheless.

THE CIVIL RIGHTS ACT OF 1991

The effort to codify the disparate impact theory was, however, to be success-ful in the 102nd Congress. The first bill introduced in the second session of the 102nd Congress was H.R. 1, the Civil Rights and Women's Equity in Employment Act. One of the strategies supporters of the House bill adopted to blunt the quota argument on which President Bush relied in vetoing the 1990 Act was to recast the new bill as a women's rights bill.[45] In this respect, Congressman Jack Brooks of Texas, who introduced the House bill, declared that "we need to extend to white women the same right to protect themselves in the workplace, just as black women have had that right for years [under Section 1981]."[46] There was, however, opposition to the strategy of emphasizing women as the prime beneficiaries of the new proposed legislation.

Prior to and after the introduction of H.R. 1, the Business Roundtable, a lobbying coalition of more than 200 corporate CEOs founded in 1972 by the CEOs of Alcoa, General Electric, United States Steel, and others, and civil rights organizations and advocates engaged in a series of discussions, meetings, and negotiations, beginning in December 1990, to try to reach a compromise on a bill that would command the two-thirds vote needed to override a poten-tial veto by President Bush.[47] The congressional supporters of the continuing effort to overturn the 1989 decisions in both the House and the Senate did not necessarily look too kindly upon these meetings, which occurred, some said, in secret and outside of the traditional congressional legislative process.[48] However, some of the proposals that resulted from these meetings were favor-ably considered by the congressional proponents in crafting a proposed bill. The negotiations between the Business Roundtable and the civil rights advo-cates ended in mid-April 1991 after White House Counsel C. Boyden Gray met with key business leaders and informed them that the Bush administration disapproved of the negotiations.[49] Civil rights lobbyists were disappointed in the collapse of the negotiations, and several Democrats and civil rights activ-ists accused the Bush administration of torpedoing the efforts to gain political mileage to continue to its quota argument to oppose a strong civil rights bill.[50]

Efforts to craft a new bill were subject to the same kind of legislative strug-gle, allegations of quotas, and interparty and intraparty conflicts among and between liberal and conservative Democrats and Republicans in the House and Senate that had occurred during the legislative maneuvering over the 1990 Act. The House eventually passed its version of the Civil Rights Act of 1991 on

June 5, 1991, by a comfortable margin, but not one that was presidential veto–proof. The legislative spotlight then turned to the Senate. Both the Democrats, led in substantial part by Senator Edward Kennedy, and the Republicans, led in substantial part by Senator John Danforth, tried in their own ways to broker a compromise that would satisfy a Democrat-controlled Congress, moderate Republicans, the Bush administration, business interests, and civil rights lobbyists. Senator Kennedy was not successful in his efforts, but Senator Danforth was more successful, and he introduced several bills in the Senate on June 27, 1991.

The issue of substance of the business necessity defense in disparate impact cases was the single most contentious issue in the two-year legislative battle that eventually led to the Civil Rights Act of 1991.[51] As an observer noted, "The proposed [1990] bill placed the burden on the employer to prove that a practice resulting in a disparate impact on women and minorities were 'essential to effective job performance.'" He continued:

> During the hearings, the business community and the [Bush] Administration relied upon the arguments originated in the opinions of three Justices of the Supreme Court: Justice Blackmun in *Albemarle* [*Paper Co. v. Moody*], Justice O'Connor in *Watson,* and Justice White in *Wards Cove,* that too stringent or narrow a definition of "business necessity" could never be proved. Thus business feared being forced to utilize a quota system to avoid unwinnable lawsuits.
>
> Business and the White House contended that an "essentiality" test of business necessity was too strict because it would be next to impossible for an employer to prove that any practice was *essential* to job performance. They also opposed the focus on an employee's "effective job performance" because it failed to take into account an employer's legitimate interest beyond the employee's performance of actual work duties. Generally, supporters of the House bill refused to accept the business community's argument.[52]

Civil rights supporters advocated a stringent test of business necessity because they believed that facially neutral employment practices were, as the Supreme Court said in *Griggs,* "artificial, arbitrary, and unnecessary barriers" to employment when they screened out a significant percentage of African Americans and other protected classes and the practices were not closely related to job performance. A close reading of *Griggs* clearly supported this view of business necessity because the Court's decision endorsing the business necessity test stated the view that employers should not be permitted to use facially neutral practices that had a substantial adverse impact on protected groups unless there was a demonstrable and measurable relationship—validation—

between the practice and the ability of job candidates to effectively perform the job.

Those, including the Bush administration, who supported the substantially weaker test of business necessity which the Court adopted in *Wards Cove* did so for several reasons. One was that a more stringent standard would be so difficult to meet that employers would adopt quotas to avoid statistical imbalances that would easily allow plaintiffs to establish a prima facie case of disparate impact; another was that in some of its post-*Griggs* cases, including *Wards Cove*, the Supreme Court had adopted a less stringent standard. A case that supported the weaker test of business necessity was the 1989 case of *New York City Transit Authority v. Beazer*. In *Beazer*, the Court defined the business necessity test as focusing on "legitimate employment goals [that] are significantly served by, even if they do not require," the challenged practice.[53] But as counsel to three of the Republican Senators intimately involved in the negotiations that led to the 1991 Civil Rights Act correctly observed, the "Bush administration supported a permanent weakening of the concept of 'business necessity' under which even Willie Griggs would not have been assured of winning his case."[54] President Bush's proposed definition of business necessity, which would essentially codify the *Wards Cove* decision, would require an employer to demonstrate that the practices it chose to defend as measures of job performance had a *significant relationship to successful job performance* and that practices an employer chose not to defend as measures of job performance had to bear a *significant relationship to a significant business objective*.

There was a major disagreement in the legislative deliberations about whether the courts, including the Supreme Court, had endorsed a less stringent test after its landmark decision in *Griggs*. To address this issue, the LDF engaged a major Wall Street law firm, Fried, Frank, Harris, Shriver & Jacobson, to prepare a study to determine whether there was a generally applied standard of business necessity the courts used during the eighteen years between *Griggs* and *Wards Cove*.[55] The LDF publicly released the Frank-Fried study in July 1991. The study was based on a computer-generated selection of 225 cases and concluded that, prior to *Wards Cove*, almost all of the disparate impact cases applied a job performance business necessity standards, even though different formulations of the standard were used.[56] These formulations included the obligation for the employer to prove that the facially neutral practice was "job related," "manifestly related to the job," "predictive of or significantly correlated with important elements of work behavior," "necessary to safe and efficient operation of the business," or "necessary to safe and efficient job performance."[57] In 217, or 96 percent, of the cases job performance standards were, in fact, applied; approximately 72 percent of the cases were decided in favor of the plaintiff; and 28 percent were decided in favor of defendants after a finding that the challenged practice resulted in a disparate impact. In eight of the cases, the standard that applied was one that did not measure ability to do the job; three of those eight were decided for the plaintiffs and four for the defendants.

When it became clear that Senator Kennedy would not be successful in his effort to gain the support he needed to move forward with a bill in the Senate, some of the Republican Senators under the leadership of Senator Danforth moved forward to introduce a Republican-sponsored bill. Negotiations between Senate Democrats under the leadership of Senator Kennedy, Senator Danforth, and the Bush administration failed to resolve the legislative impasse on an appropriate test of business necessity. However, there were two significant events that played a role in resolving the impasse. The first of these two events involved the confirmation hearings of Clarence Thomas to replace Justice Thurgood Marshall, who resigned as an Associate Justice of the Supreme Court on June 27, 1991. The second event was the success of David Duke in his bid to become the Republican candidate for governor of Louisiana. Both of these events markedly shifted the political debate in favor of a bill to undo the Court's 1989 "civil rights massacre" and influenced President Bush to sign the Civil Rights Act of 1991.

On July 1, 1991, President Bush nominated Clarence Thomas, an African American, to replace Justice Thurgood Marshall, who was the first African American appointed to the Supreme Court and whose reputation as a strong civil rights advocate before and after he was appointed to the Supreme Court is legendary, but a decidedly more conservative and Republican administration dominated national politics at the time Justice Marshall resigned. At the time of his nomination, Clarence Thomas, born in Pinpoint, Georgia, was a forty-three-year-old conservative African American Republican who received his law degree from Yale Law School. He eventually landed a job with Senator Danforth, who at that time was serving as Missouri's Attorney General. Thomas later served as a legislative aide to Senator Danforth after his election to Congress. President Reagan appointed Thomas as an assistant secretary for civil rights in the Department of Education and as chairman of the Equal Employment Opportunity Commission. President Bush then appointed him to the U.S. Court of Appeals for the District of Columbia. Because Thomas was an African American who had been selected to replace Justice Marshall, President Bush went to great lengths to explain that his decision was neither an affirmative action nor a quota appointment because he had repeatedly broadcasted his opposition to quotas as a remedy to racial discrimination throughout the two-year battle to enact the Civil Rights Act of 1991.[58]

Many civil rights activists opposed the Thomas nomination because, among other reasons, he criticized *Griggs* and opposed affirmative action,[59] even though he recognized that he had been a beneficiary of affirmative action when he gained admission to Yale Law School in 1974.[60] A number of women's organization opposed his nomination because of a concern that, if appointed, he would vote to overturn *Roe v. Wade,* the 1973 landmark Supreme Court case upholding the right to an abortion. During the Senate's confirmation proceedings, Anita Hill, an African American female, claimed that Thomas had engaged in sexual harassment against her when she worked with him at the Department of Education's Office of Civil Rights and when he was the chair of the EEOC.[61] The televised Senate hearing on Hill's allegations of sexual harassment ignited a national debate and firestorm for three days in October 1991 about sex and race discrimination, and it threatened to derail Thomas's nomination.[62] The national headlines surrounding the airing of the sexual harassment charges against Justice Thomas were brutal and ugly and raised serious questions about President Bush's sincerity in his often-stated commitment to civil rights. Thomas denounced the hearings as a "high tech lynching of an uppity black man." One legislative insider who participated in the events leading to the Civil Rights Act of 1991 concluded that the three days of hearing on the harassment charges against Thomas did more than two years of civil rights activity to communicate and dramatize the problem of discrimination against women as well as racial and ethnic minorities and instantly transformed the public and legislative debate from a fixation on quotas into a debate about workplace harassment that directly affects women.[63]

The Senate, however, eventually confirmed Thomas's nomination by a vote of 52 to 48, the narrowest margin of approval for a Supreme Court Justice in more than a century. Senator Danforth played a pivotal role in securing Justice Thomas's confirmation. It is reported that one of the reasons President Bush ultimately decided to sign the Civil Rights Act of 1991 is that he owed "a major debt" to Senator Danforth for successfully securing the confirmation of Justice Thomas,[64] and that debt included signing the Civil Rights Act of 1991.

The other event deemed to have played an important role in convincing President Bush to sign the Civil Rights Act of 1991 was the selection of David Duke, the former Ku Klux Klan Grand Wizard, as a nominee for governor of Louisiana in 1991. During the runoff election for governor, David Duke's argument in support of racial segregation paralleled, in substantial part, the same quota argument President Bush had relied upon throughout the two-year battle to overrule the 1989 massacre. This fact rendered President Bush vulnerable to criticism that he was anti–civil rights and made some Senate Republicans skittish over the impact of potential labeling of the President and Republicans as racist in the upcoming congressional elections.

Although there have been disclaimers to the contrary,[65] there is strong support for the conclusion that the Thomas-Hill confrontation and the David Duke nomination were perhaps the critical events that ultimately influenced President Bush to sign the Civil Rights Act of 1991 notwithstanding his repeated vow that he would never sign a quota bill, because the events shifted the focus of the legislative debate from quotas to civil rights for women and ethnic minorities, which produced the possibilities that both House and Senate would override a presidential veto. As explained by one commentator:

> As a result of both the duration and intensity of the attention given to the David Duke nomination and the Thomas-Hill confrontation, the nation reached its collective saturation point, and the time had come to simply remove the issue of race and gender politics from political debate and consciousness. As fate would have it, precisely because the civil rights community did not achieve their primary objective to defeat Thomas, conservative Republican senators, who in the past voted to sustain . . . [President Bush's] veto of the civil rights bill, were now free to join Danforth without having to weigh the prospect of back-to-back defeat for the Administration and of handing an important legislative victory to the very community that so fervently opposed Thomas.[66]

After these two events, the movement toward the enactment of the Civil Rights Act of 1991 was quick. On October 22, 1991, just one week after the Senate voted to confirm Justice Thomas and four days after Duke's selection as the Republican nominee for governor of Louisiana, the Senate voted 93–3 in favor of cloture on the civil rights bill. Next, there were negotiation and changes to the proposed bill, which overruled or modified the cases in the Court's "civil rights massacre." President Bush then announced his support for the bill. Congress passed the Civil Rights Act of 1991 on November 7, and President Bush signed the bill into law on November 21. In addition to overturning or modifying all of the cases affected by the Court's 1989 "civil rights massacre," including *Wards Cove, Lorance, Wilks,* and *Patterson,* the 1991 Act overturned or modified other civil rights cases, some of which were decided prior to 1989.[67] Both sides claimed victory. The congressional proponents claimed that the Act both restored the law on employment discrimination to where it was prior to the Court's 1989 "civil rights massacre" and expanded the protection for applicants and employees from discrimination in employment. The Bush administration claimed that the bill would not require employers to engage in quota hiring and promotions.[68]

The Women's Legal Defense Fund and the National Women's Law Center had proposed a provision allowing compensatory and punitive damages in intentional or disparate treatment cases brought under Title VII because it was unfair to allow such damages in Section 1981, which prohibits only racial discrimination, and not to allow similar damages in sex discrimination cases. The inclusion of compensatory and punitive damages was one of the reasons employers vigorously opposed the 1990 and 1991 civil rights bills. The proposal on awarding compensatory and punitive damages in disparate treatment employment discrimination cases under Title VII significantly extended employers' monetary liability to all protected groups. For the first time, Congress provided for awards of compensatory and punitive damages under Title VII in intentional or disparate treatment cases and for the right to jury trials, but only in disparate treatment cases, but there is still no right to a jury trial in disparate impact cases.

THE REBIRTH OF *GRIGGS*

Arguments about who won and who lost on the quota argument began almost immediately after the 1991 Act became law. However, what is not open to debate is that just over twenty years after *Griggs,* Congress, for the first time, statutorily codified the disparate impact theory. Congress clearly stated its reasons for codifying the disparate impact theory by addressing three of the rulings in *Wards Cove.* First, in *Wards Cove,* the Supreme Court held that in order to establish a prima facie case, the plaintiffs must *specifically* identify the *particular* employment practice that *caused* the disparate impact. This ruling posed a substantial proof problem for the plaintiffs in cases in which employers rely upon a group of interrelated practices in making employment decisions. The specificity/particularity/causation rule of *Wards Cove* has been characterized by some as the "cumulation" principle, and the proper application of principle was an issue on which the courts were divided.[69] Although Congress endorsed the *Wards Cove* cumulation principle, in cases in which an employer relies upon a multicriteria selection practice and the plaintiffs can prove that the employer's decision-making process is not capable of separation for analysis, then the plaintiffs are entitled to treat the decision-making process as one employment practice. The purpose of this exception is to avoid what the civil rights advocates deemed to be "death by a thousand cuts"[70] and is a partial rejection of an otherwise complete flat ban on bottom-line statistics the Court endorsed in *Wards Cove*. Second, in overruling *Wards Cove*, Congress statutorily reinstated the *Griggs* rule imposing the greater burden of proof—both the burdens of production of evidence and of persuasion—of the business necessity defense on employers.[71]

Third, the contentious debate between the Democrats' leadership, Republicans, and the Bush administration on the business necessity defense was ultimately resolved by an agreement to adopt a modified version of the defense first enacted in the Americans with Disabilities Act (ADA) of 1990, the most comprehensive federal civil rights statute protecting the rights, including the right to equal employment, of individuals with disabilities. Efforts to get Congress to enact the ADA began in 1987, before the Court had decided either *Watson* or *Wards Cove*. However, both cases were decided during the legislative process leading to the ADA. The Bush administration was committed to upholding the *Wards Cove* lenient business necessity ruling in negotiations on both the ADA and the Title VII disparate impact theory.[72] One of the nation's leading experts on disability rights law, and a key adviser to both Congress and the disability community, offered this explanation of how the standard of "job related and consistent with business necessity" evolved:

> The clear differences between the [Bush] Administration negotiators and the Senate sponsors of the ADA on the *Wards Cove* issue threatened to create an impasse on the ADA negotiations. The resolution of the conflict did not result in a particularly well written law, but it did succeed in resolving the impasse and thereby creating a bill that would ultimately become law. The negotiators agreed, as policy matter, to disagree regarding the correct standard to be applied to disparate impact claims under Title VII. At the same time, however, the negotiators agreed that the standard under the ADA would be section 504 [of the Rehabilitation Act of 1973] prior to the *Wards Cove* decision.

The negotiators agreed also not to be overly explicit regarding this policy agreement in the statute. Thus, they searched for a phrase that had some direct precedent in either section 503 or 504 regulations [under the Rehabilitation Act], or case law development under these sections that could be used as a clear "hook" to which a more explicit explanation could be attached in accompanying committee report language. The resulting phrase was "job related and consistent with business necessity."

The Committee Report . . . explanation [for the resulting phrase was that] any criteria or requirement with a disparate impact, or any medical examination or inquiry of current employees, had to be "carefully tailored [inter alia] to measure the person's actual ability to do [the] essential function[s] of the job. . . .

The compromise . . . had advantages and disadvantages for each side. On the one hand, the Administration accepted that the *Wards Cove* standard would not be imported into the ADA. On the other hand, the Senate sponsors accepted that the ADA would fail to have, within the statute itself, a clear, explicit, and understandable standard.[73]

Thus, the law on business necessity that had been adopted in pre-ADA disability cases under the Rehabilitation Act remained unchanged in the disability context, and its original meaning could be preserved without directly confronting the *Wards Cove* substantive business necessity issue.[74] Congress overwhelmingly passed the ADA with its compromise on the business necessity test, and President Bush enthusiastically championed and signed it into law in 1990.

The last-minute negotiations on the business necessity defense in the wake of the Justice Thomas confirmation hearings led to an agreement to adopt the ADA's "job related and consistent with business necessity" tests for disparate impact claims under the 1991 Act. However, the end result of the negotiations was to leave unresolved the meaning of the standard. So, anticipating this rather obvious but unanswered question as to the substantive test under the new statutory statement of the business necessity defense, Congress agreed upon legislative history that is specifically made part of the statutory codification of the disparate impact theory stating that the "terms of 'business necessity' and 'job related' are intended to reflect the concepts enunciated by the Supreme Court in *Griggs* . . . and other Supreme Court cases decided prior to *Wards Cove*."[75] The courts have yet to reach a uniform approach in defining the appropriate test of business necessity under the test Congress endorsed in the 1991 Act.[76]

The 1991 Act also codifies the alternative method by which a plaintiff may prevail under the disparate impact theory. Under this alternative, a plaintiff can prove unlawful employment discrimination by offering an alternative practice that would equally well serve the employer's legitimate business interest without a similar disparate impact on a protected group but which the employer refused to adopt even though able to satisfy the new test of business necessity under the 1991 Act.[77] The 1991 Act repudiates *Wards Cove* on this point because it provides that the determination of an acceptable alternative "shall be in accordance with the law as it existed on June 4, 1981,"[78] which is one day before the Court decided *Wards Cove*. In the LDF case of *Albemarle Paper Co. v. Moody*, the Supreme Court had endorsed the alternative evidentiary route to proving a claim under the disparate impact theory. Congress also overturned *Lorance* by providing that an unlawful employment practice of seniority discrimination occurs when the seniority system is adopted, or when an individual becomes subject to the seniority system, or when a person claiming to have been the victim of seniority discrimination is injured by the application of a facially neutral seniority system or provision of the system.[79]

The limitation *Patterson* imposed on the scope of Section 1981 was overturned by amending the statute to provide that the phrase "make and enforce contracts" include the making, performance, modification, and termination of contracts, and the enjoyment of all benefits, privileges, terms, and conditions of the contractual relationship. Left unanswered, however, was the question whether new subsection (c), which provides that rights protected under Section 1981 "are protected against impairment by nongovernmental discrimination and impairments under color of State law," overturns the Court's decision in *Jett*. In the several years after the Act's passage, the majority of courts deciding this issue held that subsection (c) does not overrule *Jett*.[80]

Another provision in the 1991 Act, Section 703(m), was enacted to overturn the Supreme Court's decision in the mixed-motive case, *Price Waterhouse v. Hopkins*. In that case, the employer, once one of the big eight accountancy firms because of its dominance in the international market, denied the plaintiff, a woman, partnership status because she did not conform to stereotypical conduct it expected of women.[81] The courts found that Price Waterhouse's reason for denying her partnership status was that she had engaged in unprofessional conduct in the workplace—a perfectly legitimate reason for the adverse decision—but that, at the same time, it had based its decision on stereotypical assumptions as to how women should look and act. The Supreme Court held that a defendant in a mixed-motive case could avoid liability under

Title VII by proving that it would have made the same decision by relying solely on the legitimate reason even if it had not taken the plaintiff's gender into account; this is the "same decision" defense. Congress overturned *Price Waterhouse* in Section 703(m) to provide that, in a mixed-motive case, a plaintiff can establish a violation of Title VII by proving that discriminatory reason was "a motivating factor" in the employment decision. The effect of Section 703(m), however, is that a plaintiff obtains only a Pyrrhic victory because the same decision defense, if proven, limits make whole relief under the principles of *Moody* and *Franks*.[82]

As to remedies, the Act provided for both punitive damages and limited compensatory damages. Punitive damages could be recovered on a showing that an employer engaged in discriminatory practices "with malice or with reckless indifference" to an individual's federally protected rights. However, the Act excluded a number of remedies from compensatory damages: back pay and interest on it, and other relief that the 1964 Act had authorized, such as injunctions and appropriate affirmative action.

In the 1991 Act, Congress also, for the first time, legislatively addressed the issue of affirmative action, albeit indirectly. Section 116 provides that nothing in the amendments to Title VII "shall be construed to affect . . . affirmation action, or conciliation agreements . . . that are in accordance with the law."[83] The phrase *in accordance with the law* strongly suggests congressional endorsement of *Weber* and *Johnson,* which are the two Supreme Court decisions that adopted a test for upholding voluntarily adopted affirmative action plans in a statutory context that is substantially less stringent than the strict scrutiny test that applies to similar plans when challenged under the Equal Protection Clause of the Constitution. While Congress overruled a number of the pre–*Wards Cove* cases that had weakened the effectiveness of laws prohibiting discrimination in employment, it did not overrule *Weber* and *Johnson,* so the principles for determining the legality of such plans remain unchanged by the 1991 Act.

The Act also overruled *Wilks,* deemed by some as the death knell for affirmative action,[84] by limiting the circumstances under which whites and males are allowed to collaterally attack affirmative action class action consent decrees. Section 703(n) of Title VII now precludes collateral attacks on litigated or consent judgments or orders that resolve claims of employment discrimination under the Constitution or federal civil rights statutes by persons who, prior to the entry of the judgment or order, had both actual notice that their interests might be affected and the opportunity to object prior to the entry of the judgment or order. This Section also precludes collateral attacks by persons whose interests were adequately represented by another person in a prior challenge to the judgment or order on the same legal grounds and with a similar factual situation. Section 703(n), however, preserves the constitutional due process rights of individuals to notice and the opportunity to be heard. The extent to which the preservation of the constitutional right to be heard limits the scope of protection from collateral attacks under Section 703(n) is a question open to debate.

15. Epilogue

It has now been more than forty years since the Supreme Court decided *Griggs*. Yet, the legitimacy, legacy, and efficacy of the disparate impact theory continue to be as hotly contested today as they were shortly after the theory's endorsement by the Supreme Court in 1971. A major purpose of this concluding chapter is to offer a few observations about the legitimacy, legacy, and efficacy of *Griggs*.

WHAT HAPPENED TO THE BLACK EMPLOYEES IN *GRIGGS*?

Willie Griggs, Willie Boyd, and the other black employees did not set out to make civil rights history when they sued Duke Power. All they really wanted was the opportunity, as provided by Title VII, to be considered for jobs that Duke Power historically had reserved for white individuals. However, they did make civil rights history when the Supreme Court endorsed the disparate impact theory in their case in 1971 and Congress later legislatively endorsed that theory of discrimination in the Civil Rights Act of 1991. The LDF, in conducting its employment discrimination litigation campaign out of which *Griggs* arose, played a major role in "standing in the gap" on behalf of the black plaintiffs, not only in landmark cases, such as *Griggs, Moody,* and *Franks,* but also in a substantial number of other employment discrimination cases on behalf of other black applicants and employees. The phrase "stand in the gap" is borrowed from softball and, as applied in employment discrimination litigation, describes the support—for example, financial and emotional support—plaintiffs received from others during the course of the many years it often takes before a case is finally over.[1]

If a case succeeds in establishing some landmark principle or precedent, then more often than not the lead plaintiff's name becomes famous because it will always be attached to the case. While the lead plaintiff's name becomes known, the plaintiff himself or herself generally fades into the background only to resurface perhaps, if at all, periodically at some future date in celebration of the anniversary of the case. Rarely discussed is what happens to plaintiffs after their cases are decided. This pattern has already manifested itself in the *Griggs* case. The black employees began to fade rather quickly soon after the Supreme Court announced its decision in *Griggs* in March 1971. Then, in 1974, the EEOC invited some of the lead plaintiffs in some of the early landmark Title VII employment discrimination cases, including Willie Griggs and Willie Boyd, to its celebration of the first decade of development under Title VII held in Atlanta, Georgia.[2] Shortly thereafter, the black employees again faded into the background. Some resurfaced in 1991, when a number of newspapers, national and local, did feature stories about some of them[3] as the disparate impact theory and its business necessity defense became major issues in light of the congressional deliberations that led to the Civil Rights Act of 1991.

But the *Griggs* story would not be complete without coverage of whether the plaintiffs in the case benefited from their landmark victory in the Supreme Court. The remedy they wanted was the opportunity to be employed in jobs historically limited to white persons, because as a court of appeals so aptly stated in one of the earliest cases in the litigation campaign, "[E]ven the most tedious physical labor is endurable and in a sense enjoyable . . . where the laborer knows that his work will be appreciated and his progress is rewarded."[4]

The story of the relief the black employees obtained begins with the court of appeals' decision because that court divided them into three groups, Groups A, B, and C as designated by Judge Gordon on remand. As explained earlier, Group A was the four black employees without a high school education who were hired after the adoption of the education-test requirements: Willie Griggs, John Hatchett, Clarence Purcell, and Eddie Broadnax. Group B was the three who met the high school education requirement: Robert Jumper, Willie Boyd, and Henry Martin. Group C was the six black employees Duke Power had hired after it adopted the education-test requirements: Junior Blackstock, William Purcell, Clarence Jackson, Eddie Galloway, Lewis Hairston, and James Tucker.

The litigation team initiated the postappellate remedies proceedings before Judge Gordon in the district court when, on June 18, 1970, it filed a motion for injunctive relief pending appeal even before the Supreme Court granted certiorari. The basis for the motion was that the black employees had informed Chambers and me that Duke Power had employed or promoted white employees for positions to which the black employees in Group C were entitled under the court of appeals' decision. After a hearing on the motion, Judge

Gordon issued his first memorandum order on relief. He noted that only the claim of Group A plaintiffs was involved in proceedings before the Supreme Court. He rejected the litigation team's argument that Group B employees were entitled to challenge any racially discriminatory practices by Duke Power that occurred subsequent to the decision by the court of appeals. The basis on which he reached that conclusion was his view that the court of appeals had determined that their claims were moot because they met the educational requirement for promotion out of the common labor/janitor category. He further ruled that the proper course the Group B employees needed to pursue for discrimination occurring after the court of appeals decision was to start the process all over again by first filing a new charge of discrimination with the EEOC.[5] The court of appeals eventually affirmed Judge Gordon on this point.[6]

The three employees who met the high school education requirement were Herman Martin and Willie Boyd—both of whom were named plaintiffs—and Jesse Martin, Herman's brother, who was not a named plaintiff. Duke Power had promoted Jesse Martin to learner in the coal-handling department on August 8, 1966, but only after the employees had filed their charge with the EEOC and just two months before the LDF filed the complaint in the district court. Duke Power later promoted him to a utility operator position on March 18, 1968. Duke Power promoted Herman Martin to watchman in March 1968, just one month after the trial, and then later to a learner's job in the coal-handling department.

Willie Boyd, the spokesperson for the black employees, satisfied the education requirement by obtaining his GED in May 1969 through the tuition remission program financed by Duke Power. He sent an invitation to his graduation to the assistant plant manager, which the plant manager accepted. Duke Power offered Boyd the position of watchman shortly after his graduation, but Boyd declined it because the pay increase over what he was earning was too small. He decided to wait for future job openings because he knew he would not have to pass the test battery. Boyd eventually became the first African American supervisor at the Dan River Steam Station when Duke Power promoted him to supervisor over the coal-handling department. Boyd was convinced that Duke Power tried to discourage him from becoming a supervisor because it wanted to preserve the position for a white person. The jobs in coal handling historically had been reserved for white employees. The discouragement was in the form of trying to convince Boyd that he was not qualified for the job. The strategy did not work. Boyd insisted on taking the job. Then Duke Power did something that was inconsistent with the notion of sound business practice: it promoted both Boyd and a white person to the position. The white "fella," as Boyd called him, worked as Boyd's co-supervisor for only about six months because he just did not like telling employees what to do. At his request, Duke Power allowed the white "fella" to return to his old job as a coal handler, thus working under the supervision of Boyd. According to Boyd, the victory in the Supreme Court in 1971 simply cemented what he and his coplaintiffs had known for a long time: given the opportunity, they would be able to perform the same jobs similarly situated white employees performed.[7]

Judge Gordon entered a fairly broad injunctive order in December 1970 in favor of the Group C employees, granting them essentially all of the relief the litigation team had requested in its motion for injunctive relief pending appeal. He ordered Duke Power to: (1) waive the education and testing requirements as to Group C employees for any promotion, demotion, or selection of employees for training; (2) consider them for future job opportunities on the basis of their total length of service (or plant seniority); (3) maintain records on the reason any of them were not considered for future vacancies and to keep such records in their personnel files and give copies to the plaintiffs; (4) "red-circle" their wages; and (5) provide the litigation team, after a written request, with copies of any personnel action affecting these plaintiffs.[8] Judge Gordon entered the same remedial order on behalf of the Group A employees after the Supreme Court March 8, 1971, decision.

After the Supreme Court handed down its decision, the litigation team renewed its motion for further relief, asking for appropriate relief for all of the employees in each group and the class on whose behalf the case was brought as certified by trial court very early in the proceedings. Judge Gordon eventually held an evidentiary hearing to determine whether further relief should be awarded to Groups B and C. After the hearing, at which I was lead counsel, the judge entered the final order in the case on January 23, 1974, about eight years after the employees first petitioned Duke Power for the opportunity to be considered for jobs that had been historically limited to white males. Judge Gordon perhaps signaled his exasperation with the case when he stated at the beginning of his memorandum opinion that the case had advanced beyond a "curious procedural phenomenon" to one that borders on the "macabre." He then went on to hold that an earlier order certifying the case as a class action was impliedly dissolved by the decision of the court of appeals. The three grounds on which he relied in dissolving the class status of the case were that the court of appeals had separated the named black employees into three groups; no court at any time had found that Duke Power had engaged in "active" discrimination, presumably intentional discrimination against African Americans after the effective date of Title VII (July 2, 1965); and the discrimination suffered by the named black employees was the residual effect of discrimination practiced by Duke Power prior to July 2, 1965. It seems a bit disingenuous that Judge Gordon would rely upon the last two grounds because the Supreme Court unequivocally held that the disparate impact theory does not require proof of intentional discrimination.

As to those in Group A, which included the lead plaintiff, Willie Griggs, Judge Gordon concluded that he had awarded them all the relief to which they were entitled in an earlier order. He also reaffirmed his earlier decision that the claims of black employees in Group B, those who had a high school education or its equivalent, were not properly before the court because they had not exhausted their administrative remedies before the EEOC. Griggs had left Duke Power in the mid-1970s; worked in New York for several years; then later returned to Reidsville and ended up working in a laborer's job on the night shift with another employer in the area performing essentially the same kind of janitorial work he had done at Duke Power.[9]

With respect to the employees in Group C, Judge Gordon concluded that none of them were entitled to further relief because Duke Power had complied with his earlier remedial order. The court found that since the date of the court of appeals decision—January 9, 1970—four of the Group C employees (Junior Blackstock, Clarence Jackson, James Tucker, and William Purcell) had been promoted out of the labor department into higher-paying previously all-white jobs in departments that provided them the opportunity to advance to some of the top-paying jobs at the steam station. Blackstock was promoted twice in the operations department; Jackson became a learner in the operations department; Tucker became a learner in the maintenance department; and Purcell became a utility operator in the operations department. Eddie Galloway, also a member of Group C, remained in his laborer job in the labor department because Duke Power rejected his bid to fill a vacant engineer's position, for two reasons: first, there was a contentious factual issue, which the court resolved in favor of Duke Power, on whether he was qualified for the vacancy, and second, he had been restricted to relatively light work because of a heart problem. Another contentious factual issue involved Lewis

Hairston's promotion, on which Judge Gordon ruled in favor of Duke Power. Duke Power had promoted Hairston to a test assistant's position in the testing department but after five weeks had demoted him back to the labor department when it deemed that he was unable to do the job that he should have been able to master in a week or less.

A number of the *Griggs* plaintiffs—all are now deceased—were interviewed in 1991 while the debate of the Civil Rights Act of 1991 was ongoing. For example, Willie Boyd, the principal mover and shaker among the plaintiffs in *Griggs*, was interviewed in a short period of time in 1991 by *USA Today*, the *Washington Post*, the *Los Angeles Times*, the *Atlanta Journal-Constitution*, and a number of local and state newspapers. A major national television network taped an extended piece on Boyd and *Griggs*, but the show was never aired because it was bumped by the Clarence Thomas confirmation hearings.[10] Reflecting many years after the Supreme Court decision, the black employees had mixed opinions about it,[11] even though they, unlike many other black employees in the case, deemed themselves "winners" because the courts had decided that they were entitled to pursue jobs at Duke Power other than the common laborer or janitorial positions to which they had been relegated because of their race. All of them, except Willie Griggs, eventually retired from Duke Power's Dan River Steam Station. Griggs, as noted earlier, left Duke Power in the 1970s, never returned, and had very little interest in the case after he left. His wife stated that whatever the case did for others, it did absolutely nothing to keep them from working anything but the night shift.[12] Most of the other plaintiffs agreed that much about the qualities of their lives in terms of having nice homes and the ability to make a good life for their families was the result of the case. One of the first things Willie Boyd did after receiving a ninety-five-cent raise when he received his first promotion in twenty years (to supervisor in coal handling) was to borrow money to help pay the educational expenses to work on his master's degree in music. Clarence Jackson, in whose house the black plaintiffs drafted their EEOC complaint, said that he accomplished what he was really working for but that during the first fifteen years, he and the other black employees were unlucky, apparently, because they were stuck in dead-end all-black positions. Willie Boyd, the spokesperson for the plaintiffs, put the case in historical perspective when he noted that "life is funny" because an earlier generation of African Americans would be amazed at the changes that took place as a result of *Griggs*, yet the generation of African

Americans who grew up after *Griggs* would also be amazed at the quality of life for blacks before the case.

THE REACH OF *GRIGGS* BEYOND TITLE VII

The legacy of *Griggs* reaches beyond Title VII. The United States has a host of laws, orders, and regulations prohibiting discrimination in employment in the public and private sectors.[13] As a general rule, most of these laws were enacted to achieve the same policy objective of implementing equality in the workplace by prohibiting those subject to the mandate of each law from engaging in conduct, when motivated by the applicant's or employee's status, that is contrary to policy objectives. In other words, most of these laws prohibit disparate treatment discrimination. Although the disparate impact theory in Title VII was first endorsed by the Supreme Court in the *Griggs* case, the courts have held that disparate impact discrimination is prohibited under some other laws, as well, and in some of these laws, Congress has legislatively endorsed the disparate impact theory, for example, the Americans with Disabilities Act of 1990. According to the legislative history of the Civil Rights Act of 1991, the Title VII provisions governing the proof structure in disparate impact cases are intended to apply also to those antidiscrimination laws that have been modeled after and interpreted consistently with Title VII. The "results" test that Congress included in voting rights legislation overturning the Supreme Court's 1980 decision in *City of Mobile v. Bolden* is analogous to the *Griggs* disparate impact theory even though it does not incorporate the *Griggs* framework. The Voting Rights Act of 1965 was the culmination of congressional effort "to banish the blight of racial discrimination in voting."[14] In *Bolden,* a plurality of the Supreme Court Justices held that proof of discriminatory intent is required to establish a violation of Section 2 of the Voting Rights Act and a constitutional violation of the Fourteenth and Fifteenth Amendments to the Constitution. Prior to *Bolden,* challenges by blacks to elections or election procedures could prevail based on a totality of the evidence showing that the procedure had the result of denying blacks or language minorities equal access to participate in the electoral process. The 1982 Amendment restored the prior legal standard that voting laws are unlawful if they have racially discriminatory effects or result in denying minorities an equal chance to participate in the electoral process.[15]

Courts have held that the disparate impact theory is applicable to claims arising under other federal statutes, even though Congress was not as explicit in legislatively endorsing the theory as it did for Title VII claims in the Civil Rights Act of 1991. Congress enacted the Age Discrimination in Employment Act (ADEA) in 1967,[16] two years after Title VII, but before the Court decided *Griggs*. But, like Title VII before the Civil Rights Act of 1991, Congress did not specifically address the issue of whether the ADEA prohibits disparate impact age discrimination. Nevertheless, in 2005, the Supreme Court, relying on *Griggs*, ruled that the ADEA prohibits disparate impact age discrimination, even though the kinds of claims that are prohibited under the statute are significantly narrower than disparate impact claims that can be brought under Title VII.[17] Although the Supreme Court has not ruled on the issue, every federal court of appeals to address the issue has held that housing discrimination cases under the federal fair housing statute, which prohibits discrimination in the sale and rental of housing, can be brought under the disparate impact theory.[18] The Supreme Court also has recognized that some forms of disparate impact claims can be brought under the Rehabilitation Act of 1973.[19]

The fact that Congress and the courts have recognized that the disparate impact theory has a broader reach than discrimination prohibited under Title VII is a testament to its influence on policies and practices to effectuate equality in the workplace, even though the manner in which it is applied is not the same as in Title VII.

GRIGGS AND STATE EMPLOYMENT DISCRIMINATION LAWS

A number of states and municipalities had enacted statutes or ordinances prior to the enactment of Title VII in 1964 that prohibited discrimination in employment.[20] However, these civil rights/human rights agencies were committed solely to the disparate treatment theory of discrimination in that they defined discrimination solely in terms of intent.[21] After *Griggs*, a number of states either adopted the disparate impact theory of discrimination or found that federal law under Title VII, including the disparate impact theory, governed in those states. At least two states, Texas and Rhode Island, explicitly endorsed and defined the disparate impact theory in their statutes.[22] Several states interpreted their fair employment practices law to support a claim for disparate impact.[23] Among these states, most have enunciated disparate impact theory in terms of federal disparate impact case law.[24] California courts, for example, specifically recognized a disparate impact claim under the California Fair Employment and Housing Act and defined disparate impact theory according to federal Title VII precedent.[25]

Several other states, although not explicitly adopting disparate impact theory in their statutes or case law, appeared ready to recognize a claim of disparate impact.[26] These states recognize that their employment discrimination statutes are similar to Title VII and should therefore be interpreted in light of Title VII precedents. Arkansas courts, for example, have not spoken on the issue of disparate impact theory in employment discrimination claims but have repeatedly indicated that "the Arkansas Civil Rights Act expressly instructs us to look to federal civil rights law when interpreting the Act."[27] As a result of this statutory instruction, Arkansas courts have looked to Title VII to determine the availability and elements of previously unrecognized causes of action under the Arkansas Civil Rights Act. Arkansas' practice of looking to Title VII for guidance when interpreting state employment discrimination law led one federal court to suggest that Arkansas recognize disparate impact claims, despite the absence of state law on the matter.[28] Colorado's Civil Rights Commission, on the other hand, has promulgated regulations adopting the disparate impact theory according to the 1978 Federal Union Guidelines on Employee Selection Procedures.[29]

Other states appear ready to apply the disparate impact theory in employment discrimination cases because they have already recognized the theory in other forms of discrimination. Indiana, for example, allows disparate impact claims in state housing and disability discrimination cases and relies upon federal precedent when applying those claims.[30] Because Indiana law considers freedom from housing discrimination, disability discrimination in employment, and Title VII–type discrimination in employment to be civil rights on equal footing,[31] it is likely that Indiana courts will also recognize disparate impact theory in Title VII–type employment discrimination claims. The fact that these states are likely to recognize a disparate impact claim under their fair employment practices statutes, however, does not mean that they will follow federal disparate impact law exactly when deciding that claim. Although these states recognize that similarities between their statutes and Title VII suggest similar statutory interpretations, these states also note that Title VII precedent is not necessarily persuasive where textual differences exist between the state and federal statutes.[32]

DISPARATE IMPACT AS AN INTERNATIONAL THEORY
OF DISCRIMINATION

Although the *Griggs* disparate impact theory "is an American innovation" because the United States was the first country to recognize it,[33] it is now an
international theory in employment discrimination law (and other civil and
human rights laws) because it either has been explicitly endorsed by other
countries or has been influential in the judicial decisions rendered by international tribunals in cases involving claims of discrimination. The LDF was well
aware of the influence of *Griggs* in the international community.[34] Outside of
the United States, the term *indirect discrimination* is often used for the disparate impact theory, and the term *direct discrimination* is often used for the disparate treatment theory, which requires proof of intentional discrimination.[35]
An early study of the favorable reception of disparate impact theory both in
other countries with similar legal heritages and in international law identified
the following as having explicitly relied upon the theory as of 1998: the United
Kingdom, Australia, New Zealand, and the Treaty of Rome, which is the fundamental constitutional document of the European Economic Community,
and the European Court of Justice, which had applied the disparate impact
theory to the issue of national origin discrimination under the Treaty of Rome
since the mid-1970s.[36] The authors report that *Griggs* had an influential rule in
the adoption of the disparate impact theory in the United Kingdom in 1974;
that Australia has incorporated the disparate impact theory in all of its antidiscrimination laws; and that the concept of "discrimination by subterfuge"
in pertinent New Zealand laws appears to be close to the concept of disparate
impact or indirect discrimination.

Like the United States prior to *Griggs,* Canada initially recognized only the
disparate treatment theory but, in 1985, judicially endorsed the disparate impact theory. However, in a 1999 case, the Supreme Court of Canada, dissatis-
fied with what it deemed to be an artificial distinction between the disparate
impact and disparate treatment theories, abolished the distinction between
the two when it adopted a new, unified theoretical and analytical approach
to employment discrimination claims.[37] The disparate impact theory first
appeared in the jurisprudence of the European Court of Justice, the highest
court of the European Union, in 1981.[38] The disparate impact theory has made
its appearance in additional European countries,[39] South Africa,[40] and Asian
countries.[41] The legacy of *Griggs* in the international community, outside of

the United States, is perhaps greater than that of *Brown v. Board of Education.*[42]

Hunter and Shoben concluded their international comparative review of the influence of the disparate impact by noting that the theory is neither a "folly"[43] nor "aberrant."[44] Rather, they conclude, the post-*Griggs* restrictive interpretation in the United States of this innovation is grossly out of step with broad acceptance and expansion upon the theory by other countries and international tribunals.[45] Others have also commented upon the fact that the reach of the disparate impact theory in the United States is much narrower than in other countries.[46]

CONCLUSION: A FEW PERSPECTIVES

The disparate impact theory, like the Court's decision in *Brown*, has generated an ongoing judicial and scholarly debate about the legitimacy of the theory and the Court's underlying rationale. As one scholar stated, "missing from the Burger Court's opinion was a clear explanation of the theory underlying disparate impact. Was the theory bottomed on the existence of past or present discrimination against minorities?"[47] Another scholar has argued that *Griggs* was wrongly decided because Congress intended to prohibit only disparate treatment discrimination.[48] As with the *Brown* decision, much of the criticism of *Griggs* is grounded at the bottom of the ongoing debate about the meaning of equality, and the debate about the meaning of equality goes back to the very beginning of this country.[49] The effort by the Legal Defense Fund in its employment discrimination litigation campaign that was responsible for *Griggs* was an attempt to move the debate about equality by reshaping the contours of the debate.

More than forty years after Congress enacted Title VII and twenty years after Congress statutorily endorsed the *Griggs* disparate impact theory, we continue to disagree about the meaning of "equality" and what constitutes "unlawful discrimination" as a social, moral, legal, and political problem. We also disagree about the extent to which discrimination on the basis of race, sex, national origin, religion, age, and disability continues and whether it is or should be a major factor in the allocation of opportunities in our society. These disagreements, like the disagreements about what *Brown v. Board of Education* did or did not do to implement our commitment to equality, are not likely to end soon. However, there appears to be a general consensus that we have now arrived at a point in our ongoing effort to remedy discrimination in employment when we can acknowledge that some progress has been made in implementing the national commitment to equality in the workplace.

Even though there is a continuing debate about how much progress we have made and what groups or classes benefit the most or the least from that theory,[50] without the *Griggs* disparate impact theory, I doubt seriously whether we could have made as much progress as we have, and not the same degree of progress made under the disparate treatment theory of discrimination alone, because the observations that the courts made in the early Title VII cases are probably as true today: "[d]efendants of even minimal sophistication will neither admit discriminatory animus nor leave a paper trail demonstrating it,"[51] and "[u]nless the employer is a latter-day George Washington, employment discrimination is as difficult to prove as who chopped down the cherry tree."[52]

There is certainly no consensus on how we should determine the efficacy of the *Griggs* disparate impact theory beyond comparing what the world of work looks like today compared to what it looked like prior to the enactment of Title VII. *Griggs* provided the first opportunity for many blacks to tell their stories of discrimination and have those stories validated by the courts. In many instances, the LDF (and others) were able to secure relief for many long-term African American employees who had suffered racial discrimination during most of their work lives to finish their careers as craft workers. For almost a decade, the present effects of past discrimination theory provided a remedy for meaningful employment opportunities to African American, who for decades before the effective date of Title VII had been locked into segregated and low-paying jobs because of their race.

Most of the empirical studies on the efficacy of Title VII generally and the disparate impact theory in particular have focused on the won-lost records of cases litigated by plaintiffs in employment discrimination cases in the federal courts and use economic analysis as the benchmark of evaluating the efficacy of Title VII.[53] Other critics of the disparate impact theory, and there are quite a few of them, often look only at court cases and make an assessment of the efficacy purely in theoretical terms.[54] However, other studies show, for example, that of the more than 17,000 employment discrimination cases that were terminated in 2005, only 535, or 3.4 percent, actually went to trial and that the overwhelming number of these cases ended in pretrial settlement.[55] And we have witnessed a number of record-breaking class action settlements in employment discrimination cases, including, among the more well known and most highly visible, settlements with Shoney's, Texaco, and Coca-Cola. Without a doubt, the disparate impact theory may be a factor that is either in the forefront or in the background of these settlements. There have also been many large class actions that have been settled that involve not only monetary relief but also programmatic and structural changes, although the efficacy of these large class action settlements is debunked with the claim that they provide little or no substantive changes in the effort to implement equality in the workplace and there are alternative or other factors that account for the win-loss records of plaintiffs in employment discrimination, including some judicial skepticism, if not outright hostility, to employment discrimination cases.[56] Moreover, there is the continuing skepticism, first expressed by Gould a half dozen years after *Griggs,* that the case is "troubling because it rests on the assumption that the employer is ultimately permitted to return to the original practice if the underlying inequality can be eliminated."[57]

Now that Congress has codified the disparate impact theory, the question that has been raised is whether the theory is likely to have the same effect in the future as it has had in the past. The perspective of the members of the LDF litigation team and others is that the judiciary was more sympathetic to Title VII claims of employment discrimination, particularly in the early years of the campaign. A number of reasons have been identified for what seems to be present underutilization of the theory.[58] The first is that the disparate impact theory may not be as attractive as the disparate treatment theory because compensatory and punitive damages are not recoverable under the disparate impact theory.[59] The second is that the impact theory is "inherently a class-based theory and class actions are difficult, if not impossible, for private parties to undertake unless they involve the possibility of very large damage awards." The third is that the world has changed since Title VII was put on the books—employers now know the rules, and "the Griggs revolution has been spectacular and employment practices across America have been influenced by the holding."[60] Indeed, employers have widely adopted diversity programs. The fourth is that the disparate impact theory was under attack, as illustrated in the split in the circuits on whether the theory applies to claims arising under the Age Discrimination in Employment Act, although the Supreme Court resolved that issue in 2005 by deciding in *Smith v. City of Jackson* that the ADEA allowed recovery in disparate impact cases. The theory is not dead, but what happens to it in the future remains to be seen.

Notes

CHAPTER ONE. INTRODUCTION

1. David B. Filvaroff and Raymond E. Wolfinger, "The Origins and Enactment of the Civil Rights Act of 1964," in *Legacies of the 1964 Civil Rights Act*, ed. Bernard Grofman (Charlottesville: University Press of Virginia, 2000), 9.

2. The most consequential of the eleven titles are Titles II, VI, and VII. Title II prohibits discrimination in places of public accommodations if their operations affect interstate commerce. *See* Richard C. Cortner, *Civil Rights and Public Accommodations: The* Heart of Atlanta Motel *and* McClung *Cases* (Lawrence: University Press of Kansas, 2001). In Title VI, Congress made broad use of its spending powers to prohibit racial discrimination in any program or activity receiving federal financial assistance.

3. *Riordan v. Kempiners*, 831 F.2d 690, 697 (7th Cir. 1987).

4. *Smith v. Chrysler Corp.*, 155 F.3d 799, 806–807 (6th Cir. 1998).

5. Robert Belton, "A Comparative Review of Public and Private Enforcement of Title VII of the Civil Rights Act of 1964," 31 *Vand. L. Rev.* 905, 908–914 (1975).

6. Abram Chayes, "The Role of the Judge in Public Law Litigation," 89 *Harv. L. Rev.* 1281 (1976).

7. Jack Greenberg, "Civil Rights Class Actions: Procedural Means of Obtaining Substance," 39 *Ariz. L. Rev.* 575 (1997).

8. Damon Keith, "*NAACP: Palladin of the People*," address before the Seventy-Fifth Annual NAACP Convention, *reprinted in* Gilbert Ware, *From the Black Bar: Voices for Equal Justice* (New York: Putnam, 1976), 32.

9. Praised: Alfred W. Blumrosen, "The Legacy of *Griggs*: Social Progress and Subjective Judgment," 63 *Chicago Kent L. Rev.* 1, 1–2 (1987) (*Griggs* is a "major instrument of social progress"); damned: Donald L. Horowitz, *The Courts and Social Policy* (Washington, D.C.: Brookings Institution, 1977), 15 (criticizing the Court's "halting and embarrassed" handling of the legislative history of Title VII); Richard Epstein, *Forbidden Grounds: The Case against Employment Discrimination Laws* (Cambridge, Mass.: Harvard University Press, 1992); Kingsley R. Browne, "*Griggs'* Folly: An Essay on the Theory, Problems, and the Origins of Adverse Impact Definition of Employment Discrimination and a Recommendation for Reform," 7 *Indus. Rel. L.J.* 429 (1985).

10. Conversation with the Chief Justice, ABC News, July 5, 1971 (TV interview of Chief Justice Warren Burger by Bill Lawrence, ABC national affairs editor; conducted on July 1, 1971, the day after the end of the October 1970 Term during which the Court decided *Griggs*). The pertinent excerpt from that interview, as provided in an ABC News transcript, is as follows:

Bill Lawrence: Could you mention a case or two that to you stand as kind of landmarks of the so-called Burger Court?

Chief Justice Burger: Well I would have to reject your characterization. The Court doesn't really warrant anybody's name being attached to it, Mr. Lawrence. I think there is one case that has been commented on a great deal by others as having been, I think one writer said, a "sleeper" (using that in quotation marks). It was Griggs against the Duke Power Company having to do with equal employment opportunities, and the limits on the kind of testing that could be used. I wouldn't want to say that was one of the terribly important cases but experts in that field of law considered it so, but it is not the kind of a case that received any public attention.

Chief Justice Burger did not mention another landmark civil rights case decided during the same Term. *Swann v. Charlotte-Mecklenburg Bd. of Ed.,* 402 U.S. 1 (1971), decided on April 20, 1971, about six weeks after *Griggs,* was the more controversial of the two cases because the Court approved of busing and racial quotas as remedies in school desegregation cases.

11. Blumrosen, *The Legacy of Griggs,* 1–2.

12. Alfred W. Blumrosen, "*Griggs* Was Correctly Decided—A Response to Gold," 8 *Indus. Rel. L.J.* 443, 450–451 (1986).

13. Alfred W. Blumrosen, "Strangers in Paradise: *Griggs v. Duke Power Co.,* and the Concept of Employment Discrimination," 71 *Mich. L. Rev.* 59, 62 (1972).

14. Hugh Davis Graham, *The Civil Rights Era: Origins and Development of National Policy* (New York: Oxford University Press, 1990), 383; William N. Eskridge, Jr., *Dynamic Statutory Interpretation* (Cambridge, Mass.: Harvard University Press, 1974), 74; H.R. Rep. No. 102-40(I), par. 1, at 23 (1991), *reprinted in* 1991 U.S.C.C.A.N. 549.

15. Epstein, *Forbidden Grounds,* 197.

16. Ibid.

17. Herman Belz, *Equality Transformed: A Quarter Century of Affirmative Action* (New Brunswick, N.J.: Transaction, 1991), 53, 54.

18. Daniel B. Rodriguez and Barry R. Weingast, "The Positivist Political Theory of Legislative History: New Perspectives on the 1964 Civil Rights Act and Its Interpretation," 151 *U. Pa. L. Rev.* 1417, 1498–1501 (2003); Kingsley R. Browne, "The Civil Rights Act of 1991: A Quota Bill, Codification of *Griggs,* a Partial Return to *Wards Cove,* or All of the Above," 43 *Case W. Res. L. Rev.* 287, 294 (1993).

19. Paul D. Moreno, *From Direct Action to Affirmative Action* (Baton Rouge, La.: LSU Press, 1997), 279–282; Epstein, *Forbidden Grounds,* 197.

20. Pub. L. No. 102-166, 105 Stat. 1071 (1991) (codified, as amended, in scattered sections of 2, 16, 29 & 42 U.S.C.). The disparate impact theory is codified in Title VII, 42 U.S.C. § 2000e-2(k).

21. One of the most definitive narratives of the *Brown* story is Richard Kluger, *Simple Justice: The History of* Brown v. Board of Education *and Black America's Struggle for Equality* (New York: Knopf, 1976). Other treatments of *Brown* include James T.

Patterson, Brown v. Board of Education: *A Civil Rights Milestone and Its Troubled Legacy* (New York: Oxford University Press, 2001); Paul E. Wilson, *A Time to Lose: Representing Kansas in* Brown v. Board of Education (Lawrence: University Press of Kansas, 1995); and Mark Tushnet, *The NAACP's Legal Strategy against Segregated Education, 1925–1950* (Chapel Hill: University of North Carolina Press, 1987).

22. Robert S. Smith, *Race, Labor, and Civil Rights:* Griggs versus Duke Power *and the Struggle for Equal Opportunity Making* (Baton Rouge, La.: LSU Press, 2008), relates *Griggs* to the civil rights movement but does not explore the legal edifice built on *Griggs* that makes its theory revolutionary and controversial.

23. *E.g.,* Graham, *The Civil Rights Era,* 244–254, 382–392; *A History of the Equal Employment Opportunity 1965–1984* (John Ross, Regional Attorney, EEOC Dallas District Office) (unpublished manuscript housed in the library of the EEOC, Washington, D.C.).

24. *See, e.g.,* Michael Selmi, "Was the Disparate Impact Theory a Mistake?," 53 *UCLA L. Rev.* 701 (2005).

25. Robert Belton, "Title VII at Forty: A Brief Look at the Birth, Death, and Resurrection of the Disparate Impact Theory of Discrimination," 22 *Hofstra L. & Empl. J.* 431 (2005); Belton, "A Comparative Review of Public and Private Enforcement," 905.

26. *See* Richard Primus, "Equal Protection and Disparate Impact: Round Three," 117 *Harv. L. Rev.* 439, 505 (2003); Samuel Estreicher, "The Story of *Griggs v. Duke Power Co.,*" in *Employment Discrimination Stories,* ed. Joel William Friedman and Stephen F. Befort (New York: Foundation Press, 2003), 153, 163 (speculating that the most important factor that explains why the Court ruled as it did in *Griggs* was the "position of the Nixon Administration, as evidenced by the Solicitor General Griswold's amicus brief in support of the plaintiffs"); Lino A. Graglia, "Lessons from the Ludicrous: How Employment Discrimination Laws Are Destroying the American Workplace," 2 *Tex. Rev. L. & Pol.* 129, 132 (1997) (book review).

27. Charles A. Sullivan, "The World Turned Upside Down? Disparate Impact Claims by White Males," 98 *Nw. U. L. Rev.* 1505, 1506 n. 6 (2004).

28. Jack Greenberg, *Crusaders in the Courts: How a Dedicated Band of Lawyers Fought for the Civil Rights Revolution* (New York: Basic Books, 1994), 412.

29. Stephen L. Wasby, *Race Relations Litigation in an Age of Complexity* (Charlottesville: University Press of Virginia, 1995), 141–169; Jack Greenberg, "Litigation for Social Change: Methods, Limits and Role in Democracy," 29 *Rec. Ass'n B. City of N.Y.,* 320, 320–322 (1974).

30. Greenberg, *Litigation for Social Change,* 29.

31. Greenberg, *Crusaders in the Courts,* 297.

32. *Griggs,* 401 U.S. at 429–430.

33. *See* Dennis Roberts, "Southern Justice," 54 *Cal. L. Rev.* 303, 304 (1966).

34. I argued a number of the early employment discrimination cases in the Fourth Circuit. One of the grand traditions that still exists in the court is that, after each argument, the panel of judges hearing the argument would descend from the bench and circle by counsel's table to shake the hands of counsel.

35. *Armstrong v. Board of Education of City of Birmingham,* 323 F.2d 333, 353 (1963) (Cameron, J., dissenting), *cert. denied, sub nom. Gibson v. Harris,* 376 U.S. 908 (1964); Jack Bass, *Unlikely Heroes: The Dramatic Story of the Southern Judges Who Translated the Supreme Court's* Brown *Decision into a Revolution for Equality* (New York: Simon & Schuster, 1981), 23–55, 231–247; Jack Bass, "The 'Fifth Circuit Four,'" *Nation,* May 3, 2004, 30–32; Jack Greenberg, "Foreword: A Civil Right Symposium Honoring Judge John Minor Wisdom," 64 *Tul. L. Rev.* 1351 (1990) (piece on influence of Wisdom on civil rights cases).

36. Alfred W. Blumrosen, "The Law Transmission System and the Southern Jurisprudence of Employment Discrimination," 6 *Industrial Rel. L.J.* 313, 324 (1984). *See also* Shirley Fingerhood, "The Fifth Circuit Court of Appeals," in *Southern Justice,* ed. Leon Friedman (New York: Random House, 1965), 214.

37. *Miller v. International Paper Co.,* 408 F.2d 283, 294 (5th Cir. 1969).

38. 515 F.2d 86 (4th Cir. 1975); 420 F.2d 1225 (4th Cir. 1970), *reversed in part,* 401 U.S. 424 (1971); 7 Empl. Prac. Dec. 9304 (M.D.N.C. 1974); 3 Empl. Prac. Dec. ¶ 8093 (M.D.N.C. 1970).

39. Greenberg, *Crusaders in the Court,* 413, 418–420.

CHAPTER TWO. THE EMERGENCE OF TITLE VII AS A
"POOR ENFEEBLED THING"

1. *Albemarle Paper Co. v. Moody,* 422 U.S. 405, 418 (1975) (citing *United States v. N.L. Indus., Inc.,* 479 F.2d 354, 379 (8th Cir. 1973)).

2. Under the direction of Professor Herbert R. Northrup, the Wharton School of Finance and Commerce, University of Pennsylvania, published a series of Ford Foundation–sponsored reports between 1967 and 1975 called "The Racial Policies of American Industry." Some of these industries were targets of opportunities in the LDF's litigation campaign. These industries include steel (Richard Rowan, *The Negro in the Steel Industry* (1968)); trucking (Richard D. Leone, *The Negro in the Trucking Industry* (1970)); railroad (Howard R. Risher, Jr., and Marjorie C. Denison, *The Negro in the Railroad Industry* (1971)); pulp and paper (Herbert R. Northrup, *The Negro in the Paper Industry* (1969)); and public utilities (Bernard E. Anderson, *Negro Employment in Public Utilities: A Study of Racial Policies in the Electric Power, Gas, and Telephone Industries* (1970)). Some of the other reports in this series are published in Herbert R. Northrup, *Negro Employment in Basic Industry: A Study of Racial Policies in Six Industries* (Philadelphia: University of Pennsylvania Press, 1970).

3. Professor Michael I. Sovern, who conducted the first comprehensive study of Title VII, coined the phrase "poor enfeebled thing" to describe the EEOC. Sovern, *Legal Restraints in Racial Discrimination in Employment* (New York: Twentieth Century Fund, 1966), 205. However, that description is equally applicable to Title VII itself.

4. 42 U.S.C. § 2000e-5(b).

5. *See* Paul Burstein, *Discrimination, Jobs, and Politics: The Struggle for Equal*

Employment Opportunity in the United States since the New Deal (Chicago: University of Chicago Press, 1985); Sovern, *Legal Restraints in Racial Discrimination;* United States Commission on Civil Rights, *Employment,* Report No. 3 (Washington, D.C., 1961); H.R. Rep. No. 1370, 87th Cong., 2d Sess. 2155–2163 (1962), *reprinted in* EEOC, *Titles VII and XI of Civil Rights Act of 1964* 2157–2163 (1968) (edited compilation of legislative documents).

6. The federal effort to remedy racial discrimination is broadly treated in John Hope Franklin and Alfred A. Moss, Jr., *From Slavery to Freedom: A History of African Americans* (7th ed.) (New York: Knopf, 1994) and Eric Foner, *Reconstruction: America's Unfinished Revolution* (New York: Harper & Row, 1988).

7. The current version of the 1866 Civil Rights Act that provides a remedy for racial discrimination in employment by private employers is 42 U.S.C. § 1981. Milton R. Konvitz and Theodore Leskes, *A Century of Civil Rights* (New York: Columbia University Press, 1961), 48.

8. Eugene Gressman, "The Unhappy History of Civil Rights Legislation," 50 *Mich. L. Rev.* 1312 (1952).

9. EEOC, *Legislative History of Titles VII and XI of the Civil Rights Act of 1964,* 1–2 (1968).

10. Timothy L. Jenkins, "A Study of Federal Effort to End Job Bias: A History, a Status Report, and a Prognosis," 14 *How. L.J.* 259, 264 (1968).

11. Reynolds Farley, "The Common Destiny of Blacks and Whites: Observations about the Social and Economic Status of the Races," in *Race in America: The Struggle for Equality,* ed. Herbert Hill and James E. Jones, Jr. (Madison: University of Wisconsin Press, 1993), 226.

12. Herbert Garfinkel, *When Negroes March: The March on Washington Movement in the Organizational Politics for FEPC* (Glencoe, Ill.: Free Press, 1959); Konvitz and Leskes, *Century of Civil Rights,* 194–197.

13. Sovern, *Legal Restraints in Racial Discrimination,* 9.

14. U.S. Commission on Civil Rights Report, *Report No. 3, Employment* 10–11 (1961).

15. Louis C. Kesselman, *The Social Politics of FEPC: A Study in Reform Pressure Movements* (Chapel Hill: University of North Carolina Press, 1948), 16.

16. Independent Offices Appropriation Act, 1945, Pub. L. No. 358, § 213, 58 Stat. 361 (1944) (current version at 31 U.S.C. § 696 (1970)).

17. FEPC, letter of transmittal and resignation to President Truman, June 28, 1946, in *Fair Employment Practices Committee, Final Report* (Washington, D.C.: U.S. Government Printing Office, 1947), vi.

18. "Summary and Conclusions," June 28, 1946, in *Fair Employment Practices Committee, Final Report* (Washington, D.C.: U.S. Government Printing Office, 1947), viii.

19. *Eyes on the Prize,* telecast on PBS in 1987, is a graphic fourteen-hour documentary of the major events of the civil rights movement from 1954 to 1965 and the violence that civil rights activists often suffered during that period.

20. James E. Jones, Jr., "The Rise and Fall of Affirmative Action, in Race in America: The Struggle for Equality," ed. Herbert Hill and James E. Jones, Jr. (Madison: University

of Wisconsin Press, 1993), 351; David L. Rose, "Twenty-Five Years Later: Where Do We Stand on Equal Employment Opportunity Enforcement Law?," 42 *Vand. L. Rev.* 1121, 1124–1126 (1989).

21. Herbert Hill, *Black Labor and the American Legal System: Race, Work, and the Law* (Madison: University of Wisconsin Press, 1977), 373–384; Sovern, *Legal Restraints in Racial Discrimination,* 9–17; Jenkins, "A Study of Federal Effort to End Job Bias," 269–274.

22. 3 C.F.R. 448 (1959–1963 Compilation). This order revived the federal effort to remedy employment discrimination. U.S. Commission on Civil Rights, *Employment* 6–17 (1961).

23. Sovern, *Legal Restraints in Racial Discrimination,* 106–108.

24. 3 C.F.R. 339 (1964–1965 Compilation). This 1965 Executive Order did not include a prohibition against sex discrimination in employment. This omission was corrected by Executive Order 11478, 3 C.F.R. 133 (1969 Compilation).

25. *See* Sovern, *Legal Restraints in Racial Discrimination,* 103–142.

26. U.S. Commission on Civil Rights, *Federal Civil Rights Enforcement Effort—A Reassessment* 74 (1973); Hill, *Black Labor,* 373–381.

27. Jenkins, "A Study of Federal Effort to End Job Bias," 269; Louis Ruchames, *Race, Jobs & Politics: The Story of FEPC* (New York: Negro Universities Press, 1953), 165–180.

28. Joseph P. Witherspoon, "Civil Rights Policy in the Federal System: Proposals for a Better Use of Administrative Process," 74 *Yale L.J.* 1171, 1173 (1965) (includes an appendix of state and local human relations commissions, their areas of competency, citations to their enabling legislation, and statistics concerning their activities).

29. Konvitz and Leskes, *Century of Civil Rights,* 203.

30. Herbert Hill, "Twenty Years of State Fair Employment Practice Committees: A Critical Analysis with Recommendations," 14 *Buff. L. Rev.* 22 (1964).

31. Arthur E. Bonfield, "The Substance of American Fair Employment Practices Legislation I: Employers," 61 *Nw. U. L. Rev.* 907, 956 (1967).

32. Jenkins, "A Study of Federal Effort to End Job Bias," 270. *See also* Kesselman, *The Social Politics of FEPC,* 228.

33. *See* Alfred W. Blumrosen, *Black Employment and the Law* (New Brunswick, N.J.: Rutgers University Press, 1971), 14–20.

34. *Hearings on S. 773, S. 1210, and S. 1937 before the Subcomm. on Employment and Manpower of the Senate Comm. on Labor and Public Welfare,* 88th Cong. 1st Sess. 228–229, 240 (1963).

35. 110 Cong. Rec. 7207 (1964).

36. Hill, "Twenty Years of State Fair Employment Practice Committees," 38.

37. *See* Sovern, *Legal Restraints in Racial Discrimination;* Hill, "Twenty Years of State Fair Employment Practices Commissions," 22. Data on enforcement under state fair employment practices commissions are reported in Hugh Davis Graham, *The Civil Rights Era: Origins and Development of National Policy* (New York: Oxford University Press, 1990), 131.

38. U.S. Commission on Civil Rights, *Report No. 3, Employment* 127–139 (1961). The

problem of racial discrimination by unions is broadly covered in William B. Gould, *Black Workers in White Unions: Job Discrimination in the United States* (Ithaca, N.Y.: Cornell University Press, 1977), and Hill, *Black Labor*.

39. 323 U.S. 192, 204 (1944). *See* Sovern, *Legal Restraints in Racial Discrimination*, 143–175.

40. *Wallace Corp. v. NLRB*, 323 U.S. 248 (1944).

41. *See, e.g., Whitfield v. Local 2708, United Steelworkers*, 263 F.2d 546 (5th Cir.), *cert. denied*, 360 U.S. 902 (1959).

42. *See* Hill, *Black Labor*, 93–169; Jonathan G. Axelrod and Howard J. Kaufman, "Mansion House Bekins Handy Andy: The National Labor Relations Board's Role in Racial Discrimination Cases," 45 *Geo. Wash. L. Rev.* 675 (1977).

43. Hill, *Black Labor*, 93.

44. Pub. L. No. 88-352, 78 Stat. 241 (codified in scattered sections of 42 U.S.C.). Some deem the modern era of employment discrimination law to have begun a year earlier, in 1963, when Congress enacted the Equal Pay Act, 29 U.S.C. § 206(d).

45. *See, e.g.,* Charles Whalen and Barbara Whalen, *The Longest Debate: A Legislative History of the Civil Rights Act of 1964* (Cabin John, Md.: Seven Locks Press, 1985); Robert D. Lowry, ed., *The Civil Rights Act of 1964: The Passage of the Law That Ended Racial Segregation* (Albany: SUNY Press, 1971).

46. "History of the Equal Employment Opportunity Commission During the Administration of President Lyndon B. Johnson: November 1963-January 1969" (unpublished document housed at the Lyndon Baines Johnson Presidential Library, Austin, Texas), 5; EEOC, *Legislative History of Titles VII and XI of Civil Rights Act of 1964*, 7–11 (1968); Francis J. Vaas, "Title VII," 7 *B.C. Indus. & Com. L. Rev.* 431, 431 (1966); Ruchames, *Race, Jobs, & Politics*, 122.

47. David Freeman Engstrom, "The Taft Proposal of 1946 and the (Non-) Making of American Fair Employment Law," 9 *Green Bag 2d* 181 (2006).

48. Norbert A. Schlei, "Foreword," Barbara Lindemann and Paul Grossman, *Employment Discrimination Law* (2d ed.) (Arlington, Va.: BNA Books, 1983), vii–viii; Mary L. Dudziak, *Cold War Civil Rights: Race and the Image of American Democracy* (Princeton, N.J.: Princeton University Press, 2000), ch. 5.

49. Schlei, "Forward," viii–xiii.

50. Nicholas deB. Katzenbach, Comment, "Twenty-Five Years of the Civil Rights Act: History and Promise," 25 *Wake Forest L. Rev.* 159, 164 (1990).

51. Schlei, "Forward," viii.

52. Stevens B. Oates, *Let the Trumpet Sound: The Life of Martin Luther King, Jr.* (New York: Harper Perennial, 1985), 239.

53. Vaas, "Title VII," 432; Katzenbach, "Twenty-Five Years of the Civil Rights Act," 164–165.

54. Richard Berg, "Equal Employment Opportunity under the Civil Rights Act of 1964," 31 *Brook. L. Rev.* 62, 64 (1964).

55. Michael Gottesman, Remarks at the EEOC 40th Anniversary Panel: Celebrating the 40th Anniversary of Title VII (June 22, 2004), "First Principles—Enacting the Civil

Rights Act and Using the Courts to Challenge and Remedy Workplace Discrimination," http://www.eeoc.gov/abouteeoc/40th/panel/40thpanels/transcript.html.

56. Katzenbach, "Twenty-Five Years of the Civil Rights Act," 163.

57. Whalen and Whalen, *The Longest Debate*, 27; Graham, *The Civil Rights Era*, 98.

58. Berg, "Equal Employment under the Civil Rights Act," 63.

59. Vaas, "Title VII," 431.

60. Berg, "Equal Employment under the Civil Rights Act," 63–64.

61. The narrative of the legislative history of the Civil Rights Act of 1964 is told in Whalen and Whalen, *The Longest Debate*.

62. Vaas, "Title VII," 450; Whalen and Whalen, *The Longest Debate*, 159–160.

63. Alfred W. Blumrosen, *Modern Law: The Law Transmission System and Equal Employment Opportunity* (Madison: University of Wisconsin Press, 1993), 47–52; Graham, *The Civil Rights Era*, 146.

64. Berg, "Equal Employment under the Civil Rights Act," 67.

65. *International Bhd. of Teamsters v. United States*, 431 U.S. 324, 336 n. 16 (1977) (citing 110 Cong. Rec. 14,270 (1964) (remarks of Senator Humphrey)).

66. 42 U.S.C. § 2000e-5(f)(1).

67. Berg, "Equal Employment under the Civil Rights Act," 63.

68. Sovern, *Legal Restraints in Racial Discrimination*, 205.

69. Blumrosen, *Black Employment*, 59.

70. The "gatekeeper" description is used in M. Isabel Medina, "A Matter of Fact: Hostile Environments and Summary Judgments," 8 *S. Cal. Rev. L. & Women's Studies* 311, 321 (1999).

71. Herbert Hill, *The Equal Employment Opportunity Acts of 1964 and 1972: A Critical Analysis of the Legislative History and Administration of the Law* (Berkeley: School of Law, University of California, 1971), 28.

72. John Ross, "A History of the Equal Opportunity Employment Commission 1965–1984" (1987) (unpublished manuscript, EEOC library, Washington, D.C.) (copy on file in library of the EEOC). Ross was the Regional Attorney in the Dallas office of the EEOC.

73. United States Commission on Civil Rights, *A Report on Federal Civil Rights Enforcement Effort*, 87–88 (1971). In a later report to the Congress, the Comptroller General concluded that the EEOC, although having some success in its enforcement efforts, a decade after the effective date of Title VII, did not appear to have made enough advances against employment discrimination to have made a real difference. Comptroller General of the United States, *Report to the Congress: The Equal Employment Opportunity Commission Has Made Limited Progress in Eliminating Employment Discrimination*, H.R. Doc. No. 147, 94th Cong., 2d Sess. (1976).

74. U.S. Commission on Civil Rights, *The Federal Civil Rights Enforcement Effort: To Eliminate Employment Discrimination* 88 (1971).

75. Blumrosen, *Black Employment*, 43–44.

76. *See, e.g., Quarles v. Philip Morris, Inc.*, 1 Empl. Prac. Dec. ¶ 9782 (E.D. Va. 1967). Charges in *Quarles* were filed in September 1965. The EEOC sent the complainant a

right to sue letter in November 1965 stating: "Since your case was presented to the Commission in the early months of the administration of Title VII of the Civil Rights Act of 1964, the Commission was unable to undertake extensive conciliation activities. Additional conciliation efforts will be continued by the Commission."

77. Comptroller General of the United States, *Report to the Congress: The Equal Employment Opportunity Commission Has Made Limited Progress in Eliminating Employment Discrimination,* H.R. Doc. No. 147, 94th Cong., 2d Sess. 8 (1976).

78. *See* Note, "The Tentative Settlement Cases and Civil Action under Title VII of the Civil Rights Act of 1964," 72 *Mich. L. Rev.* 162, 163 n. 11, 146 n. 17 (1974).

79. 181 BNA-Daily Labor Report, D1, 5 (September 17, 1974).

80. Hill, *Black Labor,* 140–142.

81. Blumrosen, *Black Employment,* ch. 2; Ross, *A History of the Equal Opportunity Employment Commission;* Nicholas Pedriana and Robin Stryker, "The Strength of a Weak Agency: Enforcement of Title VII of the 1964 Civil Rights Act and the Expansion of State Capacity, 1965–1971," 110 *Am. J. Sociology* 709 (November 2004).

82. Ross, *A History of the Equal Opportunity Employment Commission,* at 23–29. For example, the EEOC issued its first guidelines on testing in 1966, and the Supreme Court deemed these guidelines as "[e]xpressing the will of Congress." *Griggs,* 401 U.S. at 433–444. Title VII expressly provides the EEOC authority to issue procedural regulations but is silent on whether it has authority to issue substantive regulations. *See* 42 U.S.C. §2000e-12(a).

83. *See* Blumrosen, *Black Employment,* 44–47.

84. Compare *Griggs v. Duke Power Co.,* 401 U.S. 424, 433–434 (1971) (deference given to EEOC testing guidelines) with *General Elec. Co. v. Gilbert,* 429 U.S. 125 (1976) (EEOC interpretation of pregnancy disability guidelines rejected).

85. *See* EEOC, *Making a Right a Reality: An Oral History of the Early Years, 1965–1972* (EEOC pamphlet, 1990).

86. Samuel C. Jackson, "Using the Law to Attack Discrimination in Employment," 8 *Washburn L.J.* 189, 194 (1968–1969).

87. Comments of David Cashdan, "Celebrating the 40th Anniversary of Title VII: Enacting the Civil Rights Act and Using the Court to Challenge and Remedy Workplace Discrimination," http://www.eeoc.gov/abouteeoc/40th/panel/40thpanels/transcript .html (accessed June 2004). Some of the other EEOC attorneys who joined as amici in other LDF cases were Philip B. Skover, who also participated in *Griggs,* David Zugschwerdt, and Russell Specter.

88. Herbert Hill, "Black Workers, Organized Labor, and Title VII of the 1964 Civil Rights Act: Legislative History and Litigation Record," in *Race in America: The Struggle for Equality,* ed. Herbert Hill and James E. Jones, Jr. (Madison: University of Wisconsin Press, 1993), 263, 306.

89. Berg, "Equal Employment Opportunity under the Civil Rights Act," 81–88.

90. Cashdan, Remarks.

91. Brian K. Landsberg, *Enforcing Civil Rights: Race Discrimination and the Department of Justice* (Lawrence: University Press of Kansas, 1997), 108; Rose, "Twenty-Five

Years Later," 1137. (David L. Rose joined the Civil Rights Division of the Department of Justice in 1967, and from 1969 to 1987 was the chief to the section of the Civil Rights Division for enforcing Title VII and other federal laws providing for equal employment opportunities.)

92. U.S. Commission on Civil Rights, *Federal Civil Rights Enforcement Effort: To Eliminate Employment Discrimination,* 118 (1971).

93. [1965] Att'y Gen. Ann. Rep. 180–182.

94. [1967] Att'y Gen. Ann. Rep. 168, 180–182, 221. The one Title VII case was [1965] Att'y Gen. Ann. Rep. 211. The case was *United States v. Building & Constr. Trades Council,* 271 F. Supp. 447 (E.D. Mo. 1966).

95. U.S. Commission on Civil Rights, *Federal Civil Rights Enforcement Effort,* 118, 136 (1971).

96. Ibid. at 321–324.

97. Ibid. at 118.

98. Landsberg, *Enforcing Civil Rights,* 108; Rose, "Twenty-Five Years Later," 1137.

99. Compiled from the *Attorney General Annual Report* for the years 1966, 1968, 1969, 1970, and 1971.

100. U.S. Commission on Civil Rights, *Federal Civil Rights Enforcement Effort,* 136.

101. *Hearings on S. 2515, S. 2617 & H.R. 1746 Before the Subcomm. on Labor of the Senate Comm. on Labor and Public Welfare,* 92d Cong., 1st Sess. 243 (1971) (statement of Jack Greenberg, Director-Counsel, NAACP Legal Defense & Education Fund, Inc.) (a list of the Legal Defense Fund employment discrimination cases is attached to Greenberg's statement).

102. One commentator criticized the disappointment of the civil rights advocates on the grounds that civil rights advocates "do not have a monopoly on wisdom," and for that reason "[i]t is possible for them to be wrong about where their best interest lie." Blumrosen, *Modern Law,* 48.

103. Hill, "Black Workers, Organized Labor, and Title VII," 306.

104. *See* George Cooper, "Introduction, Equal Employment Law Today," 5 *Colum. Hum. Rts. L. Rev.* 263, 266 (1973).

105. Berg, "Equal Employment Opportunity under the Civil Rights Act," 96.

106. Ibid. at 67.

CHAPTER THREE. LDF'S ENFORCEMENT STRATEGY

1. U.S. Commission on Civil Rights, *Employment,* Report No. 3, 10–11 (Washington, D.C., 1961). *See also* Phillip E. Hassman, "Right to Maintain Private Employment Discrimination Action under Executive Order 11246, as Amended, Prohibiting Employment Discrimination by Government Contractors and Subcontractors," 31 A.L.R. FED. 108 (1977) (discussing the right of private action for employment discrimination through the OFCC pursuant to Executive Order 11246).

2. Michael I. Sovern, *Legal Restraints in Racial Discrimination in Employment* (New York: Twentieth Century Fund, 1966), 24.

3. In *Draper v. Clark Dairy, Inc.,* 17 Conn. Supp. 93, 96–97 (Super. Ct. 1950), the court established the rule that findings of fact of the commission are binding on the court unless the record shows that the commission acted arbitrarily or capriciously. This case reviewed most of the present rules applicable to judicial review of FEP commission actions. *See also Jeanpierre v. Arbury,* 4 N.Y.2d 238, 149 N.E.2d 882, 173 N.Y.S.2d 597 (1958); *Holland v. Edwards,* 307 N.Y. 38, 119 N.E.2d 581 (1954).

4. Jack Greenberg, *Race Relations and American Law* (New York: Columbia University Press, 1959), 154–207.

5. *Equal Employment Opportunities Enforcement Procedures: Hearings on H.R. 6228 and H.R. 13517 before the Gen. Subcomm. on Labor of the House Comm. on Education and Labor,* 91st Cong., 1st & 2d Sess. 34 (1969–1970).

6. In 1964, it was estimated that a suit involving a trial in a district court, an appeal to a circuit court, and a petition for certiorari to the Supreme Court cost between $15,000 and $18,000. Litigation in *Brown v. Board of Education,* 349 U.S. 294 (1954), cost over $200,000. 110 Cong. Rec. 6541 (1964) (remarks of Senator Humphrey in the debate over Title VII).

7. *NAACP v. Button,* 371 U.S. 415, 443 (1963).

8. *Pettway v. American Cast Iron Pipe* Co., 411 F.2d 998, 1005 (5th Cir. 1969); *Jenkins v. United Gas Corp.,* 400 F.2d 28, 33 (5th Cir. 1968).

9. NAACP Legal Defense and Educational Fund, Annual Report 1976/77, at 3.

10. Jack Greenberg, *Crusaders in the Courts: How a Dedicated Band of Lawyers Fought for the Civil Rights Revolution* (New York: Basic Books, 1994), 413.

11. Robert L. Rabin, "Lawyers for Social Change: Perspectives on Public Interest Law," 28 *Stan. L. Rev.* 207, 217 (1976).

12. Constance Baker Motley stated that when she joined the Legal Defense Fund in 1945, the then Director-Counsel, Thurgood Marshall, had two assistants and that when she left in 1965, the year Title VII became effective, there were twenty-five full-time attorneys and nearly 100 LDF cooperating attorneys around the country. Constance Baker Motley, "Standing on His Shoulders: Thurgood Marshall's Early Years," 35 *How. L.J.* 23, 36 (1991).

13. *See* Meltsner, *Cruel and Unusual: The Supreme Court and Capital Punishment* (New York: Random House, 1973), 6; NAACP Legal Defense Fund, Annual Report 1976/77; NAACP Legal Defense Fund, *30 Years of Building American Justice* (1970). *See* Rabin, "Lawyers for Social Change," 216.

14. Greenberg, *Crusaders in the Courts,* 366.

15. Rabin, "Lawyers for Social Change," 217.

16. *See* George Cooper, "Introduction: Equal Employment Law Today," 5 *Colum. Human Rights L. Rev.* 263, 266, n. 26 (1973).

17. *Equal Employment Opportunities Enforcement Act of 1971: Hearings on S. 2515, S. 2617, and H.R. 1746 before the Subcomm. on Labor of the Senate Comm. on Labor*

and Public Welfare, 92nd Cong., 1st Sess. 246–247 (1971) (statement of Jack Greenberg, Director-Counsel of the NAACP Legal Defense and Educational Fund, Inc.); NAACP Legal Defense Fund, Annual Report 1976/77, at 2.

18. James Harwood, "Battling Job Bias: Rights Groups May Ask Stiffening of '64 Law's Employment Provision," *Wall St. J.,* May 28, 1965, 1.

19. Greenberg, *Crusaders in the Courts,* 413.

20. Interview with Adam Stein, February 16, 2005; Paul Jones, "N.C.'s Employment Compliance Studied," *Charlotte Observer,* August 3, 1965, A5.

21. Robert Spearman and Hugh Stevens, *A Step toward Equal Justice: Programs to Increase Black Lawyers in the South 1969–1973: An Evaluation Report to Carnegie Corporation of New York* (1974), 17.

22. Interview with Adam Stein, February 16, 2005.

23. *E.g.,* "Workshop Planned to Explain Negro Job Rights," *St. Petersburg Times,* July 7, 1965, Section A; Ray Boone, "My Job Is to Get People to Complain," *Richmond Afro-American,* June 19, 1965; "N.C. Compliance Studied," *Charlotte Observer,* August 3, 1965, A5.

24. *See* "Workshop Planned to Explain Negro Job Rights," Section A.

25. Greenberg, *Crusaders in the Courts,* 4; "Complaints Filed under Rights Act," *New York Times,* July 30, 1965.

26. NAACP Legal Defense Fund, *30 Years of Law Which Changed America* (1970).

27. EEOC First Annual Report, at 5 (1967). *See also* EEOC, *Employment Patterns in the Textile Industry* 10 (1967). Chambers says that by July 4, 1965, there were over 5,000 charges filed with the EEOC. Julius Chambers, "Comments, Symposium on Twenty-Five Years of the Civil Rights Act: History and Promise," 25 *Wake Forest L. Rev.* 159, 170 (1990).

28. Greenberg, *Crusaders in the Courts,* 382–383, 415.

29. Meltsner's experience with the LDF is covered in his books, *The Making of a Civil Rights Lawyer* (Charlottesville: University of Virginia Press, 2006) and *Cruel and Unusual.*

30. *E.g., Adams v. School Dist. No. 5, Orangeburg County,* 271 F. Supp. 579 (D.S.C. 1967); *Brunson v. Board of Trustees of School Dist. No. 1 of Clarendon County,* 271 F. Supp. 586 (D.S.C. 1967).

31. *See* Greenberg, *Crusaders in the Courts,* 413.

32. *Griggs v. Duke Power Co.,* 420 F.2d 1225, 1238 (4th Cir. 1970) (Sobeloff, J. dissenting).

33. These race-designated help-wanted ads were published in the local newspapers the *High Point Enterprise* and the *Greensboro Daily News.*

34. D. Don Welch, *The Vanderbilt Law School: Aspirations and Realities* (Nashville, Tenn.: Vanderbilt University Press, 2008), 182.

35. The background information on Gaby is based on my interview with her and her outstanding legal career covered in Kitty Felde, "Profile of Gabrielle Kirk McDonald," 7 *Human Rights Brief* (1999).

36. The decision on the merits is *Bush v. Lone Star Steel Co.,* 373 F. Supp. 526 (E.D. Tex. 1974).

37. Sen. Comm. on Judiciary, *Hearings on the Selection and Confirmation of Federal Judges,* 96th Cong., 2nd Sess. 73–75, 93 (May 2, 1979).

38. *LeRoy v. City of Houston,* 592 F. Supp. 415 (S.D. Tex. 1984), *mandamus denied, In Re City of Houston,* 745 F.2d 925 (5th Cir. 1984); *Vietnamese Fishermen's Association v. Knights of the Ku Klux Klan,* 518 F. Supp. 1017 (S.D. Tex. 1981).

39. Greenberg, *Crusaders in the Courts,* 413–414.

40. Ibid. at 366.

41. Stephen L. Wasby, *The Supreme Court in the Federal Judicial System* (4th ed.) (Chicago: Nelson-Hall, 1993), 154–155.

42. Meltsner, *Cruel and Unusual,* 78; *see also* Greenberg, *Crusaders in the Courts,* 377–378.

43. NAACP Legal Defense Fund, Annual Report 1976/77, at 9.

44. Greenberg, *Crusaders in the Courts,* 38–41 (discussing many of the older trailblazing civil rights lawyers in the South).

45. "Panels to Press Job Rights Cases," *New York Times,* July 2, 1965, A32.

46. *Teamsters v. United States,* 431 U.S. 324, 335 n. 15 (1977) ("Undoubtedly disparate treatment is the most obvious evil Congress had in mind when it enacted Title VII.") (citing 110 Cong. Rec. 13088 (1964) (remarks of Sen. Humphrey)). The primary reason Congress enacted Title VII was to prohibit racial discrimination in employment. *See, e.g., Griggs v. Duke Power Co.,* 401 U.S. 424 (1971). Even though the elimination of race discrimination in employment was the primary reason Congress enacted Title VII, the statutory prohibition is stated in race-neutral terms. *See, e.g.,* 42 U.S.C. § 2000e-2(a)(1) and 2(a)(2); *McDonald v. Santa Fe Trail Transp. Co.,* 427 U.S. 273 (1976) (whites as well as blacks are protected from racial discrimination under Title VII).

47. 42 U.S.C. § 2000e-2(a) (2).

48. 457 U.S. 440, 447 (1982).

49. William Eskridge, "Symposium: The Department of Justice and the Civil Rights Act of 1964," 26 *Pac. L.J.* 765, 799 (1965).

50. Fair Employment Practice Committee, *First Report,* 55–57 (1945); Louis Ruchames, *Race, Jobs & Politics: The Story of FEPC* (New York: Negro Universities Press, 1953), 32–34.

51. Timothy L. Jenkins, "A Study of Federal Effort to End Job Bias: A History, a Status Report, and a Prognosis," 14 *How. L.J.,* 259, 287–268 (1968).

52. Ruchames, *Race, Jobs & Politics,* 32–33.

53. *A Tale of 22 Cities: Report on Title VII of the Civil Rights Act of 1964* (NAM 1965 Charles A. Kothe ed.), 76–94. Kothe was the vice president of NAM.

54. *See generally* William B. Gould, *Black Workers in White Unions: Job Discrimination in the United States* (Ithaca, N.Y.: Cornell University Press, 1977), 67–98.

55. 390 U.S. 400, 401–402 (1968) (per curiam).

56. Greenberg, *Crusaders in the Courts,* 414.

57. Railroad: *Rock v. Norfolk & W.R.R.,* 473 F.2d 1344 (4th Cir.), *cert. denied,* 412 U.S. 933 (1973); *English v. Seaboard Coastline R.R.,* 10 Empl. Prac. Dec. ¶ 10,476 (S.D. Ga. 1975).

58. Pulp and paper: *Albemarle Paper Co. v. Moody*, 422 U.S. 405 (1975); *Miller v. International Paper Co.*, 408 F.2d 283 (5th Cir. 1969); *Gatlin v. West Virginia Pulp and Paper Co.*, 734 F.2d 980 (4th Cir. 1984); *Jones v. International Paper Co.*, 720 F.2d 496 (8th Cir. 1983); *Myers v. Gilman Paper Corp.*, 544 F.2d 837 (5th Cir. 1977); *Watkins v. Scott Paper Co.*, 530 F.2d 1159 (5th Cir. 1976); *Rogers v. International Paper Co.*, 510 F.2d 1340 (8th Cir. 1975), *vacated and remanded*, 423 U.S. 809 (1975); *Stevenson v. International Paper Co.*, 516 F.2d 103 (5th Cir. 1975); *Long v. Georgia Kraft Co.*, 450 F.2d 557 (5th Cir. 1971); *Powell v. Georgia Pacific Corp.*, 535 F. Supp. 713 (W.D. Ark. 1982); *Miller v. Continental Can Co.*, 544 F. Supp. 210, 211 n. 2 (S.D. Ga. 1981) (noting long history of employment discrimination litigation involving the paper industry). *See* Timothy J. Minchin, *The Color of Work: The Struggle for Civil Rights in the Southern Paper Industry, 1960–1980* (Chapel Hill: University of North Carolina Press, 2001).

59. Steel: *Hardy v. United States Steel Corp.*, 371 F. Supp. 1045 (N.D. Ala. 1973).

60. Tobacco: *Patterson v. American Tobacco Co.*, 535 F.2d 257 (4th Cir.), *cert. denied*, 429 U.S. 920 (1976); *Russell v. American Tobacco Co.*, 528 F.2d 357 (4th Cir. 1975), *cert. denied*, 425 U.S. 935 (1976); *Robinson v. Lorillard Corp.*, 444 F.2d 791 (4th Cir.), *cert. dismissed*, 404 U.S. 1006 (1971); *Quarles v. Philip Morris, Inc.*, 279 F. Supp. 505 (E.D. Va. 1968).

61. Textile: *Lea v. Cone Mills*, 438 F.2d. 86 (4th Cir. 1971). *See* Timothy J. Minchin, *Hiring the Black Worker: The Racial Integration of the Southern Textile Industry, 1960–1980* (Chapel Hill: University of North Carolina Press, 1999).

62. Trucking: *Franks v. Bowman Transportation Corp.*, 424 U.S. 747 (1976); *Hairston v. McLean Trucking Co.*, 520 F.2d 226 (4th Cir. 1975).

63. Public utilities: *Griggs v. Duke Power Co.*, 401 U.S. 424 (1971); *United States v. Georgia Power Co.*, 474 F.2d 906 (5th Cir. 1973).

64. U.S. Commission on Civil Rights, *Civil Rights Enforcement Efforts*, 116 (1971).

65. *See* Jack Greenberg, "Litigation for Social Change: Methods, Limits, and Role in Democracy," 29 *Rec. N.Y.C.B.A.* 320 (1974).

66. Leroy D. Clark, "The Lawyer in the Civil Rights Movement—Catalytic Agent or Counter Revolutionary?" 19 *Kan. L. Rev.* 459, 468 (1971).

67. *See, e.g., James v. Marineship Corp.*, 25 Cal. 2d 721, 156 P.2d 329 (1944) (union with a work monopoly in an area could not enforce contract against blacks, whom it would not admit to membership because of race).

68. *See Brotherhood of R.R. Trainmen v. Howard*, 343 U.S. 768 (1952) (blacks who were in a segregated bargaining unit entitled to seek injunction against enforcement of contract to abolish their jobs); *Local 12, United Rubber Workers v. NLRB*, 368 F.2d 12 (5th Cir. 1966) *cert. denied*, 389 U.S. 837 (1967).

69. *See Alston v. School Bd.*, 112 F.2d 992 (4th Cir.), *cert. denied*, 311 U.S. 693 (1940) (school board required to pay black teachers on the same basis as white teachers).

70. *See* Stanley Mazaroff, "Surviving the Avalanche: Defendant's Discovery in Title VII Litigation," 4 *ABA Litigation* 14 (Fall 1977) ("Discovery in Title VII cases frequently is so burdensome that employers often weigh the costs of preparing their responses against the price of an early settlement.").

71. *Jenkins v. United Gas Corp.*, 400 F.2d 28, 33 (5th Cir. 1968).

72. *See* Cooper, "Introduction," 265 ("I sometimes have difficulty convincing each new generation of law students that the *Griggs* principle is a startling breakthrough in the jurisprudence of fair employment, since the result is so clearly essential to achieving the equal employment objective of Title VII."). *See also* G. Cooper, H. Rabb, and H. Rubin, *Fair Employment Litigation* (St. Paul, Minn.: West Publishing, 1975), 31.

73. *Riordan v. Kempiners,* 831 F.2d 690, 697 (7th Cir. 1987).

74. Before a federal district court can assert jurisdiction, a person claiming to be a victim of discrimination must first exhaust administrative remedies before the EEOC. *See* Robert Belton, "Title VII of the Civil Rights Act of 1964: A Decade of Private Enforcement and Judicial Developments," 20 St. Louis U. L. Rev. 225, 231–234 (1976).

75. The courts have not been uniform on the standard to be applied for appointment of counsel in Title VII cases. Compare *Davis v. Boeing Co.*, Fair Empl. Prac. Cas. 62 (W.D. Wash. 1969), with *Norpel v. Iowa Highway Patrol,* 4 Fair Empl. Prac. Cas. 391 (N.D. Iowa 1971).

76. *Brinkley v. Great Atl. & Pac. Tea Co.*, No. 65-1107 (E.D.N.C. 1965).

CHAPTER FOUR. THE LITIGATION PHASE BEGINS

1. Civil Action No. 1107 (E.D.N.C. October 18, 1965).

2. Complaint, *Brinkley v. The Great Atlantic and Pacific Tea Co., Inc.*, No. 1107 (E.D.N.C.) (complaint filed October 18, 1965).

3. Robert Belton, *Remedies in Employment Discrimination Law* (New York: Wolters Kluwer 1992); Robert Belton, "Harnessing Discretionary Justice in Employment Discrimination Cases: The *Moody* and *Franks* Standards," 44 *Ohio St. L.J.* 571 (1983).

4. The administrative exhaustion requirements under Title VII, as originally enacted, are explained in R. Wayne Walker, "Title VII: Complaint and Enforcement Procedures," 7 *B.C. Indus. and Com. L. Rev.* 495 (1965–1966).

5. *Egelston v. State Univ. College at Geneseo,* 535 F.2d 752, 754 (2d Cir. 1976).

6. *See generally* Francis Vaas, "Title VII: Legislative History," 7 *B.C. Indus. and Com. L. Rev.* 431 (1965).

7. *See Dent v. St. Louis-San Francisco Railway Co.*, 406 F.2d 399 (5th Cir. 1969) (five companion cases); *Brown v. Gaston County Dyeing Mach. Co.*, 405 F.2d 887 (4th Cir. 1968), *cert. denied,* 394 U.S. 918 (1969); *Johnson v. Seaboard Air Line Railroad Co.*, 405 F.2d 645 (4th Cir. 1968), *cert. denied sub nom; Pilot Freight Carriers, Inc. v. Walker,* 394 U.S. 918 (1969).

8. *See* Robert Belton, "Title VII of the Civil Rights Act of 1964: A Decade of Private Enforcement and Judicial Developments," 20 *St. L. U. L.J.* 225, 231–239 (1976); *Equal Opportunity Law.*

9. *Hall v. Werthan Bag Corp.*, 251 F. Supp. 184, 188 (M.D. Tenn. 1966).

10. *Miller v. International Paper Co.*, 408 F.2d 283, 290 (5th Cir. 1969).

11. *McDonnell Douglas Corp. v. Green,* 411 U.S. 792, 798 (1973).

12. *See* Belton, "Title VII of the Civil Rights Act of 1964," 228.

13. Answer of Cone Mills to the complaint, reproduced in Joint Appendix on appeal, at 26–27, *Lea v. Cone Mills*, 438 F.2d 86 (4th Cir. 1971).

14. *Robinson v. Union Carbide Corp.*, 380 F. Supp. 731, 733 (S.D. Ala. 1974).

15. Interview with Michael Meltsner, February 16, 2005.

16. *See* Jack Greenberg, "Civil Rights Class Actions: Procedural Means of Obtaining Substance," 39 *Ariz. L. Rev.* 575, 583 (1997).

17. *Equal Employment Opportunities Enforcement Act of 1971: Hearings on S. 2515, 2617 and H.R. 1746 before the Senate Subcommittee on Labor and Public Welfare,* 92nd Cong., 1st Sess., 240 (1971) (statement of Jack Greenberg, Director-Counsel, NAACP Legal Defense and Educational Fund, Inc.).

18. Complaint, *Hall v. Werthan Bag Corp.*, No. 4312 (M.D. Tenn. filed December 16, 1965), 251 F. Supp. 189 (M.D. Tenn. 1966).

19. Jack Greenberg, *Crusaders in the Courts: How a Dedicated Band of Lawyers Fought for the Civil Rights Revolution* (New York: Basic Books, 1994), 210.

20. *Lance v. Plummer,* 353 F.2d 585 (5th Cir. 1965), *cert. denied,* 384 U.S. 929 (1966); Plaintiff's Brief in Support of Motion to Intervene, *Hall v. Werthan Bag Corp.*, No. 4312 (M.D. Tenn. filed February 4, 1966).

21. Defendant's Memorandum in Opposition to Proposed Intervention by Ray Tate and on Right of Plaintiff to Maintain Class Action, *Hall v. Werthan Bag Corp.*, No. 4312 (M.D. Tenn. filed February 4, 1966).

22. *Hall v. Werthan Bag Corp.*, 251 F. Supp. 184, 186 (M.D. Tenn. 1966).

23. Ibid., 188.

24. Richard Berg, "Equal Employment Opportunity under the Civil Rights Act of 1964," 31 *Brook. L. Rev.* 62, 67, 86 (1964).

25. *See* Belton, "Title VII of the Civil Rights Act of 1964," 247–249.

26. *Jenkins v. United Gas Corp.*, 400 F.2d 28, 24 (5th Cir. 1968).

27. 398 F.2d 496 (5th Cir. 1968).

28. Ibid. at 34 and n. 14.

29. *See* Fleming James, Jr., and Geoffrey Hazard, *Civil Procedure* (Boston: Little, Brown, 1977), 500.

30. *See* "Developments in the Law—Class Actions," 89 *Harv. L. Rev.* 1318 (1976).

31. 1966 *Advisory Committee Notes, Amendments to Rules of Civil Procedure,* 39 F.R.D. 69, 102 (1969).

32. Greenberg, *Crusaders in the Courts,* 415.

33. Abram Chayes, "The Role of the Judge in Public Law Litigation," 89 *Harv. L. Rev.* 1281, 1284 (1976).

34. *See* Note, "Certifying Class Actions and Subclasses in Title VII Suits," 99 *Harv. L. Rev.* 619, 621–622 (1985).

35. *Johnson v. Georgia Highway Express, Inc.*, 417 F.2d 1122, 1124 (5th Cir. 1969).

36. *See e.g., Mack v. General Electric Co.*, 329 F. Supp. 72, 74–75 (E.D. Pa. 1971).

37. *See Equal Opportunity Law.*

38. Belton, "Title VII of the Civil Rights Act of 1964," 247–249.

39. *See Albemarle Paper Co. v. Moody,* 422 U.S. 405 (1975).

40. *See e.g., General Tel. Co. v. Falcon,* 457 U.S. 147 (1982).

41. *See* Melissa Hart, "Will Employment Discrimination Class Actions Survive?," 37 *Akron L. Rev.* 813 (2004).

42. 42 U.S.C. § 2000e-5(g).

43. Answer to Complaint, *Brinkley v. The Great Atlantic and Pacific Tea Co.,* C.A. No. 1107 (M.D.N.C. filed January 1966).

44. *Equal Opportunity Law,* 25–26.

45. Interview with Meltsner.

46. Jack Bass, *Unlikely Heroes: The Dramatic Story of the Southern Judges of the Fifth Circuit Who Translated the Supreme Court's* Brown v. Board of Education *Decision into a Revolution of Equality* (New York: Simon & Schuster, 1981).

47. Interview with Meltsner; Alfred A. Blumrosen, "The Law Transmission System and the Southern Jurisprudence of Employment Discrimination," 6 *Indust. Rel. L.J.* 313 (1984); Bass, *Unlikely Heroes;* Frank T. Read and Lucy S. McGraw, *Let Them Be Judged: Judicial Integration of the Deep South* (Metuchen, N.J.: Scarecrow Press, 1978).

48. Audrey Chin and Mark A. Peterson, *Deep Pockets, Empty Pockets: Who Wins in Cook County Jury Trials* (Santa Monica, Calif.: Rand Institute for Civil Justice, 1985), 36.

49. *See* David Benjamin Oppenheimer, "Understanding Affirmative Action," 23 *Hastings Const. L. Q.* 921, 952 (1996) (reviewing studies on racial attitudes). *See also* Patricia G. Devine and Andrew J. Eliot, "Are Racial Stereotypes Really Fading? The Princeton Trilogy Revisited," 21 *Personality and Soc. Psych. Bull.* 1139–1150 (1995) (concluding the negative stereotypes that blacks as a group have not changed since the 1930s).

50. 42 U.S.C. § 3601.

51. Legal Defense Fund's Opening Brief for Petitioner 19–24, *Curtis v. Loether,* 415 U.S. 189 (1974) (No. 72-1035).

52. 110 Cong. Rec. 14,182 (1964) (Senate rejected an amendment offered by Senator Thurman to make violations of Title VII subject to jury trial). *See also* 118 Cong. Rec. 4919–4920 (1972) (Senate rejected Senator Ervin's proposed amendment to permit either party the right to demand a jury trial in any case brought under Title VII); *see, e.g.,* 110 Cong. Rec. 8660 (Remarks of Senator Morse); 9819 (Remarks of Senator Javits); 12,595 (Remarks of Senator Humphrey).

53. *See* Charles Morgan, Jr., "Segregated Justice," in *Southern Justice,* ed. Leon Friedman (New York: Pantheon Books, 1965), 163.

54. *Anthony v. Brooks,* 67 LRRM 2897 (N.D. Ga. 1967), a case litigated with cooperating attorney Howard Moore, was the first district court case to reject defendants' demand for a jury trial. Other early LDF cases include *Hayes v. Seaboard Coast Line R.R. Co.,* 46 F.R.D. 49 (S.D. Ga. 1968); and *Lea v. Cone Mills,* C.A. No. C-176-D-66 (M.D.N.C. 1968); *Grayson v. Wickes Corp.,* 607 F.2d 1194, 1196 (7th Cir. 1979).

55. *Hubbard v. Administrator, Environmental Protection Agency,* 982 F.2d 531 (D.C. Cir. 1992) (collecting cases). The courts also denied a right to a jury trial when both parties made the demand. *See Gillin v. Federal Paper Board Co.,* 52 F.R.D. 383 (D. Conn. 1970).

56. *Cox v. Babcock and Wilcox Co.*, 471 F.2d 13 (4th Cir. 1972).

57. Milton R. Konvitz and Theodore Leskes, *A Century of Civil Rights* (New York: Columbia University Press, 1961), 48–51, 63–70.

58. *See* Note, "Racial Discrimination in Employment under the Civil Rights Act of 1866," 36 *U. Chi. L. Rev.* 615 (1968–1969).

59. *Civil Rights Cases*, 109 U.S. 3 (1883). *See also* Konvitz and Leskes, *A Century of Civil Rights.*

60. 334 U.S. 24, 31–32 (1948).

61. Interview with Meltsner.

62. *Dobbins v. Local 212, International Brotherhood of Electrical Workers*, 292 F. Supp. 413 (S.D. Ohio 1968).

63. *Culpepper v. Reynolds Metals Co.*, 296 F. Supp. 1232 (N.D. Ga. 1969).

64. 392 U.S. 409, 437 (1968).

65. *See Colbert v. H-K Corp.*, 295 F. Supp. 1091 (N.D. Ga. 1968); *Kendrick v. American Bakery Co.*, 59 CCH Lab. Cas. ¶ 9146 (N.D. Ga. 1968).

66. *Macklin v. Spector Freight Sys., Inc.*, 478 F.2d 979 (D.C. Cir. 1973); *Brady v. Bristol Myers, Inc.*, 459 F.2d 621 (8th Cir. 1972); *Caldwell v. National Brewing Co.*, 443 F.2d 1044 (5th Cir.), 405 U.S. 916 (1971); *Young v. International Tel. and Tel. Co.*, 438 F.2d 757 (3d Cir. 1971), *cert. denied*, 400 U.S. 911 (1970); *Sanders v. Dobbs Houses, Inc.*, 431 F.2d 1097 (5th Cir. 1970) (noting that "this statutory Lazarus necessarily revived the congressional prohibition against purely private discrimination in contracts of employment").

67. 421 U.S. 454, 459–460 (1975).

68. *Brown v. Gaston County Dyeing Machine Co.*, 457 F.2d 1377 (4th Cir.) (Franklin, J., dissenting), *cert. denied*, 409 U.S. 982 (1972).

CHAPTER FIVE. *QUARLES* AND THE PRESENT EFFECTS THEORY

1. *International Bhd. of Teamsters v. United States*, 431 U.S. 324, 346 n. 28 (1977).

2. Jack Greenberg, *Crusaders in the Courts: How a Dedicated Band of Lawyers Fought for the Civil Rights Revolution* (New York: Basic Books, 1994), 418.

3. *See* James P. Gannon, "U.S. Prodding Plants to Merge Negro, White Lines of Progression," *Wall Street Journal*, January 5, 1967 (noting that the LDF was involved in at least thirty-five seniority discrimination cases at that time).

4. Note, "Title VII, Seniority Discrimination, and the Incumbent Negro," 80 *Harv. L. Rev.* 1260, 1263 (1966).

5. *California Brewers Ass'n v. Bryant*, 444 U.S. 598, 606 (1980).

6. William B. Gould, *Black Workers in White Unions: Job Discrimination in the United States* (Ithaca, N.Y.: Cornell University Press, 1977), 68.

7. George Cooper and Richard Sobol, "Seniority and Testing under Fair Employment Laws: A General Approach to Objective Criteria of Hiring and Promotion," 82 *Harv. L. Rev.* 1598, 1601, n. 1 (1968).

8. *See* Benjamin Aaron, "Reflections on the Legal Nature and Enforceability of Seniority Rights," 75 *Harv. L. Rev.* 1532 (1961).

9. *United States v. Chesapeake and Ohio Ry. Co.*, 1971 WL 167 (E.D. Va. 1971).

10. William B. Gould, "Employment Security, Seniority and Race: The Role of Title VII of the Civil Rights Act of 1964," 13 *Howard L.J.* 1, 3 (1967).

11. Cooper and Sobol, "Seniority and Testing under Fair Employment Laws," 1604–1605.

12. *See* Ray Marshall, *The Negro and Organized Labor* (New York: John Wiley & Sons, 1965); Herbert Northrop, *Organized Labor and the Negro* (New York: Harper & Sons, 1944).

13. A study of the history of racial discrimination by employers and unions in the tobacco industry out of which *Quarles* arose is found in Herbert R. Northrup and Robert Ash, "The Negro in the Tobacco Industry" (1970), in Herbert Northrup, *Negro Employment in Basic Industries: A Study of Racial Policies in Six Industries* (Philadelphia: University of Pennsylvania Press, 1970).

14. Joel W. Friedman, *Champion of Civil Rights: John Minor Wisdom* (Baton Rouge, La.: LSU Press, 2009).

15. *Whitfield v. United Steelworkers, Local No. 2708*, 263 F.2d 546, 551 (5th Cir. 1959).

16. Report by the EEOC Chairman Franklin Roosevelt, Jr., on the EEOC's "first hundred days," CCH Emp. Prac. Guide ¶ 8024 (1965); *see* ibid. ¶ 8046 (1966) (speech by EEOC Commissioner Samuel C. Jackson).

17. Gould, *Black Workers in White Unions*, 71–72.

18. Herbert Hill, "Race and the Steelworkers Union: White Privilege and Black Struggles," 8 *New Politics*, No. 4 (new series), whole no. 32 (Winter 2002).

19. Gould, *Black Workers in White Unions*, 71–72; Hill, "Race and the Steelworkers Union."

20. Gould, *Black Workers in White Unions*, 20.

21. Gould, "Employment Security, Seniority and Race" (article by Gould on his report and recommendations to the EEOC). *See also* Gould, *Black Workers in White Unions*, 72.

22. *Griffin v. Illinois*, 351 U.S. 12, 17 n. 11 (1956); *Yick Wo v. Hopkins*, 118 U.S. 356 (1886).

23. *Louisiana v. United States*, 380 U.S. 145, 154–155 (1965); *Lane v. Wilson*, 307 U.S. 268, 275 (1939), *Guinn v. United States*, 238 U.S. 247 (1915). Whether this constitutional conception of discrimination survives the more recent decision in *Washington v. Davis*, 426 U.S. 229 (1976), is an open question.

24. *See* John S. Moot, "An Analysis of Judicial Deference to EEOC Interpretive Guidelines," 1 *Admin. L.J.* 213 (1987).

25. Note, "Title VII, Seniority Discrimination, and the Incumbent Negro," 1260.

26. Cooper and Sobol, "Seniority and Testing under Fair Employment Laws," 1598.

27. *Local 189 United Papermakers and Paperworkers v. United States*, 282 F.Supp. 39 (E.D. La. 1968), aff'd, 416 F.2d 980 (5th Cir. 1969), *cert. denied*, 397 U.S. 919 (1970)

(seniority discrimination); *Oatis v. Crown Zellerbach Corp.*, 398 F.2d 496 (5th Cir. 1970) (Title VII class action); *Hicks v. Crown Zellerbach Corp.*, 319 F. Supp. 314 (E.D. La. 1970) (testing).

28. The union defendant, Local 203, became a defendant in the case through the petition for intervention the litigation team filed on behalf of Ephriam Briggs, who had filed a charge of discrimination against both Philip Morris and the union. *Quarles v. Philip Morris, Inc.*, 1 EPD (CCH) ¶ 9782 (E.D. Va. 1967); *Quarles v. Philip Morris, Inc.*, 279 F. Supp. 505, 507 (E.D. Va. 1968). Briggs, the other named plaintiff, alleged that he was the victim of racial discrimination with respect to his pay. Judge Butzner found in favor of Briggs and another member of the class on the pay discrimination claim. *Quarles v. Philip Morris, Inc.*, 279 F. Supp. 505, 509–510 (E.D. Va. 1968).

29. Philip Morris hired African Americans for seasonal work in another department, stemmery, but employees in stemmery were covered by a different collective bargaining agreement. The court excluded employees in the stemmery from the class because they were seasonal employees, did not become permanent employees unless they were hired in another department, and the employer had a rational basis for distinguishing seasonal and permanent employees. *Quarles*, 279 F. Supp. at 519.

30. Judge Butzner allowed the case to go forward as a class action in an order entered in September 1966. *Quarles v. Philip Morris, Inc.*, 1 EPD (CCH) ¶ 9827 (E.D. Va. 1966); there were several other claims for which relief was sought, but Judge Butzner ruled against the plaintiffs on these claims. These claims were racial discrimination in the employment and promotion of supervisors and hiring discrimination after the effective date of Title VII. *Quarles v. Philip Morris, Inc.*, 279 F. Supp. 505, 508 (E.D. Va. 1968).

31. "Leadership Challenges in Civil Rights Law with Julian Bond and Michael Klarman," September 13, 2000, video and transcript, http://www.virginia.edu/publichistory /biographies/html (accessed August 13, 2007).

32. *E.g., Russell v. The American Tobacco Co.*, 528 F.2d 357 (4th Cir. 1975), *cert. denied*, 425 U.S. 935 (1976); *Hairston v. McLean Trucking Co.*, 520 F.2d 226 (4th Cir. 1975); *Barnett v. W. T. Grant*, 518 F.2d 543 (4th Cir. 1975); *Young v. Edgcomb Steel Co.*, 499 F.2d 97 (4th Cir. 1974).

33. Trial Brief for Plaintiffs 5, *Quarles*, filed August 14, 1967.

34. Brief of Plaintiffs at 13–14, *Quarles v. Philip Morris, Inc.*, 279 F. Supp. 505 (E.D. Va. 1968) (filed August 14, 1967).

35. The litigation team also relied upon several opinion letters issued by the EEOC Office of General Counsel in support of the present effects theory. Brief for Plaintiffs 15, *Quarles* (citing EEOC General Counsel Opinion Letter, 344–355, CCH Emp. Prac. Guide ¶ 17,251.042 (1965) and EEOC General Counsel Opinions, CCH Emp. Prac. Guide ¶ 17,252.304 (1965), *Quarles v. Philip Morris, Inc.*, 279 F. Supp. 505 (E.D. Va. 1968) (No. 4544) (filed August 14, 1967).

36. Note, "Title VII, Seniority Discrimination, and the Incumbent Negro," 1267–1268.

37. Comments of David Cashdan, "Celebrating the 40th Anniversary of Title VII:

Enacting the Civil Rights Act and Using the Court to Challenge and Remedy Workplace Discrimination," Tuesday, June 24, 2005, http://www.eeoc.gov/about eeoc/40thpanels /panel1/transcript.html (accessed July 28, 2004).

38. Brief for the United States Equal Employment Opportunity Commission as Amicus Curiae, 11–13, *Quarles v. Philip Morris, Inc.,* 279 F. Supp. 505 (E.D. Va. 1968) (filed October 9, 1967).

39. *Near v. Minnesota,* 283 U.S. 697 (1931).

40. 351 U.S. 12 (1962).

41. Reply Brief of Philip Morris to Amicus Curiae Brief of the Equal Employment Opportunity at 3–4 *Quarles* (E.D. Va. Civ. No. 4544) (filed October 31, 1967).

42. 110 Cong. Rec. 7213 (1964) (memorandum of Sen. Clark and Sen. Case, Senate floor managers of Title VII).

43. 110 Cong. Rec. 12,723 (1964) (remarks of Sen. Humphrey).

44. Local 203 of Tobacco Workers International Union, reply memo to Brief for the United States Equal Employment Opportunity 4 (filed November 1, 1967).

45. For examples of charges by some legislators that Title VII would destroy existing seniority rights, *see, e.g.,* H.R. Rep. No. 914, 64–66, 88th Cong., 1st Sess. (1963) (Minority Report); 110 Cong. Rec. 486–489 (1964) (remarks of Sen. Lester Hill); ibid. at 11471 (remarks of Sen. Javits discussing charges made by Governor George Wallace of Alabama).

46. Sadie Hawkins Day was a daylong event that first made its appearance in Al Capp's comic strip *Li'l Abner.* Sadie Hawkins was the homeliest girl in Dogpatch. When she was thirty-five years old and still a spinster because no fellows had ever sought to court her, her father, a prominent citizen of Dogpatch, decreed an annual Sadie Hawkins Day during which unmarried women pursued eligible bachelors. If caught by an unmarried woman on that day, the bachelor had to marry her.

47. *See* Note, "Title VII, Seniority Discrimination, and the Incumbent Negro," 1268.

48. 110 Cong. Rec. 7213 (1964).

49. 110 Cong. Rec. 7217 (1964). The questions and answers to Senator Dirksen's concerns on seniority are discussed extensively in the LDF case of *Franks v. Bowman Transportation Co.,* 424 U.S. 747, 760–761 (1976).

50. Posttrial Brief of Plaintiffs at 14, *Quarles v. Philip Morris, Inc.,* 279 F. Supp. 505 (E.D. Va. 1968) (filed August 14, 1967).

51. *Ford Motor Co. v. Hoffman,* 345 U.S. 330 (1953); *Humphrey v. Moore,* 375 U.S. 335 (1964).

52. Posttrial Brief of Plaintiffs at 17, *Quarles v. Philip Morris, Inc.,* 279 F. Supp. 505 (E.D. Va. 1968) (filed August 14, 1967).

53. *See* Brief of Philip Morris in response to the amicus brief of EEOC, *Quarles v. Philip Morris, Inc.,* 279 F. Supp. 505 (E.D. Va. 1967) (filed October 30, 1967).

54. Ibid. at 516.

55. Ibid. at 518–519.

56. Ibid.

57. Ibid. at 515.

58. Ibid. at 517–518.

59. *Quarles,* 279 F. Supp. at 5 (emphasis supplied).

60. Interview with Gabrielle Kirk McDonald, January 26, 2005.

61. *Clark v. Local 189, United Papermaker and Paper Workers, AFL-CIO,* 282 F. Supp. 39, 44–45 (E.D. La. 1968), *aff'd,* 416 F.2d 980 (5th Cir.), affirming, *cert. denied,* 397 U.S. 919 (1970).

62. *Local 189,* 416 F.2d at 983.

63. Jack Greenberg, *Brown v. Board of Education: Witness to a Landmark Decision* (Northport, N.Y.: Twelve Tables Press, 2004), 186; Frank Read and Lucy S. McGraw, *Let Them Be Judged: The Judicial Integration of the Deep South* (Metuchen, N.J.: Scarecrow Press, 1978).

64. Greenberg, *Brown v. Board of Education,* 186.

65. *Gomillion v. Lightfoot,* 270 F.2d 594 at 612 (5th Cir. 1969) (Wisdom, J., specially concurring); case *reversed,* 364 U.S. 339 (1970).

66. Joel W. Friedman, "The Emergence of John Minor Wisdom as Intellectual Leader of the Fifth Circuit: Reflecting Back on the Forty-Fifth Anniversary of His Joining the Court," 77 *Tul. L. Rev.* 915, 957 (2003) (citing interview the author conducted of Judge Martin L. C. Feldman, U.S. Court for the Eastern District of Louisiana, New Orleans, on November 22, 2002).

67. Friedman, *Champion of Civil Rights,* 125–130.

68. *Local 189,* 416 F.2d at 982.

69. Ibid. at 987.

70. Ibid. at 983.

71. Interview with Gabrielle Kirk McDonald, January 26, 2005; Friedman, "The Emergence of John Minor Wisdom," 957.

72. Samuel C. Jackson, "Using the Law to Attack Discrimination in Employment," 8 *Washburn L.J.* 189, 195 (1968).

73. George A. Moore, Jr., "Steel Industry Consent Decrees: A Model for the Future" 3 *Empl. Rel. L.J.* 214, 215 (1977). Moore was Assistant Vice President of Industrial Relations at Bethlehem Steel Corporation.

CHAPTER SIX. *GRIGGS*

1. Paul Burstein and Susan Pitchford, "Social-Scientific and Legal Challenges to Education and Testing Requirements in Employment," 37 *Soc. Probs.* 243, 244 (1990).

2. David Goslin, *The Search for Ability: Standardized Testing in Social Perspective* (New York: Russell Sage, 1963), 96–98.

3. Irving Kovarsky, "Some Social and Legal Aspects of Testing under the Civil Rights Act," 20 *Lab. L.J.* 346 (1969).

4. Burstein and Pitchford, "Social-Scientific and Legal Challenges," 243–244.

5. *See* Herbert N. Bernhardt, "*Griggs v. Duke Power Co.:* The Implications for Private and Public Employers," 50 *Tex. L. Rev.* 901 (1972).

6. The Decision and Order of Hearing Examiner, Charge No. 63C-127, was not officially reported but is reprinted in full in the legislative history of the Civil Rights Act of 1964. 110 Cong. Rec. at 5662 (1964), and 9 Race Rel. L. R. 1911 (Ill. F.E.P. Comm'n 1964). *Motorola v. Illinois Fair Employment Practices Commission,* 215 N.E. 2d 286 (Ill. 1966).

7. William H. Enneis, "Foreword," in William C. Byham and Morton E. Spitzer, *The Law and Personnel Testing* (New York: American Management Association, 1971), ix.

8. *Griggs,* 401 U.S. at 434 n. 10.

9. 42 U.S.C. § 2000e-2(h).

10. George Cooper and Richard Sobol, "Seniority and Testing under Fair Employment Laws: A General Approach to Objective Criteria," 82 *Harv. L. Rev.* 1598, 1638 (1969); *Business and Industry Testing: Current Practices and Test Results* (Joyce Hogan and Robert Hogan eds 1984–1990) (Austin, Tex.: Pro-Ed, 1984–1990).

11. There have been a number of studies on the discriminatory nature of ostensibly objective tests. *E.g.,* James J. Kilpatrick, Robert B. Ewen, Richard S. Barrett, and Raymond Katzell, *Testing and Fair Employment* (New York: Cambridge University Press, 1968); American Psychological Association Task Force on Employment Testing and Minority Groups, "Job Testing and the Disadvantaged," 24 *Am. Psychologist* 637 (1969).

12. EEOC, Office of Research and Reports, *Testing of Minority Group Applicants for Employment, Research Report 1966–67* at 1–2 (March 1966).

13. Ibid.

14. The report of the panel of psychologists was attached to the 1966 testing guidelines.

15. Alfred W. Blumrosen, "Strangers in Paradise: *Griggs v. Duke Power Co.* and the Concept of Employment Discrimination," 71 *Mich. L. Rev.* 59, 59–62 (1972).

16. *See* Byham and Spitzer, *The Law and Personnel Testing,* 108–120.

17. EEOC, Office of Research and Reports, *Testing of Minority Group Applicants for Employment, Research Report 1966–67* at 2 (March 1966).

18. 35 F.R. 12333 (1970); 35 C.F.R. § 1607 (1970).

19. 399 U.S. 926 (1970).

20. The information about George Cooper and Richard Sobol is based, in large part, unless otherwise noted, on an interview of Cooper by Joseph Mosnier for "Crafting Law in the Second Reconstruction: Julius Chambers, the NAACP Legal Defense Fund, and Title VII" (2004) (unpublished Ph.D. dissertation) (on file at the University of North Carolina, Chapel Hill), and my interview with Cooper.

21. George Cooper and Harriet Rabb, *Equal Employment Law and Litigation: Materials for a Clinical Course* (New York: Employment Rights Project, Columbia University, 1975); Fred Strebeigh, *Equal: Women Reshape American Law* (New York: Norton, 2009), 161–162.

22. Transcript of the Oral History Interview with Harriet Rabb, March 6, 2001 (interviewed by J. P. Ogilvy for the oral history project on clinical legal education), lib.law. cua.edu/nacle/Transcript/Rabb.pdf.

23. *E.g., Local 189 United Papermakers and Paperworkers v. United States,* 416 F. 2d

980 (5th Cir. 1969), *cert. denied,* 397 U.S. 919 (1970); *Hicks v. Crown Zellerbach,* 319 F. Supp. 314 (E.D. La. 1970).

24. Cooper and Sobol, "Seniority and Testing under Fair Employment Law," 1598.

25. George Cooper and Richard Sobol, "This Week's Citation Classic," 44 *Current Contents* 22 (November 3, 1986) (commentary by the authors). An editor's note in the comments indicates that the *Harvard Law Review* article had been cited in over 130 publications as of 1986.

26. Cooper and Sobol, "Seniority and Testing under Fair Employment Law," 1670–1673.

27. For one version of the history of Duke Power, *see* Robert F. Durden, *Electrifying the Piedmont Carolinas: The Duke Power Company, 1904–1977* (Durham, N.C.: Carolina Academic Press, 2001).

28. EEOC, *Final Investigation Report* in *Griggs,* styled *Tucker v. Duke Power Co.;* Case Nos. AT-6-4-24 through AT 6-4-41, May 26, 1966.

29. Previously, the Dan River Steam Station was located in Draper, North Carolina, which was renamed Eden when it consolidated with two other towns, Leaksville and Spray.

30. Record, Exhibit Volume, *Griggs v. Duke Power Co.,* 401 U.S. 424 (1971) (No. 124). Unless otherwise indicated, the facts are based on the findings of fact made by the trial judge, Eugene Gordon, in his opinion in *Griggs,* 292 F. Supp. 243 (M.D.N.C. 1968), and the printed Record in the Supreme Court, which consists of two volumes. The first volume is the Appendix, which includes pleadings and the trial transcript, and the second volume is in the Exhibit Volume, which also includes trial exhibits.

31. Exhibit Volume, 33b, *Griggs,* 401 U.S. 424 (No. 124) (April 28, 1966, Consolidated EEOC, Employer Information Report EEO-1).

32. Interview with plaintiff Willie Boyd, August 6, 2004.

33. These data were compiled from Duke's answers to the plaintiffs' interrogatories. Exhibit Volume, 105b–109b, *Griggs,* 401 U.S. 424 (124) (No. 124).

34. Exhibit Vol., 72b, *Griggs.*

35. Ibid.

36. *Griggs,* 292 F. Supp. 243, 245 (M.D.N.C. 1968).

37. EEOC, *Final Investigation Report, Tucker et al. v. Duke Power Co.,* Dan River Steam Station, Case Nos. At 6-4-24 through 6-4-41 (May 26, 1966).

38. Supreme Court Record, Vol. 1 at 102a, *Griggs.*

39. Exhibit Volume at 77b–83b and 126b–127b, *Griggs.*

40. Trial testimony of A. C. Thies, vice president of production, Appendix 93a, *Griggs,* 401 U.S. 424 (1971) (No. 124).

41. 327 F. Supp. 1034 (E.D. Va. 1971).

42. Testimony of Dr. Moffie, Supreme Court Record, Vol. 1, at 167a, *Griggs.*

43. Testimony of Dr. Moffie, Appendix 176a, *Griggs,* 401 U.S. 424 (1971) (No. 124).

44. The test battery included another test, General Clerical, but it was not an issue in the case.

45. The Wonderlic test, copyrighted in 1959, is a mixture of questions on vocabulary, mathematics, and other subjects, with a heavy emphasis on vocabulary and reading ability. Test-takers were expected to answer questions such as:

No. 4. Answer by printing Yes or No. Does B.C. mean "before Christ"?

No. 11. ADOPT ADEPT—Do these works have

  1. Similar meanings,

  2. Contradictory,

  3. Mean neither same nor opposite?

No. 19. REFLECT REFLEX—Do these words have

  1. Similar meanings,

  2. Contradictory,

  3. Mean neither same nor opposite?

No. 24. The hours of daylight and darkness in September are nearest equal to hours of daylight in

  1. June

  2. March

  3. May

  4. November

We specifically cited these examples in the brief the litigation team filed in the Supreme Court.

46. Dr. Moffie, letter to Duke Power, July 7, 1986.

47. Appendix 171a, *Griggs*, 401 U.S. 405 (1971) (No. 1405).

48. *Griggs*, 401 U.S. at 428 n. 3.

49. Dr. Moffie, letter to Kenneth Austin, Duke Power's Assistant Vice President, July 7, 1965.

50. Supreme Court Record, Exhibit Vol. at 137b, *Griggs*.

51. Testimony of A. C. Thies, Appendix 98a, *Griggs*, 424 U.S. 401 (1971) (saying that the company knew that the white labor foreman of the blacks did not have a high school education).

52. Barry Bearak and David Lauter, "Tense Steps to Ending Racial Bias," *Los Angeles Times*, November 3, 1991, A1.

53. The facts leading to the plaintiffs' decision to file a charge with the EEOC are based on an interview with Boyd. *See also* Mosnier, *Crafting Law in the Second Reconstruction;* Bearak and Lauter, "Tense Steps to Ending Racial Bias," A1.

54. Interview with Willie Boyd; *Russell v. American Tobacco Co.*, 528 F.2d 357 (4th Cir. 1975), *cert. denied*, 425 U.S. 935 (1976).

55. Interview with Willie Boyd; Bearak and Lauter, "Tense Steps to Ending Racial Bias," A1.

56. Reported in Bearak and Lauter, "Tense Steps to Ending Racial Bias," A1.

57. Defendant's deposition of Eddie Broadnax, *Griggs*, 292 F. Supp. 242 (M.D.N.C. 1968) (No. C-210-G-66).

58. A. C. Thies, memoranda to the file in the Duke Power materials received from Mosnier.

59. A. C. Thies to the superintendents, September 22, 1965.

60. A. C. Thies, letter to Duke Power superintendents, April 28, 1966.

61. Interview with Willie Boyd.

62. 42 U.S.C. § 2000e-2(j).

63. Duke Power (Vice President Kenneth Austin), letter to the EEOC, May 4, 1966.

CHAPTER SEVEN. *GRIGGS* IN THE DISTRICT COURT

1. Articles, commentaries, and journalistic reports about Chambers's life, the influential role he has had on civil rights law, civil rights policy, and civil rights institutions, and his status as a preeminent civil rights advocate are numerous. Some of the sources I relied upon, in addition to my own personal knowledge about Chambers, include Davidson M. Douglas, *Reading, Writing & Race: The Desegregation of the Charlotte Schools* (Chapel Hill: University of North Carolina Press, 1995), 108–109; Jack Greenberg, *Crusaders in the Courts: How a Dedicated Band of Lawyers Fought for the Civil Rights Revolution* (New York: Basic Books, 1994), 375–376; John Moxk, "An 'Optimist' Faces New Set of Challenges," *National Law Journal*, July 30, 1984, 1.

2. Julius L. Chambers, "Symposium Address: Racial Justice in the 1980s," 8 *Campbell L. Rev.* 29, 31 (1985).

3. Greenberg, *Crusaders in the Courts*, 375–376.

4. *McKissick v. Carmichael*, 187 F. 2d 949 (4th Cir.), *cert. denied*, 341 U.S. 951 (1951).

5. *See, e.g.*, Carolina Editor, *New York Times*, May 11, 1961, 36.

6. Henry Brandies, Jr., "The Law School," 41 *N.C. L. Rev.* 101–106 (1962) (Brandies was the dean at UNC Law School when Chambers was a student).

7. J. A. C. Dunn, "One Man's Achievement: A Scholar Finds His Books," *Charlotte News*, May 19, 1961, 14A (reprinted from the *Chapel Hill Weekly*); Joseph L. Mosnier, "Crafting Law in the Second Reconstruction: Julius Chambers, the NAACP Legal Defense Fund, and Title VII" (2004), 104 (unpublished Ph.D. dissertation) (on file at the University of North Carolina, Chapel Hill).

8. Chambers, "Symposium Address," 41.

9. Julius Chambers, "Comments, Panel Discussion, Twenty-Five Years of the Civil Rights Act: History and Promise," 25 *Wake Forest L. Rev.* 159, 186 (1990).

10. "Bombings Have Shocked New Bern," *Charlotte Observer*, January 31, 1965, 19A.

11. *See* "Four Charlotte Homes Hit by Bombs," *Greensboro Daily News*, November 23, 1965, 1; Chere Briggs, "Incendiary Fire Destroys Rights Lawyers' Office," *Charlotte Observer*, February 5, 1971, 1.

12. "Biracial Law Firm to Be Formed Here," *Charlotte Observer*, July 4, 1967, 10A.

13. For a study of the role of Chambers's singular contributions to the evolution of federal civil rights law, *see* Mosnier, "Crafting Law in the Second Reconstruction."

14. Vershenia M. Balance, "Conrad O. Pearson: Pioneer Defender of Civil Rights," 4 *North Carolina State Bar Quarterly* 34 (Fall 1994).

15. *Hocutt v. Wilson* (N.C. Superior Court 1933) (unreported). *See* Gilbert Ware, *William Hastie: Grace under Pressure* (New York: Oxford University Press, 1984), 46–53.

16. *Wheeler v. Durham City Board of Education,* 88 F. R.D. 27, 30 (M.D.N.C. 1980).

17. Interview with Willie Boyd.

18. The background facts on Willie Griggs are based on information in Griggs's personnel file and Mosnier, "Crafting Law in the Second Reconstruction," 344–345.

19. *Griggs,* Order on Initial Pretrial Conference, held on January 9, 1967.

20. *Griggs,* 292 F. Supp. 243, 251 (M.D.N.C. 1968).

21. Mosnier, "Crafting Law in the Second Reconstruction."

22. Appendix 11a, *Griggs v. Duke Power Co.,* 401 U.S. 422 (1971) (No. 124).

23. Validation of Employment Test, dated May 1, 1967, submitted to Kenneth Austin, vice president of Duke Power, by Dr. Moffie.

24. George Ferguson, letter to Jules Gordon, EEOC conciliator, November 21, 1966, EEOC case file Nos. 6-3-1852–1866.

25. Julius Chambers, letter to George Ferguson, October 13, 1967.

26. Mosnier, "Crafting Law in the Second Reconstruction," 374 (citing A. C. Thies, memo to Ferguson, October 19, 1967).

27. *Lea v. Cone Mills,* Civ. No. C-176-D-66 (M.D.N.C. Durham Division), order on class action entered on June 28, 1967); and *Robinson v. P. Lorillard Corp.,* Civ. No. C-141-G-1966 (M.D.N.C. Greensboro Division) (order on class action entered on January 26, 1967).

28. 347 U.S. 483, 494 n. 11 (1954). Footnote 11 in *Brown* cites articles by Kenneth Clark and others on the psychological harm of racial segregation on African American schoolchildren.

29. Obituaries: "Eugene Andrew Gordon," *Greensboro News and Record,* May 6, 2002, B8, B9, available at 2002 WL 5301159.

30. *Griggs,* Trial transcript at 39.

31. Appendix 94a–95a, *Griggs,* 401 U.S. 424 (1971) (No. 124).

32. Appendix 109a, *Griggs,* 401 U.S. 424 (1971) (No. 124).

33. Trial testimony of A. C. Thies, Appendix at 103a–104a, *Griggs,* 401 U.S. 424 (1971).

34. James J. Kilpatrick, Robert B. Ewen, Richard S. Barrett, and Raymond Katzell, *Testing and Fair Employment* (New York: Cambridge University Press, 1968).

35. Richard Barrett, *Challenging the Myths of Fair Employment Practices* (Westport, Conn.: Quorum Books, 1988), xi.

36. Appendix 126a–129a, *Griggs,* 401 U.S. 424 (1971) (No. 124).

37. Appendix 154a–156a, *Griggs,* 401 U.S. 424 (1971) (No. 124).

38. Appendix 175a–176a, *Griggs,* 401 U.S. 424 (1971) (No. 124).

39. *See* Kilpatrick, Ewen, Barrett, and Katzell, *Testing and Fair Employment.*

40. My wife, Joy, was about eight months pregnant with our first child, Keith, and spent a fair amount of time doing some of the last-minute preparations for the post-trial submissions.

41. Richard Barrett, letter to Robert Belton, April 28, 1968.

42. 42 U.S.C. § 2000e-2(h).

43. *Griggs,* 292 F. Supp. 243, 245 n. 2, 247 (M.D.N.C. 1968).

44. Posttrial brief for plaintiffs at 33–35 in *Griggs,* 292 F. Supp. 243 (M.D.N.C. 1968) (some citations omitted) (emphasis supplied).

45. *See* brief for plaintiffs in *Lea v. Cone Mills Corp.,* No. C-176-D-66 (M.D.N.C.) (plaintiff posttrial brief filed on December 23, 1968), 301 F. Supp. 97 (1969).

46. Brief for plaintiffs 17–18, *Griggs,* 292 F. Supp. 243 (M.D.N.C. 1968) (No. C-120-G-66) (filed April 16, 1968).

47. Trial brief of Duke Power Co. at 18, *Griggs,* 292 F. Supp. 243 (M.D.N.C. 1968) (No. C-120-G-66) (filed May 15, 1968).

48. Posttrial brief of Duke Power Co. at 20, *Griggs,* 292 F. Supp. 243 (M.D.N.C. 1968) (No. C-120-G-66) (filed May 15, 1968).

49. *Griggs,* 292 F. Supp. at 248, 249 (M.D.N.C. 1968).

50. Ibid.

51. Ibid.

52. Ibid. at 250.

53. Ibid.

54. The taxicab example is taken from Mark Rothstein and Lance Liebman, *Employment Law: Cases and Materials* (6th ed.) (New York: Foundation Press, 2007), 261.

55. *Griggs,* 292 F. Supp. at 251.

CHAPTER EIGHT. IN THE FOURTH CIRCUIT

1. Al Rosenthal, letter to Robert Belton, October 11, 1968.

2. George Cooper, letter to Robert Belton, October 14, 1968.

3. George Cooper and Richard Sobol, "Seniority and Testing under Fair Employment Laws: A General Approach to Objective Criteria of Hiring and Promotion," 82 *Harv. L. Rev.* 1598 (1969).

4. These cases included *Hicks v. Crown Zellerbach Corp.,* 58 CCH Lab. Cas. 9145 (E.D. La. August 8, 1968) (testing and seniority), and *United States v. Papermakers Local 189,* 282 F. Supp. 39 (E.D. La. 1968) (seniority).

5. This Week's Citation Classic, George Cooper and Richard Sobol in Current Contents, "Seniority and Testing under Fair Employment Law: A General Approach to Objective Criteria of Hiring and Promotion," *CC/Social Behavior Science,* No. 44, November 3, 1986.

6. *See* Robert Belton et al., *Employment Discrimination Law: Cases and Materials on Equality in the Workplace* (7th ed.) (St. Paul, Minn.: West Publishing, 2004), 188.

7. Al had shared some comments on the article with Cooper and Sobol prior to its publication that the authors gratefully acknowledged. Cooper and Sobol, "Seniority and Testing under Fair Employment Laws," 1598 n. **.

8. Brief for appellants 7–8, *Griggs,* 420 F.2d 1225 (4th Cir. 1970).

9. *Griggs,* 420 F.2d 1225, 1237 (4th Cir. 1970) (Sobeloff, J., concurring in part, dissenting in part).

10. Brief for appellants, 32–35 *Griggs,* 420 F.2d 1225 (4th Cir. 1970).

11. Ibid. at 20–23 (citing U.S. Bureau of the Census, U.S. Census of Population: 1960, Vol. I, Part 35, at Table 47, p. 167).

12. Ibid. at 41, 45.

13. Gary Greenberg, Civil Rights Division, Department of Justice, letter to the Clerk of the United States Court of Appeals for the Fourth Circuit, January 14, 1969.

14. Brief for the United States as Amicus Curiae, 12, *Griggs,* 420 F.2d 1225 (4th Cir. 1970) (No. 13,013).

15. Ibid.

16. Brief for appellee, 20, *Griggs,* 420 F.2d 1225 (4th Cir. 1970).

17. Reply Brief for the United States as Amicus Curiae, *Griggs,* 420 F.2d 1225 (4th Cir. 1970).

18. Brief for appellee, 12, *Griggs,* 420 F.2d 1225 (4th Cir. 1970) (No. 13,013).

19. Biographical sketches of Judges Sobeloff, Boreman, and Bryan are set out in "Remembering the Fourth Circuit Judges: A History from 1941 to 1998," 55 *Wash. & Lee L. Rev.* 471 (1998).

20. Michael Mayer, "Eisenhower and the Southern Federal Judiciary: The Sobeloff Nomination," ch. 4 in *Reexamining the Eisenhower Presidency,* ed. Shirley Anne Warshaw (Westport, Conn.: Greenwood Press, 1993); Abel J. Merrill, "Biographical Sketch," 34 *Md. L. Rev.* 491, 492 (1974).

21. Sanford J. Rosen, "Tribute to Simon E. Sobeloff: Judge Sobeloff's Public School Race Decisions," 34 *Md. L. Rev.* 498 (1974).

22. "Remembering the Fourth Circuit Judges," 510–514.

23. Judge Sobeloff's opinion in *Swann,* concurring in part and dissenting in part and joined by Judge Winter, is found at 431 F.2d 138, 148–155 (4th Cir. 1970).

24. William O. Douglas, "Tribute to Simon E. Sobeloff," 34 *Md. L. Rev.* 484, 484 (1974).

25. Abel J. Merrill, "Biographical Sketch" (in "Tribute to Simon E. Sobeloff"), 34 Md. L. Rev. 491, 493 (citing Theodore R. McKeldin).

26. "Remembering the Fourth Circuit Judges," 482.

27. Ibid. at 484.

28. 141 Cong. Rec. No. 141, pp. E1762–1763 (September 12, 1995) (naming a federal courthouse in honor of Judge Bryan).

29. Judge Sobeloff, letter to Bernard G. Segal of the ABA, General Correspondence, Bryan, Albert V., July 5, 1961, Box 9, 1958–1972, Simon E. Sobeloff Papers, Manuscript Division, Library of Congress, Washington, D.C.

30. The court of appeals generally recorded oral argument at the time *Griggs* was argued, but the disc of that argument, which I requested from the clerk of court, could not be located.

31. Judge Boreman, memo to Judges Sobeloff and Bryan, October 2, 1969, Sobeloff Papers.

32. Chief Judge Clement Haynsworth, Jr., memo to all of the circuit judges, November 13, 1969, Sobeloff Papers.

33. Chief Judge Haynsworth, Jr., memo to all of the circuit judges, April 17, 1969, Sobeloff Papers.

34. Judge Boreman, memo to Chief Judge Haynsworth and other circuit court judges, April 21, 1969, Sobeloff Papers.

35. Judge Boreman, memo to Judges Sobeloff and Bryan, October 2, 1969, Sobeloff Papers.

36. Judge Bryan, memo to Judges Boreman and Sobeloff, October 3, 1969, Sobeloff Papers.

37. Judge Sobeloff, memo to Judges Boreman and Bryan, October 22, 1969, Sobeloff Papers.

38. Judge Boreman, memo to Judges Sobeloff and Bryan, October 22, 1969, Sobeloff Papers.

39. Judge Boreman, memo to circuit judges, November 13, 1969, Sobeloff Papers.

40. Judge Sobeloff, memo to Judge Boreman, November 14, 1969, Sobeloff Papers.

41. Judge Butzner, memo to Judge Boreman and other circuit judges, November 14, 1969, Sobeloff Papers.

42. Robert Belton, letter to Samuel Phillips, clerk of the court of appeals, August 4, 1969, Sobeloff Papers.

43. *Griggs v. Duke Power Co.,* 420 F.2d at 1237, n. 2, and 1239 n 6.

44. The events surrounding the furor among the judges in the Fifth Circuit in connection with the citation of the Cooper and Sobol article in *Local 189* are recounted and documented in Joel William Friedman, *Champion of Civil Rights: Judge John Minor Wisdom* (Baton Rouge, La.: LSU Press, 2009), 135–138.

45. William F. Gardner, "The Development of the Substantive Principles of Title VII Law: The Defendant's View," 26 *Ala. L. Rev.* 1, 2–3 (1973).

46. Judge Sobeloff, memo to circuit judges, November 21, 1969, Sobeloff Papers.

47. Judge Bryan, memo to Judge Soboleff and circuit judges, November 23, 1969, Sobeloff Papers.

48. Judge Butzner, memo to circuit judges, November 24, 1969, Sobeloff Papers.

49. Judge Butzner, memo to circuit judges, December 9, 1969, Sobeloff Papers.

50. Judge Butzner, letter to Judge Sobeloff, November 19, 1969, Sobeloff Papers.

51. Judge Craven, memo to circuit judges, November 25, 1969, Sobeloff Papers.

52. Judge Winter, memo to circuit judges, November 28, 1969, Sobeloff Papers.

53. Chief Judge Haynsworth, memo to circuit judges, December 5, 1969, Sobeloff Papers.

54. Judge Boreman, memo to circuit judges, November 26, 1969, Sobeloff Papers.

55. Judge Sobeloff, memo to Judges Boreman and Bryan and circuit judges, Sobeloff Papers.

56. 420 F.2d 1225, 1230 (4th Cir. 1970).

57. Ibid. at 1231.

58. Ibid. at 1232 and n. 2.

59. Ibid. at 1235–1236.

60. Ibid. at 1229.

61. Ibid. at 1237–1238 (Sobeloff, J., concurring in part, and dissenting, in part).

62. Ibid. at 1238 (original emphasis).

63. Ibid. at 1246.

64. Ibid.

CHAPTER NINE. *GRIGGS* IN THE SUPREME COURT

1. Interview with William Robinson.

2. 422 U.S. 405 (1975).

3. George Cooper, letter to Jack Greenberg, reprinted in George Cooper and Harriet Rabb, *Equal Employment Law and Litigation: Materials for a Clinical Law Course* (1972), 497–499.

4. The story of the Pemberton letter is reported in Hugh Davis Graham, *The Civil Rights Era: Origin and Development of National Policy* (New York: Oxford University Press, 1990), 385.

5. Michael Meltsner and Philip G. Schrag, *Public Interest Advocacy: Materials for Clinical Education* (St. Paul, Minn.: West Publishing, 1974), 78.

6. Robert Belton, "A Comparative Review of Public and Private Enforcement of Title VII of the Civil Rights Act of 1974," 31 *Vand. L. Rev.* 905, 941–943 (1978).

7. Jack Greenberg, *Crusaders in the Courts: How a Dedicated Band of Lawyers Fought for the Civil Rights Revolution* (New York: Basic Books, 1994), 419.

8. This paragraph is based on Brief for Respondent in Opposition, *Griggs v. Duke Power Co.*, 401 U.S. 424 (1971), at 4–6, 13–15.

9. Bernard Kleiman, general counsel of the Steelworkers, letter to Jack Greenberg, February 12, 1970, seeking the LDF's consent to file an amicus brief urging that certiorari be granted; Jack Greenberg, letter to Michael H. Gottesman, March 11, 1970, consenting to the Steelworkers' request.

10. Motion of United Steelworkers of America, AFL-CIO for Leave to File Brief Amicus Curiae and Brief for United States Steelworkers of America, at 2, *Griggs v. Duke Power Co.*, 401 U.S. 424 (1971).

11. Ibid.

12. Gregory A. Caldeira and John R. Wright, "The Discuss List: Agenda Building in the Supreme Court," 24 *Law & Soc'y Rev.* 807, 810 (1990).

13. In 1950, Chief Justice Vinson ceased circulating the "dead list" and replaced it with the current "discuss list" practice. Artemus Ward and David L. Weiden, *Sorcerer's Apprentices: 100 Years of Law Clerks at the United States Supreme Court* (New York: New York University Press, 2006).

14. Justice John Paul Stevens gave this brief history on the past and current practice of the conferences in the fifteenth James Madison Lecture on Constitutional Law at New York University School of law, October 27, 1982, subsequently published.

John Paul Stevens, "The Life Span of a Judge-Made Rule," 58 *N.Y.U. L. Rev.* 1, 13 (1983).

15. But *see* Justice Brennan, memo to Chief Justice Burger, *Re No. 1405, Griggs v. Duke Power Co.,* Justice William Brennan Papers, Box I-200, Folder 4, Case File, O.T. 1969, Administrative File, Conference File, Library of Congress, Manuscript Division, Washington, D.C.; Bob Woodward and Scott Armstrong, *The Brethren: Inside the Supreme Court* (New York: Simon & Schuster, 1979), 122. The story of the reason Justice Brennan recused himself in *Griggs* is also reported in Paul Moreno, *From Direct Action to Affirmative Action: Fair Employment Law and Policy in America, 1933–1972* (Baton Rouge, La.: LSU Press, 1977), 276 n. 15. Neither of the authors cites supporting documentation of the reason.

16. Justice Stewart, memo to the Conference of May 21, 1970, Re No. 1405 [later changed to No. 124], Brennan Papers.

17. Special List, Conference—May 22, 1970, Petitions for Certiorari, May 20, 1970, Box 1452, Conference List, April, May, June, O.T. 1969, Justice William O. Douglas Papers, Library of Congress, Manuscript Division, Washington, D.C.

18. *Griggs v. Duke Power Co.,* 398 U.S. 926 (1970).

19. *See* Michael J. Bailey and Forrest Maltzman, "Inter-branch Communication: When Does the Court Solicit Executive Branch Views?," 3 n. 1, paper presented to Midwest Political Science Association, Chicago, Ill., 2005.

20. Greenberg, *Crusaders in the Courts,* 66.

21. Brief of the United States as Amicus in Support of Petition for Certiorari at 8, *Griggs.*

22. Ibid.

23. Law clerk, memo to Justice William O. Douglas, n.d.

24. Box 1453, Supreme Court Files, Case File, Oct. 1969, Administrative File, Docket 1400–1599, Douglas Papers. *Griggs* was originally assigned the number 1405 when the petition for certiorari was filed, but that was later changed to No. 124.

25. Brief for Petitioner, 20, *Griggs,* 401 U.S. 424 (1971).

26. Ibid., 11–12.

27. 42 U.S.C. § 2000e-5(g).

28. Brief for Petitioner, 28 n. 26, *Griggs,* 401 U.S. 424 (1971).

29. Ibid., 46–47.

30. Ibid., 46–50.

31. 5 Fed. Reg. 12222, 29 U.S.C. § 1607.1 et seq. (1970).

32. Brief for Petitioner, 23, *Griggs,* 401 U.S. 424 (1971).

33. Brief for the United States as Amicus Curiae, 12, *Griggs,* 401 U.S. 424 (1971).

34. Ibid., 21–30.

35. Motion of the United Steelworkers of America, AFL-CIO for Leave to File Amicus Curiae and Brief, 5, *Griggs,* 401 U.S. 424 (1971).

36. Brief of the Attorney General of the State of New York as Amicus Curiae in Support of Reversal, 2, 4, *Griggs,* 401 U.S. 424 (1971).

37. Brief for Respondent, 9–10, 12, 43, *Griggs,* 401 U.S. 424 (1971).

38. Ibid., 24–25.

39. Ibid., 37.

40. Brief Amicus Curiae on Behalf of the Chamber of Commerce of the United States of America, 2–3, *Griggs*, 401 U.S. 424 (1971).

41. The case where this argument bore fruit was *Wards Cove Packing Co., Inc. v. Atonio*, 490 U.S. 642 (1989).

42. Brief Amicus Curiae on Behalf of the Chambers of Commerce of the United States, 709, *Griggs*, 401 U.S. 424 (1971).

43. Order entered on October 19, 1970, *Griggs v. Duke Power Co.*, 401 U.S. 424 (1971).

44. Transcript of the oral argument, December 14, 1970, *Griggs*, 401 U.S. 424 (1971).

45. Ibid.

46. Conference notes of J. Douglas, Box 1490, Supreme Court Files, O.T. 1970, Argued Cases, 109–124, Douglas Papers. I am indebted to Del Dickson, editor of *The Supreme Court in Conference (1940–1985): The Private Discussions behind Nearly 300 Supreme Court Decisions* (New York: Oxford University Press, 2001), 732, for deciphering and editing J. Douglas's conference notes in *Griggs*.

47. Linda Greenhouse, *Becoming Justice Blackmun* (New York: Henry Holt, 2006), 31.

48. Justice Blackmun's preargument memo, dated December 14, 1970 (*Griggs v. Duke Power Co.*, No. 124), Justice Harry A. Blackmun Papers, Manuscript Division, Library of Congress, Washington, D.C., Box 125, Folder 10.

49. Harry A. Blackmun conference notes (*Griggs v. Duke Power Co.*, No. 124), Blackmun Papers.

50. As others who have reviewed Justice Blackmun's papers have observed, Justice Blackmun used extensive and idiosyncratic abbreviations. As a mathematics major at Harvard University, Justice Blackmun used mathematical symbols in his notes. For example, "-" means reverse, and "+" means affirm. In attempting to decipher Justice Blackmun's notes in *Griggs* and other cases discussed, I have also followed the convention used by others in reporting on those notes whenever I have felt comfortable that I have correctly understood or interpreted his abbreviations. Ellen Deason, "Perspectives on Decisionmaking from the Blackmun Papers: The Cases on Arbitrability of Statutory Claims," 70 *Mo. L. Rev.* 1133, 1147 n. 72 (2005).

51. The actual note reads "Er hs t B/P," which seems to translate to "employer had the burden of proof." Harry A. Blackmun conference notes (*Griggs v. Duke Power Co.*, No. 124), Blackmun Papers.

52. *See* draft of January 26, 1971, by Chief Justice Burger (*Griggs v. Duke Power Co.*, No. 124), Blackmun Papers. *Griggs v. Duke Power*, 401 U.S. 424, 429 n. 5 (1971).

53. Docket Sheet for *Griggs v. Duke Power Co.*, Box I-228, Folder 4, Case File, Administrative File, Brennan Papers.

54. Chief Justice Burger's first draft of the opinion, dated January 26, 1971, Blackmun Papers.

55. Justice White, memo to Chief Justice Burger, January 28, 1971; Justice Marshall, memo to Chief Justice Burger, February 18, 1971, Blackmun Papers.

56. Justice Stewart, memo to Chief Justice Burger, January 28, 1971, Blackmun Papers.

57. Transcript of oral argument, *Griggs*, 401 U.S. 424 (1971).

58. Chief Justice Burger's January 26, 1971, draft opinion in *Griggs* (*Griggs v. Duke Power Co.*, No. 124), Blackmun Papers.

59. *Griggs*, 401 U.S. 424, 431 (1971).

60. Justice Harlan, memo to Chief Justice Burger, February 1, 1971, Blackmun Papers.

61. Law clerk, memo to Justice Blackmun, January 26, 1971, Blackmun Papers.

62. Law clerk, memo to Justice Blackmun, January 16, 1971, Blackmun Papers.

63. *Griggs*, 401 U.S. 424, 443 n. 11, and 436 n. 12 (1971).

64. Justice Blackman, memo to Chief Justice Burger, February 10, 1971, Blackmun Papers.

65. *Griggs*, 401 U.S. 424, 431 (1971).

66. Ibid. at 432 (original emphasis).

67. Brief for Petitioners at 11, 25, *Griggs v. Duke Power Co.*, 401 U.S. 424 (1971).

68. *Griggs*, 401 U.S. 424, 430 (1971).

69. Brief for Petitioner at 19, *Griggs*, 401 U.S. 424 (1971).

70. Ibid. at 20–21.

71. *Griggs*, 401 U.S. 424, 431 (1971).

72. 411 U.S. 792, 805 (1973).

73. S. Report No. 415, 92d Cong., 1st Sess. 5 (1971), *cited with approval in Franks v. Bowman Transp. Co.*, 424 U.S. 747, 764 n. 21 (1976).

74. *Griggs* is analyzed from the perspective of the EEOC in Alfred W. Blumrosen, "Strangers in Paradise: *Griggs v. Duke Power Co.* and the Concept of Discrimination," 71 *Mich. L. Rev.* 59 (1972).

75. Woodward and Armstrong, *The Brethren*, 122–123. Another liberal decision that Chief Justice Burger authored is *Swann v. Charlotte Mecklenberg Board of Education*, 402 U.S. 1 (1971), which the Court decided a few months after *Griggs*.

76. Brad Snyder, "How the Conservatives Canonized *Brown v. Board of Education*," 52 *Rutgers L. Rev.* 383, 419–420, 419 n. 215 (1999).

77. Marcia Coyle, "Age Bias Suits at a Crossroad," *National Law Journal*, March 13, 2002 (quoting Professor Craver).

78. Judge Sobeloff, letter to Thomas Ashe Lockhart, July 27, 1971, *Robinson v. Lorillard* file, Sobeloff Papers, Library of Congress, Washington, D.C.

CHAPTER TEN. THE MATURATION OF THE *GRIGGS* THEORY

1. Stanley Klein, "Job Testing Comes under Fire," *N.Y. Times*, September 19, 1971, F5.

2. Chris Lee, "Testing Makes a Comeback," 25 *Training* 49 (December 1988).

3. William C. Byham and Morton Edward Spitzer, *The Law and Personnel Testing* (New York: American Management Association, 1971).

4. Donald J. Petersen, "The Impact of Duke Power on Testing," 51 *Personnel* 30 (March/April 1974).

5. Ruth G. Schaeffer, *Nondiscrimination in Employment: Changing Perspectives, 1963–1972,* at 20–29 (Conference Board Report No. 589 (1973) (documenting employers' reaction to *Griggs*).

6. Lee, "Testing Makes a Comeback," 52.

7. *See Equal Employment Opportunities Enforcement Act of 1971: Hearings on S. 2515, S. 2617, H.R. 1746 before the Senate Subcommittee of the Committee on Labor and Public Welfare,* 92d Cong., 2nd Sess., 243–258 (1971) (statement of Jack Greenberg, Director-Counsel, NAACP Legal Defense and Educational Fund, Inc., including list of LDF employment discrimination cases).

8. *Pettway v. American Cast Iron Pipe Co.,* 411 F.2d 998, 1005 (5th Cir. 1969).

9. *See* William B. Gould, *Black Workers in White Unions: Job Discrimination in the United States* (Ithaca, N.Y.: Cornell University Press, 1977), 35–38.

10. Other LDF attorneys who worked on employment discrimination cases during the early post-*Griggs* years included Lowell Johnston, Sylvia Drew Ivey, Vilma Martinez Singer, Elizabeth Bartholet, Charles Stephen Ralston, Franklin White, William Bennett Turner, Charles Donegan, and Eric Schnapper.

11. The Law Student Civil Rights Research Council was the first multiracial law student-run organization in the United States, founded in 1963 by northern law students who traveled south to work with civil rights lawyers supporting the civil rights movement. Over its twenty-four-year history, 5,000 law students have participated in LSCRRC's summer intern program.

12. *United States v. United States Steel Corp.,* 520 F.2d 1043 (5th Cir. 1975), *cert. denied,* 429 U.S. 817 (1976); *Ford v. United States Steel Corp.,* 638 F.2d 753 (5th Cir. 1981); *Crawford v. United States Steel Corp.,* 660 F.2d 663 (5th Cir. 1981).

13. Interview with Barry Goldstein; Brief for Plaintiffs-Appellants, *Ford v. United States Steel Corp.* at 6, No. 73-3907, consolidated with *United States v. United Steel Corp.,* 520 F.2d 1043 (1975), *cert. denied,* 429 U.S. 817.

14. *Kraszewski v. State Farm,* 1993 WL 19915 (N.D. Fla. 1993) ($240 million); *Haynes v. Shoney's, Inc.,* 1993 WL 19915 (N.D. Fla. 1993) ($135 million); *Butler v. Home Depot, Inc.,* C.A. No. C-94-4335 SI, (N.D. Cal., order entered January 14, 1998) ($87 million); *Shore v. Public Super Markets, Inc.,* No. C-92-1883 SBA (N.D. Cal.) ($81 million); *Rice v. Southern California Edison* ($18 million) and *Babbitt v. Albertson's, Inc.,* C.A. No. 92-1883 SBA (N.D. Cal. order entered October 12, 1994) ($29 million); *Weddington v. Ingles Markets, Inc.* ($16 million). For a book about the *Shoney* case, *see* Steve Watkins, *The Black O: Racism and Redemption in an American Corporate Empire* (Athens: University of Georgia Press, 1997). Barry first joined the firm of Saperstein and Seligman in Oakland, California. That firm eventually became Goldstein, Demchak, Borgen, and Dardarian.

15. The Reginald Heber Smith Community Lawyer Fellowship program began in the Office of Economic Opportunity, President Johnson's War on Poverty initiative, and was continued by the Legal Services Corporation. "Reggies" were promising

young lawyers who received fellowships to work for a year or two in legal services offices throughout the nation to provide legal services for the poor as part of the War
on Poverty.

16. Jack Greenberg, *Crusaders in the Courts: How a Dedicated Band of Lawyers
Fought for the Civil Rights Revolution* (New York: Basic Books, 1994), 48–50, 371–372.

17. Supreme Court Justice Clarence Thomas worked as a summer clerk in the Hill,
Jones, and Farrington firm after his second year at Yale Law School. Andrew Peyton
Thomas, "Clarence Thomas: The Law School Years," 35 *Journal of Blacks in Higher Edu-
cation* 106, 111–113 (Spring 2002).

18. *See* Elizabeth Bartholet, "Application of Title VII to Jobs in High Places," 95
Harv. L. Rev. 947 (1982).

19. 457 F.2d 348, 359 (5th Cir. 1972).

20. The LDF cases included *James v. Stockham Valves & Fittings, Inc.,* 559 F.2d 310
(5th Cir.1977), *cert. denied,* 434 U.S. 1034 (1978); *Robinson v. Union Carbide Corp.,* 538
F.2d 652 (5th Cir. 1976), *cert. denied,* 434 U.S. 822 (1977); *Watkins v. Scott Paper Co.,* 530
U.S. 1159 (5th Cir. 1976), *cert. denied,* 429 U.S. 861 (1976); *Pettway v. American Cast Iron
Pipe Co.,* 494 F.2d 211 (5th Cir. 1974); *Young v. Edgcomb Steel Co.,* 499 F.2d 97 (4th Cir.
1974); *Baxter v. Savannah Sugar Refining Corp.,* 495 F.2d 437 (5th Cir.), *cert. denied,* 419
U.S. 1033 (1974); *Brown v. Gaston County Dyeing Mach. Co.,* 457 F.2d 1377 (4th Cir.),
cert. denied, 409 U.S. 982 (1972).

21. *Shidakar v. Carlin,* 782 F.2d 746 (7th Cir. 1986), *cert. denied sum nom. Tisch v.
Shidakar,* 481 U.S. 1001 (1987). *See* Petition for Writ of Certiorari filed by the Solicitor
General, *Tisch v. Shidakar,* 481 U.S. 1001 (1987) (No. 86-468).

22. *Watson v. Fort Worth Bank & Trust,* 798 F.2d 791, 812 n. 25 (5th Cir. 1986).

23. *Watson v. Fort Worth Bank & Trust,* 487 U.S. 977 (1988).

24. Brief of the United States as Amicus Curiae supporting the employers.

25. Brief for the American Personnel Administration of the International Personnel Management Association and the Employment Management Association as Amicus Curiae Supporting Petitioner, *Watson v. Fort Worth Bank & Trust* 487 U.S. 977
(1988).

26. *See* Brief for Amicus Curiae, The Merchants and Manufacturers Association in
Support of Respondent, *Watson v. Fort Worth Bank & Trust,* 487 U.S. 977 (1988).

27. Brief Amicus Curiae of the Equal Employment Advisory Council in Support of
Respondent, *Watson v. Fort Worth Bank & Trust,* 487 U.S. 977 (1988).

28. Brief for the NAACP Legal Defense and Educational Fund, Inc., the Mexican
American Legal Defense and Educational Fund, Inc., the Employment Law Center,
and the Center for Law in the Public Interest, *Watson v. Fort Worth Bank & Trust,* 487
U.S. 977 (1988).

29. Robert Belton, "Reflections on Affirmative Action after *Paradise* and *Johnson,*"
23 *Harv. C.R.-C.L. Rev.* 115, 130–131 (1988).

30. *Watson,* 487 U.S. at 989, 990.

31. Ibid.

32. *Griggs,* 401 U.S. at 432.

33. Robert Belton, "Burdens of Pleading and Proof in Discrimination Cases: Toward a Theory of Procedural Justice," 34 *Vand. L. Rev.* 1205 (1981).

34. Interview with William Robinson.

35. *McDonnell Douglas Corp. v. Green,* 411 U.S. 792, 793, 802–805 (1973).

36. *See* comments of the Honorable Myron H. Bright, "In Memoriam: Judge Donald P. Lay," 92 *Iowa L. Rev.* 1551, 1555 (2007) (Judge Bright was the author of the court of appeals decision in *McDonnell Douglas* and noted in his comments that the proof scheme the Supreme Court had adopted had been cited in approximately 27,000 cases).

37. *Moody,* 422 U.S. 405, 425 (1975).

38. 401 U.S. at 432.

39. 42 U.S.C. § 2000e-2(j). This section also extends to employment agencies and labor unions.

40. The legislative history of Section 703(j) is recounted in *Local 28, Sheet Metal Workers International Assoc. v. EEOC,* 478 U.S. 421, 452–465 (1986).

41. Hugh Davis Graham, *The Civil Rights Era: The Origin and Development of National Policy* (New York: Oxford University Press, 1990), 247 (emphasis supplied). Many besides Davis have advanced the argument that Section 703(j) bars or limits the use of statistical evidence to prove claims of employment discrimination. *See* Michael E. Gold, "*Griggs* Folly: An Essay on Theory, Problems, and Origin of Adverse Impact Definition of Employment Discrimination and a Recommendation for Reform," 7 *Indus. Rel. L.J.* 429 (1985).

42. Brief for Appellee at 13, *Brown v. Gaston County Dyeing Mach. Co.,* 457 F.2d 1377 (4th Cir.), *cert. denied,* 409 U.S. 982 (1972).

43. *Pettway v. American Cast Iron Pipe Co.,* 494 F.2d 211, 218 n. 10, 220 n. 16 (5th Cir. 1974).

44. *See* David Copus, "The Numbers Game Is the Only Game in Town," 20 *How. L. Rev.* 374 (1977).

45. *Alabama v. United States,* 304 F.2d 583, 586 (5th Cir. 1962), *aff'd per curiam,* 371 U.S. 37 (1962).

46. *See Pettway v. American Cast Iron Pipe Co.,* 494 F.2d 211, 225 n. 34 (5th Cir. 1974) (collecting case). Many of the cases cited in *Pettway,* like *Pettway* itself, were some of the early cases litigated by the litigation team, *e.g., Johnson v. Goodyear Tire & Rubber Co.,* 491 F.2d 1364 (5th Cir. 1974); *Rowe v. General Motors Corp.,* 457 F.2d 348 (5th Cir. 1972); *Brown v. Gaston County Dyeing Mach. Co.,* 457 F.2d 1377 (4th Cir.), *cert. denied,* 409 U.S. 982 (1972); *Parham v. Southwestern Bell Tel. Co.,* 433 F.2d 421, 426 (8th Cir. 1970) (holding that, as a matter of law, the statistics, which revealed an extraordinarily small number of black employees, except for the most part menial laborers, established a violation of Title VII).

47. Brief for Petitioner at 22, *McDonnell Douglas Corp. v. Green,* 411 U.S. 792 (1973).

48. Ibid. at 8–9.

49. 411 U.S. 792, 805 (1973).

50. 431 U.S. 324, 339 (1977).

51. *See* Brief Amicus of the Equal Employment Opportunity Council, *Teamsters v. United States,* 431 U.S. 324, 339 n. 20 (1977).

52. 431 U.S. at 339.

53. Ibid. at 339, n. 20. The Court cited some of the leading cases litigated by the LDF. *E.g., Pettway v. American Case Iron Pipe Co.,* 494 F., 2d 211 (5th Cir. 1974); *Brown v. Gaston County Dyeing Mach. Co.,* 457 F.2d 1377 (4th Cir. 1972); *Parham v. Southwestern Bell Tel. Co.,* 433 F.2d 421 (8th Cir. 1970), all of which were cutting-edge cases.

54. *Teamsters,* 431 U.S. at 340.

55. 433 U.S. 299, 313 (1977) (Brennan, J., concurring).

56. *See* remarks of Thompson Power presented at the Proceeding of the Thirty-Seventh Annual Judicial Conference of the District of Columbia at the panel on discrimination in employment held on May 29, 1976, and reprinted in 73 F.R.D. 213 (1977) (commenting that many employers, as of that date, had not recognized that laws prohibiting discrimination in employment and particularly Title VII represented the most significant challenge to management discretion in employment practices since the rise of labor unions).

57. *Equal Opportunity Law: Defending Fair Employment Cases,* Vol. 1976, No. 10 (Chicago: Defense Research Institute, Inc., 1976).

58. Greenberg, *Crusaders in the Courts,* at 420–421.

59. 29 C.F.R. §§ 1607.16Q, 1607.28.

60. *See* Herbert Hill, "The New Judicial Perception of Employment Discrimination—Litigation under Title VII of the Civil Rights Act of 1964," 45 *Colo. L. Rev.* 243, 246 (1972); Alfred W. Blumrosen, "Strangers in Paradise: *Griggs v. Duke Power Co.* and the Concept of Employment Discrimination," 71 *Mich. L. Rev.* 59 (1972).

61. Other LDF cases involving the pulp and paper industry included *Gatlin v. West Virginia Pulp and Paper Co.,* 734 F.2d 980 (4th Cir. 1984); *Jones v. International Paper Co.,* 720 F.2d 496 (8th Cir. 1983); *Myers v. Gilman Paper Corp.,* 544 F.2d 837 (5th Cir. 1977); *Watkins v. Scott Paper Co.,* 530 F.2d 1159 (5th Cir. 1976); *Rogers v. International Paper Co.,* 510 F.2d 1340 (8th Cir. 1975), *vacated and remanded in light of Albemarle Paper Co. v. Moody,* 423 U.S. 809 (1975); *Stevenson v. International Paper Co.,* 516 F.2d 103 (5th Cir. 1975); *Long v. Georgia Kraft Co.,* 450 F.2d 557 (5th Cir. 1971); *Powell v. Georgia Pacific Corp.,* 535 F. Supp. 713 (W.D. Ark. 1982); *Miller v. Continental Can Co.,* 544 F. Supp. 210, 211 n. 2 (S.D. Ga. 1981) (noting long history of employment discrimination litigation involving the paper industry).

62. Timothy J. Minchin, *The Color of Work: The Struggle for Civil Rights in the Southern Paper Industry, 1945–1980* (Chapel Hill: University of North Carolina Press, 2001), 109–110.

63. Stipulation of Facts, Nos. 9 and 10, Appendix, Vol. II, 88–89, *Albemarle Paper Co. v. Moody,* 422 U.S. 405 (1975).

64. Stipulation of Facts, No. 23, Appendix Vol. I, 100, *Albemarle Paper Co. v. Moody.*

65. EEOC Guidelines on Employee Selection Procedures, 29 C.F.R. § 1607.5(b)(5).

66. *See* Stipulations of Facts, Appendix, Vol. I, 101–104, *Albemarle Paper Co. v. Moody.*

67. *See* Herbert Northrup, *The Negro in the Tobacco Industry, Report No. 13,*

Industrial Research Unit, Wharton School of Finance and Commerce, University of Pennsylvania, 73–74 (1970) (citing files in Northrup's possession from the New Jersey Division Against Discrimination).

68. Joseph L. Mosnier, "Crafting Law in the Second Reconstruction: Julius Chambers, the NAACP Legal Defense Fund, and Title VII" at 104 (2004) (unpublished Ph.D. dissertation) (on file at the University of North Carolina, Chapel Hill) (citing author's interview with Judge Gordon, "Settle Troubles, Judge Tells Lorillard Union," *Greensboro News and Record,* October 17, 1968; and "Judge Urges Lawyers Not to Go to Court," *Greensboro News and Record,* October 17, 1968).

69. Adam Stein, letter to Judge Gordon, January 13, 1970; *Robinson v. Lorillard Corp.,* 319 F. Supp. 835, 840 (M.D.N.C. 1970), *rev'd on other grounds,* 444 F.2d 791 (4th Cir. 1971), *cert. dismissed,* 444 U.S. 1006 (1971).

70. *Robinson v. Lorillard Corp.,* 319 F. Supp. 835, 840 (M.D.N.C. 1970), citing *Griggs v. Duke Power Co.,* 420 F.2d 1225 (4th Cir. 1970); *United States by Clark v. Local 189, etc.,* 282 F. Supp. 39 (E.D. La. 1968); *Quarles v. Philip Morris, Inc.,* 279 F. Supp. 505 (E.D. Va. 1968), *rev'd on other grounds,* 444 F.2d 791 (4th Cir. 1971), *cert. dismissed,* 404 U.S. 1006 (1971).

71. George Cooper, letter to Bill Robinson, April 27, 1970.

72. Brief for Lorillard Corp. at 49, *Robinson v. Lorillard Corp.,* 444 F.2d 791 (4th Cir. 1971), *cert. denied,* 404 U.S. 1006 (1971).

73. Judge Butzner, letter to Judge Sobeloff, June 22, 1971, Simon E. Sobeloff Papers, Box 104, Manuscript Division, Library of Congress, Washington, D.C.

74. Judge Bryan, letters to Judge Sobeloff, June 28 and 29, 1971, Sobeloff Papers.

75. *Robinson v. Lorillard Corp.,* 444 F.2d 791, 798 (4th Cir.), *cert. dismissed,* 404 U.S. 1006 (1971). Subsequently, in the wake of later Supreme Court decisions on the business necessity test, some courts began to retreat from a strict *Robinson* test of business necessity. *See, e.g., Contreras v. City of Los Angeles,* 656 F.2d 1267 (9th Cir. 1981), *cert. denied,* 455 U.S. 1021 (1982).

76. *Robinson v. Lorillard,* 444 F.2d 791, 798–800 (4th Cir.), *cert. dismissed,* 404 U.S. 1006 (1971).

77. *Pettway v. American Cast Iron Pipe Co.,* 494 F.2d 211, 246, 246 n. 92 (5th Cir. 1974) (citing *Robinson v. Lorillard,* 444 F.2d 791, 799–800 (4th Cir.), *cert. dismissed,* 404 U.S. 1006 (1971)).

78. *Bethlehem Steel,* 446 F.2d at 662.

79. Judge Sobeloff, letter to Judge Feinberg, June 30, 1971, Sobeloff Papers.

80. Judge Feinberg, letter to Judge Sobeloff, July 6, 1971, Sobeloff Papers.

81. *Robinson v. Lorillard Corp.,* 444 F.2d 791, 800 n. 10a (4th Cir.), *cert. dismissed,* 404 U.S. 1006 (1971).

82. Judge Sobeloff, letter to Judges Bryan and Butzner, June 25, 1971, Sobeloff Papers.

83. John Edwards and John Auchard, *Four Trials* (New York: Simon & Schuster, 2004), 10, 11. Edwards, who had clerked for Judge Dupree during 1977–1978, was the Democratic vice-presidential nominee in the 2004 presidential election, and was a Democratic presidential candidate in the 2008 election.

84. Comments of Julius L. Chambers, *Celebrating the 40th Anniversary of Title VII, Panel 1, First Principles: Enacting the Civil Rights Act and Using the Courts to Challenge and Remedy Workplace Discrimination,* http//www.eeoc.gov/abouteeoc/40 /panel/40thpanels/panel1/transcript.html.

85. Appendix, Vol. I, 2–3, Chronological List of Relevant Docket Entries, *Albemarle Paper Co. v. Moody,* 422 U.S. 405 (1975) (Nos. 74-389 & 74-428).

86. *Moody v. Albemarle Paper Co.,* 4 FEP Cases (BNA) 561 (E.D.N.C. 1971).

87. Appendix, Vol. I, 114–115, *Albemarle Paper Co. v. Moody,* 422 U.S. 405 (1975).

88. Portions of Drs. Tiffin's and Barrett's testimony are reproduced in Appendix, Vol. 1, 160–185, 196–211, *Albemarle Paper Co. v. Moody,* 422 U.S. 405 (1975) (Nos. 74-389 & 74-428).

89. 4 FEP Cases (BNA) 56 (E.D.N.C. 1971).

90. *Moody v. Albemarle Paper Co.,* 4 FEP Cases (BNA) 570 (E.D.N.C. 1971).

91. E. F. Wonderlic & Associates, Inc., *Negro Norms: A Study of 38,452 Job Applicants for Affirmative Action Programs,* 3 (1972). The court of appeals cited the Wonderlic Study in its opinion. *Moody,* 474 F.2d 134, 138 n. 1 (4th Cir. 1973).

92. Robert Belton, letter to the clerk of the court of appeals. *See* Docket Sheet, *Moody v. Albemarle Paper Co.,* 474 F.2d 134 (4th Cir. 1973).

93. *Moody,* 474 F.2d 134, 138 n. 1 (4th Cir. 1973).

94. *James v. Stockham Valves & Fittings Co.,* 559 F.2d 310, 335 (5th Cir. 1977), *cert. denied,* 434 U.S. 1034 (1978); *Young v. Edgcomb Steel Co.,* 363 F. Supp. 961 (M.D.N.C. 1973), *rev'd on other grounds,* 499 F.2d. 97 (4th Cir. 1974).

95. 474 F.2d 134 (4th Cir. 1973).

96. Ibid., 138.

97. Ibid., 139.

98. Box 1678, Supreme Court File, Case File, O.T. 1974, Argued Cases, 74-363 to 74-389, Justice William O. Douglas Papers, Manuscript Division, Library of Congress, Washington, D.C.

99. Brief of Employer at 28–31, *Albemarle Paper Co. v. Moody,* 422 U.S. 405 (1975).

100. Ibid., 41 and n. 42.

101. Brief of the American Society for Personnel Administration as Amicus Curiae at 28–30, *Albemarle Paper Co. v. Moody,* 422 U.S. 405 (1975) (Nos. 74-389 & 74-428).

102. In a later Title VII case involving the issue of the legality of voluntarily adopted affirmative action plans, the Court recognized that numerous judicial findings of racial discrimination in some instances are a proper subject for judicial notice. *Steelworkers v. Weber,* 443 U.S. 193, 198 n. 1 (1978).

103. Transcript of the oral agreement of Frank Lowden on behalf of Albemarle, *Albemarle Paper Co. v. Moody,* 422 U.S. 405.

104. Notes from the Conference of April 28, 1975, Justice William Brennan Papers, Box I-335, Folder 10, Case File, O.T. 1974, Administrative File, Assignments, Manuscript Division, Library of Congress, Washington, D.C.

105. *Moody,* 422 U.S. at 431 (citing the EEOC Guidelines, 29 CFR § 1607.4 (c)).

106. Ibid. at 433.

107. Ibid. at 433 n. 32.

CHAPTER ELEVEN. MAKE WHOLE REMEDIES

1. Robert Belton, *Remedies in Employment Discrimination Law* (New York: Wolters Kluwer, 1992), ix.

2. 422 U.S. 405, 418 (1975).

3. *United States v. Burke*, 504 U.S. 229, 239 (1992).

4. Pub. L. No. 102-166, 105 Stat. 1073 (1991), codified at 42 U.S.C. § 1981a.

5. Reginald C. Govan, "Honorable Compromises and the Moral High Ground: The Conflict between the Rhetoric and the Content of the Civil Rights Act of 1991," 46 *Rutgers L. Rev.* 1, 35–36 (1993).

6. S. Rep. No. 92-415, p. 5 (1971); *Franks*, 424 U.S. at 764.

7. *See Robinson v. Lorillard Corp.*, 319 F.2d 835 (M.D.N.C. 1970) (class exceeded 200 members).

8. Belton, *Remedies in Employment Discrimination Law*, §§ 4.4–4.5.

9. *See United States v. United States Steel Corp.*, 520 F.2d 1043, 1053–1054 (5th Cir. 1975); *Baxter v. Savannah Sugar Refining Corp.*, 495 F.2d 437, 443–444 (5th Cir. 1974).

10. *Ellison v. Rock Hill Printing and Finishing Co.*, 64 F.R.D. 415, 419 (D.S.C. 1974). The court in *Ellison* specifically cited the LDF's case of *Robinson v. Lorillard Corp.*, 444 F.2d 791 (4th Cir. 1971), *cert. dismissed*, 404 U.S. 1006 (1971), a case that was settled with the assistance of Senator Edward Brooke of Massachusetts.

11. *Cooper v. Federal Reserve Bank*, 467 U.S. 867, 872 (1984); *Firefighters Local Union No. 1784 v. Stotts*, 467 U.S. 561, 615 (1984) (Blackmun, J., dissenting).

12. *Teamsters v. United States*, 431 U.S. 324, 361 (1977).

13. *See Clark v. American Marine Corp.*, 304 F. Supp. 603, 607 (E.D. La. 1969).

14. *James v. Stockham Valves and Fitting Co.*, 559 F.2d 310, 354 (5th Cir. 1977), *cert. denied*, 434 U.S. 1034 (1978).

15. Courts have consistently enjoined the use of these practices. For some LDF cases, see *Kirkland v. New York State Dep't of Correctional Servs.* 711 F.2d 1117, 1122 (2d Cir. 1983), *cert. denied*, 405 U.S. 1005 (1984) (corrections officer exam); *Detroit Police Officers' Ass'n v. Young*, 608 F.2d 671, 681 (6th Cir. 1979), *cert. denied*, 452 U.S. 938 (1981) (police exam); *James v. Stockham Valves & Fittings Co.*, 559 F.2d 310, 334 (5th Cir. 1977), *cert. denied*, 434 U.S. 1034 (1978) (Wonderlic, Bennett, and Tabaka exams); *Watkins v. Scott Paper Co.*, 530 F.2d 1159, 1185 (5th Cir.), *cert. denied*, 429 U.S. 861 (1976) (Kopas and Wonderlic exams); *Robinson v. Union Carbide Corp.*, 538 F.2d 652 (5th Cir. 1976), *cert. denied*, 434 U.S. 822 (1977) (Bennett exam); *Young v. Edgcomb Steel Co.*, 499 F.2d 97, 100 (4th Cir. 1974) (Wonderlic Test), a case I argued; *Duhon v. Goodyear Tire & Rubber Co.*, 494 F.2d 817, 819 (5th Cir. 1974) (Wonderlic and Bennett tests); *Pettway v. American Cast Iron Pipe Co.*, 494 F.2d (5th Cir. 1974), *cert. denied*, 439 U.S. 1115 (1979) (general intelligence and California

Mental Maturity exams); *United States v. Georgia Power Co.*, 474 F.2d 906 (5th Cir. 1973) (tests battery and high school education), in which the LDF represented the private plaintiffs; *Chance v. Board of Examiners*, 458 F.2d 1167, 1175 (2d Cir. 1972) (New York City school supervisor exam). However, not all written employment tests were invalidated by courts. *See, e.g., Cormier v. PPG Indus.*, 702 F.2d 567, 568 (5th Cir. 1983) (no adverse impact); *Pegues v. Mississippi State Employment Serv.*, 699 F.2d 760 (5th Cir. 1983); *Buckner v. Goodyear Tire & Rubber Co.*, 339 F. Supp. 1108, 1115–1116 (N.D. Ala. 1972), *aff'd*, 476 F.2d 1287 (5th Cir. 1973) (Wonderlic and Bennett tests upheld as job-related).

16. *United States v. Georgia Power Co.*, 474 F.2d 906, 917–918 (5th Cir. 1973).

17. *Local 189 Papermakers and Paperworkers v. United States*, 416 F.2d. 980, 988 (5th Cir. 1969), *cert. denied*, 397 U.S. 919 (1970).

18. *Moody*, 422 U.S. at 418–419; *Pettway v. American Cast Iron Pipe Co.*, 494 F.2d 211, 236 n. 56 (5th Cir. 1974).

19. Note, "Title VII, Seniority Discrimination and the Incumbent Negro," 80 *Harv. L. Rev.* 1260 (1967).

20. *Pettway v. American Cast Iron Pipe Co.*, 494 F.2d 211, 243–244 (5th Cir. 1974); *Tippett v. Liggett & Myers Tobacco Co.*, 402 F. Supp. 934, 951 n. 3 (M.D.N.C. 1975). Judge Gordon, who rejected the *Quarles* present effect of past discrimination in *Griggs*, later recognized in *Tippett* that *Quarles* indeed had become a landmark decision.

21. *Quarles*, 279 F. Supp. at 510.

22. Order entered January 4, 1968, *Quarles v. Philip Morris, Inc.* No. 4544 (E.D. Va.).

23. *Quarles*, 279 F. Supp. at 519–521.

24. *Local 189*, 416 F.2d at 988.

25. Ibid.

26. *Pettway v. American Cast Iron Pipe Co.*, 494 F.2d 211, 243 and n. 84 (5th Cir. 1974).

27. *United States v. Allegheny-Ludlum Indus., Inc.*, 517 F.2d 826, 847 (5th Cir. 1975), *cert. denied sub nom NOW v. U.S. on other grounds*, 425 U.S. 944 (1976).

28. Frank T. Read and Lucy S. McGraw, *Let Them Be Judged: The Judicial Integration of the Deep South* (Metuchen, N.J.: Scarecrow Press, 1978), 34.

29. *Dent v. St. Louis–San Francisco R.R. Co.*, 406 F.2d 399 (5th Cir.), *cert. denied sub nom. Hyler v. Reynolds Metals Co.*, 403 U.S. 912 (1969).

30. *Pettway*, 494 F.2d at 248–249 (citations omitted).

31. *See James v. Stockham Valves & Fitting Co.*, 559 F.2d 310, 356 (5th Cir. 1977); *Hill v. Western Electric Co.*, 13 FEP Cases (BNA) 1157 (E.D. Va. 1976).

32. *Pettway*, 494 F.2d at 250.

33. *Robinson v. Lorillard Corp.*, No. C-141-G-66 (M.D.N.C. July 30, 1970) (judgment); *EEOC v. Kansas City Power & Light Co.*, 32 FEP Cases (BNA) 1396, 1399–1401 (W.D. Mo. 1981).

34. *See Russell v. American Tobacco Co.*, 528 F.2d 357, 364 (4th Cir.), *cert. denied*, 425 U.S. 935 (1976).

35. *See* decree entered in *United States v. Georgia Power*, 1974 WL 110 (N.D. Ga. 1974), on remand from *United States v. Georgia Power Co.*, 474 F.2d 906 (5th Cir. 1973) (the LDF represented the private plaintiffs in the case).

36. Plaintiffs' Motion for Entry of Findings of Fact, Conclusion of Law and Judgment, *Robinson v. Lorillard Corp.*, 319 F. Supp. 835 (M.D.N.C. 1970) (filed January 12, 1970).

37. *Robinson v. Lorillard Corp.*, 318 F. Supp., at 843.

38. 444 F.2d 791 (4th Cir. 1971), *cert. dismissed*, 404 U.S. 1006 (1971).

39. Appendix at App. 45–47 (Order entered June 18, 1971), *Albemarle Paper Co. v. Moody*, 422 U.S. 405 (1975) (Nos. 74-389 & 74-428).

40. However, in *Gulf Oil Co v. Bernard*, 452 U.S. 89 (1981), another employment discrimination case, the LDF successfully challenged before the Supreme Court the imposition of a broad gag order similar to the one Judge Dupree entered in *Moody*.

41. The statement in the published version of *Robinson* is found at 444 F.2d at 800.

42. Judge Dupree's notation on *Robinson* in *Moody v. Albemarle Paper Co.*, No. 989, available in Records of the United States District Court for the Middle District of North Carolina, Wilson Division, Record Group, National Archives and Records Administration, Southeast Region, Morrow, Georgia.

43. The notice Judge Dupree ordered to be published and mailed is set out in Appendix, App. 53-App. 56 (Notice of Pendency of Class Action), *Albemarle Paper Co. v. Moody*, 422 U.S. 405 (1975).

44. For a discussion of the use of gag orders and proof of claim orders in employment discrimination litigation, *see* Richard Seymour, "Proof of Claim Forms and Gag Orders in Employment Class Actions," 10 *Conn. L. Rev.* 920 (1978).

45. Judge Dupree's handwritten notes on his call to Judge Gordon about *Robinson* in *Moody v. Albemarle Paper Co.*, No. 989, available in Records of the United States District Court for the Middle District of North Carolina, Wilson Division, Record Group, National Archives and Records Administration, Southeast Region, Morrow, Georgia.

46. *Moody v. Albemarle Paper Co.*, 4 FEP Cases (BNA) 561, 570–571 (E.D.N.C. 1971).

47. Brief for Plaintiffs-Appellants 81–82, *Moody v. Albemarle Paper Co.*, 474 F.2d 134 (4th Cir. 1973).

48. *Moody*, 474 F.2d, at 142.

49. *William v. General Foods Corp.*, 492 F.2d 399 (7th Cir. 1974); *Pettway v. American Cast Iron Pipe Co.*, 494 F.2d 211 (5th Cir. 1974).

50. *E.g.*, *Rasimas v. Michigan Dep't of Mental Health*, 714 F.2d 614, 626 (6th Cir. 1983).

51. *E.g.*, *Kober v. Westinghouse Electric Corp.*, 480 F.2d 240, 246–247 (3d Cir. 1973).

52. *Johnson v. Goodyear Tire & Rubber Co.*, 491 F.2d 1364, 1375 (5th Cir. 1974); *Franks v. Bowman Transportation Co.*, 495 F.2d 398, 421–422 (5th Cir. 1974) (LDF), affirmed on other grounds 424 U.S. 747 (1976); *Baxter v. Savannah Sugar Refining Corp.*, 495 F.2d 437, 442–445 (5th Cir. 1974), *cert. denied*, 419 U.S. 1033 (1974) (LDF); *Head v. Timken Roller Bearing Co.*, 496 F.2d 870, 876–877 (6th Cir. 1973).

53. Box I, Folder 10, Case File, O.T. 1974, Administrative File, Assignments, Justice Brennan Papers, Manuscript Room, Library of Congress, Washington, D.C.

54. *Moody*, 422 U.S., at 417–418 (citing *United States v. N. L. Industries, Inc.*, 479 F.2d 354, 379 (8th Cir. 1973)).

55. Brief for Respondent 57–58, *Albemarle Paper Co. v. Moody*, 422 U.S. 405 (1975).

56. *Moody*, 422 U.S. at 421.

57. Brief for Respondents 57–58, *Albemarle Paper Co. v. Moody*, 422 U.S. 405 (1975).

58. *Moody*, 422 U.S., at 422.

59. 494 F.2d, at 258–263. *See* Belton, *Remedies in Employment Discrimination Law*, § 9.1–12.15.

60. 494 F.2d, at 260–261.

61. *See* "Special Project—Back Pay in Employment Discrimination Cases," 35 *Vand. L. Rev.* 893 (1982).

62. The case had been filed under Title VII and Section 1981, and the LDF sought review of this question under both provisions. The Court specifically did not decide this issue with respect to the Section 1981 claim, stating that "[i]n view of our decision [under Title VII] we have no occasion to address that claim." *Franks*, 424 U.S. 747, 750 n. 1 (1975).

63. Ibid., 788 (Powell, J., dissenting).

64. *Griggs*, 401 U.S., at 429–430.

65. Interview with Morris J. Baller.

66. Transcript of oral argument in *Franks*, argued November 3, 1975.

67. Notes on the conference, Box 215, Supreme Court File, Appellate/IFP, O.T. 1975, Opinions, 74–728, *Franks v. Bowman Transportation* (2 of 2), Justice Blackmun Papers, Manuscript Division, Library of Congress, Washington, D.C. *See also* Case Status Sheet, Box 365, Folder 2, Case File, Administration File, Assignment List (2 of 3), Brennan Papers, Library of Congress, Washington, D.C.; Folder 1701, Sup. Ct. File, Case File, O.T. 1975, Argued Cases, 74-676 to 74-1445, Justice William O. Douglas Papers, Library of Congress, Washington.

68. *Franks*, 424 U.S., at 761–762. Justice Brennan also concluded that his view was apparently in accord with the unanimous view of the legal commentators. Ibid., 762 (citing, among others, the Cooper and Sobol *Harvard Law Review* article that the courts found most helpful on the seniority and testing issues).

69. *Franks*, 424 U.S., at 771.

70. 424 U.S. 724, 777 (1976).

71. In *Firefighters Local Union 1784 v. Stotts*, the Court noted the uniformity among the lower courts in the application of the no-bumping rule in the context of the seniority discrimination cases.

72. *Pettway v. American Cast Iron Pipe Co.*, 494 F.2d 211, 260 (5th Cir. 1974).

73. Ibid., 261–263.

74. Ibid., 259.

75. 532 F.2d 336, 341 (4th Cir. 1975). The various methods for computing back pay including back pay in class action cases are treated in Belton, *Remedies in Employment Discrimination Law* §§ 9.28–9.33.

76. *Teamsters v. United States*, 431 U.S. 324, 361–362 (1977).

77. 42 U.S. C. 2000e-5(k).

78. *See, e.g., Griggs v. Duke Power Co.,* 401 U.S. 424 (1971) (six years); *Johnson v. Georgia Highway Express, Inc.,* 488 F.2d 714 (5th Cir. 1974) (four years).

79. Brief for Petitioner 14, *Newman v. Piggie Park Enterprises, Inc.,* 390 U.S. 400 (1968).

80. *See, e.g., Clark v. American Marine Corp.,* 320 F. Supp. 709, 711 (E.D. La. 1970), *aff'd,* 437 F.2d 959 (5th Cir. 1971).

81. *Lea v. Cone Mills Corp.,* 467 F.2d 277 (4th Cir. 1972). Another reason on which the court of appeals relied was the fact that the trial judge in the case had died subsequent to his order on counsel fees.

82. 444 F.2d 791, 804 (4th Cir. 1971), *cert. dismissed,* 444 U.S. 1006 (1971).

83. Brief of the NAACP Legal Defense and Educational Fund, Inc., 5–8, *Christiansburg Garment v. EEOC,* 434 U.S. 412 (1978) (No. 76-1383).

84. 434 U.S., at 421, 422; *Blue v. U.S. Dept. of Army (In re Julius Chambers),* 914 F.2d 525 (4th Cir. 1990), *cert. denied sub nom. Chambers v. U.S. Army,* 499 U.S. 959 (1991).

85. *Christianburg Garment,* 434 U.S. at 421–422.

86. Brief of the NAACP Legal Defense and Educational Fund, Inc., 10, *Christiansburg Garment v. EEOC,* 434 U.S. 412 (1978) (No. 76-1383).

87. *EEOC v. L. B. Foster Co.,* 123 F. 3d 746, 751 (3d Cir. 1997).

88. 488 F.2d, at 719 (citing, inter alia, *Clark v. American Marine Corp.,* 437 F.2d 959 (5th Cir. 1971), affirming 320 F. Supp. 709 (E.D. La. 1970).

89. *Hensley v. Eckerhart,* 461 U.S. 424 (1983).

90. 42 U.S.C. § 1988.

91. *See* Mary Frances Derfner, "One Giant Step: The Civil Rights Attorney's Fees Act of 1976," 21 *St. L. U. L.J.* 441 (1977).

92. *Alyeska Pipeline Service Co. v. Wilderness Society,* 421 U.S. 240 (1975).

93. *See James v. Stockham Valve and Fittings Co.,* 559 F.2d 310, 359 (5th Cir. 1977), *cert. denied,* 434 U.S. 1034 (1978); *Baxter v. Savannah Sugar Refining Corp.,* 495 F.2d 437, 447 (5th Cir. 1974).

94. *See, e.g., Hensley v. Eckerhart,* 461 U.S. 424, 428 (1983); *Kelley v. Metropolitan Cty. Bd. of Ed.,* 558 F. Supp. 468, 477 (M.D. Tenn. 1983), *aff'd in part, rev'd in part,* 773 F.2d 677 (6th Cir. 1985), *cert. denied,* 474 U.S. 1083 (1986). Some courts have now adopted rules that require that statutory awards of fees requests must be based on contemporaneous records. *E.g., Grendel's Den, Inc. v. Larkin,* 749 F.2d 945, 952 (1st Cir. 1984); *Ramos v. Lamm,* 713 F.2d 546, 553 (10th Cir. 1983); *New York State Ass'n for Retarded Children, Inc. v. Carey,* 711 F.2d 1136, 1147 (2d Cir. 1983).

CHAPTER TWELVE. *GRIGGS* AND AFFIRMATIVE ACTION

1. Robert Belton, "Discrimination and Affirmative Action: An Analysis of Competing Theories of Equality and *Weber,*" 59 *N.C. L. Rev.* 531, 534–535 (1981).

2. *See* ibid. at 534–538.

3. *See* Bob Zelnick, *Backfire: A Reporter's Look at Affirmative Action* (Washington, D.C.: Regnery Publishing, 1996), 4.

4. *See, e.g.,* James E. Jones, Jr., "The Origins of Affirmative Action," 21 *U.C. Davis L. Rev.* 383 (1987); Eric Schnapper, "Affirmative Action and the Legislative History of the Fourteenth Amendment," 71 *Va. L. Rev.* 753 (1985), which is revised from his brief for the LDF's amicus brief in *Regents of the University of California v. Bakke,* 438 U.S. 265 (1978).

5. *See* Paul D. Moreno, *From Direct Action to Affirmative Action* (Baton Rouge, La.: LSU Press, 1997), 189 (*New Deal legislation*).

6. Hugh Davis Graham, *The Civil Rights Era: Origins and Development of National Policy* (New York: Oxford University Press, 1990), 28.

7. *See* David J. Garrow, "The Evolution of Affirmative Action and the Necessity of Truly Individualized Admission Decisions," 34 *J. of College and Univ. L.* 1 (2007).

8. Richard Berg, "Equal Employment under the Civil Rights Act of 1964," 31 *Brook. L. Rev.* 62, 76 (1965).

9. 42 U.S.C. § 2000e-(j). *See* Berg, "Equal Employment under the Civil Rights Act of 1964," 76–77; Francis J. Vaas, "Title VII: Legislative History," 7 *B.C. Indus. & Com. L. Rev.* 431, 450 (1965–1966).

10. David Benjamin Oppenheimer, "Distinguishing Five Models of Affirmative Action," 4 *Berkeley Women's L.J.* 42 (1988–1989).

11. Morris B. Abram, "Affirmative Action: Fair Shakers and Social Engineers," 99 *Harv. L. Rev.* 1312, 1312 (1986). I suppose that I am one of those civil rights "social engineers" because the author cites one of my articles as an example of one of those individuals who has abandoned the equal opportunity theory of equality. Ibid. at 1317 n. 15 (citing my article "Discrimination and Affirmative Action," 531).

12. *See* Randall Kennedy, "Persuasion and Distrust: A Comment on the Affirmative Action Debate," 99 *Harv. L. Rev.* 1327 (1986).

13. Herbert Hill, "Black Workers, Organized Labor, and Title VII of the Civil Rights Act of 1964: Legislative History and Litigation Record," in *Race in America: The Struggle for Equality,* ed. Herbert Hill and James E. Jones, Jr. (Madison: University of Wisconsin, 1993), 327.

14. *See Adarand Constructors v. Pena,* 515 U.S. 200 (1995); *City of Richmond v. J. A. Croson Co.,* 488 U.S. 469 (1989).

15. *United States v. Paradise,* 480 U.S. 149 (1987); *Local 28, Sheet Metal Workers International Ass'n v. EEOC,* 478 U.S. 421 (1986).

16. *Steelworkers v. Weber,* 443 U.S. 193 (1979); *Johnson v. Transportation Agency, Santa Clara County,* 480 U.S. 616 (1987).

17. *See Contreras v. City of Los Angeles,* 565 F.2d 176 (9th Cir. 1981), *cert. denied,* 455 U.S. 1021 (1982); Note, "Business Necessity: Judicial Dualism and the Search for Adequate Standards," 15 *Ga. L. Rev.* 376 (1981).

18. *Watson v. Fort Worth Bank and Trust Co.,* 487 U.S. 977, 998 (1988).

19. James Gwartney, Ephrain Asher, Charles Haworth, and Joan Haworth, "Statistics, the Law and Title VII: An Economist's View," 54 *Notre Dame L. Rev.* 633, 643

(1979); Barbara Lerner, "Employment Discrimination: Adverse Impact, Validity and Equality," 1979 *Sup. Ct. Rev.* 17, 18 n. 6 (reporting that an adequate criterion-related validation study generally costs between $100,000 and $400,000 and requires approximately two years to complete).

20. Comments of Thompson Powers, *Panel Discussion on Discrimination in Employment,* May 29, 1976, Proceedings of the Thirty-Seventh Annual Judicial Conference of the District of Columbia Circuit, *printed in* 73 F.R.D. 213 (1977).

21. *See* David L. Rose, "Twenty-Five Years Later: Where Do We Stand on Equal Employment Opportunity?" 42 *Vand. L. Rev.* 1121, 1145 (1989). A plurality of the Supreme Court captured this either-or situation in a case in which the employer urged the Court, without success, to decline to extend the disparate impact theory to subjective criteria. *Watson v. Fort Worth Bank & Trust* 478 U.S. 977, 991–992 (1988).

22. *See Contractors Association,* 442 F.2d 159, 172 (3d Cir. 1971) ("[t]he unions, it is said, refer men from the hiring hall on the basis of seniority, and the Philadelphia Plan interferes with this arrangement since few minority tradesmen have high seniority"), *cert. denied,* 404 U.S. 854 (1971).

23. 442 F.2d at 173.

24. Alfred W. Blumrosen, *How the Courts Are Handling Reverse Discrimination Claims,* Draft Report on Reverse Discrimination Commissioned by the Labor Department, 1995 DLR 147 (April 1, 1995).

25. By 1977, there were 107 complaints of "reverse discrimination awaiting decision by the EEOC, arising mainly under Affirmative Action plans which had been developed by government contractors under Executive Order No. 11,246." *See* Alfred W. Blumrosen, "The Bottom Line in Equal Employment Guidelines: Administering a Polycentric Problem," 33 *Admin. L. Rev.* 323, 338 and n. 46 (1981) (citing a September 19, 1977, memorandum to the chair of the EEOC).

26. Brief for the NAACP Legal Defense and Educational Fund, Inc., the National Urban League, and Howard University as Amicus Curiae at 59–84, *Steelworkers v. Weber,* 443 U.S. 193 (1979).

27. *Weber v. Kaiser Aluminum & Chemical Corp.,* 443 U.S. 193, 210 (1979) (Blackmun, J., concurring).

28. *See* Reply Brief for the United States and the Equal Employment Opportunity Commission at 3–5, *Steelworkers v. Weber,* 443 U.S. 193 (1979).

29. Brief for Petitioner (Kaiser) at 4, *Weber v. Kaiser Aluminum & Chemical Corp.,* 443 U.S. 193 (1979).

30. *Burrell v. Kaiser Aluminum & Chemical Co.,* No. 67–86 (M.D. La.) (consent decree filed February 24, 1975).

31. *Parsons v. Kaiser Aluminum & Chemical Co.,* 575 F.2d 1374 (5th Cir. 1978).

32. *Weber v. Kaiser Aluminum & Chemical Corp.,* 415 F. Supp. 761, 765 (E.D. La. 1976).

33. *See Ford v. United States Steel Corp.,* 638 U.S. 763 (5th Cir. 1981); *James v. Stockham Valves and Fitting Co.,* 559 F.2d 310 (5th Cir. 1977), *cert. denied,* 434 U.S. 1034 (1978); *United States v. United States Steel Corp.,* 520 F.2d 1043 (5th Cir. 1975) (the LDF

represented the private plaintiffs), *cert. denied,* 429 U.S. 817 (1976); *Rodgers v. United States Steel Corp.,* 508 F.2d 152 (3d Cir.), *cert. denied,* 423 U.S. 832 (1975). *See* Herbert Hill, *Race and the Steelworkers Union: White Privilege and Black Struggles;* Judith Stein, "Running Steel, Running America," 8 *New Politics* 174 (Winter 2002).

34. *See United States v. Allegheny-Ludlum Industries, Inc.,* 517 F.2d 826 (5th Cir. 1975), *cert. denied,* 425 U.S. 944 (1976); George A. Moore, Jr., "Steel Industry Consent Decree—A Model for the Future," 3 *Empl. R. L.J.* 214 (1977).

35. William B. Gould, *Black Workers in White Unions: Job Discrimination in the United States* (Ithaca, N.Y.: Cornell University Press, 1977), 395.

36. 415 F. Supp. 761, 764–765 (E.D. La. 1976).

37. 563 F.2d 216 (5th Cir. 1977).

38. Ibid., 227 (Wisdom, J., dissenting).

39. *McDonald v. Santa Fe Trail Transp. Co.,* 427 U.S. 273, 281 n. 8 (1976).

40. 443 U.S. 193, 200 (1979) (original emphasis).

41. *See* Justice Powell's January 2, 1979, memo to the conference, Justice Harry A. Blackmun Papers, Box 294, Folder 1, Sup. Ct. File, Appellate/IFP Opinion, No. 78-432, 2 of 4, *United Steelworkers v. Weber,* Library of Congress, Manuscript Division, Washington, D.C.; Justice White, memo to Justice Brennan, May 7, 1979, Blackmun Papers.

42. *See* Curt Matthews, "2 Justices to Be Absent in Bias Case," *Sun,* March 16, 1979, A6 (Baltimore); copy in Brennan Papers, Box I-487, Folder 5, Case File. O.T. 1978, Opinions, No. 78-432, *United Steelworkers v. Weber,* Library of Congress.

43. Ibid.; Justice Powell, memo to Justice Brennan, March 8, 1979, requesting that the opinion specifically note that he took no part in the consideration or decision in the case, Brennan Papers.

44. *See* Justice Powell, memo to the conference, January 2, 1979, Blackmun Papers.

45. Chief Justice Burger, memo to the conference, March 30, 1979, Blackmun Papers.

46. Chief Justice Burger, memo to the conference, April 1, 1979, Brennan Papers.

47. Justice Brennan, memo to Justices Stewart, White, Marshall, and Blackmun, April 30, 1979, Blackmun Papers.

48. Justice Blackmun, memo to Justice Brennan, May 8, 1979, Blackmun Papers.

49. 443 U.S., at 202–204.

50. Law clerk, memo to Justice Blackmun, May 14, 1979, Blackmun Papers, Box 294, Folder 1.

51. Brief for the NAACP Legal Defense and Educational Fund, Inc., National Urban League, and Howard University as Amici Curiae 62, *Steelworkers v. Weber,* 443 U.S. 193 (1979).

52. *Weber,* 443 U.S., at 205–206.

53. Justice Brennan, memo to Justices Stewart, White, Marshall, and Blackmun, May 2, 1979, Blackmun Papers.

54. *Weber,* 443 U.S., at 209 n. 9.

55. Ibid., 208–209.

56. 443 U.S., at 212. In *Wygant v. Jackson Bd. of Education,* 476 U.S. 267 (1986), the Supreme Court applied strict scrutiny to the public employment arena. The Court

held that "societal discrimination" itself is not enough to justify racial classifications and that the government must show the existence of some discrimination, although a finding of actual discrimination is not required.

57. Ibid., 220–222 (Rehnquist J., dissenting).

58. Ibid., 215 (Blackmun, J., concurring).

59. Ibid., 218 (Burger, C.J., dissenting).

60. 770 F.2d 752 (9th Cir. 1985).

61. Interview with Morris J. Baller.

62. Ibid. *See* Melvin L. Urofsky, *Affirmative Action on Trial: Sex Discrimination in Johnson v. Santa Clara* (Lawrence: University Press of Kansas, 1997), 119.

63. 480 U.S. 616, 627 n. 6 (1987).

64. *Wygant v. Jackson Board of Education,* 476 U.S. 276 (1986).

65. 480 U.S., at 632–633.

66. Ibid., 633 (citing *Weber,* 433 U.S., at 204).

67. Ibid., 657 (White, J., dissenting).

68. For a perspective of one of the participants in the efforts to resolve the impasse among the federal agencies on the bottom-line principle, *see* Blumrosen, "The Bottom Line in Equal Employment Guidelines," 323.

69. Uniform Guidelines on Employee Selection Procedures, 29 C.F. R. 1607.161 (1981); *Connecticut v. Teal,* 457 U.S. 442, 453 n. 12 (1981).

70. Ibid., 447 n. 8.

71. Ibid., 455, 458 (Powell, J., dissenting).

CHAPTER THIRTEEN. THE DEATH KNELL FOR *GRIGGS*

1. *See* Office of Legal Policy, U.S. Department of Justice, Report to the Attorney General, *Redefining Discrimination: Disparate Impact and the Institutionalization of Affirmative Action* (November 1, 1987).

2. *Chance v. Board of Examiners,* 330 F.2d 203 (S.D.N.Y. 1971), *aff'd,* 458 F.2d 1167 (2d Cir. 1972). The district court decided *Chance* on July 14, 1971, about five months after the Supreme Court decided *Griggs.*

3. Michael J. Perry, "The Disproportionate Impact Theory of Racial Discrimination," 125 *U. Pa. L. Rev.* 540, 544–548 (1977) (discussing the cases).

4. Their equal protection claim was based on the Fifth Amendment to the Constitution. Unlike the Fourteenth Amendment, which applies only to state and local governments and has an Equal Protection Clause, the Fifth Amendment, which applies only to the federal government, does not. However, the Supreme Court has held that the equal protection principle is included in the Due Process Clause of the Fifth Amendment. *Bolling v. Sharpe,* 347 U.S. 497 (1954). The plaintiffs also relied upon two other grounds for relief, 42 U.S.C. § 1981 and a District of Columbia statutory provision that prohibits racial discrimination in employment. The majority opinion in *Washington v. Davis* did not address these claims. In a later case, the Court held that

Section 1981 is inapplicable to claims against the federal government. *Brown v. General Servs. Admin.*, 425 U.S. 820 (1976).

5. Transcript of the Oral Argument, March 1, 1976, *Washington v. Davis*, 426 U.S. 229 (1976) (No. 74-1492) (report of the oral argument by Hoover Reporting Co., Inc., but the names of the Justices who raised the issues are not clear from the transcript).

6. *Personnel Administrator of Massachusetts v. Feeney*, 422 U.S. 256, 273–274 (1976).

7. *Washington v. Davis*, 426 U.S. at 247–248.

8. 431 U.S. 324 (1977).

9. Herbert Hill, "Black Workers, Organized Labor, and Title VII of the Civil Rights Act: Legislative History and Litigation Record," in *Race in America: The Struggle for Equality*, ed. Herbert Hill and James E. Jones, Jr. (Madison: University of Wisconsin Press, 1993), 269–271.

10. For a broad overview of the courts' approach to seniority discrimination cases prior to *Teamsters* and a view that the results in *Teamsters* could hardly be unexpected, *see* James E. Jones, Jr., "Title VII, Seniority and the Supreme Court: Clarification or Retreat," 26 *U. Kan. L. Rev.* 1 (1997).

11. Hill, "Black Workers, Organized Labor, and Title VII," 306.

12. *Teamsters*, 431 U.S., at 349–350.

13. Ibid., 352–353.

14. Ibid., 346 n. 28.

15. *Pullman Standard v. Swint*, 456 U.S. 273, 289 (1982).

16. *Sprogis v. United Airlines, Inc.*, 444 F.2d 1194 (7th Cir. 1971).

17. Ibid., 608.

18. *See, e.g., Harris v. Bekins Van Lines*, 1996 WL 57019 (D. Kan. Sept. 27, 1996) (possession of a chauffeur's license part of a seniority system).

19. *E.g., Anderson v. City of Bessemer*, 470 U.S. 564 (1985), argued in the Supreme Court by cooperating attorney Jonathan Wallace.

20. *E.g., Harvey by Blackshear v. United Transportation Union*, 878 F.2d 1235 (10th Cir. 1989), *cert. denied*, 493 U.S. 1074 (1990).

21. Employers and unions: *Younger v. Glamorgan Pipe and Foundry Co.*, 621 F.2d 96 (4th Cir. 1980), *affirming*, 1979 WL 31 (W.D. Va. 1979); *Alexander v. Aero Lodge No. 725, International Association of Machinists and Aerospace Workers*, 565 F.2d 1364, 1367 (6th Cir. 1977). Litigation team: *United States v. Georgia Power Co.*, 695 F.2d 890 (5th Cir. 1981) (the litigation team represented private plaintiffs in the case); *Terrell v. United States Pipe and Foundry Co.*, 1985 WL 56648 (N.D. Ala. 1985) (on remand from 696 F.2d 1132 (5th Cir. 1983)).

22. David L. Rose, "Twenty-Five Years Later: Where Do We Stand on Equal Employment Opportunity?," 42 *Vand. L. Rev.* 1121 (1989).

23. *See* Drew S. Days III, "The Court's Response to the Reagan Civil Rights Agenda," 42 *Vand. L. Rev.* 1003 (1989); Norman C. Amaker, *Civil Rights and the Reagan Administration* (Washington, D.C.: Urban Institute Press, 1988).

24. 1980 Republican Platform, *reprinted*, in 36 Cong. Q. Almanac 58-B, 62-B (1980).

25. William Bradford Reynolds, "The Reagan Administration and Civil Rights: Winning the War against Discrimination," 1986 *U. Ill. L. Rev.* 1001.

26. Office of Legal Policy, U.S. Department of Justice, Report: *Redefining Discrimination*, i.

27. Ibid., ii.

28. Ibid., 77 (quoting Robert Belton, "Discrimination and Affirmative Action: An Analysis of Competing Theories of Equality and *Weber*," 59 *N.C. L. Rev.* 531, 542 (1981)).

29. *See* Joel L. Selig, "The Reagan Justice Department and Civil Rights: What Went Wrong," 1985 *U. Ill. L. Rev.* 785, 823 (collecting case on the Civil Rights Division's cases urging affirmative action in litigated cases).

30. *Bob Jones University v. United States,* 461 U.S. 574 (1983).

31. *United States v. Birmingham, Michigan,* 538 F. Supp. 819, 827 n. 9 (E.D. Mich. 1982), *aff'd as modified,* 727 F.2d 560 (6th Cir.), *cert. denied,* 469 U.S. 821 (1984).

32. *See* Drew S. Days III, "Turning Back the Clock: The Reagan Administration and Civil Rights," 19 *Harv. C. R.-C. L. L. Rev.* 309 (1984).

33. *Oversight Hearings on Equal Employment Opportunity and Affirmative Action, Part 1: Hearings before the Subcomm. on Equal Employment Opportunities of the House Comm. on Education and Labor,* 97th Cong., 1st Sess. 132, 134 (testimony of William Reynolds).

34. Gary McDowell, "Affirmative Action: The Brock-Meese Standoff in Federal Racial Quotas," 48 *Policy Rev.* 32 (1989).

35. *See* Selig, "The Reagan Justice Department and Civil Rights," 823.

36. EEOC Chides Justice for "Deplorable" Action on New Orleans Police Case, Daily Lab. Rep. (BNA) No. 22, at A-2 (February 1, 1983).

37. Statement of Assistant Attorney General Reynolds before the National Foundation for the Study of Equal Employment Policy (November 4, 1984) (quoted in Julius Chambers and Barry Goldstein, "Title VII at Twenty: The Continuing Challenge," 1 *Lab. Law.* 235, 252 (1985)).

38. David Rose, "Twenty-Five Years Later: Where Do We Stand on Equal Employment Law Enforcement," 42 *Vand. L. Rev.* 1121, 1155 (1989).

39. Howard Kurtz, "Reynolds Nomination Voted Down," *Washington Post,* June 28, 1985, A1.

40. Chester Finn, "'Affirmative Action' under Reagan," *Commentary,* April 1982, at 28.

41. Jack Greenberg, "Civil Rights Enforcement Activity of the Department of Justice," 8 *Black L.J.* 60, 61 (1983).

42. Lee Cokorinos, *The Assault on Diversity: An Organized Challenge to Racial and Gender Justice* (Lanham, Md.: Rowman & Littlefield, 2003); Selig, "The Reagan Justice Department and Civil Rights," 785.

43. Days, "Turning Back the Clock," 309.

44. Theodore M. Shaw, "Introduction," in Cokorinos, *The Assault on Diversity,* vii.

45. *See* Herman Schwartz, *The Rehnquist Court: Judicial Activism on the Right* (New York: Farrar, Straus & Giroux, 2002).

46. Albner J. Mikva and Jeff Bleich, "When Congress Overrules the Court," 79 *Cal. L. Rev.* 729, 739 (1991).

47. 487 U.S. 977, 991–992 (1988).

48. Ibid., 993.

49. Ibid., 993–994 (plurality opinion).

50. Ibid., 1001 (Blackmun, J., dissenting).

51. Ibid., 998 (plurality opinion).

52. Ibid., 987.

53. 490 U.S., at 663 n. 4 (Stevens, J., dissenting).

54. Ibid., 662 (Blackmun, J., dissenting).

55. 490 U.S., at 649 n. 4.

56. *See* Robert Belton, "The Dismantling of the Griggs Disparate Impact Theory and the Future of Title VII: The Need for a Third Reconstruction," 8 *Yale L. & Pol'y Rev.* 223, 224 (1990).

57. 490 U.S., at 658–660.

58. Ibid., 661.

59. *Furnco Construction Corp. v. Waters,* 438 U.S. 567 (1978).

60. Belton, "The Dismantling of the Griggs Disparate Impact Theory," 237.

61. The *New York Times* repeatedly referred to *Wards Cove* as "overruling" the eighteen-year-old unanimous precedent of *Griggs. See, e.g.,* Linda Greenhouse, "The Year the Court Turned to the Right," *N.Y. Times,* July 7, 1989, A1 ("*Griggs v. Duke Power* . . . was effectively overruled this term."); Editorial, "A Red Herring in Black and White," *N.Y. Times,* July 23, 1990, A14 ("[L]ast year in the *Wards Cove* case, a 5-to-4 majority overruled *Griggs* and placed new, heavy burdens on civil rights plaintiffs."); Adam Clymer, "President Rejects Senate Agreement on Rights Measure," *N.Y. Times,* August 2, 1991, A1 ("For more than a year arguments over civil rights legislation have focused on how to interpret a 1971 Supreme Court decision, *Griggs v. Duke Power Company,* which was overruled by the Court in 1989 in *Wards Cove v. Antonio.*"). *See also* Reginald Alleyne, "Smoking Guns Are Hard to Find," *L.A. Times,* June 12, 1989, Pt. 2, p. 5 (the Supreme Court's "underlying dislike" for Title VII "is openly revealed by the illogic of the reasoning" of *Wards Cove*); Marcia Coyle and Fred Strasser, "Is the High Court Hiding Reversals on Rights?," *Nat'l L.J.,* June 19, 1989, 5 (quoting Isabelle K. Pinzler, director of the American Civil Liberties Union Women's Rights Project: "The most fascinating aspect of the decision was its dishonesty. . . . They have overruled *Griggs* but they deny it. . . . The doors of opportunity opened by *Griggs* have been slammed shut. We're not out of business, but ironically, Title VII will become the vehicle that prevents the remedying of systemic employment discrimination.").

62. 457 U.S. 440, 447 n. 8 (1982).

63. 490 U.S., at 662 (Blackmun, J., dissenting).

64. *See* Brief Amici Curiae of NAACP Legal Defense and Educational Fund, Inc., Women's Legal Defense Fund, National Women's Law Center, and International Association of Black Professional Firefighters in Support of Petitioners, *Martin v. Wilks,* 490 U.S. 755 (1989).

65. *United States v. Jefferson County,* 720 F.2d 1511, 1516 (5th Cir. 1984).

66. *See* Petition for a Writ of Certiorari on behalf of John Martin, *Martin v. Wilks,* 490 U.S. 755 (1989).

67. Arthur S. Hayes, "Job-Bias Litigation Wilts under High Court Rulings," *Wall St. Journal,* August 22, 1989, 1 (quoting LDF attorney Eric Schnapper).

68. *General Building Contractors Ass'n v. Pennsylvania,* 458 U.S. 375 (1982).

69. *See* Theodore Eisenberg and Stewart Schwab, "The Importance of Section 1981," 73 *Cornell L. Rev.* 596 (1988).

70. 491 U.S. at 212 (Brennan, J., concurring in part, dissenting in part).

71. *See* Petition for a Writ of Certiorari, *Patterson v. McLean Credit Union,* 491 U.S. 164 (No. 87-107).

72. 485 U.S. 617 (1988); *Runyon v. McCrary,* 427 U.S. 160 (1976).

73. *See, e.g.,* Stuart Taylor, Jr., "Court 5–4 Votes to Restudy Rights in Minority Suits," *N.Y. Times,* April 26, 1988, A1; Al Kamen, "High Court to Review Bias Ruling: Revisiting 1976 Case Provokes Unusually Sharp Dissent," *Washington Post,* April 26, 1988, Al.

74. *See Patterson,* 491 U.S. 164, n. *164 (1989); Stuart Taylor, Jr., "High Court Getting Unusual Plea Not to Reverse Key Rights Ruling," *N.Y. Times,* June 24, 1988, A1.

75. *See* "Symposium: Patterson v. McLean," 87 *Michigan L. Rev.* 1–137 (1989); "Symposium on Reconsideration of *Runyon v. McCrary,*" 67 *Wash. U. L. Q.* 1–58 (1989); "Review Essay and Comments, Reconstructing Reconstruction," 99 *Yale L.J.* 519–595 (1989).

76. Brief for Petitioner on Rehearing at 22–23, 40–47, 50–51, *Patterson v. McLean Credit Union,* 491 U.S. 164 (1989).

77. Brief for sixty-six Members of the United States Senate and 118 Members of the United States House of Representative Amici Curiae at 28, *Patterson v. McLean Credit Union,* 491 U.S. 164 (1989).

78. Michael Zimmer, Charles Sullivan, and R. Richards, *Employment Discrimination* § 21.1 (2d ed.) (Boston: Little, Brown, 1988), 467.

79. Julius Chambers, Comments, "Twenty-Five Years of the Civil Rights Act: History and Promise," 25 *Wake Forest L. Rev.* 159, 174 (1990).

CHAPTER FOURTEEN. THE RESURRECTION OF *GRIGGS*

1. Julius Chambers, Comments, "Twenty-Five Years of the Civil Rights Act: History and Promise," 25 *Wake Forest L. Rev.* 169, 173 (1990).

2. Charles Stephen Ralston, Comments, "Symposium, The Supreme Court and Local Government: 1988–89 Term, Employment Discrimination," 6 *Touro L. Rev.* 55, 55–56 (1989).

3. *NAACP Attorney's Assessment of Activist Court Rulings,* Fair Employment Practices, July 20, 1989, at 88 and *Departing Remarks of NAACP Goldstein,* 131 Lab. Rel. Rep. Rep. (BNA) 371–372 (July 17, 1989).

4. Bruce Fein, "Civil Rights Duplicity?," *Washington Times,* August 1, 1989, 3 (Commentary).

5. "Marchers Protest 'Legal Lynching': NAACP Urges Lawmakers: Counter 4 Top Court Rulings," *Chicago Tribune*, August 27, 1989, 1.

6. William P. Murphy, "Supreme Court Review," 5 *Lab. L.* 679, 680 (1989).

7. Ralph G. Neas, "The Civil Rights Legacy of the Reagan Years," *USA Today*, March 1990, 19.

8. Peter Leibold, Stephen A. Sola, and Reginald E. Jones, "Civil Rights Act of 1991: Race to the Finish—Civil Rights, Quotas, and Disparate Impact in 1991," 45 *Rutgers L. Rev.* 1043, 1056 (1993). The authors were counsel to three key Republican senators.

9. Marian Dozier, "A March In Time: NAACP to Protest Recent Rulings by High Court," *Seattle Times*, July 14, 1989, A2.

10. Robert Belton, "The Dismantling of the Griggs Disparate Impact Theory and the Future of Title VII: The Need for a Third Reconstruction," 8 *Yale L. & Pol'y Rev.* 223 (1990); Mark S. Brodin, "Reflections on the Supreme Court's 1988 Term: Employment Discrimination and the Abandonment of the Second Reconstruction," 31 *B. C. L. Rev.* 1 (1989).

11. *Dred Scott*, 60 U.S. at 407 (the Court reviewed more than 100 years of colonial legal treatment of African Americans in reaching its decision that African Americans had been a subordinate and inferior class and dominated by whites). The background and decision are described in detail in Don E. Fehrenbacher, *The Dred Scott Case: Its Significance in American Law and Politics* (New York: Oxford University Press, 2001).

12. *See* John Hope Franklin, *Reconstruction: After the Civil War* (Chicago: University of Chicago Press, 1961); Eric Foner, *Reconstruction: America's Unfinished Revolution, 1877–1883* (New York: Harper & Row, 1989); C. Vance Woodward, "From the First Reconstruction to the Second," *Harper's*, April 1965, 25.

13. Norman C. Amaker, *Civil Rights and the Reagan Administration* (Washington, D.C.: Urban Institute, 1998), 3–4.

14. *See* Foner, *Reconstruction;* Derrick Bell, *Race, Racism, and American Law* (5th ed.) (New York: Aspen Law and Business, 2004), 37–39; C. Vann Woodward, *Reunion and Reaction* (New York: Little, Brown, 1951).

15. *See* John H. Franklin and Alfred A. Moss, Jr., *From Slavery to Freedom: A History of African Americans* (7th ed.) (New York: Knopf, 1994), 225, 232–246, 259–263. Black codes generally refer to a body of laws, statutes, and rules enacted after the Civil War to regain control over the freed slaves, maintain white supremacy, and ensure the continued supply of cheap labor obtained through slavery.

16. *See* Manning Marable, *Race, Reform and Rebellion: The Second Reconstruction in Black America, 1945–1990* (Oxford: University Press of Mississippi, 1991), 39. Marable states that the Second Reconstruction actually began on the afternoon of February 1, 1960, with the onset of the sit-ins that began in Greensboro, North Carolina. The beginning of the Second Reconstruction also has been stated to have started with the enactment of the Civil Rights Act of 1964. D. Marvin Jones, "No Time for Trumpets: Title VII, Equality, and the Fin De Siecle," 82 *Mich. L. Rev.* 2311, 2317 (1994).

17. *See Monroe v. Pape*, 365 U.S. 167 (1961) (extending 42 U.S.C.§ 1983 to individual state actors); *Runyon v. McCrary*, 427 U.S. 160 (1976) (extending 42 U.S.C. § 1981 to private parties).

18. Sondra Hemeryck, Cassandra Butts, Laura Jehl, Adrienne Koch, and Matthew Sloan, Note, "Reconstruction, Deconstruction and Legislative Response: The 1988 Supreme Court Term and the Civil Rights Act of 1990," 25 *Harv. C.R. C.L .L. Rev.* 475, 477 (1990).

19. The editors of an important anthology of critical race theory define this school of thought as "challeng[ing] the ways in which race and racial power are constructed and represented in American legal culture and, more generally, in American society as a whole." Kimberlé Crenshaw et al., *Critical Race Theory: The Key Writings That Formed the Movement* (New York: New Press, 1995), xiii. "This comprehensive movement in thought and life—created primarily, though not exclusively, by progressive intellectuals of color—compels [the critical race theorists] to confront critically the most explosive issue in American civilization: the historical centrality and complicity of law in upholding white supremacy (and concomitant hierarchies of gender, class, and sexual orientation)." Ibid. at xi.

20. Bell, *Race, Racism, and American Law,* 18. *See also* Derrick Bell, *And We Are Not Saved: The Elusive Quest for Racial Justice* (New York: Basic Books, 1987); Linda S. Greene, "Race in the 21st Century: Equality through Law," 64 *Tul. L. Rev.* 1515, 1517 (1990) ("The civil rights decisions of the 198[8] Term force us to refocus on a question time and time again, before and after *Dred Scott:* whether meaningful equality can be obtained for African Americans through law.").

21. Eric Foner, "An Unfinished Revolution," in *The Return of Jim Crow: The Bitter Fruit of the Reagan Court in* Patterson v. McLean (New York: National Lawyers Guild, 1988).

22. Belton, "The Dismantling of the Griggs Disparate Impact Theory," 248; Alan Freeman, "Antidiscrimination Law: The View from 1989," 64 *Tul. L. Rev.* 1407, 1407 (1990) ("the impact of the 1989 decision was so dramatic as to parallel those of the post–Civil War Reconstruction Era").

23. The Civil Rights Act of 1875 provides that "[a]ll persons within the jurisdiction of the United States shall be entitled to the full and equal enjoyment of the accommodations, advantages, facilities, and privileges of inns, public conveyances on land and water, theaters, and other places of public amusement, subject only to the conditions and limitation established by law, and applicable alike to citizens of every race and color, regardless of any previous condition of servitude." The 1875 Act parallels, in some respects, the public accommodation provision of Title II of the Civil Rights Act of 1964, 42 U.S.C. § 2000a.

24. 109 U.S. 3, 25 (1883).

25. *Wards Cove,* 490 U.S. at 662 (Blackmun, J., dissenting).

26. *See City of Richmond v. J. A. Croson,* 488 U.S. 469, 694 (1989) ("'[the] guarantee of equal protection cannot mean one thing when applied to one individual and something else when applied to a person of a different color.'") (quoting *University of California Regents v. Bakke,* 438 U.S. 265, 289–290 (1978) (Powell, J.) (plurality opinion)); Belton, "The Dismantling of the Griggs Disparate Impact," 247–249.

27. Leibold, Sola, and Jones, "Civil Rights Act of 1991," 1043, 1045.

28. Reginald C. Govan, "Honorable Compromises and the Moral High Ground: The Conflict between the Rhetoric and the Content of the Civil Rights Act of 1991," 46 *Rutgers L. Rev.* 1 (1993). Govan, a young African American attorney, was a House Democratic staff member and counsel who participated in the legislative process that culminated in the enactment of the 1991 Civil Rights Act. *See also* Roger Clegg, "Introduction, A Brief Legislative History of the Civil Rights Act of 1991," 54 *La. L. R.* 1459 (1993). Clegg was the Deputy Assistant Attorney General, Civil Rights Division, U.S. Department of Justice, from 1987 to 1991.

29. *See* President George Bush, *Message to the Senate Returning without Approval the Civil Rights Act of 1990,* 2 Pub. Papers 1437, 1438 (October 22, 1990); Fred Barnes, "Quota, Unquota," *New Republic,* November 19, 1990, 10, 11.

30. *E.g.,* Civil Rights Attorney's Fees Award Act of 1976, Pub. L. No. 94-559, 90 Stat. 2641, codified at 42 U.S.C. § 1988 (overturning *Alyeska Pipeline Service Co. v. Wilderness Society,* 421 U.S. 240 (1975)); Pregnancy Discrimination Act., Pub. L. No. 95-555, 92 Stat. 2076, codified as an amendment to Title VII, at 42 U.S.C. § 2000e(k) (overturning *General Electric Co. v. Gilbert,* 429 U.S. 125 (1976), which held that discrimination because of pregnancy is not sex discrimination under Title VII); Voting Rights Act Amendments of 1982, Pub. L. 97-205, 96 Stat. 131, codified at 42.S.C. 1973 § 1973 (overturning *Mobile v. Bolden,* 446 U.S. 55 (1980), in which the Court rejected the disparate impact theory in voting rights cases); Handicapped Children Protection Act of 1986, 20 U.S.C. §§ 1415(e)(4)(B)(g) (1982 ed., Supp. V) (overturning *Smith v. Robinson,* 468 U.S. 992 (1984)); *see* H.R. Rep. No. 99-296, p. 4 (1985); Civil Rights Restoration Act of 1987, Pub. L. No. 100-259, 102 Stat. 28, note following 20 U.S.C. 1687 (overturning *Grove City College v. Bell,* 465 U.S. 555 (1984); *see, e.g.,* S. Rep. No. 100-64, p. 2 (1987).

31. Fair Employment Reinstatement Act, S. 1261, 101st Cong. 1st Sess. 135 Cong. Rec. S. 7512–7513 (statement of Senator Metzenbaum); "Metzenbaum Seeks Reversal of Wards Cove," 131 *Lab. Rel. Rep.* (BNA) 309 (July 3, 1989); Govan, "Honorable Compromises and the Moral High Ground," 33.

32. Equal Justice, LDF News: *A Report from the NAACP Legal Defense and Educational Fund, Inc.,* Vol. 11, No. 2, p. 1, Winter 1989; Arthur S. Hayes, "Job-Bias Litigation Wilts under High Court Rulings," *Wall St. J.,* August 22, 1989, B1.

33. Govan, "Honorable Compromises and the Moral High Ground," 31–33.

34. *Hearings on H.R. 4000, the Civil Rights Act of 1990, Joint Hearings before the Comm. on Educ. and Labor, and Subcomm. on Civil and Constitutional Rights of the Comm. on the Judiciary,* 101st Cong. 2d Sess., at 46–140 (February 20 and 27, 1990) (statement of John H. Buchanan) (study entitled "The Overall Impact of the Supreme Court's 1989 Decisions on Title VII of the Civil Rights Act" prepared by Barbara Holden-Smith and Dawn Jablonski of Arnold and Porter and Elliot M. Minceberg of the People for the American Way).

35. Ibid. at 140–200 (February 20 and 27, 1990) (statement of Julius L. Chambers) (study entitled "The Impact of *Patterson v. McLean Credit Union*" prepared by Eric Schnapper, then assistant counsel with the LDF).

36. *Joint Hearings before the Comm. on Educ. and Labor, and Subcomm. on Civil and*

Constitutional Rights of the Comm. on the Judiciary, Hearings on H.R. 4000, the Civil Rights Act of 1990, 101st Cong. 2d Sess., at 46–140 (February 20 and 27, 1990) (statement of Barbara Arnwine) (study entitled *"Impact of the Supreme Court in* Martin v. Wilks," prepared by Stephen L. Spitz).

37. Govan, "Honorable Compromises and the Moral High Ground," 31–33.

38. *See* ibid., 46–47.

39. This account draws on ibid., 59–61.

40. 136 Cong. Rec. S16, 457 (1990). A few commentators have provided a detailed discussion of the failed 1990 civil rights legislation. *See* Leland Ware, "The Civil Rights Act of 1990: A Dream Deferred," 10 *St. Louis. U. Pub. L. Rev.* 1 (1991); Cynthia Alexander, Note, "The Defeat of the Civil Rights Act of 1990: Wading through the Rhetoric in Search of Compromise," 44 *Vand. L. Rev.* 595 (1990); Patricia A. Pattison and Philip E. Varca, "The Demise of the Disparate Impact Theory," 29 *Am. Bus. L.J.* 413, 438–443 (1991) (discussing the battle between Congress and President Bush on the Civil Rights Act of 1990).

41. Those other decisions are *Crawford Fittings Co. v. J. T. Gibbons,* 482 U.S. 437 (1987); *Evans v. Jeff D.,* 475 U.S. 717 (1986); *Library of Congress v. Shaw,* 478 U.S. 310 (1986).

42. House Names Conferees for Omnibus Civil Rights Legislation, Daily Lab. Rep. (BNA), No. 182, at A-7 (September 19, 1990).

43. Message from the President of the United States Returning without My Approval S. 2104, The Civil Rights Act of 1990, S. Doc. No. 35, 101st Cong., 2d Sess. (1990); 136 Cong. Rec. S16, 589 (daily ed. October 24, 1990).

44. Govan, "Honorable Compromises and the Moral High Ground," 148–149; Ruth Marcus, "The Shifting Sands of George Bush's Civil Rights Positions," *Washington Post, National Weekly Edition,* August 24–30, 1992, 8.

45. Govan, "Honorable Compromises and the Moral High Ground," 177.

46. Steven A. Holmes, "New Battle Looming as Democrats Reintroduce Civil Rights Measure," *N.Y. Times,* January 3, 1991, A1. *See also* Joan Biskupic, "New Struggle over Civil Rights Brings Shift in Strategy," 49 *Cong. Q. Wkly.* 336, 367 (1991) (quoting Congressman Brooks).

47. *See* Sharon LaFraniere and Gary Lee, "Behind Closed Doors: Civil Rights Compromise," *Wash. Post,* April 10, 1991, 16 (noting growing concern that Democrats and business groups might unite on a bill and gain enough momentum to override a presidential veto).

48. Govan, "Honorable Compromises and the Moral High Ground," 186, n. 814 (citing a letter from Representative Craig A. Washington to Ralph G. Neas, Executive Director of the Leadership Conference on Civil Rights criticizing the negotiations because no members of Congress were part of the negotiations and noting that negotiations must not take place on behalf of legislators).

49. Gary Lee and Sharon LaFraniere, "Business Coalition Pulls Out of Civil Rights Talks," *Wash. Post,* April 20, 1991, A.

50. Steven Holmes, "Business and Rights Groups Fail in Effort to Draft Bill on Job Bias," *N.Y. Times,* April 20, 1991, A1.

51. *See* Leibold, Sola, and Jones, "Civil Rights Act of 1991," 1044.

52. Govan, "Honorable Compromises and the Moral High Ground," 54–56.

53. 440 U.S. 568, 587 n. 31 (1979).

54. Leibold, Sola, and Jones, "Civil Rights Act of 1991," 1070.

55. Memorandum to NAACP Legal Defense and Educational Fund, Inc., *From Griggs to* Wards Cove: *Job Performance, A Uniformly Applied Standard in Title VII Cases* (July 26, 1991) (authored by Leon Silverman, Arthur Lazarus, Jr., John Sullivan, and Natalie Chetlin) (copy available at Vanderbilt Law School library).

56. The 225 cases in the study are listed in Exhibit A to the study. Cases excluded from this number were those that did not involve Title VII; education and housing discrimination cases; disparate treatment cases; cases in which the courts articulated but did not apply the business necessity test because the plaintiffs did not prove a prima facie case of disparate impact; and cases in which the district courts' analyses of business necessity were reversed on appeal or the appellate court decided that the disparate impact analysis did not apply. However, the analysis included some cases in which the courts questioned the plaintiffs' proof of disparate impact but went on to apply the business necessity test anyway.

57. Memorandum *From* Griggs *to* Wards Cove at 14.

58. *See* Maureen Dowd, "The Supreme Court; Conservative Black Judge, Clarence Thomas, Is Named to Replace Marshall's Court Seat," *N.Y. Times,* July 2, 1991, A1.

59. *See* Clarence Thomas, "Affirmative Action, Goals and Timetables: Too Tough? Not Tough Enough!," *Yale L. & Pol'y Rev.* 402 (1987).

60. Clarence Thomas, *My Grandfather's Son: A Memoir* (New York: HarperCollins Perennial, 2007), 74–75.

61. Anita Hill, *Speaking Truth to Power* (New York: Anchor Books, 1997); Thomas, *My Grandfather's Son;* John Danforth, *Resurrection: The Confirmation of Clarence Thomas: A Story of Friendship and Faith* (New York: Viking, 1994).

62. *See* Timothy M. Phelps and Helen Winternitz, *Capitol Games: Clarence Thomas, Anita Hill, and the Story of a Supreme Court Nomination* (New York: Hyperion, 1992).

63. Govan, "Honorable Compromises and the Moral High Ground," 224.

64. Jane Mayer and Jill Abramson, *Strange Justice: The Selling of Clarence Thomas* (New York: Plume, 1994), 351; Danforth, *Resurrection.*

65. *See, e.g.,* Clegg, "A Brief History of the Civil Rights Act," 1469–1470.

66. Govan, "Honorable Compromises and the Moral High Ground," 225.

67. Some of the other cases overturned or modified by the 1991 Act include *Independent Fed'n of Flight Attendants v. Zipes,* 491 U.S. 754 (1989); *Price Waterhouse v. Hopkins,* 490 U.S. 228 (1989); *Crawford Fittings Co. v. J. T. Gibbons, Inc.,* 482 U.S. 437 (1987); *Library of Congress v. Shaw,* 478 310 (1986); *Evans v. Jeff D.,* 475 U.S. 717 (1986); *EEOC v. Arabian American Oil Co.,* 499 U.S. 244 (1991); *West Virginia Univ. Hospitals, Inc. v. Casey,* 499 U.S. 83 (1991); *Marek v. Chesny,* 473 U.S. 1 (1985).

68. Statement on Signing the Civil Rights Act of 1991, 27 Weekly Comp. Pres. Doc. 1701, 1701 (November 21, 1991); *see also* C. Boyden Gray, "Civil Rights: We Won, They Capitulated," *Wash. Post,* November 14, 1991, A22.

69. Leibold, Sola, and Jones, "Civil Rights Act of 1991," 1050–1053. The label "cumulation" is apparently based on the Court's reference to "cumulative comparative" statistics relied upon by the plaintiffs in *Wards Cove*, 490 U.S. at 656. The cumulation principle was sometimes referred to in the legislative debates as involving a group of interrelated employment practices that produces a single employment decision, and the elements of the decision-making process are not capable of separation for analysis. *See also* Govan, "Honorable Compromises and the Moral High Ground," 127–128 (discussion of the negotiations on this issue during the legislative discourse on the 1990 Act).

70. Leibold, Sola, and Jones, "Civil Rights Act of 1991," 1050, 1064–1065.

71. 42 U.S.C. § 2000e-2(k) provides that upon proof of a prima facie case of disparate impact, a defendant loses if it is unable to "demonstrate" that the challenged practice is job related and consistent with business necessity. The 1991 Act defines "demonstrate" to mean the burdens of production and persuasion. 42 U.S.C. § 2000e(l).

72. Chai Feldblum, "Medical Examination and Inquiries under the Americans with Disabilities Act: A View from the Inside," 64 *Temp. L. Rev.* 521, 546 (1991).

73. Ibid. at 546–547.

74. Arlene Mayerson, "Title I—Employment Provisions of the Americans with Disabilities Act," 64 *Temp. L. Rev.* 499, 510–513 (1991); Feldblum, "Medical Examination and Inquiries," 545–548.

75. The Civil Rights Act of 1991, Pub. L. No. 102-166, 105 Stat. 1071, Sec. 3(2) (1991); 137 Cong. Rec. S15, 276 (daily ed. October 25, 1991) (statement of Senator Danforth).

76. *See, e.g., Lanning v. Southeastern Pa. Transp. Auth.*, 181 F.3d 478 (3d Cir. 1999), *cert. denied*, 528 U.S. 1131 (2000); Linda Lye, Comment, "Title VII's Tangled Tale: The Erosion and Confusion of Disparate Impact and the Business Necessity Defense," 19 *Berkeley J. Empl. & Lab. L.* 315 (1998); Philip Runkel, Note, "The Civil Rights Act of 1991: A Continuation of the Wards Cove Standard of Business Necessity?," 35 *Wm. & Mary L. Rev.* 1177 (1993).

77. 42 U.S.C. § 2000e-2(k)(1)(A)(ii).

78. 42 U.S.C. § 2000e-2(k)(1)(C).

79. 42 U.S.C. § 2000e-5(e)(2).

80. *McGovern v. City of Philadelphia*, 554 F.3d 114 (3d Cir. 2009) (collecting cases).

81. Hopkins tells the story of her case in Ann Branigar Hopkins and Mary Roth Walsh, *So Ordered: Making Partner the Hard Way* (Boston: University of Massachusetts Press, 1996).

82. Section 706(g)(2)(B), 42 U.S.C. § 2000e(g)(2)(B). *See Stevens v. Gravette Medical Center Hospital*, 998 F. Supp. 1011 (W.D. Ark. 1998); Robert Belton, "Mixed Motive Cases in Employment Discrimination Law Revisited: A Brief Updated View of the Swamp," 51 *Mercer L. Rev.* 651 (2000).

83. Civil Rights Act of 1991, Pub. L. No. 102-166, § 116, 105 Stat. 1071, 1079 (1991).

84. Owen M. Fiss, "The Allure of Individualism," 78 *Iowa L. Rev.* 965 (1993).

CHAPTER FIFTEEN. EPILOGUE

1. *See* Andrea Giampetro-Meyer, "Standing in the Gap: A Profile of Employment Discrimination Plaintiffs," 27 *Berkeley J. Lab. L.* 431 (2006)

2. EEOC, *The First Decade* (1974).

3. Barry Bearak and David Lauter, "Tense Steps to Ending Racial Bias," *Los Angeles Times,* November 3, 1991, A1; Drew Jubera "How Willie Griggs Changed the Workplace," *Atlanta Constitution,* July 1, 1991, B1.

4. *Miller v. International Paper Co.,* 408 F.2d 283, 294 (5th Cir. 1969).

5. *Griggs v. Duke Power Co.,* 1970 WL 160 (M.D. N.C. December 23, 1970).

6. 515 F.3d 87 (4th Cir. 1975).

7. Robert S. Smith, *Race, Labor & Civil Rights:* Griggs v. Duke Power *and the Struggle for Equal Employment Opportunity* (Baton Rouge, La.: LSU Press, 2008), 178–179.

8. *Griggs v. Duke Power Co.,* 1970 WL 160 (M.D. N.C. Dec. 23, 1970).

9. Jubera, "How Willie Griggs Changed the Workplace."

10. Smith, *Race, Labor & Civil Rights,* 188–189.

11. The comments about the reflections of the black employees are based on my interview with Willie Boyd; Smith, *Race, Labor & Civil* Rights; and a newspaper article, Jubera, "How Willie Griggs Changed the Workplace," B1.

12. Jubera, "How Willie Griggs Changed the Workplace."

13. *See* Robert Belton, *Remedies in Employment Discrimination Law* (New York: Wolters Kluwer, 1992), § 1.1.

14. *South Carolina v. Katzenbach,* 383 U.S. 301, 308 (1966).

15. *See* Frank R. Parker, "The 'Results' Test of Section 2 of the Voting Rights Act: Abandoning the Intent Standard," 69 *Va. L. Rev.* 715 (1983).

16. 42 U.S.C. §§ 621–634.

17. *Smith v. City of Jackson,* 544 U.S. 238 (2005).

18. *See Tenants Ass'n v. District of Columbia,* 444 F. 2d 673, 679 (D.C. Cir. 2006) ("[S]ince *Griggs,* every one of the eleven circuits to have considered the issue has held that the FHA similarly prohibits discrimination, not only intentional housing discrimination, but also housing actions have a disparate impact.") (citing John F. Stanton, "The Fair Housing Act and Insurance: An Update and the Question of Disability Discrimination," 31 *Hofstra L. Rev.* 141, 174 n. 180 (2002)); Dana L. Kaersvang, "The Fair Housing Act and Disparate Impact in Homeowners Insurance," 104 *Mich. L. Rev.* 1993, 2007 n. 17 (2006) (listing cases from the courts of appeals that have so held).

19. 29 U.S.C. §§ 701–797(h); *Alexander v. Choate,* 469 U.S. 287 (1985).

20. Joseph P. Witherspoon, "Civil Rights Policy in the Federal System: Proposals for a Better Use of Administrative Process," 74 *Yale L.J.* 1171, 1173 (1965) (includes an appendix of state and local human relations commissions, their areas of competency, citations to their enabling legislation, and statistics concerning their activities).

21. *See* Michael I. Sovern, *Legal Restraints on Racial Discrimination in Employment* (New York: Twentieth Century Fund, 1966); Herbert Hill, "Twenty Years of State Fair Employment Practices Commissions: A Critical Assessment with Recommendations,"

14 *Buff. L. Rev.* 22 (1964). Data on enforcement under state fair employment practices commission are reported in Hugh Davis Graham, *The Civil Rights Era: Origins and Development of National Policy* (New York: Oxford University Press, 1990), 131.

22. Tex. Lab. Code § 21.122; *Texas Parks & Wildlife Dept.*, 240 S.W. 3d 330, 353 (Tex. App. 2007); R.I. Gen. Laws § 28–57.2. *See Connelly v. R. I. Bd. of Governors*, 110 F.3d 2, 6 (1st Cir. 1997) (treating the Rhode Island Fair Employment Practices Act (RIFEPA) and Title VII disparate impact claims identically after noting that Rhode Island courts look to Title VII for guidance in construing RIFEPA claims).

23. These states include Alaska, Arizona, California, Connecticut, Florida, Idaho, Illinois, Massachusetts, and Tennessee. *See Thomas v. Anchorage Telephone Utility*, 741 P.2d 618 (Alaska 1987); *Civ. Rights Div. of Ariz. Dept. of Law v. Amphitheater Unified School Dist. No. 10*, 680 P.2d 517 (Ariz. App. 1983); *Frank v. County of Los Angeles*, 57 Cal. Rptr. 3d 430 (Cal. Ct. App. 2007); *Levy v. Comm'n on Human Rights and Opportunities*, 671 A.2d 349 (Conn. 1996); *Florida State University v. Sondel*, 685 So. 2d 923 (Fla. App. 1996); *Bowles v. Keating*, 606 P.2d 458 (Idaho 1979); *People v. R. L.*, 634 N.E. 2d 733 (Ill. 1994); *School Committee of Braintree v. Mass. Comm'n Against Discrimination*, 386 N.E.2d 1251 (Mass. 1979); *Moore v. Nashville Elec. Power Bd.*, 72 S.W. 643 (Tenn. Ct. App. 2001).

24. *E.g., Thomas v. Anchorage Telephone Utility*, 741 P.2d 618, 628 (Alaska 1987) (citing *Griggs* and *Teamsters* for the elements of a disparate impact case).

25. *Frank v. County of Los Angeles*, 57 Cal. Rptr. 3d 430, 440 n. 3 (Cal. Ct. App. 2007); *Carter v. CB Richard Ellis, Inc.*, 122 Cal. App. 4th 1313, 1321 (Cal. Ct. App. 2004) (relying on *Griggs* and *Watson v. Fort Worth Bank and Trust*, 487 U.S. 977 (1988), to formulate the test for the disparate impact theory).

26. These states include Arkansas, Colorado, Delaware, Hawaii, and Indiana. *See generally Island v. Buena Vista Resort*, 103 S.W. 3d 671 (Ark. 2003); 30 Colo. Code Regs. § 708-1 (2007); *Quaker Hill Place v. Saville*, 523 A.2d 947 (Del. Super. 1987) (recognizing disparate impact claim in fair housing case); *French v. Hawaii Pizza Hut, Inc.*, 99 P.3d 1046 (Haw. 2004); *Civil Rights Comm'n v. County Line Park, Inc.*, 738 N.E.2d 1044 (Ind. 2000).

27. *Island v. Buena Vista Resort*, 103 S.W. 3d 671, 675 (Ark. 2003).

28. *Robinson v. Sears, Roebuck, & Co.*, 111 F. Supp. 2d 1101, 1118 n. 9 (E.D. Ark. 2000) (noting Arkansas courts' previous application of Title VII jurisprudence to state law employment discrimination claims and that recognition of a disparate impact claim would be consistent with the language of the state employment discrimination statute).

29. 30 Colo. Code Regs. § 708-1, Rules 90.0–90.16 (2007).

30. *Civil Rights Commission v. County Line Park, Inc.*, 738 N.E.2d 1044, 1048–1049 (Ind. 2000) (housing discrimination); *Robinson v. Dana Corp.*, 656 N.E.2d 540, 545–546 (Ind. App. 1995) (disability discrimination).

31. Ind. Code 22-9-1-2 (2007) ("Equal education employment opportunities and equal access to and use of public accommodations and equal opportunity for acquisition of real property are hereby declared to be civil rights.... [D]enying these rights.... shall be considered as discriminatory practices.").

32. *E.g., Shoppe v. Gucci America, Inc.,* 14 P.3d 1049, 1058 (Haw. 2000) ("We have also recognized, however, that federal employment discrimination authority is not necessarily persuasive, particularly where a state's statutory provision differs in relevant detail."). This is particularly important because most states' employment discrimination statutes—although similar to Title VII in substance—depart from the exact language of Title VII. *See Parker v. Warren County Utility Dist.,* 2 S.W.3d 170, 172–173 (Tenn. 1999) (noting that, despite a general policy of interpreting Tennessee employment discrimination law coextensively with Title VII, Tennessee courts "are neither bound by nor limited by the federal law when interpreting our state's anti-discrimination statute"); *Spann v. Abraham,* 36 S.W.3d 452, 463 (Tenn. App. 1999) (noting that Tennessee courts are not bound or limited by federal law but should "giv[e] the fullest possible effect to Tennessee's own human rights legislation").

33. Rosemary C. Hunter and Elaine W. Shoben, "Disparate Impact Discrimination: American Oddity or Internationally Accepted Concept?," 19 *Berkeley J. Empl. & Lab. L.* 108, 109 (1998).

34. *See* Departing Attorney Urges Civil Rights Action, 131 DLR A-4 (July 11, 1989) (statement by Barry L. Goldstein).

35. Katerina Linos, "Path Dependence in Discrimination Law: Employment Cases in the United States and the European Union," *Yale J. Intern'l L.* 114, 117 (2010).

36. Hunter and Shoben, "Disparate Impact Discrimination," 108.

37. *See* Joseph A. Steiner, "Disentangling Disparate Impact and Disparate Treatment: Adapting the Canadian Approach," 25 *Yale L. & Pol'y Rev.* 95 (2007).

38. Case 96/80, *Jenkins v. Kingsgate (Clothing Prods.) Ltd.,* 198 (E.C.R. 911). *See* Linos, "Path Dependence in Discrimination Law," 134–136.

39. *See D.H. v. The Czech Republic (Grand Chamber),* Application No. 57325/00 (Eur. Ct. H.R. November 13, 2007) (citing *Griggs* in a case involving a denial of rights to education without regard to race or ethnic origin).

40. *See* Chief Justice Arthur Chaskalson, "*Brown v. Board of Education:* Fifty Years Later," 36 *Colum. Hum. Rts. L. Rev.* 503, 510–511 (2005) (noting that proof of intention is not a requirement to prove discrimination and, in this respect, South Africa chose to follow the decisions of the Canadian Supreme Court and the European Court of Justice rather than the rule in the United States in *Washington v. Davis,* 426 U.S. 229 (1976), which requires proof of intent in constitutional equal protection cases).

41. Holning Lau, "Sexual Orientation & Gender Identity: American Law in Light of the East Asian Developments," 31 *Harv. J. L. & Gender* 67 (2008) (Hong Kong and South Korea).

42. *See* Justice Richard J. Goldstone and Brian Ray, "The International Legacy of *Brown v. Board of Education,*" 35 *McGeorge L. Rev.* 105 (2004).

43. *See* Michael E. Gold, "*Griggs's* Folly: An Essay on the Theory, Problem, and Origins of the Adverse Impact Theory Definition of Employment Discrimination and a Recommendation for Reform," 7 *Indus. Rel. L.J.* 429 (1985).

44. Richard A. Epstein, *Forbidden Grounds: The Case against Employment Discrimination Laws* (Cambridge, Mass.: Harvard University Press, 1992).

45. Hunter and Shoben, "Disparate Impact Discrimination," 143–152.

46. Linos, "Path Dependence in Discrimination Law," 117.

47. Brian K. Landsberg, "Race and the Rehnquist Court," 66 *Tul. L. Rev.* 1267, 1281 (1992).

48. Gold, "*Griggs's* Folly," 429. Richard Epstein, one of the harshest critics of employment discrimination law, has argued, "If in 1964 any sponsor of the Civil Rights Act had admitted Title VII on the ground that it adopted the disparate impact test read into it by the Supreme Court in *Griggs,* Title VII would have gone down to thundering defeat." *Forbidden Grounds,* 197.

49. *See, e.g.,* Derrick Bell, *Race, Racism and American Law* (New York: Aspen Law and Business, 2004), ch. 2.

50. *See* Julius L. Chambers and Barry Goldstein, "Title VII: The Continuing Challenge of Establishing Fair Employment Practices," 49 *Law & Contemp. Probs.* 9 (1986).

51. *Rodman v. Kempner's,* 831 F.2d 690, 697 (7th Cir. 1987).

52. *Thornbrough v. Columbus & Greenville R.R.,* 760 F.2d 633, 638 (5th Cir. 1985).

53. *See* Kevin M. Clermont and Stuart J. Schwab, "How Employment Discrimination Plaintiffs Fare in Federal Court," 1 *J. Empirical Legal Stud.* 429 (2004); Kevin M. Clermont and Stewart J. Schwab, "Employment Discrimination Plaintiffs in Federal Court: From Bad to Worse," 3 *Harv. L. & Pol'y Rev.* 102 (2009).

54. *See* Michael Selmi, "Was the Disparate Impact Theory a Mistake?," 53 *UCLA L. Rev.* 701 (2006).

55. Minna J. Kotkin, "Outing Outcomes: An Empirical Study of Confidential Employment Discrimination Settlements," 64 *Wash. & Lee L. Rev.* 111 (2007).

56. Michael Selmi, "The Price of Discrimination: The Nature of Class Action Employment Discrimination and Its Effects," 81 *Tex. L. Rev.* 1249 (2003); *see* Trina Jones, "Anti-Discrimination Law in Peril," 75 *Mo. L. Rev.* 423 (2010).

57. William B. Gould, *Black Workers in White Unions: Job Discrimination in the United States* (Ithaca, N.Y.: Cornell University Press, 1977), 98.

58. Elaine Shoben, "Disparate Impact Theory in Employment Discrimination: What's *Griggs* Still Good For? What Not?," 42 *Brandeis L.J.* 579 (2004).

59. *See* 42 U.S.C. § 1981a (b).

60. Shoben, "Disparate Impact Theory in Employment Discrimination," 598.

Table of Cases

Index